Theology and the Enlightenment

Theology and the Enlightenment

A Critical Enquiry into Enlightenment Theology and Its Reception

Paul Avis

t&tclark
LONDON • NEW YORK • OXFORD • NEW DELHI • SYDNEY

T&T CLARK
Bloomsbury Publishing Plc
50 Bedford Square, London, WC1B 3DP, UK
1385 Broadway, New York, NY 10018, USA
29 Earlsfort Terrace, Dublin 2, Ireland

BLOOMSBURY, T&T CLARK and the T&T Clark logo are trademarks of Bloomsbury Publishing Plc

First published in Great Britain 2023

Copyright © Paul Avis, 2023

Paul Avis has asserted his right under the Copyright, Designs and Patents Act, 1988, to be identified as Author of this work.

Cover image: Kevin Carden/Adobe Stock

All rights reserved. No part of this publication may be reproduced or transmitted in any form or by any means, electronic or mechanical, including photocopying, recording, or any information storage or retrieval system, without prior permission in writing from the publishers.

Bloomsbury Publishing Plc does not have any control over, or responsibility for, any third-party websites referred to or in this book. All internet addresses given in this book were correct at the time of going to press. The author and publisher regret any inconvenience caused if addresses have changed or sites have ceased to exist, but can accept no responsibility for any such changes.

A catalogue record for this book is available from the British Library.

A catalog record for this book is available from the Library of Congress.

	ISBN:	
	HB:	978-0-5677-0565-5
	PB:	978-0-5677-0564-8
	ePDF:	978-0-5677-0567-9
	eBook:	978-0-5677-0566-2

Typeset by Integra Software Services Pvt. Ltd.
Printed and bound in Great Britain

To find out more about our authors and books visit www.bloomsbury.com and sign up for our newsletters.

CONTENTS

Preface vi
Abbreviations xii

1 Engaging the Enlightenment 1
2 Scapegoating the Enlightenment 33
3 A virtuous Enlightenment 67
4 The Enlightenment and religion 137
5 The Anglican Enlightenment 209
6 Enlightenment history and the Bible 273
7 The Enlightenment in the frame of Christian theology 335

Bibliography 356
Index of Names 395

PREFACE

I have found myself drawn again and again since my teenage years to the Enlightenment and to the lives and thoughts of its main protagonists. I have increasingly felt the need, as a Christian theologian, to come to some kind of reckoning with it. This book is my attempt to get to grips with the theological dimension of the Enlightenment and, correspondingly, with the frequently inadequate, misleading and ill-informed ways in which that theological dimension has been interpreted by historians, philosophers and theologians themselves. So this book ventures well beyond even the capacious boundaries of theology into the reception of the Enlightenment in the disciplines of history, philosophy and literature.

The trigger for this book was the growing exasperation that I felt as I saw the Enlightenment stereotyped, caricatured and misrepresented by Christian writers, including scholars who should have known better. References to the Enlightenment in theological literature tend to be ball-park generalizations that show little acquaintance with the sources or even with the main lines of interpretation. But what is worse, if possible, is that such references are studded with vague and undefined 'scare' phrases like 'Enlightenment rationalism' and 'Enlightenment secularism', or – even more far-fetched – 'Enlightenment atheism', which all bear minimal relation to the facts of the case.

As I will show conclusively, building on recent decades of revisionist history, the ideological centre of the Enlightenment in England, Scotland, Germany and the Netherlands was firmly religious, Christian and even ecclesiastical. Deism was prevalent in France among the *philosophes* and existed in England, while Scottish 'Moderate' theology was tinged with it. But deism is a religious faith and a reduced form of Christianity, with the supernatural and redemptive aspects toned down. There was a sprinkling of atheists, especially in France. In England, which enjoyed more intellectual liberty than most countries after 1689, Enlightenment conceptual paradigms were absorbed relatively calmly into the cultural and ecclesiastical mainstream. But a number of early modern and Enlightenment thinkers, whom it has been fashionable to call harbingers of a modern, secular, rationalist and even atheist future – Montaigne, Charron, Spinoza, Simon, La Peyrère, Bayle, Hobbes, Locke, Middleton – were nothing of the sort. In fact quite the reverse: they were all passionately religious, God-obsessed people, and all but Spinoza (a Jew) were Christian and some were clergy. If historians, philosophers and – yes – even theologians knew more theology and were better acquainted with the Christian tradition in all its richness and diversity, they would not make such blunders. Some interpreters seem to think that if 'reason' is invoked, revelation is excluded, and that if 'criticism' is deployed, faith goes out of the window. The Enlightenment certainly saw a fresh emphasis on reason and criticism, on investigation and evidence. The traditional theological authorities of Bible and church were challenged, reinterpreted and reshaped, but not abandoned or abolished. Christian thinkers took these developments in their stride, as they had always done, and in fact normally took the lead intellectually. In Christian theology, reason and revelation, criticism and faith have gone hand in hand, from the early apologists to the medieval schoolmen, through the Renaissance and the Reformation, to the Enlightenment and modern critical theology, right up to the present day. Theology is not fazed by such challenges, but rather stimulated. Christianity is continually evolving into something that is capable of being believed, just like every ideology there has ever been. In doing so, Christianity continually shows its capacity to respond to human need by adapting to changing cultural and social norms. It is not static, not fossilized, but alive and dynamic. The Enlightenment continues.

As my title suggests, I begin from theology and view the Enlightenment from that perspective. I come to the task as a (mainly) historical theologian, but also as one who is not helpless when biblical, systematic and philosophical skills are called for. I do not pose as an expert on the Enlightenment who then attempts to relate it to theology. This book is that *rara avis*, a Christian theological assessment of the theologies of the Enlightenment and of their reception in scholarship. I range over historical, philosophical, theological and literary territory and offer running commentary from a Christian theological perspective.

I have long been intrigued by the Enlightenment. I began some sporadic reading of Enlightenment material in the sixth form, including Basil Willey's well-known *Background* books which hold their value.[1] In reading Leonard Woolf's five-volume autobiography in the mid-sixties, I was struck by the fact that, after leaving Cambridge and well before he met Virginia, Woolf took with him to Ceylon (as it then was), as a raw imperial administrator, the seventy-volume set of the works of Voltaire (in French obviously). Why would he do that, I wondered.[2] Soon afterwards I devoured Rousseau's *Confessions* and Voltaire's *Candide*.[3] My first proper taste of a passionate, partisan Enlightenment ideology was Paul Hazard's *The European Mind 1680–1715* (ET 1964), which I read uncritically.[4] I relished the whole of Boswell's life of Samuel Johnson in my early twenties, though I had no idea at the time that I was being immersed in the British Enlightenment.[5] In those days I understood little of the significance of what I was reading, but I began to be captivated by the energy, vision and courage of the Enlightenment thinkers, though I resisted anything hostile to Christianity, as I knew it, in their work.

The Enlightenment has had a bad press among Christian writers. As I show early on, theologians have tended to scapegoat an undefined and undifferentiated Enlightenment as responsible for much of our modern social, political and ideological ills at the hands of such supposedly aggressive forces as 'rationalism', 'secularism', 'atheism', 'individualism' and 'liberalism'. This stance

---

[1] Basil Willey, *The Seventeenth Century Background* (Harmondsworth: Peregrine, 1962 [1934]); id., *The Eighteenth-Century Background: Studies in the Idea of Nature in the Thought of the Period* (Harmondsworth: Peregrine, 1962 [1940]).
[2] Leonard Woolf [1880–1969], *Growing: An Autobiography of the Years 1904–1911* (London: Hogarth Press, 1960), vol. 2 of Woolf's autobiography.
[3] Jean-Jacques Rousseau, *Confessions*, trans. and intro. J. M. Cohen (Harmondsworth: Penguin, 1953 [1781]); Voltaire, *Candide*, trans. John Butt (Harmondsworth: Penguin, 1947 [1759]).
[4] Paul Hazard, *The European Mind 1680–1715*, trans. J. Lewis May (Harmondsworth: Penguin, 1964 [1953]).
[5] James Boswell, *Life of Johnson*, ed. R. W. Chapman (London: Oxford University Press, 1953).

is understandable if their reading has been confined to interpreters such as Paul Hazard and even Isaiah Berlin (not to mention the four heavy-weight volumes of Jonathan Israel which I do not suppose such writers have ever embarked on).[6] I challenge head-on this stock, off-the-peg, negative Christian interpretation and I set out an alternative landscape of the Enlightenment in relation to Christian theology. In particular I show that historians and philosophers who tend to get excited about non-mainstream theological ideas (which they love to call 'heterodox'), in such authors as Charron, Spinoza, Hobbes, Locke, Bayle and some deists, lack much sense of the breadth, diversity and richness of Christian theological positions and traditions. I object to devoutly Christian thinkers like Locke or Vico being labelled 'heterodox', without sufficient justification or explanation. The variety of genuine Christian belief through history is quite astonishing; historians and philosophers who pontificate about Christian thinkers need to be aware of this.

This project represents some unfinished business in my research and writing programme. My first approach to the Enlightenment (*Foundations of Modern Historical Thought: From Machiavelli to Vico* (1986/2016),[7] which I wrote as a young priest in a parish, followed an historical track which – apart from a chapter which I could not resist, on Giambattista Vico – ran out of time and space on the verge of Enlightenment historiography. I returned to the Enlightenment more broadly, but with a focus on theological methodology, in the book *In Search of Authority: Anglican Theological Method from the Reformation to the Enlightenment* (2014)[8] where the spotlight finally rested on 'the Anglican

---

[6] Jonathan Israel, *Radical Enlightenment: Philosophy and the Making of Modernity 1650–1750* (Oxford: Oxford University Press, 2001); id., *Enlightenment Contested: Philosophy, Modernity and the Emancipation of Man 1670–1752* (Oxford: Oxford University Press, 2006); id., *Democratic Enlightenment: Philosophy, Revolution, and Human Rights 1750–1790* (Oxford: Oxford University Press, 2011); id., *Revolutionary Ideas: An intellectual history of the French Revolution from the Rights of Man to Robespierre* (Princeton, NJ: Princeton University Press, 2014).
[7] Paul Avis, *Foundations of Modern Historical Thought: From Machiavelli to Vico*, 2nd edn (London and New York: Routledge, 2016 [1986]), abbreviated in this book to *FMHT*.
[8] Paul Avis, *In Search of Authority: Anglican Theological Method from the Reformation to the Enlightenment* (London and New York: T&T Clark, 2014), abbreviated in this book to *ISOA*.

Enlightenment', a nomenclature that requires some justification, which I trust it receives in the present volume. But that all-too-short treatment left me unsatisfied and I knew that I needed to return to the subject. The present effort began as the draft of a linking chapter of the planned sequel to *In Search of Authority*, a sequel that will be devoted to the transformations of Anglican theology in the nineteenth century, an age of Romanticism and revolutions, which begins unusually by making connections between literature and theology in English Romanticism. But, as an opening chapter, it got a bit out of hand!

So some of the (probably few) faithful followers of my work may wonder what the relationship of the present volume is to the series that I began with *In Search of Authority* (I am often asked when the sequel is to appear). The answer has to be that this book broadly follows the planned trajectory, and fits, not altogether neatly, between *In Search of Authority* and its nineteenth-century sequel, which is yet to be completed. Although the present work sits somewhat to one side of the planned series, it is also connected to it. There is a substantial chapter here on the Anglican Enlightenment, showing why it is sometimes considered as 'unique'. But that epoch of Anglicanism can be understood only within the context of the Enlightenment as a pan-European and even transatlantic phenomenon. That is why my discussions of the wider context, especially the chapters on the Enlightenment and religion and on Enlightenment history and the Bible, are necessary.

I am all too conscious of the selective nature of the material and the limitations of scope of this book. The main focus is on England and therefore necessarily France also. There are reasonably substantial discussions of the German *Aufklärung* (mainly Kant and Lessing), the Netherlands (Spinoza and Bayle), Scotland (Hume, Ferguson, Smith and Robertson). I regret that it has not proved possible to extend the parameters of this study to include the impact of the Enlightenment on America. Enlightenment research is a major historical and philosophical industry. The literature is infinite, in the sense that new editions of primary works and fresh secondary studies (books and articles) are pouring from the presses all the time. No-one can keep up with it all. Reluctantly, I thought it best to draw a line at this point. Reviewers love to ask why the author did not mention such and such an aspect of their subject, or such and such a book or seminal article about it and I tend to do that myself a bit. I can only say here, rather apologetically, that I am probably well aware of the work or works that such hypothetical reviews might have in mind, but no-one can cover all bases where the Enlightenment is concerned.

My warm thanks go to the editorial staff at Bloomsbury/T&T Clark: Lalle Pursglove, Anna Turton and Sinead O'Connor. But above all to my beloved wife Susan for her continuing forbearance, massive practical support and enduring love.

Paul Avis
Shrove Tuesday 2022

ABBREVIATIONS

AACC	Paul Avis, *Anglicanism and the Christian Church: Theological Resources in Historical Perspective*, 2nd edition (London and New York: T&T Clark, 2002).
FMHT	Paul Avis, *Foundations of Modern Historical Thought: From Machiavelli to Vico*, 2nd edition (London and New York: Routledge, 2016 [1986]).
H&T	*History and Theory*
ICC	*International Critical Commentary*
ISOA	Paul Avis, *In Search of Authority: Anglican Theological Method from the Reformation to the Enlightenment* (London and New York: T&T Clark, 2014).
JEH	*Journal of Ecclesiastical History*
JHI	*Journal of the History of Ideas*
JTS	*Journal of Theological Studies*
KJB	King James Bible (Authorized Version)
ODNB	*Oxford Dictionary of National Biography* (Oxford: Oxford University Press, 2004).
SVEC	*Studies on Voltaire and the Eighteenth Century*

1

Engaging the Enlightenment

For the past three and a half centuries, the whole of Western thought – including the sciences, the humanities and our general culture – has been evolving in the wake of the Enlightenment. The portmanteau term 'the Enlightenment' designates the international, transatlantic, movement of critical rationality, investigative enquiry and liberated public argument, which took its rise in England and Holland in the second half of the seventeenth century and reached its sharpest and most subversive form in France in the reforming agenda of the *philosophes* in the middle decades of the eighteenth. In the nineteenth and twentieth centuries the legacy of the Enlightenment fed into the emergence of the social sciences and critical theory and that legacy continues to mutate to this day. In this first chapter we begin to encounter and engage critically with the phenomenon of the Enlightenment, both in the words and deeds of its protagonists at the time and in the writings and views of its modern and contemporary interpreters: philosophers, historians and theologians.

The inescapable Enlightenment

The generative power of the Enlightenment, both by attraction and by repulsion, is at least as great as ever it was, if not greater. As Lloyd has put it, 'The Enlightenment has become the touchstone for highly emotional – often contradictory – articulations of contemporary western values. We of the west [sic] may proudly claim it as our heritage; we may also blame it for our contemporary woes. Whether we praise or deride it, we now live in its shadows and must reckon with what it has bequeathed us. Western thought is haunted by the Enlightenment.'[1] For us in the twenty-first century, whatever our personal beliefs or academic specialism, the Enlightenment is simply *inescapable*.

There is a tendency to look back in time towards 'the Enlightenment', as a discrete historical event, as though it belonged firmly in the past and had a beginning and an end. Perhaps this is a temptation for historians, especially those working in political and social history, though surely not for historians of ideas or historical theologians. But to see the Enlightenment as an historical episode that has now come to an end would be an illusion. The Enlightenment is not stuck in past time. We are not detached from it, nor are we in a position to assess it objectively, as a phenomenon outside of ourselves. The Enlightenment and its impact continues. It is part of us and we are part of it, whether we like it or not. We have all internalized the Enlightenment. All of us in the modern, Westernized world – whatever we think of the Enlightenment – are and remain its children; religious believers, Christians and even theologians though we may be.

Christian theology in the cultural West has not escaped from the wake and wash of the Enlightenment, nor can it do so. Theological reflection is always compelled to ply its trade within a given cultural environment and the prevailing conceptual paradigms. If we are Christian thinkers and theologians, we are called to be 'in' the world, if not 'of' it. All modern Christian theology is theology shaped and marked by the Enlightenment and its continuing impact. This is just as true of conservative evangelical or conservative Roman Catholic or Anglo-Catholic theology as it is of progressive or 'liberal' theology. It is notorious that evangelical Fundamentalism was and is deeply marked by Enlightenment rationality, even though it purported to repudiate it. All Western theology is still being pursued 'within' the Enlightenment precisely because the Enlightenment is 'within' us as theologians and within our churches.

Of course, as students of theology, we do not need to submit meekly and uncritically to the dictates of cultural trends and dominant ideas. We should remain alert to the ideological forces

---

[1] Genevieve Lloyd, *Enlightenment Shadows* (Oxford: Oxford University Press, 2013), p. 1 (Prologue).

that are at work in the societies that we inhabit, shaping their intellectual products and cultural artefacts. Theology can critique culture and can hope to influence it. But theology cannot pretend to do this from some Olympian perspective, outside culture and above it.[2] It has never been the case that theology has been completely disengaged from culture and from the intellectual environment. Even the most conservative and ostensibly counter-cultural theologians have engaged with the intellectual milieu and have often been highly 'cultured' persons themselves (Karl Barth springs immediately to mind). It is impossible to withdraw comprehensively from the intellectual environment, however much some theologians try to make a virtue of being counter-cultural or of swimming against the current, or posing egotistically as 'prophetic' over against the age to which they belong. More positively, theology needs to be open and receptive to fresh developments in areas of research and thought – collateral disciplines – that in principle are relevant to the formal tasks and material content of theology. Theologians wrestle with the truths of the Christian faith in dialogue with the cultural world around them, working dialectically by way of assimilation or reaction to what they find there. They are compelled to engage with it and, if they are truly 'enlightened' thinkers, they will acknowledge that the culture is not external to them but is firmly installed within their psyche, distributed among their mental furniture and pervading it. So with the Enlightenment: Christian thinkers of the past three centuries, up to the present day, have in no way been insulated from its impact, but have pursued their calling unavoidably within its ample and ambiguous wake. So we have to confess that Christian theology too has been pursued in the wake of the Enlightenment. But, given that there are several 'Enlightenments', what do we mean by 'the Enlightenment' within the scope of this book?

Rival theories of the Enlightenment

The first thing to be said about 'the Enlightenment' is that it eludes simple definition. It was a many-stranded, profoundly variegated and dynamic movement, marked by the internal turbulence of

---

[2]H. Richard Niebuhr, *Christ and Culture* (New York: HarperSanFrancisco, 2001 [1951]).

tensions and contradictions. The Enlightenment was a continuing state of intellectual, emotional and cultural ferment. It was an ongoing, internal, dialectical process. It cannot be caught in a snapshot; it cannot be freeze-framed. No single aspect of the Enlightenment should be taken as definitive – certainly not the work of the *philosophes*, favoured by leading interpreters, especially Peter Gay. There are reductionist interpretations a-plenty, but the historical Enlightenment eludes them all. To use the phrase 'the Enlightenment' as a univocal, 'catch-all' term, as though it referred to a homogeneous cultural phenomenon, as some historians and philosophers do (in its favour) and not a few Christian theologians do (to its condemnation), is misleading. A monolithic reference can point to only one dimension of this multi-faceted phenomenon: which one shall it be? The singular use of the term 'Enlightenment' can be defended only if we acknowledge that we are being selective – and not everybody does that.[3]

Jonathan Israel distinguished two forms or versions of Enlightenment: 'radical Enlightenment' and 'moderate Enlightenment'. But he makes it clear that for him the true and authentic – though not the only – Enlightenment is the 'radical Enlightenment'. The 'radical Enlightenment', he argues, tended inevitably to scepticism, naturalism, materialism, secularism and atheism. It was therefore the only kind of Enlightenment fit for modernity.[4] A consequence of this selective, confessedly tendentious approach, is that Israel's 'radical Enlightenment' does not include Locke, Hume, Voltaire or Gibbon, who were all conservative

---

[3]Useful surveys of historical and contemporary trends in the interpretation of the Enlightenment include: Vincenzo Ferrone, *The Enlightenment: The History of an Idea*, trans. Elizabeth Tarantino (Princeton, NJ: Princeton University Press, 2015); John Robertson, *The Case for the Enlightenment: Scotland and Naples 1680–1760* (Cambridge: Cambridge University Press, 2005), ch. 1; Alan Charles Kors, *Encyclopedia of the Enlightenment*, 4 vols (Oxford: Oxford University Press, 2003), art. 'Enlightenment Studies' (by Lynn Hunt with Margaret Jacob) – a brilliant compressed narrative of the reception, impact and fate of Enlightenment ideas, though it does go over the top about materialism when it gets to Darwin. B. W. Young, 'Enlightenment Political Thought and the Cambridge School', *The Historical Journal* 52.1 (2009), pp. 235–51.
[4]Jonathan I. Israel, *Radical Enlightenment: Philosophy and the Making of Modernity 1650–1750* (Oxford: Oxford University Press, 2001); id., *Enlightenment Contested: Philosophy, Modernity and the Emancipation of Man 1670–1752* (Oxford: Oxford University Press, 2006).

thinkers and opposed to ideas that were religiously and politically subversive.⁵ Israel's is therefore a 'radically' truncated Enlightenment.

On the other hand, some writers (notably John Pocock) prefer to speak of 'Enlightenment' without the definite article, or of 'Enlightenments', in the plural. Thus in a recent article Pocock states: '"Enlightenment" is a word or signifier, and not a single or unifiable phenomenon which it consistently signifies. There is no single or unifiable phenomenon describable as the "Enlightenment", but it is the definite article rather than the noun which is to be avoided.'⁶ The late Roy Porter accepted the logic of this view in theory, but wisely admitted that it was difficult to put into practice, believing that the generic use 'Enlightenment' distorts and conceals as much as it explains and reveals.⁷

There is a third position – which I find persuasive – articulated notably by Hugh Trevor-Roper and John Robertson who believe that the various national and cultural expressions of the Enlightenment have more than enough in common to justify the singular use, provided that we recognize the internal differentiations and the powerful tensions within it.⁸ Robertson writes:

> The unrestricted definition of Enlightenment, or its alternative, the admission that there were multiple Enlightenments, has rendered the subject so blurred and indeterminate that it is impossible to reach any assessment of its historical significance. Even if this is an effective response to those who imagined that there was a clear-cut 'Enlightenment project', it is a response close to conceding that the Enlightenment is no longer worth arguing over.⁹

---

⁵Israel, *Enlightenment Contested*, p. 58 (I have added Gibbon).
⁶J. G. A. Pocock, 'Historiography and Enlightenment: A View of Their History', *Modern Intellectual History* 5 (2008), pp. 83–96, at p. 83.
⁷Roy Porter, *Enlightenment: Britain and the Creation of the Modern World* (London: Penguin, 2000).
⁸Ibid.; John Robertson, *The Enlightenment: A Very Short Introduction* (Oxford: Oxford University Press, 2015). Anthony Padgen, *The Enlightenment and Why It Still Matters* (Oxford: Oxford University Press, 2013), refers to 'the Enlightenment project', a phrase that probably originated with Alasdair MacIntyre.
⁹Robertson, *The Case for the Enlightenment*, p. 43. See also James Alexander, 'Radical, Sceptical and Liberal Enlightenment', *Journal of the Philosophy of History* 14 (2020), pp. 257–83. Alexander provides a stimulating taxonomy and analysis of the uses of Enlightenment in Israel, Pocock and Robertson.

Robertson favours, therefore, referring to the 'Enlightenment in the singular, with or without the definite article'.[10] He is helped to do this by his insistence that 'it is as a movement of thought that the Enlightenment possesses historical significance, for good or ill' and by narrowing the aims of the Enlightenment to the goal of the betterment of humankind.[11] To this extent only, Robertson aligns himself with Israel, of whom he is otherwise critical. Edelstein also makes a robust defence of 'the Enlightenment' as a unified concept, though he also is sharply critical of other aspects of Israel's overall scheme.[12] I concede that we can hardly avoid using 'the Enlightenment' as a convenient term of periodization and as shorthand for the world of thought of the late seventeenth and much of the eighteenth century and I am using it in that sense myself quite a lot, though not to impose sweeping generalizations on it and always with the caveat that 'the Enlightenment' was a highly diverse and often contradictory phenomenon.

Given all that, it is obviously hazardous to try to encapsulate the 'essence' of the Enlightenment in a single formula. However, interpreters of the Enlightenment have not been shy of doing so. There is no *a priori* reason why there should not be some common thread or key theme that runs through the Enlightenment in all its diversity. I find it in the connections between three aspirations: freedom, confidence and progress.[13] (a) Freedom: the liberation of the human mind and heart from enforced dogma, the power of prejudice, the exercise of censorship, the threat of persecution and pervasive social and economic oppression opens the door to (b) confidence: what Peter Gay called 'the recovery of nerve', the confidence to harness knowledge, skills and energy, belief in the autonomy of reason, and therefore (c) progress: the possibility of mastering natural forces and resources and turning them to the advantage and benefit of humankind and its well-being, which in turn can make social and material progress possible. I have used

---

[10]Robertson, *The Case for the Enlightenment*, p. 45.
[11]Ibid., p. 21.
[12]Dan Edelstein, *The Enlightenment: A Genealogy* (Chicago: University of Chicago Press, 2010).
[13]This analysis is prompted by Peter A. Schouls, *Descartes and the Enlightenment* (Edinburgh: Edinburgh University Press, 1989), p. 3.

the word 'autonomy', just as others have done,[14] but it is in reality an inadequate word for the heart of the cultural and intellectual sea change that we call the Enlightenment, because a sense of dependence always remains and is ineradicable – dependence on transmitted knowledge and skills and dependence on others for collaborative working (as in the case of the *Encyclopédie*). So we have to qualify autonomy, by pointing out that critical enquiry was not seen by the *philosophes* in an individualistic sense – they did not seek to emulate Descartes when he shut himself upon (or in) his famous stove to think things through alone from a supposed intellectual ground zero – but was understood as a collective project. Right across the board, members of the European intelligentsia thought of themselves as participating in a new movement, one that was marked by the supreme authority of reason in enquiry and in argument, freedom of speech and publication, toleration of dissenting convictions and, above all, the flowering of scholarship, science, art and literature in a reborn civilization. Where they did not already enjoy such privileges, they fought for them.

The shadow of the Enlightenment

Every shining light, when it encounters an object, casts a shadow. We see the shadow against the light. Where there is no light, there is no shadow. So to speak of the 'shadow of the Enlightenment' is not to deny or negate the chequered light that shone and still shines from that cultural epoch. The Enlightenment lit up many dark corners of eighteenth-century European and American civilization. It spread knowledge, explanation and understanding in the realms of science, history, philosophy, religion and society.

---

[14]Ira O. Wade, *The Intellectual Origins of the French Enlightenment* (Princeton, NJ: Princeton University Press, 1971), p. 659: 'Descartes' one fundamental idea, which was accepted by every one of the subsequent philosophers, was the autonomy of thought.' Ernst Cassirer, *The Philosophy of the Enlightenment*, trans. A. Koelln and J. P. Pettegrove (Princeton, NJ: Princeton University Press, 1951 [1932]), had previously made this point. But 'the autonomy of reason' for the Enlightenment was the autonomy, authority and sufficiency of critical, investigative, empirical and experimental reason, not of rational speculation (not that I have anything against the latter, in its place).

It upheld canons of justice, liberty and tolerance, where church and state had failed to do so. It allowed people to think of society not as a divinely ordained static, hierarchical order, but in terms of moral, educational and material improvement and it provided the tools to bring this about. It defended the claims of reason to probe areas of ecclesiastical and monarchical privilege that had been fenced off from such investigation. It gave birth to the critical-historical method in theology, especially in biblical scholarship. In England it provided the matrix for the unprecedented novels of Daniel Defoe, Samuel Richardson, Henry Fielding, Tobias Smollett and Laurence Sterne and for the poetry of (the Roman Catholics) John Dryden and Alexander Pope, and also of Thomas Gray, the Dissenters Isaac Watts and Philip Doddridge, the music of Henry Purcell and Georg Frideric Handel. It enriched Christian discourse in the hands of, among many others, Samuel Johnson, William Law, John Wesley, Joseph Butler, Joseph Addison and Edmund Burke – all certainly Enlightenment figures. It gave us the gem of catalogued natural observation in Gilbert White's *The Natural History of Selborne* (1789).[15]

While the French spoke of *les lumières* and the Germans of *der Aufklärung*, the term 'Enlightenment' was not applied to eighteenth-century English thought until the following century. But it has deservedly stuck. These Anglican writers were all robustly rational, though there was far more to them than the reasoning faculty. Their rationality was imbued with self-abasing devotion in the case of Johnson; intellectual humility and sharp moral insight in the case of Butler; mysticism and asceticism in the case of Law; organizing mastery, as well as surprising credulity, in the case of Wesley; and high-principled idealism in the case of Burke. It is absurd to dismiss and discard as 'rationalistic' this flowering of English culture, which within Anglicanism was not only mainly clerical, but at the same time and for that reason, impressively learned, intellectually innovative and profoundly devout (as William Bulman for one has emphasized). I am content with Bulman's working definition of the Anglican Enlightenment, which he says, denotes 'the participation of conforming members of the Church of England in the Enlightenment, under a variant of the

---

[15] Gilbert White, *The Natural History of Selborne* (Oxford: Oxford University Press, 1937).

Enlightenment's characteristic conditions', conditions that in this case comprise the following: the aftermath of the British Civil War and Interregnum, the Restoration of the monarchy in 1660, followed by the restoration of the Established Church, the Glorious Revolution of 1688, the Toleration Act of 1689, the rise of Dissent and freethinking, and the acquisition of an empire.[16]

However, the Enlightenment had a shadow side, especially in the anti-Catholic and anti-clerical legacy of the *philosophes*. Many elements that are commonly attributed to the thinkers and publicists among the *philosophes* had their origins elsewhere, especially in radical, dissident Christian writers and activists, as we shall note. The influence of the *philosophes* on the first phase of the French Revolution – constitutional reform – is generally acknowledged and in fact a number of the *philosophes'* demands for humanitarian and social reform were implemented before, during and following the Revolution.[17] But the ideological warfare of the revolutionaries against Roman Catholicism lost them popular support. As Nigel Aston puts it, 'The price paid by revolutionary activists for their militancy against Christianity and the Churches was to turn support for the Revolution into a minority activity for the rest of the 1790s.'[18] The extent to which those earlier French intellectuals were indirectly responsible for the later populist degradation of the principles of *Liberté, égalité, fraternité* in the exaltation of the goddess of Liberty in the Temples of Reason, which were former

---

[16] William J. Bulman, *Anglican Enlightenment: Orientalism, Religion and Politics in England and Its Empire, 1648–1715* (Cambridge: Cambridge University Press, 2015), p. xiv.
[17] On the *philosophes* and their possible influence on the French Revolution and after: John Lough, *The Philosophes and Post-Revolutionary France* (Oxford: Clarendon Press, 1982); John McManners, *The French Revolution and the Church* (London: SPCK, 1969); id., *Church and Society in Eighteenth-Century France*, 2 vols (Oxford: Oxford University Press, 1998); Douglas Johnson (ed.), *French Society and the Revolution* (Cambridge: Cambridge University Press, 1976); E. E. Y. Hales, *Revolution and Papacy 1769–1846* (London: Eyre & Spottiswoode, 1960); Nigel Aston, *Christianity and Revolutionary Europe, 1750–1830* (Cambridge: Cambridge University Press, 2002); Dale K. Van Kley, *The Religious Origins of the French Revolution: From Calvin to the Civil Constitution, 1560–1791* (New Haven, CT: Yale University Press, 1996).
[18] Nigel Aston, *The French Revolution, 1789–1804: Authority, Liberty, and the Search for Stability* (Basingstoke: Palgrave Macmillan, 2004), p. 256.

churches throughout France, notably Notre-Dame Cathedral in Paris in 1793, and even more so the Terror, or the ensuing Napoleonic Europe-wide tide of aggression, is still argued over. Some have seen the totalitarian horrors of the twentieth century – especially National Socialism (Nazism) in Germany and the Communist revolutions in Russia and China and particularly the Holocaust – as the nemesis of the Enlightenment because they were godless, anti-Christian movements, in thrall to false gods.

Dialectic of Enlightenment

In *Dialectic of Enlightenment* Max Horkheimer and Theodor Adorno, two of the principal founders of the Critical Theory pioneered by the Frankfurt School, portray the Enlightenment as turning upon itself and devouring its own children.[19] They accuse it of promising freedom, yet delivering bondage. The Enlightenment, they write, 'has always aimed at liberating men from fear ... yet the fully enlightened earth radiates disaster triumphant'. The Enlightenment's programme was 'the disenchantment of the world, the dissolution of myths and the substitution of knowledge for fancy'. Following Francis Bacon's empirical scientific methodology, the human mind was to hold sway over a disenchanted nature. In this agenda, 'Knowledge, which is power, knows no obstacles'. The ironic and tragic result is ideological 'totalitarianism' – 'a patriarchal domination of the world according to the criteria of computation and utility, in which the natural environment is ruthlessly exploited and the distinctive particularities of human nature are ironed out, with oppressive and even lethal consequences for those whose difference is a sign of opposition: women, black people, Jews'.[20] Horkheimer and Adorno's startling thesis invites some basic observations.

---

[19]Max Horkheimer and Theodor Adorno, *Dialectic of Enlightenment*, trans. John Cumming (New York: Herder and Herder, 1972; London: Allen Lane, The Penguin Press, 1973). There is a more recent translation, based on the definitive text from Horkheimer's collected works, by Edmund Jephcott (Stanford, CA: Stanford University Press, 2002).
[20]Horkheimer and Adorno, *Dialectic of Enlightenment*, pp. 3–6.

We note, first, that Horkheimer and Adorno speak of the Enlightenment in the present tense, as something that is not confined to the eighteenth century but is still going on now. They believe that we are being held – or trapped – within the trajectory of the Enlightenment, caught up in its irresistible wake. As we read them, we are also aware that, especially by virtue of being German and Jewish, their thinking is irreparably traumatized by Fascist and Stalinist tyranny (or 'domination') and by the devastation and oppression that it brought to Europe during and after the Second World War and especially by the destruction that was meted out to the Jewish people. In the Holocaust, technological mastery and industrial power, motivated purely by hate-filled, paranoid fantasies, became the means, the instruments, of genocide on an unprecedented scale. The early phase of the Cold War perpetuated a mass terror of mutual destruction, this time in the form of a thermo-nuclear conflagration.[21] But Horkheimer and Adorno were not trapped in the past and its consequences for the present: their vision also embraced the future and the fate of the natural world at the hands of rapacious humankind. They could not have been expected to anticipate the threat to civilization brought by global warming, but they prophetically warned – without offering any hope – against the consequences of the reckless exploitation of natural resources.

It is also obvious that, in their diatribe against the legacy of the Enlightenment, Horkheimer and Adorno are using the key principles or axioms of the Enlightenment itself and its critical tools, though considerably refined, to expose the shortcomings and deficiencies of the Enlightenment. They are emulating its unmasking of myth and illusion to themselves unmask the 'Enlightenment' myth and illusion of technological domination of nature, masterminded subsequently by the process-driven technocrats of mass industrial production. The exponents of Critical Theory are holding on to the Enlightenment ideal of the courageous individual using their reason, conscience and judgement in defiance of enthroned,

---

[21]The basic work was first circulated in 1944 under the title *Philosophische Fragmente* (New York: Social Studies Association, Inc.). A revised version under the title *Dialektik der Aufklärung* was published in 1947 (Amsterdam: Querido Verlag). It was reissued in 1969 by S. Fischer Verlag.

unchallengeable authority, but they are doing so without the *hubris* of many of the Enlightenment publicists. They thus reveal themselves to be unquestionably products of the Enlightenment. In this respect, Connerton insists, 'In the Frankfurt School the aspirations of the Enlightenment remain but its illusions have been lost' and 'Critical Theory is the Achilles heel of the Enlightenment brought to light'.[22] In this respect, Horkheimer and Adorno are following a well-worn path of the enemies of the Enlightenment, the Counter-Enlightenment, which we will discuss shortly. There is plenty of evidence to suggest that, in the late eighteenth and early nineteenth centuries, 'some of the most ferocious critics of the Enlightenment were, none the less, deeply indebted to it'.[23]

Subverters of the Enlightenment

It could be said that the Enlightenment invited such treatment; it deserved to have the tables turned against it. As a movement of critical investigation, it could not complain (so to speak) if critique were to be applied to it in turn. Since it exalted critical reason, it was only fitting that it should be subjected to the scrutiny of critical reason. It was to be expected that reason would fight back, as it were under the motto *Tu quoque*, 'The same to you', or 'You said it first'. As the Enlightenment developed, elements within it began to subvert it and elements outside it attacked it head-on. Its confidence in criticism produced self-criticism.

---

[22]Paul Connerton, *The Tragedy of Enlightenment: An Essay on the Frankfurt School* (Cambridge: Cambridge University Press, 1980), p. 119.
[23]Peter Hulme and Ludmilla J. Jordanova (eds), *The Enlightenment and its Shadows* (London: Routledge, 1990), pp. 2–3. See further Reinhart Koselleck, *Critique and Crisis: Enlightenment and the Pathogenesis of Modern Society*, trans. Keith Tribe (Oxford, New York, Hamburg: Berg, 1988 [1959]). Terry Eagleton's, *Reason, Faith, and Revelation: Reflections on the God Debate* (New Haven, CT: Yale University Press, 2009), especially pp. 68–76, 94–5, mainly consists of variations on the theme of *Dialectic of Enlightenment*, namely that the Enlightenment gave rise to the opposite of its intention, which was the betterment and flourishing of human social existence, but all the same, we still need its values. Unfortunately, Eagleton's rhetoric boils over continually; to change the metaphor, he drastically over-eggs the pudding, inadvertently obscuring his message.

Some of the major figures of the French Enlightenment, such as Denis Diderot and Jean-Jacques Rousseau, contributed to this undermining from within. Shaped by the classical Pyrrhonist tradition of philosophical scepticism, Diderot held that 'scepticism' (in another version, 'incredulity') was the first step towards truth. He hungered for all that was factual, concrete and mundane, regarding it as the raw material of philosophy. But in spite of himself, he could not deny transcendence completely and so he also thirsted for the Gothic, the macabre, the sublime, the numinous, for which he looked to the poets and artists of early Romanticism. His word to poets was, in effect, 'Make my flesh creep'.[24]

Rousseau, the outsider who has been described as 'the first enemy of the Enlightenment', critiqued his fellow *philosophes* for courting the great autocrats of the age and in his *Discourse of Inequality* highlighted the human cost of the material, technological progress so trumpeted by the *philosophes*, among others.[25] The claim has been made that, in effect, Rousseau mounted a 'Counter-Enlightenment'.[26] This designation is only accurate to the extent that Rousseau is seen as critiquing the *philosophes* from within the basic ideology of the French Enlightenment. As Robertson says, 'he was by no means exceptional, or external, or "counter" to Enlightenment'.[27] Hulliung proposes that Rousseau progressed step by step from *philosophe* to ex-*philosophe* to counter-*philosophe*, but all within the French version of the Enlightenment. According to Hulliung, he never even for a moment defected from the Enlightenment, remaining 'staunchly loyal to the ideals of freedom, individual autonomy and toleration'.[28] But, Hulliung believes

---

[24] Peter France, *Diderot* (Oxford: Oxford University Press, 1983), pp. 29–30; Denis Diderot, *Selected Philosophical Writings*, ed. John Lough (Cambridge: Cambridge University Press, 1953); Hulme and Jordanova (eds), *The Enlightenment and Its Shadows*, p. 2.
[25] Jean-Jacques Rousseau, *A Discourse on a Subject Proposed by the Academy of Dijon: What Is the Origin of Inequality among Men, and Is It Authorized by Natural Law?*, in id., *The Social Contract and Discourses*, trans. and intro. G. D. H. Cole (London: Dent; New York: Dutton, 1913), pp. 143–229.
[26] Graeme Garrard, *Rousseau's Counter-Enlightenment: A Republican Critique of the Philosophes* (New York: State University of New York Press, 2003), p. 120.
[27] Robertson, *The Enlightenment: A Very Short Introduction*, p. 72.
[28] Mark Hulliung, *The Autocritique of Enlightenment: Rousseau and the Philosophes* (Cambridge, MA: Harvard University Press, 1994), p. 242.

that, in the end, Rousseau represented an alternative version or expression of the French Enlightenment, forcing the Enlightenment to question itself.[29] I would say that, in Rousseau, the French Enlightenment was thirsting for, reaching out to, and beginning to taste what Romanticism would deliver.

It is said of David Hume, the most sceptical of eighteenth-century philosophers, a weakly convinced deist who seemed completely indifferent to Christianity, that he 'saw through' the Enlightenment. By means of reason, he undermined reason by showing that it would always give way in the face of emotion – and that it was right that it should.[30]

Obviously, it would be foolish to first define the Enlightenment as 'the age of reason' – where, unpardonably, reason is not defined – and then to transfer all that did not match that definition to the dawning of Romanticism. Gay, the exponent of the secular drive of the Enlightenment, nevertheless draws attention to the vitalism of Diderot, the emotional passion of Rousseau and the cool scepticism of Hume. All three were firmly embedded in the Enlightenment, but they nevertheless call into question any identification *tout court* of that movement with the primacy of reason, understood in purely empirical, critical and analytical terms that could be applied universally.[31]

Then there were those alienated and more radical intellectuals, on the fringe of eighteenth-century cultural life, who became disenchanted by the tendency of certain of the *philosophes*, d'Alembert, Diderot and Voltaire, to put their faith in the so-called enlightened despots or absolute monarchs, Frederick the Great of Prussia, Catherine the Great of Russia and Joseph II of Austria-Hungary. While employing 'enlightened' ideas to reform the structures of administration and drag their backward subjects into the modern age, they remained ruthless autocrats with highly mixed motives.[32] Diderot's five-month sojourn at the court of the Empress

---

[29]Ibid., p. 4.
[30]Robert Ginsberg, 'David Hume versus the Enlightenment', *SVEC* LXXXVIII (1972), pp. 599–650.
[31]Peter Gay, *The Enlightenment: An Interpretation, Vol. 1: The Rise of Modern Paganism* (London: Weidenfeld and Nicolson, 1966), p. xii.
[32]H. M. Scott (ed.), *Enlightened Absolutism: Reform and Reformers in Later Eighteenth-Century Europe c. 1750–1790* (Basingstoke: Macmillan, 1989).

Catherine of Russia ended in misunderstanding, disillusionment and mutual alienation.[33] The more radical and dissenting intellectuals, on the other hand, envisaged the overthrow of the institution of monarchy altogether in favour of a new republican Europe of the future. With monarchy would fall the Catholic Church and the Christian faith itself, which were often replaced in their vision by a naturalistic creed, centred on nature and reason in harmony and given ritual expression in Freemasonry. In England, the radicals stood aside from the informal alliance of the Established Church and 'The Royal Society of London for the Improvement of Natural Knowledge' (founded 1662–3; now simply 'The Royal Society'), which for a time was dominated by moderate, latitudinarian churchmen and bishops.[34]

The occult fringe

We might readily imagine that radical, sectarian or puritan groups stood aside from the current of Enlightenment ideas and values, but that was not necessarily so. For example, Madeleine Pennington has recently demonstrated the interaction of Quaker writers and publicists with the English Enlightenment and has shown that radical religious groups (in her case the late seventeenth-century Quakers), far from being displaced to the periphery of intellectual life, were actively engaged with it, the issues at stake being not only socio-political but theological, particularly christological. Extreme dissenters though they were, theologically, ecclesiastically and politically, Quaker leaders were embroiled with Enlightenment ideas and culture.[35]

---

[33]Robert Zaretsky, *Catherine and Diderot* (Cambridge, MA: Harvard University Press, 2019).

[34]Margaret C. Jacob, *The Radical Enlightenment: Pantheists, Freemasons and Republicans* (London: George Allen and Unwin, 1981); John Redwood, *Reason, Ridicule and Religion: The Age of Enlightenment in England 1660–1750* (London: Thames and Hudson, 1976); John V. Fleming, *The Dark Side of the Enlightenment: Wizards, Alchemists, and Spiritual Seekers in the Age of Reason* (New York: W. W. Norton and Company, 2013).

[35]Madeleine Pennington, *Quakers, Christ, and the Enlightenment* (Oxford: Oxford University Press, 2021).

Beyond the frontiers of political and religious radicalism there existed a thriving realm of atavistic and occult belief and experimentation concerned with such phenomena as superstitions, apparitions, miracles of healing, powers of foretelling the future (second sight), astrology, alchemy, levitation, self-starved women, demons, ghosts, spirits, fairies and poltergeists, and (assumed) witchcraft, much of it shot through with an ascent into the realm of mystery and the mystical. Far from being overtly anti-Christian (though heterodox of course), biblical and theological themes were appropriated and seamlessly combined with pagan ones in its theory, practice and iconography.[36] Moreover, its practitioners, rather than reacting against Enlightenment rational and empirical methods, sought to align themselves with the Enlightenment and to bathe in reflected glory, believing (or pretending) that they were contributing, by their experimental shortcuts, to the advancement of science and the perfection of humankind. This lurid aspect of English fringe culture is often designated as the dimension of 'irrationality' within the Enlightenment.[37] But that categorization is misplaced and is now widely rejected. Such beliefs as the existence of witches and occult powers may seem irrational to us today, but many in 'the age of reason' regarded them as purported natural phenomena that demanded to be investigated, assessed and sometimes corroborated by the methods of empirical investigation and rational judgement. John Wesley was far from being the only churchman or cleric who took such claims seriously.

Miracle claims were evaluated both empirically and metaphysically. Contrary to a popular assumption, David Hume's famous essay 'On Miracles', which first appeared in 1748 as Section X of *An Enquiry Concerning Human Understanding* and was subsequently published separately in various forms, was not responsible for the wave of controversy. It came at the tail end of the great national debate and made little impact at the time, the debate

---

[36]Paul Kléber Monod, *Solomon's Secret Arts: The Occult in the Age of Enlightenment* (New Haven, CT: Yale University Press, 2013); Euan Cameron, *Enchanted Europe: Superstition, Reason and Religion, 1250–1750* (Oxford: Oxford University Press, 2010).
[37]For example, H. E. Pagliaro (ed.), *Irrationalism in the Eighteenth Century* (Cleveland, OH: Case Western Reserve University Press, 1972), especially George Rosen, 'Forms of Irrationality in the Eighteenth Century' (pp. 255–88).

being at its height in the 1720s. It is also questionable whether the Baconian-Newtonian scientific revolution in itself generated doubts about miracles, though that assumption is well embedded in the secularization narrative.[38] Bacon advocated the collecting and categorizing of empirical evidence, not the making of metaphysical conclusions from it; Newton's cosmology required periodic divine intervention. Those most in touch with the new horizons of physical science were sometimes the most robust defenders of the possibility of miracles and they were generally the ones who instigated the debate in response to the deists' sceptical reductionism about the nature of divine revelation.[39]

Jane Shaw, building on the work of R. M. Burns, has shown that the upsurge of bizarre supernaturalistic claims and phenomena, from the British Civil War and Commonwealth periods onward, provided 'natural philosophers', physicians and churchmen with fascinating raw material for empirical investigation and reasoned evaluation. The result was not always to dismiss miraculous claims. Some leading natural philosophers, including Robert Boyle himself, accepted the possibility of modern miracles, but would judge them on the evidence. Apologists pointed to these inexplicable phenomena, some of which lack any obvious religious significance, in order to establish the reality of the supernatural in the midst of the natural realm and to refute 'atheists' – that is to say, usually deists. The deists, however, made great play of the fact that the 'evidence' for miracles is always elusive and at best ambiguous. And if you, as a churchman, are going to approach contemporary claims for miracles in a rigorous, enquiring, open-minded way, why not examine the miracles of the Gospels in the same spirit also, even the resurrection of Christ? Altogether, the supernatural or miraculous was a hot topic of the Enlightenment era, to be investigated, debated and evaluated, mostly seriously and responsibly, according to the lights of the time. Jane Shaw's term 'Enlightenment miracles' is deliberate and telling.[40]

---

[38]E.g., Herbert Butterfield, *The Origins of Modern Science* (New York: Free Press, 1965 [1949]); Richard S. Westfall, *Science and Religion in Seventeenth-Century England* (New Haven, CT: Yale University Press, 1958).
[39]R. M. Burns, *The Great Debate on Miracles from Joseph Glanville to David Hume* (Lewisburg, PA: Bucknell University Press, 1981), pp. 9–12; Jane Shaw, *Miracles in Enlightenment England* (New Haven, CT, and London: Yale University Press, 2006).
[40]Shaw, *Miracles in Enlightenment England*, p. 18.

An alternative option

Isaiah Berlin singled out Vico, Hamann and Herder as subverters of the Enlightenment from within and as prophets of pluralism.[41] This trinity of thinkers began their intellectual and emotional lives within the matrix of the Enlightenment, but burst forth into a better light. However, the real enemies of the aggressive French form of the Enlightenment were not those such as G. B. Vico, who transcended Enlightenment paradigms, or Rousseau, who was a passionate critic from within, but the politically and theologically right-wing opponents of the *philosophes* who deplored their arrogance and vanity and the way that they were lionized in elegant and sophisticated society. These declared enemies of the *philosophes* worked for the restoration of the monarchy and the Gallican church, throne and altar. Their campaign continued beyond the Revolution and the Napoleonic era, most notably in the passionate outpourings of Joseph de Maistre (1753–1821). However, de Maistre should not be stereotyped as simply the antithesis of the French Enlightenment, for he was also (as the editors of a revisionist collection of studies suggest) 'an heir and practitioner of the Enlightenment', deploying its tools against itself and taking its best ideals forward. Moreover, 'as soon as one stops thinking of the Enlightenment as a strictly secular phenomenon, as soon as one allows that some of its strands were fundamentally theological in character, it becomes difficult to continue to perceive Maistre as the apotheosis of Counter-Enlightenment'.[42] De Maistre stood in a relationship of obvious discontinuity and of less obvious continuity with the thought and work of the *philosophes*,

---

[41]Isaiah Berlin, *Three Critics of the Enlightenment: Vico, Hamann, Herder*, ed. Henry Hardy (Princeton: Princeton University Press, 2013); id., *The Magus of the North: J. G. Hamann and the Origins of Modern Irrationalism* (London: John Murray, 1993); Ronald Gregor Smith, *J. G. Hamann 1730–1788: A Study in Christian Existence with Selections from His Writings* (London: Collins, 1960); Laurence Brockliss and Ritchie Robertson (eds), *Isaiah Berlin and the Enlightenment* (Oxford: Oxford University Press, 2016).

[42]Carolina Armenteros and Richard A. Lebrun (eds), *Joseph de Maistre and the Legacy of Enlightenment* (Oxford: Voltaire Foundation, 2011), pp. 6–7 (editors' 'Introduction').

correcting and supplementing their programme. His early and deep engagement with the writings of Jean-Jacques Rousseau permanently shaped the structure of his thought.[43] The counter-attack on the *philosophes* was premised in part on a rejection of the central underlying epistemology of the *philosophes*, the sensationalism of Locke, somewhat systematized by Condillac. De Maistre attacked the 'grossness' of Locke's philosophy as too crude for the task it was attempting. He deplored the mundane reductionism that was characteristic of Locke's favourite metaphors, such as memory as a box for storing ideas and the mind as dark room with a few windows to let in the light.[44] De Maistre's Ultramontanist works, *Du Pape* (1819) and *De l'Eglise gallicane* (1821), indicate how the attacks of the *philosophes* on the Catholic Church and its theological traditions provoked and stimulated a renewal of Gallican ecclesiology.

Well before 1789 the conservative publicists were predicting in 'apocalyptic rhetoric' that the Enlightenment in France would lead to regicide, civil anarchy and the destruction of religion. They were vindicated with a vengeance.[45] However, as William Doyle has written, 'In condemning the chaos and blind destruction which the revolution had brought, they evoked a contrasting Ancien Régime arcadia of calm, harmony, and deference, where everybody knew their place under the rule of a paternalistic nobility, a clergy offering the consolations of true religion, and a benign monarchy.' Doyle adds: 'It was a caricature, but perhaps no more than the picture of tyranny and hopeless inertia and misery favoured by the revolutionaries.'[46] The reality, both before and after 1789, was more mixed, more elusive, than the propagandists of the time claimed.

---

[43]Carolina Armenteros, 'Maistre's Rousseaus', in Armenteros and Lebrun (eds), *Joseph de Maistre and the Legacy of Enlightenment*, pp. 79–103.
[44]E. D. Watt, '"Locked In": De Maistre's Critique of French Lockeanism', *JHI* XXXII.1 (1971), pp. 129–32.
[45]Darrin M. McMahon, *Enemies of the Enlightenment: The French Counter-Enlightenment and the Making of Modernity* (New York: Oxford University Press, 2001).
[46]William Doyle in id. (ed.), *The Oxford Handbook of the Ancient Régime* (Oxford: Oxford University Press, 2012), p. 5.

Discriminating appreciation

While there is nothing surprising in the idea that a movement as dynamic, diverse and complex as the Enlightenment should contain the elements of its own subversion, the irony is all too apparent. The critics of the Enlightenment are using the very methods of analysis and critique, based on investigation and evidence, to denounce the intellectual movement that, beginning with Bacon, given a seminal impetus by Locke and crowned by Newton, gave birth to those methods and deployed them, for the first time, in an organized, programmatic way. These critics misguidedly condemn the Enlightenment for its hostility to tradition, overlooking the fact that the Enlightenment not only had its favoured, selective traditions, but has now actually created its own tradition which, precisely on their premises, should be respected as such. So, continuing with the question of the Enlightenment and tradition, I will now give a few examples of 'discriminating appreciation' in modern times, beginning with the philosopher of knowledge and of hermeneutics Hans-Georg Gadamer (1900–2002).

Gadamer on Enlightenment and prejudice

Hans-Georg Gadamer's assessment of the Enlightenment, especially with regard to the value and authority of tradition, appears at first sight to be judiciously even-handed. He sees the Enlightenment as an attack on the power of prejudice in thinking, in enquiry. However, Gadamer points out, 'there is one prejudice of the Enlightenment that is essential to it: the fundamental prejudice of the Enlightenment is the prejudice against prejudice itself, which deprives tradition of its power'.[47] He does not dispute that the distinction, drawn by many Enlightenment thinkers, is a legitimate one: that is between faith in authority, whether of the church or of 'the ancients' or classical antiquity, Aristotle being the paradigm of this deference

---

[47]H.-G. Gadamer, *Truth and Method*, trans. and ed. Garrett Barden and John Cumming (London: Sheed and Ward, 1975), pp. 239–40.

to authority in matters of knowledge, on the one hand, and the use of one's own reason, on the other. He concedes that, if the prestige of authority takes the place of one's own judgement, or supersedes it, then authority is indeed the source of damaging prejudice. But Gadamer insists that authority may also be the source of truth. He claims that this insight was concealed from the Enlighteners by their prejudice against authority and their consequent denigration of it. Thus the very notion of authority became distorted, being defined as opposition to reason and freedom and tantamount to demanding blind obedience. But, Gadamer insists, that is to severely distort the idea of authority. The exercise of personal authority is not based on the intellectual subjugation of other minds, nor does it demand that they abdicate their own reasoning powers. It postulates the possibility of other minds coming to acknowledge a superior understanding, insight and judgement in those in the position of authority and so benefiting from it.[48]

Gadamer has somewhat overstated the Enlightenment approach to the question of authority and specifically to the authority of tradition. The Enlighteners had their own genealogies of ideas and values. Those who influenced their thinking formed their favoured traditions, whether they were philosophers of antiquity, especially Aristotle and Cicero, Humanist scholars of the Renaissance such as Erasmus, or radical thinkers of more recent times including Castellio, Montaigne, Charron and Bayle. They did not take up arms against authority as such, authority *tout court*, but against 'superstitions' of all kinds and especially the authority claimed for church dogma. They were over-awed by the authority of Bacon, Locke and Newton and they revered classical culture, especially its literature. What they repudiated was the overbearing authority of the Roman Catholic Church (and other intolerant churches, whether Lutheran, Reformed or Anglican), which was reinforced by censorship, persecution and the suppression of free public discussion and debate. They found the Old Testament generally distasteful, but their humanitarian instincts led them to respect the primitive Christian impulse, grounded in the Gospels, of compassion for human need and this was a continuing inspiration for many.

---

[48]Ibid., pp. 247–8.

MacIntyre, the Enlightenment and tradition

Alasdair MacIntyre's (b. 1929) critique of the Enlightenment follows similar lines to Gadamer's. It can be expressed in a syllogism. First, MacIntyre's central claim, which I fully endorse, is that there can be no rationality without the indwelling of tradition; we work within a tradition in order to progress in understanding. Second, the Enlightenment rejected the whole concept of tradition. The 'Enlightenment project' was (MacIntyre claims) to provide an independent rational justification for moral norms and social flourishing. But, third, this project has clearly failed, for without drawing on tradition, 'the legacy of the Enlightenment has been ... an ideal of rational justification which it has proved impossible to attain'.[49] MacIntyre does not deny that the Enlighteners possessed rationality of a sort, albeit a deficient rationality and one that did not work for the benefit of humankind in the long-term. And since he believes – correctly – that rationality can emerge only within a tradition, it seems clear from MacIntyre's own argument that the Enlighteners not only operated within a tradition of some kind but also that they were aware of doing so – how could they not be? The traditions in which they found wisdom and inspiration, over against received authority in church and state and an imposed ecclesiastical tradition, were the empiricist tradition of Bacon and Locke, the sceptical or Pyrrhonist tradition of two thousand years, the humanist (i.e. humane literature) tradition of the Renaissance, the Ciceronian tradition of classical antiquity. So I detect some sleight of hand in MacIntyre's accusation that the Enlightenment rebelled against tradition *per se*, when what they actually did – or at least aimed to do – was to exchange one tradition for another (as I will show below).

---

[49]Alasdair MacIntyre, *After Virtue*, 2nd edn (London: Duckworth, 1988), p. 6.

Edward Shils and intellectual emancipation

Edward Shils (1910–95) has usefully stressed that the Enlightenment continues in the sense that its legacy is part of the mental framework of us all. The Enlightenment is now an ineradicable part of the Western intellectual, cultural, politico-economic tradition. It follows that any critique of the Enlightenment that we may wish to make cannot be undertaken as a merely historical, detached and objective exercise, looking down on the Enlightenment from a supposedly superior position (*de haut en bas*), but will be one in which we are fully involved, intellectually and emotionally. Therefore, Shils insists, any critique must take place within an ongoing 'discriminating appreciation of traditions'.[50] Shils's assessment of the Enlightenment is an example of just the kind of 'discriminating appreciation' that he commends and is much more favourable than that of Horkheimer and Adorno, or Gadamer and MacIntyre. In his work *Tradition* Shils draws up a simple balance sheet of the pros and cons, the advantages and disadvantages, of the Enlightenment for human kind. First he designates the Enlightenment's 'tradition of emancipation from traditions' – that is from blind submission to traditional authority – as 'among the most precious achievements of our civilization', adding: 'It has made citizens out of slaves and serfs. It has opened the imagination and the reason of human beings; it has opened to them the possibility of the good life.' The Enlightenment in Europe and America should therefore be judged to be 'one of the noblest epochs in the history of the human race'. In sum, 'Its instrument was reason and its end was emancipation.' Thus Shils is not at all deterred by Horkheimer's and Adorno's indictment in their *Dialectic of Enlightenment*, assuming, that is, that he had read that earlier work (1972).

---

[50]Edward Shils, *Tradition* (London: Faber. 1981), p. 330. Shils devotes an insightful essay to a sociological, psychological and conceptual analysis of tradition, but without mentioning the Enlightenment, in Edward Shils, *Center and Periphery: Essays in Macrosociology, Selected Papers of Edward Shils, II* (Chicago, IL: The University of Chicago Press, 1975), pp. 182–218.

On the other side of the balance sheet, however, Shils places the nemesis of the Enlightenment that Horkheimer and Adorno had portrayed in such memorably lurid colours. Shils writes: 'The emancipation of mankind from superstition and from belief in magic has been carried so far that it has destroyed for many persons the idea of a morally ordered universe in which some things are sacred.' For Shils, hallowed or sacred traditions are maps to guide us safely through the perilous journey of life together. So 'the destruction or discrediting of these cognitive, moral, metaphysical and technical charts is a step into chaos'. Altogether, Shils judges, 'Destructive criticism which is an extension of reasoned criticism, aggravated by hatred, annuls the benefits of reason and restrained emancipation.'[51]

Noting elsewhere that 'the program of the enlightenment [sic]' (the programme is not further specified) provided the basis of 'traditional [sic] liberalism', Shils – the academic champion of the free and equal society – goes on in an essay on 'Tradition and Liberty: Antinomy and Interdependence' to dispute what he regards as the general assumption of the Western intelligentsia that tradition is the enemy of liberal values and that to uphold the virtues of a free and equal liberal democracy, one must oppose the authority of tradition. On the contrary, Shils insists, it is the responsibility of professed liberals to accept the challenge of reconciling their liberal convictions with the claims of 'normal tradition', because tradition is not only a source of wisdom, but is actually inescapable; it is our intellectual and moral milieu.[52]

Daphne Hampson: The Enlightenment as ideological liberation

Daphne Hampson (b. 1944) is a striking example of a formerly ardent Christian believer who renounced the Christian faith, rebuilt her religious beliefs and then promoted and expounded a

---

[51] Shils, *Tradition*, p. 326.
[52] Edward Shils, *The Virtue of Civility: Selected Essays on Liberalism, Tradition, and Civil Society*, ed. Steven Grosby (Indianapolis, IN: Liberty Fund, 1997), pp. 9, 103–22.

'post-Christian' theology. Hampson (at least partly) attributed her deliverance from Christianity to 'the Enlightenment'. In *Christianity and Feminism*[53] Hampson deconstructed the traditional and biblical paradigm of Christianity as patriarchal, androcentric and sexist. Unlike Christian feminist theologians, such as Sarah Coakley and Elaine Graham, Hampson holds that the received biblical and traditional worldview, so intrinsically oppressive to women, was essential to Christianity and ineradicable from its world of thought. She does not believe that Christian theology can be purged of these vices, that in other words, it could, be reformed, reconstructed and articulated in fresh ways that were not open to these undeniable objections which remain to trouble the conscience of all reflective Christians. We could say that Hampson was not persuaded (as I am) of the validity of the dictum, sometimes attributed to T. S. Eliot, that Christianity is constantly evolving into something that is capable of being believed.

Nevertheless, Hampson remains a theist, continuing to believe in the efficacy of prayer and feeling the attraction of some aspects of Lutheran (or at least German Protestant theology). In *Christian Contradictions: The Structures of Lutheran and Catholic Thought* (2001) Hampson points out that Lutheran and Roman Catholic theologies are separated by opposing structures of thought.[54] Their views of salvation therefore reflect these opposing structures. Martin Luther's soteriology was a theology of action, of experience; the Council of Trent's soteriology was a theology of nature, of metaphysics. Luther's was primarily biblical; Trent's was primarily philosophical. In this work she shows how little Roman Catholics have ever truly understood Luther and she traces certain ways in which his thought has been interpreted and developed by Protestant scholars. Although Hampson has ceased to believe in the Christian revelation and carries out her scholarly work outside the church, she makes no secret of the fact that questions of salvation were once of great personal moment for her. It is not the doctrines of salvation, but the ideas of selfhood and the self's relation to God that fascinate her now, according to her writings. It is against

---

[53] Daphne Hampson, *Christianity and Feminism* (Oxford: Blackwell, 1990).
[54] Daphne Hampson, *Christian Contradictions: The Structures of Lutheran and Catholic Thought* (Cambridge: Cambridge University Press, 2001).

that personal and intellectual background that we may note her interpretation of the Enlightenment.

In *After Christianity* (1996) Hampson credits 'the Enlightenment' with having decisively destroyed, on different grounds to feminist arguments, the conceptual credibility of Christianity – an outcome which, of course, she welcomes.[55] First, she claims that the Enlightenment overthrew (as she puts it) the oppressive paradigm of transcendent power and authority that is intrinsic to Christian theology. The heteronomy of divine sovereignty over against the world, she insists, is ethically objectionable (p. 2). In asserting the inherent autonomy of human beings, the Enlightenment enabled them to 'come into their own' (p. 2). The Enlightenment's mental framework of empiricism, universalism and uniformitarianism ruled out the supposed moments of unique particularity on which traditional Christian doctrine rests, which renders one age 'closer to God' than another – an invidious and unacceptable idea (p. 8). We know, Hampson protests, that there are no unique events in history such as might be caused by divine intervention (p. 8). At least since the Enlightenment, she confidently asserts, 'it has been known that there can be no such particularity' (p. 12). So the Enlightenment is our criterion of judgement and truth.[56]

Without wishing at all to respond to Daphne Hampson's argument in any hostile way, I could make the following brief and cumulative comments.

(a) Hampson tends to treat 'the Enlightenment' as one thing and in an *en bloc* way. Not all 'Enlightenment' thought was orientated to the canons of universality and uniformity. Vico, Hamann, Rousseau and Herder, to name but a few eighteenth-century super-heavyweights, pointed in another direction, in fact towards a grasp of particularity and the emotional, imaginative and intuitive – rather than ratiocinative – resources that enable our discovery and apprehension of truth. We should not over-generalize about 'the

---

[55] Daphne Hampson, *After Christianity* (London: SCM Press, 1996); page references in my main text.
[56] For a concise and sympathetic exposition of her views see Daphne Hampson, 'Freedom and Human Emancipation', in Nicholas Adams, George Pattison and Graham Ward (eds), *The Oxford Handbook of Theology and Modern European Thought* (Oxford: Oxford University Press, 2013), ch. 6.

Enlightenment' in the way that Hampson does; it was a complex, multi-faceted, diverse and sometimes contradictory movement.

(b) The conceptual paradigms that form the central core of the Enlightenment worldview – rationality (not rational*ism*), universality and uniformity in combination – are, I believe, incompatible with the feminist values that Hampson so ably and courageously defends. In eighteenth-century thought these paradigms were infused with the patriarchal, androcentric and sexist value-laden ideology that Hampson rightly deplores. I suggest that the Enlightenment paradigms that she commends are not actually her allies.

(c) In any case, these canons began to break down as the dynamic of the Enlightenment itself, in its mode of empirical investigation, gave impetus to historical study and eventually to the philosophy of historicism, and stimulated the emergence of such empirical and comparative academic disciplines as ethnography, anthropology, sociology, social psychology and the more specialized disciplines of gender and sexuality studies. The modern philosophy of science, as we see it in both the physical and the social sciences, is only the step-daughter of the Enlightenment; the Romantic recovery of the creative imagination made modern scientific method possible.

(d) It is true that, as Hampson avers, the metaphysical paradigm of Christianity throughout history has been dominantly transcendent and, in terms of divine governance of the world, heteronomous or 'over-against', with an emphasis on divine sovereignty in creation, providence and the moral law. But there are countervailing witnesses within the Christian theological tradition, including Thomas Aquinas, Franciscan theology including Bonaventure, Martin Luther, Friedrich Schleiermacher (whom Hampson particularly appreciates, although he was not a Lutheran but the theologian of the politically imposed union of the Prussian Lutheran and Reformed Churches that took place in 1817); and there are also the mystics both medieval and early modern. The influence of Romanticism in theology was a massive correction in the direction of a theology of divine immanence, as was philosophical idealism in Germany and England with its theological fruits in Anglican theology. The symposium *Lux Mundi* of 1889 and the work of J. R. Illingworth and the early Charles Gore began to reshape Anglican theology so that divine immanence was brought back into the frame and a balancing polarity of transcendence and immanence was affirmed and reached a high point in the philosophical theology of William Temple.[57] The Process Theology, that has been influenced by Henri Bergson and A. N. Whitehead, has taken this trajectory further and we see an attempted integration with orthodox Christian theology in the panentheistic theology of the late John Macquarrie.[58] In place of divine heteronomy over the created order, we see emerging a new theological cosmology of divine presence, guidance and sustenance, innate creative vitality, and cooperation, communion and love between God and those human persons who seek to be in tune with God. And that is very close, I would tentatively suggest, to the kind of religion that Hampson herself espouses. So there may be the possibility of a meeting point, of convergence.

Taking stock of the Enlightenment

The word 'Enlightenment' is loaded with irony for us in the twenty-first century. Many of us are acutely conscious that our intellectual and cultural life is overcast by the shadow of the Enlightenment. The intense light of moral, intellectual and spiritual awakening – which is what 'the Enlightenment' set out to be – sheds a correspondingly dark shadow. We are the legatees of the mixed heritage of the Enlightenment, in which light and darkness mingle. Hence the Enlightenment-consciousness, that imbues intellectual and cultural life in the West, is bifurcated. The virtues or principles of critical enquiry, justice, freedom, tolerance and open discussion are rightly championed. They may well derive ultimately from the biblical revelation within the Judaeo-Christian tradition and there were many 'enlightened' Christian thinkers and writers who acknowledged that fact, explicitly or implicitly. But the Christian church itself through the ages has not conspicuously exhibited

---

[57]Charles Gore (ed.), *Lux Mundi: A Series of Studies in the Religion of the Incarnation*, 10th edition with additions by Gore (London: John Murray, 1890 [1889; 15th edn, 1904]); J. R. Illingworth, *Divine Immanence: An Essay on the Spiritual Significance of Matter* (London: Macmillan, 1898); William Temple, *Nature, Man and God: Gifford Lectures 1932–33, 1933–34* (London: Macmillan, 1934).
[58]John Macquarrie, *In Search of Deity: An Essay in Dialectical Theism*, Gifford Lectures, 1983–4 (London: SCM Press, 1984).

them, so that the more subversive 'enlighteners' believed that they needed to promote them outside the boundaries of the church and against the church.

But there is an equal and countervailing reaction against the Enlightenment, found especially in conservative theological publicists: Roman Catholic, Orthodox, Protestant and Anglican. They hold the Enlightenment responsible for the moral disease and decadence of our culture, politics and capitalist economic ideology. In particular, they focus on the stereotyped characteristics of the Enlightenment and its legacy: rampant individualism, the cult of self-expression and consumer gratification, corrosive criticism of all established institutions and disdain for tradition, alienation from the natural environment and reckless exploitation of the creation. The Enlightenment has become the *bête noire*, the whipping boy and the scapegoat of conservative voices of all philosophical and religious stripes.

The biggest problem with the stance of those who champion the Enlightenment and the stance of those who blame it for all our ills is that they assume that 'the Enlightenment' is essentially *one thing* and that we know what that thing is. I will be arguing, *au contraire*, that the Enlightenment was a highly diverse and often self-contradictory phenomenon that eludes crude labelling and refuses to lend itself to propagandizing. I will be advocating a stance of critical, dialectical, solidarity with the Enlightenment, as far as that is possible with this diverse and elusive movement. And that will mean an approach marked above all by discriminating scholarly attention. I will assert that it is meaningless to repudiate 'the Enlightenment' as such, as some do, for at least two reasons. (i) The Enlightenment was and is a highly diverse and differentiated phenomenon and therefore cannot meaningfully be either embraced or repudiated *en bloc*. (ii) We are all children of the Enlightenment now in as much as we have all, at least in the West, I believe, embraced and imbibed the epistemological axioms and ethical principles of the Enlightenment. Let me expand this second point. I do not think that there can be one modern Western person who does not believe that they have a right and duty to make up their own minds, rather than blindly deferring to authority. There is not one critic of the Enlightenment framework who does not believe that we should investigate the evidence for any claim that we are asked to accept, rather than accepting it unquestioningly because we are told to do so. And there is not one writer, posturing as a champion of traditional beliefs, who would admit to rejecting the principle of toleration and freedom of speech, publication and association and instead advocate using forcible sanctions to silence those who disagree with them, or would care to defend the Inquisition! Those who critique the Enlightenment today do so within the Enlightenment's hard won world of thought and with the tools that the Enlightenment has handed on to them.

The thesis that I am defending in this theological enquiry is threefold. First, that the Enlightenment is a massive, unavoidable, simply inescapable, presence in our intellectual environment and that, in the theological enterprise, we cannot either go round it like some kind of road-block, or go back behind it to some supposed pre-Enlightenment age of critical innocence. Second, that with its *chiaroscuro* of light and shade, moral courage and intellectual *hubris*, creative insight and blatant blind spots, the Enlightenment comprises a mixed blessing in the inheritance of modernity, especially for theology and consequently for the church and therefore requires a discerning and discriminating approach and a consistently nuanced interpretation. And third, that the attitude and stance *vis-à-vis* the Enlightenment that is appropriate and required of thinking Christians and theologians is, at the least, one of *ambivalent engagement* and at the highest one of *critical appropriation*. In this chapter I have majored on what I believe we must designate from a Christian perspective as the objectively *ambiguous* character of the Enlightenment, eliciting a subjective attitude of intellectual engagement and ethical wrestling infused with *ambivalence* from us as its legatees and recipients. In Chapter 3, 'A Virtuous Enlightenment', I will show why I believe that critical appreciation and appropriation of the Enlightenment is called for and required.

But, before we get to the 'virtuous' aspects of the Enlightenment, I think that I need to show exactly why a fresh examination of its philosophies, religious thought and theology, its pioneering efforts in historical method and biblical research, not forgetting its socio-economic reform programmes, is needed. And that particular task is mandated precisely because the character of the Enlightenment has been misunderstood and misrepresented by many of its interpreters, past and present, whether they saw themselves as speaking generally 'for' the Enlightenment or 'against' it. The Enlightenment has hotly divided its interpreters, whether historians, philosophers or theologians, and it continues to do so. Among theologians the Enlightenment has found few defenders or champions. In reading modern theological works one comes across, without officiously searching them out, many examples of ill-informed, tendentious and even quite vicious portrayals of the Enlightenment. In these instances it is accused of setting modern thought on the wrong track and therefore of being the source of most of the supposed ills and woes of modernity, especially 'secularism', 'rationalism', 'liberalism' and 'atheism'. There are numerous examples of a jejune form of the genetic fallacy applied to the Enlightenment, namely that because someone, or a group of someones, had a bad idea long ago, everything in thought and culture has gone badly wrong ever since. To the unpleasant phenomenon of 'scapegoating the Enlightenment' I will turn in the next chapter.

2

Scapegoating the Enlightenment

In recent years Christian writers, including theologians, have lined up to condemn 'the Enlightenment' for much that has gone wrong with modern civilization and in Christian theology. These writers tend to refer in blanket terms to such vague entities as 'Enlightenment reason', 'Enlightenment rationalism' and 'Enlightenment secularism', and they do so in a global, undefined and unqualified way, not excluding the Enlightenment in England. In his influential work *History of English Thought in the Eighteenth Century*, Leslie Stephen was responsible for promoting, if not originating, the warped perception that the Anglican divines of the seventeenth-century Restoration Church of England were 'rationalist to the core'.[1] And the lapsed (or renegade) Tractarian Mark Pattison wrote of these divines: 'Reason was at first offered as the basis for faith, but gradually became its substitute. The mind never advanced as far as the stage of belief, for it was increasingly engaged in reasoning up to it', and much more in the same vein.[2] Though quite wrong, such judgements have had a long afterlife. The anti-Enlightenment animus has become quite a bandwagon, with an accompanying raucous chorus of 'rationalism', 'secularism', 'liberalism' and even 'atheism'. Even in the eyes of Christian writers,

---

[1] Leslie Stephen, *History of English Thought in the Eighteenth Century*, 2 vols (London: Harbinger, 1962 [1902]), vol. 1, p. 76.
[2] Mark Pattison, 'Tendencies of Religious Thought in England, 1688–1750', in *Essays and Reviews*, 9th edn (London: Longman, Green, Longman, and Roberts, 1861), pp. 254–329, at p. 260.

some quite eminent and others by no means insignificant, whom I will regretfully have to mention before long, 'the Enlightenment' has been singled out as the scapegoat, for many of the ills that modernity is heir to, philosophy and theology included. It seems to be implied in these disparaging comments that, if the Enlightenment had never happened, the world would be a much better place and a purer theology, uncontaminated by 'rationalism', 'secularism', 'liberalism' and 'atheism', would be possible.

In the face of this barrage of anti-Enlightenment rhetoric, some of which is merely formulaic and uttered parrot-fashion, I propose to ask a few searching questions. Do these Christian scholars, who campaign against the Enlightenment and its legacy, wish that we could go back to a pre-Enlightenment state of affairs in European civilization with a pre-Enlightenment philosophy and theology? The pre-Enlightenment world – typified by, but not confined to, the *ancien régime* in France – was a Europe ruled by absolute monarchs nationally and by grand landowning aristocrats locally. It meant actual serfdom for many and ceaseless toil for most of the population. The polity or political structure of *ancien-régime* Europe was a confused, irrational jumble of customs, jurisdictions and economic restrictions; its economy was mainly agrarian and lacked even basic mechanization. Moreover, do such deriders of the Enlightenment still hanker for a monopolistic, intolerant, state church, as existed in most countries of Europe, wielding legal sanctions against dissent, whether Christian dissent or non-Christian? When we are considering the Enlightenment, we should also bear in mind that, in France, the Catholic Church owned a sixth of all land and enjoyed feudal rights over much more. It was a church populated in its higher echelons by the nobility; it enforced its authority with censorship and persecution.[3] The Revocation by Louis XIV in 1685 of the Edict of Nantes, which had afforded toleration to the French Protestants, the Huguenots, provoked an outcry across the rest of Europe, indicating that a groundswell of educated, élite opinion was already turning against absolutist ideology in church and state. But, before showing why I find this tendency to distort and disparage the Enlightenment among (mainly) religious writers misconceived and

---

[3] See at large William Doyle (ed.), *The Oxford Handbook of the Ancient Régime* (Oxford: Oxford University Press, 2012).

objectionable, I will mention a few examples of the scapegoating of the Enlightenment in theological writings that have crossed my path in recent years.

Karl Barth on the Enlightenment

Karl Barth (1886–1968) was one of the most profoundly cultured of all modern theologians, a lover of beauty in nature, music and literature.[4] He had an affirmative theology of culture and in particular a love affair with the music of that Enlightenment masonic genius Wolfgang Amadeus Mozart.[5] Barth had a close, empathetic knowledge of eighteenth-century philosophy, theology and artistic culture, as he demonstrates particularly and at length in *Protestant Theology in the Nineteenth Century*. Nevertheless, in spite of his sensitive appreciation of Enlightenment thought, Barth is not innocent of polemical and tendentious accusations of 'rationalism' with regard to the Enlightenment.

For example, in his sixty-page essay, in that volume, on Jean-Jacques Rousseau's theological significance, Barth consistently calls Rousseau a 'rationalist' and one who inaugurated the movement of 'theological rationalism'.[6] Since Barth devotes many pages of that essay in expounding Rousseau's unique sensibility and emotional sensitivity and in establishing him as a precursor of Johann Wolfgang von Goethe who was for Barth the supreme representative of the superior form of Romanticism, I do not understand what Barth can mean by the terms 'rationalist' and 'rationalism' in this context. Barth could not have meant

---

[4]For a fine comparison of Barth and Hans Urs von Balthasar on beauty in theology see Jason A. Fout, *Fully Alive: The Glory of God and the Human Creature in Karl Barth, Hans Urs von Balthasar and Theological Exegesis of Scripture* (London and New York: Bloomsbury T&T Clark, 2015).
[5]Some of Barth's shorter tributes are collected in Karl Barth, *Wolfgang Amadeus Mozart*, trans. Clarence K. Pott, foreword John Updike (Eugene, OR: Wipf and Stock, 2003).
[6]Karl Barth, *Protestant Theology in the Nineteenth Century*, trans. Brian Cozens and John Bowden, foreword Colin Gunton (London: SCM Press, 2001), Chapter 5 'Rousseau', esp. p. 219: 'It is from Rousseau onwards and originating from Rousseau that the thing called theological rationalism, in the full sense of the term, exists.'

'rationalism' in the usual sense of philosophical speculation and system building, which we associate with Descartes, Hobbes, Spinoza, Malebranche and Berkeley. Nor could he have intended 'rationalism' to refer (in the more popular sense) to the secular, materialistic, atheistic thought of extreme elements of the French Enlightenment. Rousseau repudiated and detested both kinds of 'rationalism'. What infused Rousseau's thought was a profoundly personal and subjective source of feeling and intuition in relation to nature and 'the heart'. In the context of that work, I suspect that Barth means to point to Rousseau's humanism, his unwavering focus on the human being, on human existence in the world and on the human spirit and self-consciousness, what Barth calls Rousseau's 'anthropology' (i.e. theological anthropology, the theology of human being and human nature, created in the image and likeness of God). However, as we shall see in a later chapter, Rousseau's undeniable humanism is not a humanism without a loving God, creation, providence and immortality, nor is it without prayer, praise and worship of a kind. That is hardly 'rationalism'.

Lesslie Newbigin's cultural diagnosis

In the UK, the movement 'The Gospel and our Culture', associated with the late, much respected, Bishop Lesslie Newbigin (1909–98), was in the forefront of attacks on the Enlightenment. In his earlier writings on the theme of the gospel and culture, Newbigin reacted shrilly to the legacy of the Enlightenment. But in his later writings he slightly toned down the polemical rhetoric, though he still summarized its legacy as 'Enlightenment rationalism'. Newbigin admitted that it would be perverse to criticise the Enlightenment without first acknowledging the enormous debt that we owe to it. We have to confess, he frankly admitted, that, by the eighteenth century, the authority of the Bible and of the church had become 'fetters upon the human spirit'; that the removal of barriers to freedom of conscience and of intellectual enquiry was achieved in the teeth of opposition from the ecclesiastical authorities; that the Enlightenment programme led to the ending of much cruelty, ignorance and oppression; and that the scientific and technological advances which that liberation made possible have been immensely beneficial to humankind; and finally, that much remains still to be done to fulfil the Enlightenment's constructive agenda.[7]

After that catalogue of what the Enlightenment has done for us, it would seem churlish indeed to indict the Enlightenment, but Newbigin has several serious charges to bring. Commenting on the quasi-religious utopian visions of Enlightenment thinkers – their alternative eschatology – so effectively deflated by Carl Becker in *The Heavenly City of the Eighteenth-Century Philosophers*, Newbigin comments that we can only read of these hubristic fantasies 'with a sorrow which is hard to express'.[8] He adds that the Enlightenment regarded the Christian doctrine of Original Sin as 'the most dangerous and destructive of all the dogmas which have perverted human reason'.[9] I am tempted to interject that, if we consider the doctrine of Original Sin in its traditional, full-blooded, that is to say Augustinian, form, we might be inclined to sympathize with the thinkers of the eighteenth century. That doctrine included the notion, based on a bad Latin translation of the Greek of St Paul's letter to the Romans that Augustine was using, of the imputation of the *guilt*, not simply the consequences, of Adam's transgression to his posterity, by means of the act of sexual intercourse because the passion that it involves is transgressive, not fully under the control of our reason and will.

However, Newbigin's main accusation, which he owes particularly to his reading of Michael Polanyi and Polanyi's principle of fiduciary knowledge,[10] is that the Enlightenment reversed the proper roles of doubt and faith in enquiry, doubt being 'elevated [by the Enlightenment] to a position of honour as the first principle of knowledge'.[11] Newbigin appears to have in mind

---

[7]Lesslie Newbigin, *The Other Side of 1984* (Geneva: World Council of Churches, 1983), pp. 15–16. Similar sentiments abound in some of Newbigin's other late writings, especially *Foolishness to the Greeks: The Gospel and Western Culture* (Grand Rapids, MI: Eerdmans/London: SPCK, 1986); *The Gospel in a Pluralist Society* (London: SPCK/Grand Rapids, MI: Eerdmans/Geneva: World Council of Churches, 1989); and *Truth to Tell: The Gospel as Public Truth* (London: SPCK, 1991).
[8]Newbigin, *The Other Side of 1984*, p. 3; Carl Becker, *The Heavenly City of the Eighteenth-Century Philosophers*, 2nd edn (New Haven, CT: Yale University Press, 2003 [1932]).
[9]Newbigin, *The Other Side of 1984*, p. 3.
[10]Michael Polanyi, *Personal Knowledge: Towards a Post-critical Philosophy* (London: Routledge, 1958).
[11]Ibid., p. 19.

Descartes' celebrated philosophical methodology of systematic doubt. In this respect Descartes inspired several of the *philosophes*, notably d'Alembert, who credited Descartes with showing how 'to shake off the yoke of scholasticism, opinion, and authority ... of prejudice and barbarism'.[12] But the method of systematic doubt and distrust of authority in philosophy does not disqualify Descartes as a Christian thinker. He brings God pivotally into his famous argument, that culminates in *Cogito ergo sum*, to guarantee the veridicality of the knowledge that he cannot doubt – it is not an illusion – and he frequently professed his adherence to Christianity and remained a devout Roman Catholic.[13] Newbigin overlooks the fact that the Cartesian influence was superseded by the mid-eighteenth century in France by the method and tradition of Francis Bacon, John Locke and Isaac Newton, the method of empirical, experimental and inductive investigation of phenomena which, contrary to Newbigin's assertion, precisely teaches the investigator to trust the data.

Newbigin's real quarrel is probably not with the rationalistic, Cartesian, phase, which was not typical of the Enlightenment, nor with the empirical, inductive method, which is the basis of modern science including medicine, albeit much refined especially in relation to the role of theory, models and testing in scientific method. But what troubled him was probably a third aspect of the Enlightenment, that of 'redemptive optimism', with its visionary programmes for the amelioration of the human condition, an amelioration that was in fact not only (I do not say, merely) material, but intellectual and moral. Newbigin saw this dimension as the origin and begetter of the brash hedonism of twentieth-century Western culture.[14] But in this respect too, he misjudged the Enlightenment. As we will see in due course, one of its main motivations was indeed social and economic – including material – progress and the spread of happiness, which was largely intended

---

[12] D'Alembert, *Discours préliminaire* (of the *Encyclopédie*), cited Peter A. Schouls, *Descartes and the Enlightenment* (Edinburgh: Edinburgh University Press; Montreal: McGill-Queens University Press, 1989), p. 11.
[13] Schouls, *Descartes and the Enlightenment*, p. 37.
[14] Cf. Charles Vereker, *Eighteenth-Century Optimism: A Study of the Interrelations of Moral and Social Theory in English and French Thought between 1689 and 1789* (Liverpool: Liverpool University Press, 1967).

to replace the cruelty, oppression, injustice and physical hardship endured throughout history by the mass of humankind and which the church had endorsed as the punishment and consequence of original sin. That men and women had a right to be happy and to enjoy their lives free from want and oppression, and could attain this state upon earth, was the great new idea of the Enlightenment. I do not hear modern Christian writers deploring this ideal. They do not argue that God wants us to do without the machinery that eases the burden of labour or the medical and surgical help that can enable us to live longer, happier and more productive lives. I do not hear any Enlightenment-bashers claiming that God wants God's children to grow up without education and to suffer hunger, sickness and injustice. The Enlightenment vision of human, social well-being and happiness has been absorbed into modern Christianity.[15]

Colin E. Gunton: Enlightenment and alienation

The late Colin Ewart Gunton (1941–2003) belonged to the rare breed of British systematic theologians and it was his calling, as a systematician or dogmatician, standing consciously in the Reformed tradition of John Calvin, Karl Barth and Thomas F. Torrance, that led him to write a book about the Enlightenment, which he saw as a road block on the path to recovering a sound Reformed theology. In *Enlightenment and Alienation* (1985)[16] Gunton highlights the experience of 'alienation' within post-Enlightenment Western culture: alienation from ourselves, from one another, from the natural world and from God. Gunton aims to make a balanced and nuanced theological assessment of the Enlightenment, carefully avoiding misrepresentation and caricature. But we should bear in mind that he was not an historical theologian and that his sweeping generalizations about the history

---

[15]Crane Brinton, *Ideas and Men: The Story of Western Thought* (New York: Prentice Hall, 1950), p. 369 quotes the ardent French revolutionary activist Louis Saint-Just (1767–94): 'le bonheur est une idée neuve en Europe'.
[16]Colin E. Gunton, *Enlightenment and Alienation: An Essay towards a Trinitarian Theology* (Basingstoke: Marshall, Morgan & Scott, 1985).

of philosophy and theology sometimes need to be taken with a pinch of scepticism. He deployed the big metaphysical ideas, but the historical foundations were often rather shaky, as his former students and other interpreters admit.[17] In this work, Gunton, like Newbigin, identifies the nemesis of Enlightenment thinking in its supposed detached, extrinsic epistemology, in the divorce of subject and object and an instrumental idea of reason. Again, like Newbigin, he finds the philosophical antidote to what he regards as the toxic elements of Enlightenment epistemology in Michael Polanyi's notion of 'personal knowledge', with its key concepts of 'tacit knowing' and 'indwelling' with regard to the rapport between the knower and the known.[18] Gunton believes that 'post-critical philosophy', especially that of Polanyi, represents an alternative epistemology to that of the Enlightenment. It is an approach that is grounded in an essentially 'fiduciary' relationship to the tradition of enquiry in which we stand and which mediates to us key pathways of knowledge. The words of St Augustine, echoed by St Anselm, point to the fiduciary pathway: 'Unless you believe, you will not understand.'

In Gunton's Oxford Bampton Lectures for 1992, *The Three, the One and the Many*, he developed the argument of *Enlightenment and Alienation*.[19] Gunton's thesis is that modernity is characterized by 'disengagement' from one another as persons and by a consequent 'fragmentation' of culture and society. In a word, 'modern disengagement has engendered alienation'. He claims that, while the Enlightenment demolished aspects of traditional Christianity that were ripe for deconstruction, it failed to build a sustainable civilization in its place.[20] He claims that our existential state of alienation can be overcome only by recovering the truth that human flourishing depends on meaningful societal inter-relationships, based on a recognition that our lives are interconnected. True human being-in-the-world is defined by

---

[17]Andrew Picard, Myk Habets and Murray Rae (eds), *T&T Clark Handbook of Colin Gunton* (London and New York: T&T Clark, 2021).
[18]Polanyi, *Personal Knowledge*.
[19]Colin E. Gunton, *The Three, the One and the Many: God, Creation and the Culture of Modernity* (Cambridge: Cambridge University Press, 2003).
[20]Ibid., p. 130.

'habitation', which is an echo of Polanyi's concept of 'indwelling'.[21] Gunton's rather clotted and indigestible argument in this book is somewhat flawed by the running together, as though they were synonymous, of 'modernity' – a descriptive term that refers to a cultural era that stems from the Enlightenment – and 'modernism' – the name of a prescriptive ideology that promotes certain aspects of the modern era – notoriously, untrammelled individualism and unconstrained self-expression amounting to self-creation, which both Gunton and I regard as detrimental to human and social well-being.[22] His sweeping generalizations also include the completely unsustainable claim that the Enlightenment was responsible for the 'loss of a concept of God' (see below).[23]

I have absolutely no quarrel with Gunton's post-critical, personalist model of the knowing subject who imaginatively indwells the tradition in a trustful way and I have expounded it myself. However, I think that a balancing and corresponding stance, informed by a hermeneutic of interrogation and suspicion, is also needed.[24] But where I demur from Gunton's analysis is with regard to his failure to apply precisely this principle of indwelling to the Enlightenment itself. As I have pointed out in Chapter 1, we are not in the hypothetically privileged position of detached, external observers of the Enlightenment, so that we can weigh it up impartially and attribute blame to it, as though it were another sphere of reality. We are not detached from the Enlightenment tradition. It is internal to us and has shaped us. We stand in the mid-stream of the tradition (yes, tradition!) that derives from the Enlightenment. We should aim to understand it better by empathetic indwelling, recognizing that we can criticize it only from within. In the era of modernity, we are all children of the Enlightenment. In coming to know the Enlightenment better, from the inside, we shall come to know ourselves better.

---

[21]Ibid., p. 14.
[22]Ibid., see especially p. 1.
[23]Ibid., p. 141.
[24]See further Paul Avis, *Ecumenical Theology and the Elusiveness of Doctrine* (London: SPCK, 1986); id., *God and the Creative Imagination: Metaphor, Symbol and Myth in Religion and Theology* (London and New York: Routledge, 1999).

Alister E. McGrath: An influential misreading

The Bampton Lectures immediately prior to those of Colin Gunton were delivered by Alister E. McGrath, then in his late thirties, in 1990. McGrath has been a huge influence on Evangelicals – especially but not exclusively Anglican Evangelicals – an influence that is probably second only to that of C. S. Lewis and exceeds that of John Stott. For many years McGrath has been regarded understandably by Evangelicals as the paradigm and paragon of a sound, learned and brilliant Evangelical scholar. Rather like Francis Schaeffer in a previous generation (the founder of the L'Abri Fellowship in 1955, who died 1984), McGrath was (and still is) looked to by Evangelical students for their cultural and theological bearings. In his analysis of the failings of modernity Schaeffer consistently demonized the Enlightenment.[25] McGrath vastly excels Schaeffer (an amateur) in the range and depth of his scholarship, his intellectual energy and his published output (which in the number of theological titles may be a record in modern theology). I am referring to McGrath's eminence in historical and doctrinal theology, in the relations of theology and science and in the task of apologetics – that is to say, outside the realm of biblical interpretation, where Evangelicals also have their favourite exegetes and guides, who can be trusted not to question, doubt or make uncomfortable. (These are often those scholars who, especially in the area of 'Biblical Introduction', that is to say the provenance, authorship, structure, purpose and text of the biblical books, after going through the motions of reviewing the standard interpretations, including the most radical and far-fetched, come to the most conservative conclusions that are possible within the span of reasonable opinion, especially favouring apostolic authorship and an early date, and at the same time fighting shy of pseudepigraphy in authorship and myth in genre, which are viewed as a scholarly 'bridge too far'.) McGrath's theology and scholarship have become more profound, sophisticated and judicious as his

---

[25]Francis Schaeffer, *The Complete Works of Francis A. Schaeffer* (Illinois: Crossway Books, 1985). Cf. Nathan W. Hinkle, 'A Critique of the Enlightenment Doctrine on Progressivism through the Writings of Francis A. Schaeffer': https://core.ac.uk/reader/58824379 (accessed 2 March 2022).

academic trajectory has risen over the years,[26] but in his early work he chose to appear as a hammer of the Enlightenment. Entitled *The Genesis of Doctrine*, McGrath's Bampton Lectures contain a sustained attack on 'the Enlightenment'. But, although the French and German versions of the Enlightenment are distinguished, that cultural moment or movement is not actually delineated or defined.[27] In the Bamptons, which impress by their breadth of reading and reference, McGrath is essentially advocating a return to tradition as a resource for enquiry and a retrieval of 'the past', as an authority, though not of course an absolute one, to guide that enquiry, whether it be in the realm of physical science or, as is his concern here, of theology. McGrath's premise is the incontrovertible one that 'a communal tradition is central to religious epistemology' (p. 189). McGrath claims that the Enlightenment was blind to this truth and despised tradition. He alleges that it embarked on a wholesale, doctrinaire repudiation of the past (p. 138), that it dismissed the past as dead and gone (p. 171) and treated it as defunct (p. 137). The Enlightenment, we are told, had no time for the idea of historically mediated truth (p. 141). 'As a matter of principle, tradition is declared to be epistemologically bankrupt, a source of intellectual enslavement rather than liberating knowledge' (p. 179). The Enlightenment thinkers, we are told, regarded doctrinal formulations as historically conditioned and limited in their relevance to a different socio-cultural situation (p. 137). It was the Enlightenment that introduced the corrosive framework of historical relativism which was later deployed by historians of dogma, by the questers for the 'historical Jesus' and by modern theological liberals, who have (he claims) embraced relativism in order to deprive Jesus Christ of his divine authority and to eliminate the possibility of firm and abiding doctrinal truth (pp. 138–51). In reclaiming the validity of tradition (I would not simply say 'the past' which is not a manageable or intelligently deployable concept),

---

[26]E.g., Alister E. McGrath, *A Fine-Tuned Universe: Science, Theology, and the Quest for Meaning* (Louisville, KY: Westminster John Knox Press, 2011); id., *Darwinism and the Divine: Evolutionary Thought and Natural Theology* (Oxford: Wiley Blackwell, 2011).
[27]Alister E. McGrath, *The Genesis of Doctrine: A Study in the Foundations of Doctrinal Criticism* (Oxford: Blackwell, 1990); page references to this work are in my main text.

McGrath invokes the same post-critical luminaries as Newbigin and Gunton do: Polanyi, Gadamer and MacIntyre, and I certainly would not criticize him for that.

However, much of the strong anti-Enlightenment polemic of *The Genesis of Doctrine* is very wide of the mark. McGrath seems to have relied, at that time, more on tendentious modern interpretations of the Enlightenment, especially that of Jeffrey Stout in his *The Flight from Authority* (1981), than on either first-hand acquaintance with eighteenth-century texts (other than some texts by English deists and German rationalist theologians, the 'Neologists') or the more reliable assessments of the Enlightenment by historians who have specialized in eighteenth-century thought (though McGrath has an unrivalled capacity to hoover-up vast tracts of documentation and put it to good use when he wants to). McGrath quotes Stout approvingly and uncritically as showing that the Enlightenment was the sworn enemy of authority *tout court* and of the authority of tradition in particular. So I think I now need to make a short critical excursion into Stout's claims.

Jeffrey Stout: Tendentious theorist of the Enlightenment

In his arrestingly written but deeply flawed work *The Flight from Authority*, Stout asserts (and McGrath quotes this in part) that 'modern thought was born in a crisis of authority, took shape in flight from authority, and aspired from the start to autonomy from all traditional influence whatsoever' and that the modern 'quest for autonomy was also an attempt to deny the historical reality of having been influenced by tradition'.[28] Stout accuses the Protestant Reformers of rejecting authority, presumably meaning the authority of the Catholic Church and particularly the papal magisterium, though what they actually did was to submit to an alternative authority, that of Scripture (or perhaps we should say, of a range of

---

[28]Jeffrey Stout, *The Flight from Authority: Religion, Morality and the Quest for Autonomy* (Notre Dame, IN: Notre Dame University Press, 1981), pp. 2–3. Cf. McGrath, *Genesis of Doctrine*, p. 179.

particular interpretations of Scripture) read in the light of the new texts and tools of Renaissance Humanist scholarship. Moreover, the early or 'primitive' church was also an authority for Reformation theology.[29] Not content with complaining that the Reformers and the proponents of the Enlightenment rejected certain specific traditions (i.e. of the Catholic Church and medieval philosophical theology), Stout asserts that they sought to free themselves 'from all traditional influence whatsoever' – which, as we know from all the arts and sciences is something that no-one can ever do; it is not within the realms of possibility.

Stout makes a number of wild and unsubstantiated assertions, such as that Martin Luther mounted 'a full-scale attack on the traditional rule of faith' (McGrath, who has written several books on the Reformation, could never agree with that!); that the Huguenots and the Jansenists alike in early modern France contributed to the repudiation of authority (they had their authorities, especially St Augustine for both groups, and in the case of the French Protestants, also John Calvin); and that eighteenth-century deism was tantamount to atheism (in that era many stripes of nonconforming religion were dubbed 'atheists'; it was the ultimate insult; but it does not follow that they were actually atheists; almost all were not).[30] But what Stout never does is to explain what he means by authority and which authorities he has in mind, nor does he specify which tradition or traditions the Reformers and the thinkers of the Enlightenment are said to have 'overcome'.[31]

Stout's work is subtitled *Religion, Morality, and the Quest for Autonomy* and his genealogy of the dire effects of the quest for 'autonomy' in the Enlightenment is traced back to Descartes' method of systematic doubt, as set out in his *Discourse on Method* and *Meditations*. But, for a number of reasons, it is highly misleading (as I have pointed out before) to claim Descartes as the originator of 'the quest for autonomy' via 'the repudiation of tradition'.

1. Descartes (1596–1650) was engaged in a thought experiment for heuristic purposes in his search for sound and reliable

---

[29] *ISOA*, chs 1–3.
[30] Stout, *Flight from Authority*, pp. 3, 10, 41.
[31] Ibid., p. 257.

foundations for knowledge.[32] The foundation that he found was twofold. (i) First, he finds the indubitable reality of the thinking self: *Cogito ergo sum*. This crux of Descartes' method shows that, at that moment, he was relying on and building on the tradition of Christian and humanist values and doctrines. He does not say, 'I breathe, therefore I am' or 'I sweat and therefore I am' (he was in or on a stove at the time!). Thinking is good; as an activity of the human person, thinking has a value that other activities do not have. It is the classical tradition, the medieval scholastic tradition (especially St Thomas Aquinas) and the Renaissance Humanist tradition that tell us with one voice that thinking is a worthy, indeed noble, thing to do and that it is one of the highest activities of the human being. (ii) Second, Descartes explicitly relies on belief in the God who would not allow the thinking self to be fundamentally deceived. This is the coping stone of his progressive logic and enables us to trust our thought processes. The fact that Descartes chose to invoke the faithfulness of the Creator shows that he was not attempting any kind of Promethean detachment from his Christian culture and tradition. He was not cutting himself off from church, theology and Christian faith. The whole of the Enlightenment cannot feasibly be enclosed with Descartes, in the way that Stout implies, in that famous oven where he undertook that thought experiment! The Enlightenment was much more complex and diverse than any simplistic identification with Descartes' thought experiment would suggest.

2. As several eminent interpreters (whom we will meet later) of the Enlightenment have pointed out, the driving force of the French Enlightenment, among the *philosophes*, was precisely a reaction and revolt against speculative reason, as employed by Descartes, Malebranche, Spinoza, Christian Wolff and others, and an attempt to come back down to

---

[32]René Descartes, *Discourse on Method* and *Meditations*, trans. F. E. Sutcliffe (Harmondsworth: Penguin, 1968). Cf. John Cottingham, 'A New Start? Cartesian Metaphysics and the Emergence of Modern Philosophy', in John Cottingham, *Cartesian Reflections: Essays on Descartes's Philosophy* (Oxford: Oxford University Press, 2008), pp. 53–74.

earth with critical, empirical enquiry. Most Enlightenment thinkers did not trust Descartes or wish to follow the route he took. It is perverse to see him as the prime begetter of the Enlightenment.

3. It is also highly questionable whether the Enlightenment was the real source of the doctrine of historical relativism (sometimes misleadingly called 'historicism'), especially when historical relativism is escalated into a relativism of all truth claims, whether in philosophy, ethics or theology. One of the fundamental tenets of the Enlightenment, in most of its expressions because there were exceptions, was uniformitarianism: the invariability of human nature and human social dynamics across cultures and across historical epochs. Although there are intimations of the notion of historical relativism in Renaissance Humanism, in its developed form it emerges from the hermeneutical methods that stemmed from Romanticism and Idealism. I will attempt to clarify the principles and programmes of some key Enlightenment thinkers shortly. But I have said enough to show that Stout's diatribe against the Enlightenment (and the Reformers to boot) is highly tendentious and offers no sound basis for any theological enterprise.

Alister E. McGrath again: Still grappling with the Enlightenment

In some of his subsequent writings, McGrath continued to engage with the Enlightenment and its legacy. Only three years' after the Bamptons, McGrath edited an *Encyclopedia of Modern Christian Thought*, to which, naturally, he contributed various articles, including 'Enlightenment'. Here we find already a self-correcting tendency at work including a welcome effort to recognize the intellectually diverse and geographically variegated character of the Enlightenment.[33] McGrath writes: 'the Enlightenment is now

---

[33]Alister E. McGrath (ed.), *The Blackwell Encyclopedia of Modern Christian Thought* (Oxford: Blackwell, 1993), art. 'Enlightenment'. Incidentally, I contributed the article on 'Ecclesiology' to this volume.

recognized to be intellectually heterogeneous, including a remarkable variety of anti-rational movements'. He even advises that the term 'rationalism' should be used with caution and should be avoided as catch-phrase for an optimistic 'belief in scientific and social progress'. Furthermore, he correctly points out that the rational approach of Descartes, Spinoza, Leibniz and Wolff, in the first stage of the Enlightenment, was superseded by the empirical method based on John Locke's sensation-based epistemology. What is missing here is Isaac Newton, the sun in the firmament of eighteenth-century thought, and the enormous impetus that Newtonian science, as an all-conquering paradigm, gave to intellectual activity in other cultural spheres, even including literature. But McGrath has more than compensated for that neglect since then.

McGrath's very first account, as far as I am aware, of the Enlightenment generally is perhaps his most reliable and useful treatment of it, in my opinion, apart from what he had already written with reference to German Christology.[34] It comes in volume 1 of *The History of Christian Theology* that I initiated and edited in the mid-1980s: *The Science of Theology*, which also had major contributions by Gillian R. Evans and Allan D. Galloway.[35] However, in McGrath's contribution a certain tension with regard to the assessment of the Enlightenment in relation to Christian belief persists. On the one hand we read that 'the widespread belief in the omnicompetence of reason reached its zenith in the eighteenth-century Enlightenment, as the "superstitions" of Christianity were exposed to the full power of rational criticism'. But on the other hand, we learn that 'Although the Enlightenment is usually regarded as characterised by a highly critical and sceptical attitude towards religion ... this is a dangerous simplification.' Then McGrath adds: 'While this judgement is certainly valid in the case of the French Enlightenment, it is far from clear that it can be applied to the movement as a whole, as, for example, it occurred in England or Germany', where religious belief was modified and adapted, rather than rejected wholesale.[36] But that

---

[34]Alister E. McGrath, *The Making of Modern German Christology* (Oxford: Blackwell, 1986).
[35]Paul Avis (ed.), *The History of Christian Theology, Volume 1: The Science of Theology* (Basingstoke: Marshall Pickering; Grand Rapids, MI: Eerdmans, 1986). McGrath writes on the Enlightenment on pp. 206–29.
[36]Ibid., p. 206.

is the whole point: Christian belief, like Christian practice, has always been adapted or modified or developed in response to changing cultural and social norms. The history of theology is one of continual adaptation, modification and development in response to evolving worldviews. Of course, every change should be subject to evaluation – but by what criteria? I cannot pursue any further here that debate, which was launched by John Henry Newman in his *Essay on the Development of Christian Doctrine* in the mid-nineteenth century,[37] and continues unabated today. But I will simply say that the question of doctrinal development lies at the heart of the theological enterprise, generating much of the theological dynamic within Christianity as it attempts to respond to changing cultural norms. It is a virtue of the Enlightenment that it engaged critically and constructively with the Christian tradition in its various forms and sought to make it responsive, relevant and credible in a changing culture.

I now contrast that recognition of the adaptability of Christian faith with another statement of McGrath that must have been written about the same time as the essay mentioned immediately above. In his substantial and indispensable history of the doctrine of justification, first published in 1986 and revised several times, McGrath outlines the fate of that doctrine during the Enlightenment period, majoring on Germany and the English deists again and bringing out the moral (or 'moralizing', as he sometimes puts it) concerns of the leading figures. He concludes ominously: 'By the year 1780, therefore, the foundations of the Christian doctrine of justification had been subjected to such destructive criticism by the Enlightenment in England, France and Germany that it appeared impossible that they could ever be restored.'[38] But that judgement seems to assume that 'the Christian doctrine of justification' is univocal, that is to say that there is only one Christian doctrine of justification. If justification be taken to refer to reconciliation

---

[37]John Henry Newman, *An Essay on the Development of Christian Doctrine; The Edition of 1845*, ed. and intro. J. M. Cameron (Harmondsworth: Penguin, 1974).
[38]Alister E. McGrath, *Iustitia Dei: A History of the Christian Doctrine of Justification* [2 vols], *Vol. II: From 1500 to the Present Day* (Cambridge: Cambridge University Press, 1986), pp. 136-48, at p. 148. A comprehensively revised 4th edition was published in 2020, but I have not had the opportunity to consult it. In the period in question, McGrath's emphasis is on 'moralism' and 'rationalism'.

or salvation, it is clear that the theologians of the Enlightenment, though they tended to challenge certain aspects of tradition that they had inherited, whether Tridentine Roman Catholicism or Lutheran scholasticism, and especially the Augustinian doctrine of Original Sin, nevertheless recognized in their different ways that humankind needed salvation, that it needed to be reconciled to God. There have been – and are – in fact a number of versions of the doctrine of justification and several of them were articulated by the thinkers of the Enlightenment. We have only to think of Lessing's identification of salvation with enlightenment (a model that has precedent in Augustine and Aquinas, so it can hardly be thrown out as unchristian), Joseph Butler's highly ethical teaching about the way of salvation, William Law's mystical theology and John Wesley's doctrine of Christian perfection.[39]

Louis Dupré: Ambivalence and distortion

The prolific Flemish Roman Catholic scholar Louis Dupré (b. 1925), who has taught at the Universities of Georgetown and Yale, is an exponent of the history of ideas and of the critique of modernity. His *forté* is broad-brush – I might say sweeping – generalizations about intellectual trends and influences. In his study of the Enlightenment, I find both ambivalence on his part because there is not a little of giving with one hand and taking away with the other and also (unintentional) distortion in his interpretation. I will briefly discuss some aspects of his genealogical account of the Enlightenment worldview and its legacy for modernity as expounded in his book of 2004 with the alluring title *The Enlightenment and the Intellectual Foundations of Modern Culture*.[40]

First, on a puzzling historical note, Dupré rejects the connection, pioneered by Jacob Burckhardt and Hugh Trevor-Roper, that the

---

[39]For Locke, Butler, Law, Wesley and Burke (and in passing, Addison and Johnson) as Enlightenment thinkers see *ISOA*, chs. 8 and 9.
[40]Louis Dupré, *The Enlightenment and the Intellectual Foundations of Modern Culture* (New Haven, CT: Yale University Press, 2004); page references in my main text.

Enlightenment had important roots in the classical humanism of the Renaissance. While Trevor-Roper traces a direct line back to Erasmus, Dupré insists that 'no direct causal succession links the humanism of the fifteenth century with the Enlightenment'. We should not repeat, he says, 'the mistake made by Jacob Burckhardt in *The Civilisation of the Renaissance in Italy*, and often repeated in the twentieth century, of interpreting the Renaissance as the first stage of the Enlightenment' (p. xi).[41] Dupré's robust assertion goes against a substantial scholarly consensus. It is important for us to grasp the connection between the Renaissance and the Enlightenment in order to do justice to the theme of Christian belief that runs through Enlightenment thought.

Erasmus and the tribe of Renaissance humanist scholars were devout Christians and Catholics, dedicated to the reform and renewal of the church through the fertilizing influence of the original texts of the Scriptures and the early Fathers. Erasmus' alternative to Luther's theology was the fervent but quietist path of the *philosophia christi*.[42] Nearly fifty years ago it was said that 'Recent scholarship has emphasized that it is difficult, if not impossible, to find a humanist of the fifteenth or sixteenth centuries who was not a Christian.'[43] Most of the sixteenth-century Protestant and Catholic Reformers were trained in humanist studies and methods. Erasmus's own scholarly methods prefigured those of the Enlightenment scholars, especially the eighteenth-century historians (who are praised by Dupré), in the areas of philology, scepticism towards sources, a sense of historical perspective and cultural relativism, and notions of development. The seeds of these methodological norms, that are associated with Enlightenment historiography, are apparent in the Renaissance, particularly in the

---

[41]Jacob Burckhardt, *The Civilisation of the Renaissance in Italy* (London: Phaidon, 1965).
[42]Desiderius Erasmus, *Enchiridion Militis Christiani* (London: Methuen, 1905; repr. of edn by Wynkyn de Worde, 1533 [1501]).
[43]Myron P. Gilmore, 'Italian Reactions to Erasmian Humanism', in Heiko A. Oberman and Thomas A Brady, Jr. (eds), *Itinerarium Italicum: The Profile of the Italian Renaissance in the Mirror of Its European Transformations, Dedicated to Paul Oskar Kristeller on the Occasion of His 70th Birthday* (Leiden: Brill, 1975), pp. 61–115, at p. 61; cf. pp. 62–3.

work of the Italian priest Lorenzo Valla (1407–57) and the French layman Guillaume Budé (1467–1540).[44] These attributes are also strongly present, in a mature and sophisticated form, in the work of Jean Bodin (1530–96) who wrote history and the philosophy of history.[45] On the other hand, national identities meant little to Erasmus, who was a citizen of the known civilized world (Christendom) and he sat light to periodicity (which would become important in the Enlightenment which favoured stadial theories of society).[46] Recent scholarship has taken up the theme of Erasmus' influence on the humanist tradition of his time and subsequently and on radical religious thought in the early modern period.[47] However, Dupré seems to believe that the Enlightenment rejected the tradition of classical humanism because (he seems to think) the Enlightenment was hostile to Christianity; therefore there could be no direct continuity between the two. But his assumption (if that is what it is) that the Enlightenment generally was hostile to Christianity is mistaken, as we shall see. The Enlightenment,

---

[44]Donald R. Kelley, *Foundations of Modern Historical Scholarship: Language, Law and History in the French Renaissance* (New York: Columbia University Press, 1970), pp. 45–6; George Huppert, *The Idea of Perfect History: Historical Erudition and Historical Philosophy in Renaissance France* (Urbana, IL: University of Illinois Press, 1970).

[45]Jean Bodin, *Method for the Easy Comprehension of History*, trans. Beatrice Reynolds (New York: Columbia University Press, 1945); John L. Brown, *The Methodus ad Facilem Historiarum Cognitionem of Jean Bodin: A Critical Study* (New York: AMS reprint, 1969 [1939]); Julian H. Franklin, *Jean Bodin and the Sixteenth-Century Revolution in the Methodology of Law and History* (New York: Columbia University Press, 1963); Donald R. Kelley, 'The Development and Context of Bodin's Method', in Horst Denzer (ed.), *Jean Bodin: Verhandligen der internationalen Bodin Jagung in München* (München: Verlag C. H. Beck, 1973), pp. 123–50.

[46]Peter G. Bietenholz, *History and Biography in the Work of Erasmus of Rotterdam* (Geneva: Groz, 1966); George Huppert, 'The Renaissance Background of Historicism', *H&T* 5 (1966), pp. 48–60; Joseph M. Levine, *Humanism and History: Origins of Modern English Historiography* (Ithaca, NY: Cornell University Press, 1987).

[47]Peter G. Bietenholz, *Encounters with a Radical Erasmus: Erasmus' Work as a Source of Radical Thought in Early Modern Europe* (Toronto: University of Toronto Press, 2009); Gregory D. Dodds, *Exploiting Erasmus: The Erasmian Legacy and Religious Change in Early Modern England* (Toronto: University of Toronto Press, 2009); Erika Rummell (ed.), *Biblical Humanism and Scholasticism in the Age of Erasmus* (Leiden: Brill, 2008).

even in its militant French variant among the *philosophes*, was a development, within a different milieu, of classical humanism, even Christian humanism.

Second, Dupré belongs to the noisy school of interpretation that holds that a key characteristic of the Enlightenment was 'contempt for tradition' (p. 4). In this chapter and the previous one I have critiqued this view and in the next chapter I will outline some aspects of the Enlightenment's various attitudes to tradition. So I will leave it there for now, except to say in summary that the Enlightenment tended to reject some traditions (especially those of medieval Catholicism) and to admire others (especially those of Classical Antiquity and the Renaissance). However, Dupré is correct to designate the Enlightenment as 'first and foremost a breakthrough in critical consciousness'; and he is sound when he comments (as I have done, citing notably Horkheimer and Adorno) that those who criticize the Enlightenment for taking criticism too far 'ought to remember that they attack the movement with the very weapon forged by the object of their attack: that of critical reflectiveness' (p. xiii).

Dupré properly insists that it is a gross over-simplification to identify the Enlightenment with 'rationalism'. There were countervailing tendencies, including an emphasis on sensibility. 'One might just as well describe the Enlightenment as an era of sentimentality' (p. xiii). But this is one point at which I detect ambivalence (to put it kindly): it is in his explanation of 'rationalism' that I think Dupré goes astray. Pointing out that 'the dual meaning of the term "rationalism" has led to misunderstandings', Dupré explains that 'rationalism'

> refers to a philosophical doctrine that insists on the primacy of a priori concepts in the process of knowledge. As such it is opposed to empiricism according to which the origin of our ideas lies in experience. Historically the former was embodied in the theories of Descartes, Spinoza, Leibniz, and Wolff. Yet those who refer to the Enlightenment as a 'rationalist' period usually understand this to include philosophical empiricists as well as rationalists [in the above sense]. This use of the term assumes that the human mind is the sole source of truth and hence must reject faith as a possible source of truth.
>
> (p. 7)

There are a couple of puzzling assumptions in this statement. First, while it is true that one often finds the supreme empiricist, John Locke, accused of 'rationalism', the empirical method in scientific enquiry stands at the opposite pole to any system that takes 'the human mind [as] the sole source of truth'. Empiricism – while of course it cannot function without explanatory hypotheses – is concerned to study a reality that is already given, 'out there', awaiting our inspection. It is the opposite of solipsistic, subjective and inward looking. Second, it is misleading to suggest that 'faith' as such can be a 'source of truth'. I may have faith in any person or any belief system. Muslim suicide-bombers have great faith, but they lack intellectual and moral truth. Although 'faith' is often used in the mass-media as a politically correct euphemism for religious belief, Dupré is not a journalist and I think that when he says 'faith', he must mean 'divine revelation' considered as a source of truth – which, for Christians and other theistic believers, it is. But the point of Enlightenment methodology is that biblical revelation, while it remains a source of truth about realities beyond mere human investigation, is not a source of the truth that can be discovered about the natural or the human world, the world that is studied by empirical scientific methods. That battle was won some time ago (shades of Galileo), as Dupré would, surely agree.

Dupré also asserts that Descartes for whom, he affirms, 'the ground of reality as well as of truth' was a transcendent, objective reality, 'nonetheless created the conditions for an ideological rationalism when he transferred the question of truth from its traditional ontological basis (according to which truth resides primarily in the nature of the real) to an epistemic one whereby it becomes the result of a method of thinking' (p. 7). I think Dupré is mistaken in taking Descartes's famous mind experiment as an exercise in displacing ontology (cf. p. 16) Rather, as I have already mentioned, the *Cogito ergo sum* was a heuristic exercise which Descartes undertook against the background of the sceptical or Pyrrhonist tradition that derived from antiquity and had flourished again in the Renaissance and afterwards, even among Christian thinkers. Descartes embarked on his experiment precisely in order to regain a solid footing in objective ('ontological') reality. For Descartes, the truth that there was such an 'external' reality – the veridicality of our apprehension of it – was guaranteed by the God of the Christian church who would not allow us to be so fundamentally deceived. As I will show, the Enlightenment was not typically rationalist in a speculative sense, postulating a reality out of the philosopher's mental contents, but was critical, empirical and ethical in its approach to questions of knowledge. But the rationalist philosophers, such as those mentioned by Dupré (who were all Christians bar Spinoza, but he was on the fringe of radical Protestant thought), who worked on the eve of the Enlightenment, did not attempt to replace ontological doctrine with naked human subjectivity.

The Enlightenment in some recent theology

In recent a book review I praised and supported a programmatic study of Christian apologetics by the Anglican feminist theologian Elaine Graham.[48] I found a great deal to agree with, but I regretted one flaw in her case, which illustrates once again the prevalent misconceptions of the Enlightenment in much recent theology. I regretted the multiple references, in disparaging terms, to 'the Enlightenment' in this book, such as the expressions 'Enlightenment reason' (p. 15), 'Enlightenment secularism' (p. 57), 'a rationalist post-Enlightenment mindset' (p. 66), and most comprehensively in the statement: 'the eighteenth-century Enlightenment view that in order to flourish, humanity must be free of God, church, religion, superstition, and anything that prevents them from having freedom to exercise their reason' (p. 49). That really takes my breath away. Stigmatization of 'the Enlightenment' in such sweeping and unqualified terms is completely unjustified and historically incorrect, as I will shortly show.

Another recent example, also in a book that I have reviewed, comes from *The Oxford Handbook of the Oxford Movement*.[49]

---

[48]Elaine Graham, *Apologetics without Apology: Speaking of God in a World Troubled by Religion* (Eugene, OR: Cascade Books, 2017). My review appeared in *Ecclesiology* 15.1 (2019), pp. 97–9.
[49]Stewart J. Brown, Peter B. Nockles and James Pereiro (eds), *The Oxford Handbook of the Oxford Movement* (Oxford: Oxford University Press, 2017). My Article Review appeared in *Ecclesiology* 16.2 (2020), pp. 243–53: Paul Avis, 'Towards a Richer Appreciation of the Oxford Movement'.

That otherwise superb volume is marred here and there by a less than assured handling of eighteenth-century thought, including the now familiar caricature of the Enlightenment as 'rationalistic'. Here we find frequent unqualified, 'global' references to 'rationalism', 'liberalism' and 'the 'Enlightenment', as though they were each one thing and we knew what that thing was. This kind of usage lacks the sophistication and nuanced exposition that is called for by the complex and diversified character of eighteenth-century European thought. It does poor justice not least to the variegated complexion of 'the Enlightenment', which was not typically rationalistic, neither was it generically anti-Christian – far from it – and in fact received various Christian expressions, of varying degrees of orthodoxy.

Rousseau the scapegoat

Although Voltaire was thoroughly demonized by Christian writers, in his own time and since, it is Jean-Jacques Rousseau who has been particularly victimized. Rousseau has sometimes been depicted as the ultimate source, the *fons et origo*, of all that has apparently gone wrong with Western civilization. For example, in his dazzlingly erudite work of 1919, *Rousseau and Romanticism*, the American intellectual and academic Irving Babbitt (1865–1933) held up Rousseau as the epitome of subjectivism, cultural decadence, self-indulgent spontaneity and free-wheeling fantasizing – in a word, Babbitt accused Rousseau of the sacrifice of *form*. It was Rousseau, according to Babbitt, who led the profane attack on the classical and Christian inheritance of Western culture, an onslaught from which it has never recovered.[50]

In similar fashion, but more recently, Frances Ward took Rousseau as the paradigm of what was most wrong with Britain in particular, in a work of 2013 which she intended as a tract for the times: *Why Rousseau Was Wrong: Christianity and the Secular Soul*.[51] Here Rousseau, along with John Locke and Thomas Hobbes, was

---

[50]Irving Babbitt, *Rousseau and Romanticism*, intro. Claes G. Ryn (New Brunswick, NJ, and London: Transaction Publishers, 1991 [1919]).
[51]Frances Ward, *Why Rousseau Was Wrong: Christianity and the Secular Soul* (London and New York: Bloomsbury, 2013).

taken to represent 'Enlightenment thinking' which (it was further claimed) had shaped the 'secular soul' of modern culture. The Enlightenment mindset, according to Ward, has generated a legacy of individualism, instrumentalism and an obsession with identity that is detrimental to human flourishing because human flourishing needs transcendent roots and reference points. While I passionately share Ward's antipathy to individualism and instrumentalism, together with her longing for human community, her affirmation of the need for roots[52] and her preference for the mind and method of Edmund Burke over most of his contemporaries, I have strong reservations about the historical narrative or genealogy that she invokes to support her argument (support for what I say here will be provided substantially in subsequent chapters). (i) Although Rousseau can be counted among the *philosophes*, he is by no means representative of them. His writings were scorned by Voltaire and other *philosophes*; his feelings of persecution by fellow *philosophes*, though somewhat paranoid, were not completely without foundation; and he bitterly attacked these *philosophes* in turn. He should be somewhat distanced from them, not tarred with their brush. (ii) It is misleading to dub Rousseau a 'secular' thinker, if 'secular' has its usual modern meaning of a God-free world, because Rousseau was a passionately religious man in his own way, with an overwhelming sense of the sacred in nature and the human heart, though of course he was not an orthodox Christian and had no time for an authoritarian, intolerant church. For Rousseau the world and the human heart were filled with God. (iii) Hobbes and Locke are not representative of the Enlightenment either. Hobbes was born in the sixteenth century and remained a maverick political philosopher who was feared as an ideological bogey-man by many and remains very difficult to place in relation to Christianity. Locke was more of a precursor or forerunner of the Enlightenment than a fully fledged exponent of its platform. Moreover, Locke was a Christian and Anglican lay philosopher and biblical theologian, and even Hobbes was an Anglican, a pillar of the established church and an expositor of the Bible, as I and others have argued. I do not accept the argument that Hobbes was a covert atheist. The

---

[52]Simone Weil, *The Need for Roots: Prelude to a Declaration of Duties towards Mankind*, trans. Arthur Wills, preface T. S. Eliot (London: Routledge, 1952 [1949]).

least convincing argument for Hobbes's 'atheism' that I have come across is in David Berman's, *Atheism from Hobbes to Russell*, a claim which is based largely on Hobbes's insistence in *Leviathan* that (a) we cannot possess a true idea of God in our minds and that (b) 'existence' cannot be literally attributed to God. But these tenets are both truisms of orthodox negative theology (*via negativa*) and a staple of the philosophy of religion. They form the premise of the venerable Thomist analogical approach to speech about God.[53] Altogether, Hobbes, Locke and Rousseau are like apples, oranges and bananas; they are all 'fruit', but look and taste very different. 'Enlightenment thinking' was just as diverse – it was not one thing.

Rowan Williams on Isaiah Berlin

Rowan Williams is obviously one of the most personally admired, widely read and deeply appreciated of contemporary theologians. More's the pity, then, that in a published lecture, 'Faith and Enlightenment', Williams seizes on one strand of Enlightenment thought, that of 'coercive universal rationalism', highlighting the oppressive, totalitarian implications and potential consequences of the uniformitarian ideology of the *philosophes*.[54] Williams would be the last person on earth to defend any kind of unchallengeable authority or to suggest that there are certain questions which should never be asked. On the contrary, he consistently seeks a middle path of a cultural and political pluralism of convictions within which rational conversation and debate can freely flourish. Who among us would not say, 'Amen' to that? Williams's focus on the Enlightenment in this chapter of *Faith in the Public Square* stems

---

[53]David Berman, *Atheism from Hobbes to Russell* (London: Routledge, 1988), pp. 64–9; *ISOA*, pp. 175–201 (Hobbes), 269–75 (Locke). In addition to the bibliography on Hobbes in that volume, see the balanced account in R. W. Hepburn, 'Hobbes on the Knowledge of God', in Maurice Cranston and Richard S. Peters (eds), *Hobbes and Rousseau: A Collection of Critical Essays* (Garden City, NY: Doubleday, 1972), ch. 4 (pp. 85–108).
[54]Rowan Williams, *Faith in the Public Square* (London and New York: Bloomsbury, 2011), ch. 9. Cf. William's more dense exposition of the nemesis of Enlightenment in *Lost Icons: Reflections on Cultural Bereavement* (London and New York: T&T Clark, 2003), pp. 199–203.

from the fact that he was giving the 2010 Isaiah Berlin Lecture at the Hampstead Synagogue, so it was natural and right for him both to begin by acknowledging Berlin as 'one of the leading canonical voices of liberal modernity' and then to take Berlin's work on the 'Counter-Enlightenment' as his starting point.[55] Unfortunately, there are serious problems with Berlin's interpretation of the Enlightenment; he is not overall a safe guide.

Isaiah Berlin held a narrow and partial perspective on the Enlightenment.[56] Being imaginatively gripped by the genealogies and interactions of ideas and ideologies and their proponents (or creators, as he tended to see it), Berlin understood the Enlightenment, especially that segment of it represented by the *philosophes*, as intellectually rationalistic and universalistic and to that extent tending to authoritarianism and totalitarianism, regimes that are inevitably defined for him, as for us, by Nazi Germany and the Soviet Union. Berlin stated that 'the central doctrines of the progressive French thinkers, whatever their disagreements among themselves, rested on the belief, rooted in the ancient doctrine of natural law',

> that human nature was fundamentally the same in all times and places; that local and historical variations were unimportant compared with the constant central core ... that there were universal human goals; that a logically connected structure of laws and generalisations susceptible of demonstration and verification could be constructed and [could] replace the chaotic amalgam of ignorance, mental laziness, guesswork, superstition, prejudice, dogma, fantasy, and, above all, the 'interested error' maintained by the rulers of mankind and [which was] largely responsible for the blunders, vices and misfortunes of humanity.[57]

---

[55]Isaiah Berlin, *Against the Current: Essays in the History of Ideas*, ed. Henry Hardy, intro. Roger Hausheer (Oxford: Oxford University Press, 1981), ch. 1: 'The Counter-Enlightenment' (pp. 1–24). This essay appears to have been written in the late 1960s.
[56]See further Laurence Brockliss and Ritchie Robertson (eds), *Isaiah Berlin and the Enlightenment* (Oxford: Oxford University Press, 2016) and Joseph Mali and Robert Wokler (eds), *Isaiah Berlin's Counter-Enlightenment* (Philadelphia, PA: American Philosophical Society, 2003).
[57]Berlin, *Against the Current*, p. 1.

Noting that the *philosophes* also believed that 'methods similar to those of Newtonian physics, which had achieved such triumphs in the realm of inanimate nature, could be applied with equal success to the fields of ethics, politics and human relationships in general, in which little progress had been made', Berlin added that it was believed that, as a result, 'irrational and oppressive legal systems and economic policies' would be swept away and replaced by the rule of reason, so setting mankind on the path to wisdom, virtue and happiness.[58]

The ambiguities in Berlin's deployment here of the terms 'reason', 'rational' and 'rationalist' in relation to the French Enlightenment are palpable and do not all arise directly from eighteenth-century usage. John Robertson has claimed that 'although Berlin thought of himself as a historian of ideas, his Counter-Enlightenment was deliberately abstracted from historical context'.[59] Berlin's target was a particular philosophical outlook – rationalistic, universalistic and uniformitarian – which was typical to one degree or another of the *philosophes*, which he then in effect attached to the Enlightenment in general. The consequence of this definition was that he was forced to exclude such figures as Vico, Rousseau, Hamann, Herder and Burke from the Enlightenment itself. Berlin designated them as 'irrational' thinkers (though he slightly qualified this description in the cases of Rousseau and Burke), and postulated a concurrent 'Counter-Enlightenment' in which to locate them all. The part-subtitle of Berlin's study of Hamann is telling: *[T]he Origins of Modern Irrationalism.*[60] Hamann's *forte*, according to Berlin, was to contrast 'the intuitive insight, the imaginative grasp of reality, with the lifeless material of the systematisers and the dissecters' (p. xv) – that is, the German rationalists and the French *philosophes*. Berlin may be correctly summarizing Hamann, but the summary is seriously unfair to the French Enlightenment: its vast *oeuvre* was hardly 'lifeless', nor were Voltaire, Diderot or Rousseau systematizers or dissectors – quite the reverse – though there were *philosophes* who fitted

---

[58]Ibid.
[59]Robertson, *The Enlightenment*, p. 122.
[60]Isaiah Berlin, *The Magus of the North: J. G. Hamann and the Origins of Modern Irrationalism*, ed. Henry Hardy (London: John Murray, 1993); page references in my main text.

that description, especially d'Holbach and La Mettrie perhaps. As I will show in this book, on good authority and with ample evidence, the Enlightenment – even the French Enlightenment – was not 'rationalistic' or even merely 'rationalist'. The dominant epistemology was sceptical, empirical, pragmatic and ethical. The *philosophes* were eminently practical thinkers – polemicists, moralists, social reformers and propagandists. Berlin's stereotype (which was certainly not unique to him, as I have demonstrated already in this chapter) has been thoroughly discredited by scholarship since he formed his paradigm of the Enlightenment in the 1950s (before he lectured on Hamann in the 1960s), but it was extreme and tendentious even then.

More to the point, it is a travesty of the endowment of reason to set it over against the endowments of intuition and imagination, as though we had to choose between them. To work with the whole mind and heart is not irrationalism, but the highest form of rationality. You do not need to be a paid-up Romantic to have a holistic grasp of the nature of reason. But Berlin dubs Hamann 'the true founder of a polemical anti-rationalist tradition' and '[t]he most passionate, consistent, extreme and implacable enemy of the Enlightenment and, in particular, of all forms of rationalism of his time' and 'the pioneer of anti-rationalism in every sphere' (pp. xv, 1, 4). Hamann was indeed outrageous and extreme in thought and speech, a self-styled 'genius' and 'prophet' who despised all convention. But in their perception of the Enlightenment, both he and Berlin were tilting at windmills much of the time.

It is also genuinely perplexing that Berlin styles Hamann's thought 'secular'. Hamann began, he says, 'the secular resistance to the eighteenth-century march of enlightenment and reason' (p. 4); the book jacket blurb makes the same claim. What can Berlin mean by 'secular' here? True, Hamann was not a priest (how could he be in Protestant Königsberg, the city of Immanuel Kant?) or even a Protestant pastor. But that does not make him 'secular' as there are 'secular priests', those who are not 'religious' (members of a religious order). To the extent that Hamann was suspicious of institutional religion – in his case the Lutheran church, though he was devoted to the person and the theological insights of Luther and had a friend and disciple in Herder, a church leader as well as a philosopher of genius – does not make him a 'secular' thinker, any more than a similar stance makes the Catholic mystical guides Madame Guyon and Angelus Silesius 'secular'. Berlin knows that Hamann was not what we usually mean by a 'secular' thinker – a sceptical unbeliever who wants a world without God. Berlin suggests that the expression that is often applied to Spinoza, 'a God-intoxicated man', was more applicable to Hamann. 'For Hamann everything – all there is and all that could be – is not only created by God, and serves his inscrutable purposes, but speaks to us, his creatures, made in his image. Everything is revelation. Everything is a miracle' (p. xiv). The Scriptures, the writings of the church fathers, the lives of the saints, were also sources of revelation (ib.). Hamann did not need to harmonize them; he despised system; he revelled in the unharmonized diverse voices of God, speaking to the heart. As Berlin notes, rather superfluously, Harmann was 'never an atheist or an agnostic' (p. 13). Hardly a secular thinker then. Those more recent interpreters of the Enlightenment, especially Jonathan Israel, who see it as essentially a movement towards secularity, scepticism and unbelief, seem to have an equally mistaken predecessor in Isaiah Berlin.

Hamann abhorred Descartes's deductive method. We do not need intellectual inferences. Reality presses upon us and in it God does too. In place of Descartes's *Cogito ergo sum* (I think, therefore I am), Hamann proposed *Est ergo cogito* – literally 'It is, therefore I think'. Experience and the world are given inescapably and we reflect on them, finding God in them and in our thinking of them. Hamann was drawn to Hume's privileging of passion over cerebration. He revelled in Hume's mocking jest, in his *Enquiry Concerning Human Understanding*, that just as the birth of Christianity was accompanied by miracles, so today it cannot be believed without one! Hamann seized on this as a true insight. Living faith is a gift of God and an inward miracle of the Holy Spirit.[61]

There was in fact a genuine 'Counter-Enlightenment' ideological movement, especially in France, as a reaction to the posture of the *philosophes* and concurrent with them though gaining fresh momentum from the way that reforming impulses turned out, in the Revolution, the Terror and the Napoleonic aggression. The worldview of the Counter-Enlightenment was reactionary: Catholic, monarchist and aristocratic. It hankered nostalgically for

---

[61]Ronald Gregor Smith, *J. G. Hamann 1730–1788: A Study in Christian Existence; With Selections from his Writings* (London: Collins, 1960), pp. 50–1.

the restoration of the essentials of the *ancien régime*. It was far from sympathetic to the ideas of Berlin's heroes.

In *The Roots of Romanticism*, Berlin identifies two Rousseaus. One is a 'father' of the Romantic movement. But the other, whose connection with Romanticism is far from obvious, is the Rousseau whose *Du Contrat Social: ou, Principes du droit politique* (1762), which (according to Berlin) promotes 'the reign of universal reason', rather than divisive emotions, in order to bring human beings together, and inspired the Jacobins and Robespierre.[62] Berlin's claim of a double Rousseau is implausible and its cogency deserves to be probed. I suspect that, as we have already seen immediately above, it rests on a false antithesis between reason and emotion. In the same work, Berlin describes the Enlightenment mindset as distrustful of revelation, of tradition, of Christian doctrine and of introspection. In place of those supposed sources of knowledge, the Enlightenment substituted, he says, 'the correct use of reason, deductively as in the mathematical sciences, inductively as in the sciences of nature'.[63] If Berlin's interpretation is imbibed uncritically, it leads inescapably to the assumption that the Enlightenment was typically 'rationalist' or 'rationalistic' and therefore hostile to Christianity. It would be more correct, however, to say that the Christian – or at least religious – thinkers of the eighteenth century, who were in the majority, used reason as a tool to evaluate the claims of revelation, tradition, doctrine and so on (as we all do), and formed their own conclusions. Bishop Butler for one explicitly says that we should do so. It by no means follows that the thinkers of the Enlightenment, because they took critical reason as their guide, generally had no room for revelation, tradition and church doctrine. Many did, all the time.

Isaiah Berlin's exponent, John Gray, popularized the former's interpretation of the Enlightenment in a series of tracts for the times, blaming the Enlightenment's supposed dogmatic,

---

[62]Isaiah Berlin, *The Roots of Romanticism: The A. W. Mellon Lectures in the Fine Arts, 1965, The National Gallery of Art, Washington, DC*, ed. Henry Hardy (London: Pimlico, 2000 [1999]), p. 7. Jean Jacques Rousseau, *The Social Contract and Discourses*, trans. and intro. G. D. H. Cole (London: Dent; New York: Dutton, 1913); id., *The Social Contract*, trans. and intro. Maurice Cranston (Harmondsworth: Penguin, 1968).
[63]Berlin, *The Roots of Romanticism*, p. 22.

universalistic rationalism, for the (alleged) failures of modern political and economic liberalism. In a collection of these pieces, *Enlightenment's Wake* (1995), which has had an extended life in various editions, Gray paradoxically claims that the Enlightenment is both 'irreversible' and 'exhausted'.

This rationalist and universalist tradition of liberal political philosophy runs aground, along with the rest of the Enlightenment project, on the reef of value-pluralism – on the truth that the values embodied in different forms of life and human identity, and even within the same form of life and identity, may be rationally incommensurable. The truth of value-pluralism suggests another mode of liberal theorizing, in which not rational choice but radical choice among incommensurables is central, and in which the particularistic character of human identity and reasoning is fundamental.[64]

Gray offers naught for our comfort: he unceremoniously dispatches all the available options: 'the Enlightenment project', modern liberalism, the conservative political tradition, Western metaphysics, modernity and post-modernity, the scientific worldview and the aspiration towards a unified scientific theory, and Christian theology to boot.[65] In their place he privileges the values of personal fulfilment, individual freedom and imaginative creation, which he derives from the Romantic reaction to the Enlightenment. But he does so without providing rational, ethical or theological parameters for our indulgence of those values or our enjoyment of them. Berlin's doctrine of the incommensurability of values across and within cultures is clearly pivotal to Gray's ruthless critique of the Enlightenment, as he understands it, and to his antidote and remedy. But I would say that, on the contrary, we should be grateful to the Enlightenment thinkers for insisting on universally applicable rational and ethical criteria of judgement for human behaviour and enterprise. The alternative would be anomie and social chaos.

---

[64]John Gray, *Enlightenment's Wake: Politics and Culture at the Close of the Modern Age* (London and New York: Routledge, 1995), p. 68. See also id., *Isaiah Berlin: An Interpretation of His Thought; With a New Introduction by the Author* (Princeton, NJ: Princeton University Press, 2013 [1995]).
[65]Gray, *Enlightenment's Wake*, pp. 155–6.

Now to revert to Rowan Williams: by taking Isaiah Berlin as a handy starting point for a lecture to a Jewish audience, he may have given succour inadvertently to the widespread misapprehension among his extensive readership, and especially among Christian and Anglican readers, including students and scholars, that the Enlightenment as a whole can be dismissed, from their faith perspective, as rationalistic, secular and ungodly and therefore uncongenial to thinking Christians. Williams's ascription of 'coercive universal rationalism' to the Enlightenment and his highlighting of the oppressive, totalitarian implications of the uniformitarian ideology of the *philosophes* savours of Gray's attack. Much historical scholarship of the Enlightenment era has been battling to combat this cluster of misconceptions for several decades now. A better informed and more nuanced understanding of the Enlightenment than we find in philosophers of ideas, such as Berlin and Gray, and Christian theologians such as Newbigin, Gunton and the early McGrath, together with various other theological interpreters, some of whom I have mentioned in this chapter, is needed. This I will endeavour to provide, in summary form, in the next chapter.

3

A virtuous Enlightenment

In this chapter I am going to qualify and complexify how I understand the portmanteau term 'the Enlightenment'. I will not be joining the dismal chorus of those who attribute to the Enlightenment all the woes and wrongs of modernity. On the contrary, I will be highlighting certain aspects of the Enlightenment which I regard as not vicious faults but virtuous achievements. These points may strike some readers – those who have been taught to look askance at the Enlightenment – as counter-intuitive and perversely revisionist. However, in truth they reflect the far-reaching reassessment of the Enlightenment that has taken place over the past several decades, first in historiography, then in philosophy (up to a point) but hardly at all in theology. I aim to begin to put that right.

First, however, I should explain what I mean by describing certain aspects of the Enlightenment as 'virtuous'. Needless to say, I do not mean to imply that the protagonists of the Enlightenment were saintly figures or paragons of virtue or that such figures as Voltaire, Diderot and Rousseau should have gleaming haloes over their heads. Not at all. But I do mean to point to aspects of the Enlightenment that I regard as salutary and beneficial for human well-being. There was a definite humanitarian thrust to much of the Enlightenment's projects and programmes. They were infused with an ethical agenda. Justice and virtue were the prime ethical criteria by which it assessed the Christian tradition, the Catholic Church, social institutions and governing regimes. Francis Bacon, a major begetter of Enlightenment methodology, was contemptuous of abstract ethical theories; ethical principles should require action and should result in an improvement in the conditions of human life.[1] Before the rise of biblical criticism, one of the main weapons in the armoury of deists was an ethical critique of the Old Testament. Bernard de Fontenelle, the philosopher, scientist and historian, insisted that 'history is good for nothing if it is not allied to ethics'.[2] Samuel Johnson, though a man of awesome parts, was primarily a moralist. Edmund Burke consistently applied ethical criteria to the momentous events of his age. Across Europe the Enlightenment ethic combatted ignorance, oppression, superstition, prejudice and fanaticism. It fought for the spread of knowledge and understanding, for improvement in agriculture and husbandry, for personal liberty in speech, print and association, for reform of the dark corners of the *ancien régime* symbolized by the Bastille. We can allow for blind spots, inconsistencies, hypocrisy and self-righteousness; they do not negate the virtuous, commendable and admirable aspects of the Enlightenment. In view of all the aspersions that the Enlightenment has attracted in some quarters, I think we do well to remember some of these strong points, without which we would all be the poorer in mind, body and estate.

A conservative Enlightenment

The first point of orientation to establish within our theological perspective is that the mainstream of the Enlightenment, particularly in England and Germany, and even in France, was not politically, socially or religiously subversive, but on the contrary moderate and conservative in its tendency and significantly clerical in its constituency.[3] The Enlightenment was

---

[1] Paolo Rossi, *Francis Bacon: From Magic to Science* (London: Routledge and Kegan Paul, 1968), p. 109.
[2] Cited Leonard M. Marsak, *Bernard de Fontenelle: The Idea of Science in the French Enlightenment* (Philadelphia: Transactions of the American Philosophical Society, 1959), p. 435.
[3] J. G. A. Pocock, 'Conservative Enlightenment and Democratic Revolutions: The American and French Cases in British Perspective', *Government and Opposition* 24.1 (Winter 1989), pp. 81–105. I have not been able to obtain his slightly earlier article 'Clergy and Commerce: The Conservative Enlightenment in England', in R. J. Ajello et al. (eds), *L'Età dei Lumi: studi storici sul sul settecento europeo in onore di Franco Venturi* (Naples: Jovene Editore, 1985), vol. 1, pp. 523–68.

generally conservative of religious faith and of social structures and institutions. This fact may come as a surprise to those who have uncritically imbibed the recent rhetoric of a militantly ungodly, secular and rationalistic Enlightenment, but it has acquired massive and incontrovertible scholarly authority in the past several decades, notably that of the weighty 'senior' scholars Hugh Trevor-Roper, J. G. A. Pocock, J. C. D. Clark and Knud Haakonssen, as well as a host of more recent writers, some of whom I shall mention shortly.

In his seminal essay 'The Religious Origins of the Enlightenment' (1967) Hugh Trevor-Roper countered the view that orthodox Protestantism, especially Calvinism, by its purposefulness, energy and intellectual rigour, had prepared the way for the Enlightenment.[4] On the contrary, he claimed, enlightened ideas flourished only where Calvinism had been repulsed or repressed, not where it was dominant. For Trevor-Roper, religious thinkers did indeed prepare the ground for the Enlightenment, but they were at first dissident intellectuals, moving around Europe to escape persecution for 'heresy', and only later well-established groups and tendencies within society when political stability had been achieved. The genealogy that Trevor-Roper traces begins with Erasmus where he quotes Gibbon: 'Erasmus may be considered as the father of rational theology.'[5] Following Gibbon, Trevor-Roper traces the lineage of the Enlightenment through Socinianism, Arminianism and (in England) Latitudinarianism and the Anglican establishment, even to Archbishop Tillotson in Lambeth Palace.[6] It is intriguing that Jonathan Israel tracks a very similar succession of allegedly dissident, heterodox and alienated religious thinkers, especially Montaigne, Charron, Spinoza and Bayle, and sees this series of radical thinkers as leading to a secular, rationalistic and

---

[4]Hugh Trevor-Roper, 'The Religious Origins of the Enlightenment', in id., *Religion, the Reformation and Social Change* (London: Macmillan, 1967), ch. 4.
[5]Ibid., p. 200.
[6]See also the succinct analysis of origins of the Enlightenment, which comes to a similar conclusion, in Helena Rosenblatt, art. 'Calvinism', in Alan Charles Kors (ed.), *Encyclopedia of the Enlightenment*, 4 vols (Oxford: Oxford University Press, 2002).

even atheistic Enlightenment.[7] (Note that I do not accept Israel's basic assessment of these figures, as being distinguished by their unbelief, as will become clear.) Trevor-Roper, on the other hand, finds the Enlightenment's parentage in genuine and heartfelt, if sometimes marginal, religious thought. As he puts it, 'the eighteenth-century Enlightenment grew slowly out of seventeenth-century heresy'.[8] 'Heresy', which is an ideological term of opprobrium and not a stable concept by any measure, is nevertheless by definition formally integral to Christianity as an ideology and is a version of its theology, not a repudiation of it. Paradoxically, heresy conserves religion and keeps it moving.

According to Pocock, seconded by Haakonssen, the English constitution, especially after the Glorious Revolution (1688) made it possible for moderate Enlightened attitudes and ideas to be absorbed and integrated into public discourse, rather than marginalized as a threat to the *status quo*. In this way, the momentum of the Enlightenment actually served and supported the preservation of the establishment in church and state. Pocock is slightly guarded in his claims, but the thesis is clear: that 'among the phenomena which "Enlightenment" connotes for us there are some whose effect may be termed "conservative" in the sense that it was to strengthen existing elites – some of them clerical – in their capacity for civic control'.[9] Pocock supports his point by asserting that the British had shown themselves to be 'deeply counter-revolutionary in their behaviour' since the upheavals of the seventeenth century, 'if not before', so that the English prototypes (especially Locke) of the continental *philosophes* 'saw themselves as coming after an age of fanaticism and disorder rather than one of the despotism of tradition, and that the work of what we call Enlightenment was promoted by clerical elites as well as by sceptics

---

[7]Jonathan I. Israel, *Radical Enlightenment: Philosophy and the Making of Modernity 1650–1750* (Oxford: Oxford University Press, 2001); id., *Enlightenment Contested: Philosophy, Modernity and the Emancipation of Man 1670–1752* (Oxford: Oxford University Press, 2006). Israel's 'radical Enlightenment' does not include the great luminaries of the age, Locke, Newton, Hume and Voltaire, who all opposed religiously, socially and politically subversive ideas (*Enlightenment Contested*, p. 58).
[8]H. R. Trevor-Roper, 'The Historical Philosophy of the Enlightenment', *SVEC* XXII (1963), pp. 1667–87, at p. 1671.
[9]Pocock, 'Conservative Enlightenment and Democratic Revolutions', p. 82.

and subversives'. In essence Pocock is 'challenging the paradigm of Enlightenment as radical liberation which [he notes in passing] has made it so hard to speak of an English Enlightenment at all'.[10] Clearly, if you begin by defining the Enlightenment as a radical movement of intellectual and political emancipation, as Israel does, you have to search for it on the further reaches of English intellectual life. Its pervasiveness is one reason why the English Enlightenment is difficult to pinpoint in order to say, 'It's right there!' As Pocock concludes, the Enlightenment in England, where collective memories of the destruction and bloodshed of the Civil War and the ensuing chaos and deluded fanaticism ('enthusiasm') of the subversive sects during the Protectorate were still raw, was 'often a conservative and Anglican force, designed in the defence of the magisterial and clerical elites against the subversive claims of the spirit'.[11]

So much so that the French Revolution, as it ran its course to the execution of King Louis XVI and Queen Marie Antoinette and then the Terror with its mass guillotinings, far from appearing as an inevitable outcome and product of the Enlightenment, was seen at the time by many English intellectuals, led by Edmund Burke, as an attack on Enlightenment values and principles and as a relapse into barbarism and 'enthusiasm', which staunch Anglican thinkers saw at work, not only in the fanaticism of the sectaries of the mid-seventeenth century, but most recently and currently (for them) in aspects of the Methodist movement within the Church of England.[12] George Lavington, Bishop of Exeter, produced a three-volume *Enthusiasm of Methodists and Papists Compared* (1749–51), citing the extreme ascetical practices of John Wesley himself and some of his early followers, as well as Wesley's editing and promotion of Roman Catholic devotional literature. Lavington drew a rather obvious parallel between the outdoor preaching of the friars and the 'field preaching' of the Methodists that dispensed with consecrated

---

[10]Ibid., pp. 82, 84.
[11]Ibid., p. 85.
[12]Knud Haakonssen in id. (ed.), *Enlightenment and Religion: Rational Dissent in Eighteenth-Century Britain* (Cambridge: Cambridge University Press, 1996), 'Enlightened Dissent: An Introduction', pp. 1–11, at pp. 2–3. See also John Gascoigne, 'Anglican latitudinarianism, Rational Dissent and political radicalism in the late eighteenth century', in id., ch. 9.

buildings and disregarded parish boundaries. Lavington was followed by others such as Thomas Green's *Dissertation on Enthusiasm* (1755), which similarly deployed popular anti-Catholic sentiment as a weapon against the new movement.[13] Enlightenment intellectuals across Europe similarly recoiled in horror from what the Revolution had become by 1793. The sensitive and retiring Rousseau, had he lived to see it, would have been appalled at the use being made of his armchair political theories. The Revolution appeared as a profoundly reactionary and atavistic movement, pitted against enlightened, progressive modernity.[14]

Edward Gibbon, who was deemed by the eminent scholar of the Enlightenment Franco Venturi (in an exaggeration that makes the point) to be the only true Enlightenment figure to come out of England (so, in Venturi's terms, an authentic voice of the Enlightenment),[15] deplored the fanaticism and dogmatism of the *philosophes*. In his *Memoirs*, which were drafted after the French Revolution had begun, Gibbon wrote of his experience in France: 'Nor could I approve the intolerant zeal of the philosophers and Encyclopaedists [sic], the friends of d'Olbach and Helvetius: they laughed at the scepticism of Hume, preached the tenets of Atheism with the bigotry of dogmatists, and damned all believers with ridicule and contempt.'[16] In his posthumously published autobiography or memoirs, Gibbon aligned himself with Burke's condemnation and castigation of the Revolution: 'I beg leave to subscribe my assent to Mr. Burke's creed of the revolution of France. I admire his eloquence, I approve his politics, I adore his chivalry [in defence of the French royal family, especially Marie Antionette]', adding sardonically 'and I can almost excuse his reverence for church establishments'.[17] Unfortunately, Burke's *Reflections on the Revolution in France*

---

[13] I am grateful to Dr Peter Nockles for these references.
[14] Pocock, 'Conservative Enlightenment and Democratic Revolutions', p. 100.
[15] Franco Venturi, *Utopia and Reform in the Enlightenment* (Cambridge: Cambridge University Press, 1971), p. 132.
[16] Gibbon, from Draft B of his *Memoirs* (not included in popular editions of the *Autobiography*: cited David Womersley, *Gibbon and the 'Watchmen of the Holy City': The Historian and His Reputation, 1776–1815* (Oxford: Oxford University Press, 2002), p. 351, from Gibbon, *Miscellaneous Works* (1796), vol. 1, pp. 203–4.
[17] Edward Gibbon, *Autobiography* (London: Dent; New York: Dutton, 1911), p. 178.

(1790) was not a reliable analysis of recent events in France, though prophetic of their outcome. For Cobban they are 'magnificent ... as anything but history'.[18]

The moderate, deistic *philosophes* justifiably rejected the accusation that their ideas were subversive of political stability and civil order. In particular one might imagine – and many have – that Rousseau's political writings helped to stoke up revolutionary fervour. The Second Part of his *Discourse on the Origins of Inequality* begins with what appears to be an attack on property, in the case of the (imagined) 'first man who, having enclosed a piece of ground, bethought himself of saying, "This is mine", and found people simple enough to believe him'.[19] And the Second Part ends with the ringing declaration: '[I]t is plainly contrary to the law of nature, however defined, that children should command old men, fools wise men, and that the privileged few should gorge themselves with superfluities, while the starving multitude are in want of the bare necessities of life.'[20] Nothing could be more stirring and awakening than the words near the beginning of *The Social Contract*: 'Man was born free; and he is everywhere in chains.'[21] Marx and Engels echo Rousseau's words in the last paragraph of *The Communist Manifesto*: 'The Communists ... openly declare that their ends can be attained only by the forcible overthrow of all existing social conditions. Let the ruling classes tremble at a Communist revolution. The proletariat have nothing to lose but their chains. They have a world to win.' There follows the revolutionaries' rallying cry: 'Working men of all countries unite!'[22]

---

[18] Edmund Burke, *Reflections on the Revolution in France* (London: Dent; New York: Dutton, 1910). Alfred Cobban, *Historians and the Causes of the French Revolution* (London: Routledge and Kegan Paul for the Historical Association, 1958), p. 6.
[19] Jean-Jacques Rousseau, *The Social Contract and Discourses*, trans. and intro. G. D. H. Cole (London: Dent; New York: Dutton, 1913), p. 192.
[20] Ibid., p. 221.
[21] Jean-Jacques Rousseau, *The Social Contract*, trans. and intro. Maurice Cranston (Harmondsworth: Penguin, 1968), p. 49. I prefer Cranston's translation at this point to that of Cole in Rousseau, *The Social Contract and Discourses*, p. 3.
[22] Karl Marx and Friedrich Engels, *The Communist Manifesto*, ed. and intro. A. J. P. Taylor (Harmondsworth: Penguin, 1967 [1888]), pp. 120–1. The final sentence is in capitals in Taylor's text.

However, the subversive effect of Rousseau's political writings is discounted by historians. It was Cobban's view that *Du Contrat Social* had no detectable influence before the Revolution and only a highly debatable influence during it.[23] Rousseau's *Discourse on Political Economy* (originally written for the *Encyclopédie*) castigates tyranny and implicitly undermines absolute rulers, but it gives no succour to radically subversive political doctrines and in fact offers much sound advice to those who bear the rule.[24] Diderot and Voltaire respectively colluded with the 'enlightened despots', Catherine the Great of Russia and Frederick the Great of Prussia – that is to say, they attended their courts and advised them when commanded to do so. Gay comments that the *philosophes* were 'servile' towards their great patrons. Even in France, they worked within the existing system, not against it. 'There were few revolutionaries before the fact; the *philosophes* were reformers within the system.'[25]

In reaction to the bloodshed and devastation of the European religious wars of the sixteenth and seventeenth centuries and the pervasive *odium theologicum* both between the major churches and within them, the *philosophes* and Gibbon saw polemical clerical religion and obscurantist theology, not philosophical enquiry, as the cause of political instability and recurring periods of the decline of civilization. Voltaire claimed: 'It is not Montaigne, nor Locke, nor Bayle, not Spinoza, nor Hobbes, nor Lord Shaftesbury, nor Mr Collins, nor Mr Toland [both regarded as notorious deists], etc., who have carried the torch of discord into their countries, it is in the main the theologians.'[26]

---

[23]Alfred Cobban, 'The Enlightenment and the French Revolution', in E. R. Wasserman (ed.), *Aspects of the Eighteenth Century* (Baltimore: Johns Hopkins University Press, 1965), pp. 305–15, at p. 309.
[24]Rousseau, *The Social Contract and Discourses*, ed. Cole, pp. 233–69.
[25]Peter Gay, 'Why Was the Enlightenment?' in id. (ed.), *Eighteenth-Century Studies Presented to Arthur M. Wilson* (Hanover, NH: The University Press of New England, 1972), pp. 61–71, at p. 67.
[26]Voltaire, *Letters on England*, trans. Leonard Tancock (Harmondsworth: Penguin, 1980), p. 67. French text in Voltaire, *Lettres Philosophiques*, intro René Pomeau (Paris: Garnier-Flammarion, 1964), p. 88.

A 'secular' Enlightenment?

The most eminent advocates of the supposedly secular character of the Enlightenment are, I suppose, Paul Hazard, Peter Gay, Jonathan Israel and Margaret Jacob. For them, the essence of the Enlightenment, the authentic Enlightenment itself, was an unbelieving revolt against orthodox religious belief and ecclesiastical authority. It is particularly Hazard, Gay and Israel who venture beyond their brief as historians to promote with evangelistic zeal the Enlightenment (actually selected aspects of it) as launching their much vaunted secular modernity. Hazard presents the Enlightenment as an unprecedented new revelation.[27] Gay gave his first volume the ludicrous subtitle *The Rise of Modern Paganism*.[28] Israel finds the source of liberal, democratic modernity in the *Radical Enlightenment*, an historical niche of selected writers, basically misinterpreted.[29] Faced with that formidable phalanx of historians, my aim in this chapter is to bring out what I regard as the 'virtuous' aspects of the Enlightenment. For me, that means the conservation and purification, not the eradication, of religious faith and worship, accompanied by the vitality of theological enquiry.

Probably no-one has fewer illusions than I have about the dark underside of religion and the chequered history of the churches or is more appalled by the gruesome elements in the unfolding of Christian theology. I have frequently castigated the churches for their sins, crimes and failures and I have pointed out a pathway to repentance, reform and development.[30] But, notwithstanding the downside of Christianity, I continue to believe in it; I work

---

[27]Paul Hazard, *The European Mind 1680–1715*, trans. J. Lewis May (Harmondsworth: Penguin, 1964 [*La Crise de la conscience européenne*, 1953]).
[28]Peter Gay, *The Enlightenment: An Interpretation, Vol. 1, The Rise of Modern Paganism* (London: Weidenfeld & Nicolson, 1967).
[29]Israel, *Radical Enlightenment*.
[30]See especially Paul Avis, *Reconciling Theology* (London: SCM Press, 2022), ch. 5: 'Unreconciled Church – Counter-sign of the Kingdom', and more briefly Paul Avis, 'Overcoming "The Church as Counter-Sign of the Kingdom"', in Mark D. Chapman and Vladimir Latinovic (eds), *Changing the Church: Transformations of Christian Belief, Practice, and Life* (Cham, Switzerland: Palgrave Macmillan, 2021), pp. 243–9.

for an intelligent, informed, inclusive faith and for an ethically orientated Christian discipleship. I love the church and its liturgy and I continue fervently to believe that what it offers us is 'the best we know' and that means the best for human well-being. To be uncomfortably aware of the doubtful and dark side of the church as an institution through time does not equate to wanting to see it disappear. So I do not want to see secularism prevail and I think that the familiar depiction of the Enlightenment as a great movement of secularity needs to be seriously qualified. In fact I think that secularism is grossly misleading as an overall characterization of the Enlightenment. I will take the latest major discussion from the 'pen' of the distinguished Enlightenment scholar Margaret C. Jacob as a test case.[31]

In *The Secular Enlightenment* (2019) Jacob argues that the Enlightenment 'made the secular world its point of departure'. She acknowledges that the Enlightenment 'did not necessarily deny the meaning or emotional hold of religion', but she argues that 'it gradually shifted attention away from religious questions toward secular ones'. She claims intriguingly that the Enlightenment was 'seeking answers in secular terms – even to many religious questions' and so 'vastly expanded the sphere of the secular, making it, for increasing numbers of educated people, a primary frame of reference' (p. 1). Jacob insists that she does not mean 'to downplay the many religious manifestations found in the age' and that she is not claiming that 'religion was en route to being cast aside' (p. 1). However, she thinks that the fact that people generally could now live their lives 'without constant reference to God', freed them to experiment and innovate in a way that was not possible before (p. 1).

But what does Jacob mean by 'secular' and secularity? She does not explicitly define this key term of her book, but we can glean her meaning from the context. 'In a secular setting', she explains, 'the purpose of human life takes shape without necessary reference to a transcendent order'. Temporal well-being and temporal happiness is the aim and living in the here and now is what matters (pp. 2–3). The effect of the Enlightenment was that transcendent, spiritual

---

[31] Margaret C. Jacob, *The Secular Enlightenment* (Princeton, NJ: Princeton University Press, 2019); page references in my main text.

realities began to fade. 'Sin, hell, and salvation became less real, or to be attended to less urgently' (p. 265). In summary:

> In some minds, the clergy could be disdained, churches avoided or viewed only for their physical beauty; even the founders of the great monotheistic religions could be mocked. By 1800, space and time on earth were filled by fewer miracles, saints, and prophecies than had been the case in 1700. The secular with which we still live had become all pervasive, even if offensive to the religiously observant.
>
> (p. 265)

I would like to make some preliminary comments on Jacob's use of the term 'secular' and its application to the Enlightenment.

(a) I cannot expand here on the essential distinction between 'secularism' (a militant ideology) and 'secularization' (a socio-economic process) or attempt to tease out the various confusing meanings of 'secular' in academic writing ('the secular clergy' are non-monastic priests, while 'the secularization of church lands' refers to the removal of assets from ecclesiastical oversight). The slang academic phrase 'a secular society' usually refers to a society where religious belief and practice has declined and the churches have a low public profile. Colloquially, 'secular' is used to mean a kind of God-free cultural and ideological space. Jacob does not enter into these distinctions; she allows her meaning to emerge from the context.

(b) Etymologically, of course, 'secular' means 'of the present age' (Latin *saeculum*; French siècle) and by a natural extension it normally refers to this world, rather than specifically to the present age of the world. Undoubtedly elements of the eighteenth-century intelligentsia (especially the *philosophes*) turned their attention mainly or entirely to the world and this focus stimulated improvements and innovations in husbandry and the 'cottage industries' of artisans (the industrial revolution not yet having arrived). The turn to this world may also have given impetus to natural science, political economy and historiography.

(c) Yet we find that those who are universally acknowledged as the greatest minds of the Enlightenment in fact studied this world in the light of another world, earth in the light of heaven, and time in the light of eternity. This is true of Bacon, the founder of the inductive scientific method, and of Locke, its greatest exponent in epistemology, as well as of Newton and Boyle, physicist and chemist respectively. It also applies to Vico, the most brilliant of Enlightenment philosophers of history. But it is true not only of those who were unquestionably Christians, but also of those whose relationship to Christianity has been thought tenuous at best and hostile at worst: Descartes the devout Catholic; Hobbes the political theologian; Bayle the sceptical Protestant historian and polemicist; Voltaire the passionate deist; Rousseau obsessed with the presence of the God of nature within and around himself; and Spinoza whose mind was filled with God. It is arguable that all of these thinkers or writers shaped our perception of the world in the way that they did because the reality of a greater and better world impinged on their spirits.

(d) The more weight we give to the influence of classical, Christian Humanism on Enlightenment thought, the more we are compelled to recognize that a focus on the concerns of this world were not new and were in fact far from unprecedented. Renaissance Humanism had drawn not only on Aristotle, Cicero and Seneca, but also on the Augustinian tradition of political theology. Although Augustine had worked, in *The City of God*, with a dualism of the earthly and heavenly cities, the natural and spiritual spheres, he had not taught that Christians should abandon the affairs and responsibilities of this world (as the sectarian Montanists and Donatists had).[32] As Pocock has argued, Augustine neutralized the temporal realm, leaving it weak and ripe for occupation.[33] The rise

---

[32] Augustine, *The City of God*, ed. David Knowles; trans. Henry Bettenson (Harmondsworth: Penguin, 1972).

[33] J. G. A. Pocock, *The Machiavellian Moment: Florentine Political Thought and the Atlantic Republican Tradition* (Princeton, NJ: Princeton University Press, 1975), pp. 42ff; R. A. Markus, *Saeculum: History and Society in the Theology of St Augustine*, 2nd edn (Cambridge: Cambridge University Press, 1988 [1970]).

of civic Humanism, with its ethical ideal of the *vita activa* of the citizen, began to fill the vacuum left by Augustinian political theology. Civic Humanism emerged from within the Christian cosmos and worldview; it was in no way anti-Christian though it was certainly anti-scholastic and anti-hierarchical. Thomas Aquinas, whose theology was indebted above all to Augustine and Aristotle (as well as to the Bible and the teachings of the church), provided the theological underpinnings for civic Humanism. As Ullmann puts it, 'Precisely because Thomas rehabilitated natural man [*sic*], his doctrines can be said ... to constitute the opening bars of Renaissance humanism.'[34] Medieval Christian Humanism already affirmed the worth of the natural realm (*naturalia*), human concerns (*humana*) and this-worldly occupations (*mundana*). The validity of the natural order and of our responsibilities towards it belongs to the essence of medieval Humanism.[35] The secular-minded members of the eighteenth-century intelligentsia were its inheritors; they did not invent it. What is significant in the Enlightenment is not its attention to the secular in the sense of the temporal and mundane, but the attempt by some to detach this outlook, this imperative, from its previous Christian, Catholic, framework. We should also note that the Protestant theological ethics and political theology of Luther and Calvin also affirmed the Christian's responsibility towards 'worldly' affairs and duties in terms of the Christian's calling (*vocatio*). Reformation theology furnished a source for Spinoza, Locke, Hobbes and Bayle. The Enlightenment's concerns with the present world are linked back, via Catholic and Protestant streams of tradition, to Renaissance Humanism, medieval scholasticism and civic thought.

---

[34]Walter Ullmann, *Medieval Foundations of Renaissance Humanism* (London: Elek, 1977), p. 100; Cf. Jerrold E. Seigel, *Rhetoric and Philosophy in Renaissance Humanism: The Union of Eloquence and Wisdom, Petrarch to Valla* (Princeton, NJ: Princeton University Press, 1968), p. 241.
[35]R. W. Southern, *Medieval Humanism* (Oxford: Oxford University Press, 1970), p. 57; *FMHT*, pp. 4–5.

There is another perplexing aspect of Jacob's view of the secular Enlightenment. She refers to Spinoza's 'identification of God with Nature'. Although that is a literal paraphrase of *deus sive natura*, it needs explicating, since *natura* for Spinoza encompasses all reality; it is not simply the nature of the Romantic nature poets, such as Wordsworth and Coleridge. Jacob then invites us to 'fast-forward to the 1780s in both England and Germany, where thinkers with obviously religious sentiments like the Lutheran Johann Herder, or the poet of Dissenting ... background, Samuel Taylor Coleridge, could imagine a universe infused with the divine' (p. 3). Thus 'within three generations', she comments 'one of the foundations of Christian metaphysics, the absolute separation of Creator from Creation, of spirit from matter, had disaggregated' (p. 4). This statement calls for some commentary. The assumption that Christian metaphysics holds to 'the absolute separation of Creator from Creation' and of 'spirit from matter' is astonishing. Christianity entertains no such doctrine. To do so would be Manichaeism, a heretical dualism that would destroy the whole Christian scheme of creation, revelation, inspiration, incarnation, salvation, sanctification, sacraments, all of which require the interaction and interpenetration of God and the world.

Christian theology teaches the immanence, the indwelling, as well as the transcendence, of God, the presence within as well as the element of over-againstness. The interpenetration and indwelling of God in the creation and therefore in human being forms a large part of the doctrine of the Holy Spirit. I can hardly even begin to document this truth from Scripture, the work of theologians and the church's liturgy. Thomas Aquinas teaches that God is within all created things (and that all creation is in God) by power, presence and essence: 'God is in all things by his power, inasmuch as all things are subject to his power; he is by his presence in all things, as all things are bare and open to his eyes; he is in all things by his essence, inasmuch as he is present to all as the cause of their being.'[36] The saints and mystics have testified to the indwelling presence of God. The Anglican poet and priest Thomas Traherne (1636–74) who lived wholly within Spinoza's own lifetime (1632–77) described a world suffused with the presence, beauty and glory of the Creator

---

[36]Thomas Aquinas, *Summa Theologiae* (Blackfriars Latin/English edition; London: Eyre & Spottiswoode; New York: McGraw-Hill, 1964), Prima Pars, Q.8.3.

and knew this within himself. The *Gloria in Excelsis*, which is used in the eucharistic liturgy is drawn from Isaiah 6:3 and first appears in the fourth century AD: 'Holy, holy, holy, Lord God of hosts, The whole earth is full of thy glory. Glory be to thee, O Lord most High'.

Enlightenment 'rationalism'?

'I refute it thus!', declaimed Samuel Johnson, kicking a stone in response to Boswell's question whether he could refute Bishop Berkeley's idealist philosophy, that reality was all 'in the mind'. By so doing, Dr Johnson in no way refuted Berkeley, but he did reveal that he shared the Lockean empiricist-experiential (or in the currency of the day 'experimental') approach that was characteristic of Enlightenment epistemology.[37] Enlightenment thinkers typically asked themselves: 'Do we have sufficient evidence for what we believe?' and 'Do others have sufficient evidence for the claims that they make of us?' The core of the much vaunted 'Enlightenment reason' was the insistence that all beliefs and claims should be subject to assessment on the basis of evidence.[38] It does not follow, of course, that the protagonists of Enlightenment reason were not swayed by bias, prejudice, egotism, interests or emotional moods in applying these tests or that they always or even usually applied this principle in an objective and impartial way. But rational examination of claims, arguments and evidence was unquestionably the ideal to which Enlightenment thinkers aspired, as opposed to taking them on the authority of church teaching, unchallenged tradition or the texts of antiquity. Classical writers, especially Aristotle, Cicero and Seneca, were still a source of wisdom, moral example and how the good life may be lived, but not of uncorroborated scientific or historical knowledge.

Contrary to the strident claims of those who rely on tendentious and simplistic second-hand interpretations of the Enlightenment,

---

[37]James Boswell, *Life of Johnson*, ed. R. W. Chapman (London: Oxford University Press, 1953), pp. 333–4.
[38]Cf. Frederick C. Beiser, *The Sovereignty of Reason: The Defense of Rationality in the Early English Enlightenment* (Princeton, NJ: Princeton University Press, 1996), p. ix.

its typical intellectual methods were not rationalistic, in the sense of deductive, speculative and system-building; neither were they generally secularist, reductionist or hostile to Christianity. The methods of the Enlightenment, including the methods of most of the *philosophes*, were (ideally) practical, pragmatic, ethical, empirical, inductive and critical. And this was true in philosophy, science, technology, historiography and theology. The *philosophes*' guiding lights were English and Anglican (as Voltaire described them): Francis Bacon (*le père de la philosophie expérimentale*); John Locke (*un esprit plus sage, plus méthodique, un logicien plus exact*); and Isaac Newton who (according to Voltaire) 'saw into the mind of God'. These three pioneered the empirical, critical exploration of (respectively) the natural world, the human mind and the cosmos.[39]

If we are urged to reject this cluster of methodological principles as 'rationalistic', as ideological critics of the Enlightenment claim, there would not be much left of the knowledge that we all rely on from day to day and which as academics we seek and teach with a good conscience – and we could close down our universities with all their departments! In its intellectual aspect, the Enlightenment represented a vigorous reaction against the highly rational, speculative metaphysics of Descartes, Malebranche, Spinoza, Leibniz, Berkeley and Wolff. I am saying nothing against metaphysics except that it was not the choice of the Enlightenment. Voltaire, in particular, was generally outspokenly hostile to Descartes. 'Our Descartes', he wrote, was 'born to uncover the errors of antiquity but to substitute his own, and spurred on by that systematizing mind which blinds the greatest of men' (including Malebranche with 'his sublime illusions').[40] In the Preface to his prizewinning First Discourse, *On the Moral Effects of the Arts and Sciences*, Rousseau disdains all 'metaphysical subtleties', but, in the practical

---

[39]French quotations from Voltaire, *Lettres Philosophiques*, pp. 78, 82; cf. 104. In his *Discours Préliminaire* to the *Encyclopédie*, d'Alembert puts Fontenelle (1657–1757) on a par with Bacon, Descartes, Locke and Newton as the main shapers of enlightened thinking.

[40]Voltaire, *Letters on England*, p. 63. Voltaire had been first drawn to the study of philosophy by reading not 'infidel' literature, but (in 1723) the Oratorian priest, philosopher and apologist Nicolas Malebranche's *Recherche de la vérité*; see Ira O. Wade, *The Intellectual Development of Voltaire* (Princeton, NJ: Princeton University Press, 1969), pp. 711–19.

spirit of the Enlightenment, he turns to address 'those [practical] truths on which the happiness of mankind depends'.[41]

However, all of these metaphysical thinkers were Christians and wrote to defend basic Christian belief, except Spinoza whose beliefs stood at a distance from Christian theology, though they were not untouched by it. Beiser points out that 'the motives, problems, and content of seventeenth-century rationalism was almost entirely religious'.[42] Even Immanuel Kant (1724–1804), the greatest philosopher of the *Aufklärung* and of the whole Enlightenment, used philosophical reasoning precisely to show the limitations of reason and to advocate 'practical reason', guided by the moral sense. According to Onora O'Neil, '[N]o thinker of the Enlightenment was more deeply aware that reason might be an illusory and self-destroying authority than Immanuel Kant.'[43]

So when some modern Christian writers throw around the phrase 'Enlightenment rationalism', as a term of disparagement, almost of abuse, they are doing a great disservice to the memory and reputation of some of the greatest Christian philosophers and apologists of modern times. In England, Anglican thinkers and writers, notably John Locke, William Law, Joseph Addison, Samuel Johnson, Joseph Butler, Jonathan Swift and John Wesley, all typically appealed to the tribunal of 'reason', just as much as the critics of orthodox Christianity did; they were all men of the Enlightenment. The shibboleth of 'reason' was not the sole prerogative of anticlerical deists and free-thinkers, but was endemic. However, there were various modes of reason. The 'reason' of these devout Anglican authors was not the speculative, deductive reason of Descartes, Malebranche and Spinoza; nor was it a sceptical, deconstructive, even purely empirical kind of reason (though empiricism remained crucial, especially in Locke's psychology and epistemology and in

---

[41]Rousseau, *The Social Contract and Discourses*, ed. Cole, p. 118.
[42]Beiser, *The Sovereignty of Reason*, p. 17.
[43]Onora O'Neil, 'Enlightenment as Autonomy: Kant's Vindication of Reason', in Peter Hulme and Ludmilla J. Jordanova (eds), *The Enlightenment and Its Shadows* (London: Routledge, 1990), p. 185; Immanuel Kant, *Critique of Pure Reason*, trans. J. M. D. Meiklejohn, ed. A. D. Lindsay (London: Dent; New York: Dutton, 1934); id., *Religion within the Limits of Reason Alone*, trans. and intro. Theodore M. Greene and Hoyt H. Hudson, with a new essay 'The ethical Significance of Kant's Religion' by John R. Silber (New York and London: Harper & Row, 1960 (1934]).

the thought of all who were influenced by it), such as influenced the *philosophes*. It was an idea of reason open to divine revelation, grounded in the lessons of experience and infused with heavenly light. It derived from the tradition of Richard Hooker, the Tew Circle (especially Lord Falkland, William Chillingworth and John Hales) and the Cambridge Platonists for whom reason was (quoting the Book of Proverbs) 'the candle of the Lord'. These Anglican thinkers, as Beiser comments, 'made it a religious duty to enquire into the grounds of their faith', though they unwittingly prepared the ground for deism and freethinking by validating religious truth by means of rational and ethical criteria.[44] Enlightenment thinkers were not cold cerebrating machines, but in many cases fervent and passionate people of faith who dreamed, struggled and suffered. A common misconception about Enlightenment thinkers is that they privileged reason over against feeling and imagination. Not so; sensibility played a key role. Voltaire ruefully acknowledged that emotion trumped reason in human experience, while Rousseau gloried in that fact and Hume said it was right that it should. In an essay entitled 'In Search of the Age of Reason', George Boas insists that 'Age of Sentiment' would be an equally appropriate name, noting that Lord Shaftesbury (d. 1713) and Francis Hutcheson (d. 1746) founded their ethical theories on sentiment.[45]

However, reason had the capacity to fight back against blind instinct and unruly passions. Voltaire wrote in the *Essai sur les Moeurs*: 'God has endowed us with a principle of universal reason ... [which] is so constant that it asserts itself despite all the passions which threaten it, despite the tyrants trying to drown it in blood, despite the impostors endeavouring to destroy it by superstitions.'[46]

---

[44]Beiser, *The Sovereignty of Reason*, pp. 7, 132–3. I have described the Anglican dimension of the Enlightenment, with special attention to Richard Hooker, Francis Bacon, John Locke, William Law, John Wesley, Joseph Butler and Edmund Burke in *ISOA*, chs 7–9. See especially B. W. Young, *Religion and Enlightenment in Eighteenth-Century England: From Locke to Burke* (Oxford: Oxford University Press, 1998). For Falkland, Chillingworth and Hales (and more on Hooker) see *AACC*, pp. 31–51, 85–97.
[45]George Boas, 'In Search of the Age of Reason', in Earl Reeves Wasserman (ed.), *Aspects of the Eighteenth Century* (Baltimore, MD: Johns Hopkins University Press, 1965), pp. 1–19, at p. 10.
[46]Cited from Voltaire, *Essai sur les Moeurs* in Jerome Rosenthal, 'Voltaire's Philosophy of History', *JHI* XVI.2 (1955), pp. 151–78, at p. 167.

We see the importance of reason for the Enlightenment when we see what it was opposed to: the crimes, vices, errors and superstitions that rage in history, not least in the history of the church. Reason was the civilising faculty.

It will help us to gain a clearer understanding of what the thinkers of the Enlightenment, including the *lumiéres*, meant by 'reason' when we see that 'reason' was assimilated to 'nature' across the board of intellectual enquiry. Reason and nature were equated and identified, becoming mutually interpretative. Together they were the antidote to the fanaticism ('enthusiasm') of the mid-seventeenth-century civil wars and the sects that arose in their wake. But what is particularly significant here is that nature was the subject of empirical, critical and inductive investigation in the tradition of Francis Bacon and Isaac Newton and in line with Locke's privileging of sense experience in epistemology. Thus 'natural law' was understood as reason working in the field of human interaction and natural processes; natural morality was reason applied to ethics; and natural religion was the result of reason working in the field of religious belief.[47] Moreover, as several interpreters of the Enlightenment point out, 'reason' stands not for a set of conclusions or beliefs, but for a method and approach to questions and phenomena that invite investigation. It was a method of critical thinking, of analysis and synthesis, leading to the formulation of the results into 'laws'.[48]

Enlightened 'reason' was dedicated to the amelioration of the human condition and the removal of everything, however hallowed by tradition, that stood in the way of that imperative. Peter Gay, the pioneer champion of the radical Enlightenment, entitled a collection of his studies of the French Enlightenment *The Party of Humanity* (a quotation from Diderot).[49] The 'reason' of the Enlightenment, especially of the *philosophes*, was an appeal to common sense, practical reality and a moral sense of the good. Gay roundly rejects the title 'The Age of Reason': 'The *philosophes*' glorification of criticism and their qualified repudiation of metaphysics make it obvious that the Enlightenment was not an Age of Reason, but a revolt against Rationalism.' Gay adds that the *philosophes*' claim

---

[47]Wade, *Intellectual Origins of the French Enlightenment*, p. 22.
[48]Ibid., pp. 22–4.
[49]Peter Gay, *The Party of Humanity: Studies in the French Enlightenment* (London: Weidenfeld & Nicolson, 1964).

for 'the omnicompetence of criticism was in no way a claim for the omnipotence of reason. It was a political demand for the right to question everything, rather than the assertion that all could be known or mastered by rationality.'[50] Redwood points out that the 'much vaunted rise of rationalism in the early eighteenth century should not be taken as a sufficient or even a real cause of Enlightenment questions concerning God, man [sic] and society'. The word 'reason' (Redwood continues) 'reflected a disparate number of prejudices and preconceptions' on the part of the individuals who invoked it.[51] In other words, the initially impressive terms 'reason' and 'rationalism', undefined and un-nuanced, are not only inadequate but seriously misleading to account for Enlightenment thought.

Tradition and the Enlightenment

Paul Hazard, whose book *The European Mind 1680–1715*, was one of the first to awaken my lively interest, as a school-leaver, in the Enlightenment, claimed that Enlightenment thinkers abandoned all tradition and respect for the past, especially for antiquity. 'The Past abandoned; the Present enthroned in its place.'[52] Why, he asked, did a whole section of Europe's *intelligentsia* suddenly drop the cult of antiquity? The answer is that it did not. It is a gross misrepresentation to assert, as Hazard did as long ago as 1935, and as Jonathan Israel has been doing in recent decades and as many theological writers (some discussed in Chapter 2) have claimed, that the Enlightenment rejected tradition and aspired to make start *de novo*. The Enlightenment was not hostile to tradition as such and the writers of the eighteenth century knew as well as we do that, without the resources furnished by tradition, there can be no knowledge or thought and that enquiry cannot progress. They were often avid readers of the Greek and Roman classics.

---

[50]Gay, *The Enlightenment: An Interpretation, Vol. 1, The Rise of Modern Paganism*, p. 141.
[51]John Redwood, *Reason, Ridicule and Religion: The Age of Enlightenment in England 1660–1750* (London: Thames and Hudson, 1976), p. 215.
[52]Hazard, *The European Mind 1680–1715*, p. 47.

As we have noted earlier, the Enlightenment in England was a largely Anglican affair with a conservative tendency. It leaned wholeheartedly on its favoured traditions. Try to imagine the mind and work of Johnson, Swift, Pope, Dryden, Addison, Gray, Sterne, Wesley and Burke after subtracting 'tradition' or 'antiquity'! The idea is fatuous. These writers were fluent in the classics: Pope superbly translated Homer; Gray was a consummate Latinist; Johnson knew few limits and composed the best verse of his age in Greek and Latin; the young John Wesley had the classics for breakfast, almost literally, on certain days of the week. Sterne sprinkled classical tags throughout *Tristram Shandy*. When we place Edmund Burke, as with Brian Young and others I believe we should, within the spacious precincts of the Enlightenment, as well as seeing him as a harbinger and pioneer of Romanticism, then we have a formidable defender, on the basis of first principles, of the claims of tradition ('prescription' or enduring precedent), alongside and certainly not against the authority of reason.[53]

The Dissenting academies were the redoubtable scholarly alternative to the Anglican foundations of Oxford and Cambridge Universities, though there were significant correspondences in educational quality, text books and general culture between the two sets of institutions, many of the first tutors of the academies being 'Oxbridge' graduates. The academies were equally infused with Enlightenment ideals of reasoned argument, toleration and intellectual and social advancement, but they diverged into orthodox and rationalistic branches, the orthodox remaining in continuity with the Christian doctrinal tradition and its classical sources.[54] But the love of ancient learning was not confined to England, as we shall see, though first we must consider the ambivalent attitude towards tradition of the most radical element within mainstream Enlightenment thought.

---

[53] On Burke see *ISOA*, pp. 326–39; Young, *Religion and Enlightenment in Eighteenth-Century England*.
[54] David L. Wykes, 'The Contribution of the Dissenting Academy to the emergence of Rational Dissent', in Haakonssen (ed.), *Enlightenment and Religion: Rational Dissent in Eighteenth-Century Britain*, ch. 5.

The *philosophes* and tradition

The *philosophes* did indeed spurn the particular tradition of Christian theology with which they were most familiar, that of the Roman Catholic Church, regarding with contempt, as so much logic-chopping, what seemed to them its interminable scholastic squabbles over terminological minutiae and at the same time disdaining its punitive enforcement of dogma and obedience. The *philosophes*' aversion from the enforced dogma and discipline of the church was stiffened by disgust at what they witnessed or knew of religious conflict – conflict between Catholics and Protestants, Jesuits and Jansenists, Lutheran and Reformed. Louis XIV's Revocation of the Edict of Nantes (1685), which had given protection to the Huguenots, his suppression of the Jansenists and the condemnation of Quietism exacerbated the tensions. Some of those thus alienated from the Roman Catholic Church, in its tense alliance with the repressive state, were drawn to deism and a few to atheism. But the aversion of the *philosophes* to the *status quo* did not mean the abrogation of all debts to tradition. Even the *philosophes* had their favoured traditions which they revered, drew inspiration from and adopted as their models. These traditions were fourfold.

First, the *philosophes* were consciously influenced by the tradition of scepticism and criticism that takes its name from the Greek philosopher Pyrrho of Elis (c. 370–c. 272 BC) and which was recovered at the Renaissance when the texts of Sextus Empiricus (AD c. 160–c. 210) in particular, became available. These Greek philosophers perfected the technique of pitting argument against argument and taught that to maintain an open mind and hold back from commitment (ἐπέχω, *epochē*) in the face of inconclusive evidence and insoluble intellectual problems was not defeatist but virtuous. Pyrrhonist assumptions and methods were deployed notably by Michel de Montaigne (1533–92), Pierre Charron (1541–1603) and Pierre Bayle (1647–1706).[55] These writers have been widely assumed

---

[55]Richard H. Popkin, *The History of Scepticism: From Savonarola to Bayle*, 2nd edn (Oxford: Oxford University Press, 2003 [1960]). Lorraine Daston, 'Probability and Evidence' (ch. 31; pp. 1106–44) and Charles Larmore, 'Scepticism' (ch. 32; pp. 1145–92), in David Garber and Michael Ayers (eds), *The Cambridge History of*

to be unbelievers, but in reality they were sincerely Christian in their way. Montaigne expounds both natural and revealed religion in his *Apologie de Raimonde Sabonde*. He also goes on pilgrimage, collects relics, lights candles and says his prayers.[56] With regard to Charron, I have written elsewhere: 'Charron has been claimed as an atheist and to read some accounts you would never guess that he was a dedicated priest, who published sermons and writings on the Eucharist, was favoured and promoted by his bishop, and was an apologist for Christianity and the Roman Catholic Church.'[57] Bayle, for his part, employed in essence an ethical, empirical form of critique, especially of the intellectual and moral foundations of the Catholic Church, to prepare the ground for a commitment to a liberal and minimal version of Reformed Christianity.[58]

These three writers – Montaigne, Charron and Bayle – whom some have seen as pioneers of a secular, atheistic Enlightenment, actually belong within the turbulent, variegated history of the questioning, probing and doubting, but by no means unusual, version of Christian thought. They have their place in a long tradition of radical, adventurous, subversive, sometimes dissenting or sectarian Christianity.[59] Erasmus and Pascal also have affinities to the sceptical tradition, but that hardly makes them non-Christian writers.[60] There are elements of Fideism – the willingness to believe

---

Seventeenth-Century Philosophy, 2 vols (Cambridge: Cambridge University Press, 2008), vol. 2. See also my defence of these sceptical thinkers' Christian allegiance in *ISOA*, ch. 6. A robust presentation of Charron as a denier and opponent of the Christian faith is made by Tullio Gregory, 'Pierre Charron's "Scandalous Book", in Michael Hunter and David Wootton (eds), *Atheism from the Reformation to the Enlightenment* (Oxford: Oxford University Press, 1992), ch. 3 (translated from, *Etica e religione nella critica libertina*, Naples, 1986), but Gregory's one-sided interpretation of Charron distorts and ultimately reverses his overall position.
[56]The *Apology*, together with the essay on prayer, is included in Michel de Montaigne, *The Complete Essays*, trans. and intro. M. A. Screech (Harmondsworth: Penguin, 1991).
[57]*ISOA*, p. 214.
[58]On Bayle see *ISOA*, pp. 230–4.
[59]See notably, Dominic Erdozain, 'A Heavenly Poise: Radical Religion and the Making of the Enlightenment', *Intellectual History Review* 27.1 (2017), pp. 71–96.
[60]Nietzsche placed Erasmus on the 'banner' of the Enlightenment, together with Petrarch and Voltaire – just those three: Friedrich Nietzsche, *Human, All Too Human: A Book for Free Spirits*, trans. R. J. Hollingdale, intro. Erich Heller

and to adhere to the faith against evidence and in the face of arguments and a readiness to set aside reason in order to make room for faith – in Montaigne, Charron, Pascal, Bayle and even Lessing (each in his own idiosyncratic way).[61] Thus a troubled awareness of the difficulties of faith need not lead to loss of faith but to a different approach to faith; argument and evidence are not the only sources of belief.

Those, like Jonathan Israel, who place Montaigne, Charron and Bayle outside the pale of mainstream Christian tradition, designating them torch-bearers for the coming of a secular, atheistic Enlightenment, tend to overlook the broad, generous, radical and adventurous scope of the history of Christian thought.[62] Benedict Spinoza is Israel's central figure and hero in his genealogy of the Enlightenment. But Spinoza's key formula *deus sive natura* ('God or nature') does not make him an atheistic materialist, as Israel, Robertson and others assume, but more correctly a panentheist. While strict *pantheism* is by no stretch of theological liberality Christian, because it identifies God and the cosmos absolutely and without remainder, pan*en*theism ('All things in God' or 'God in all things'), a high form of divine immanence, does fall within the

---

(Cambridge: Cambridge University Press, 1986), p. 26 (1.26). On Pascal's famous 'Wager' argument for Christian commitment see, *inter alia*, Ian Hacking, *The Emergence of Probability: A Philosophical Study of Early Ideas about Probability, Induction, and Statistical Inference* (Cambridge: Cambridge University Press, 1975), ch. 8. Pascal was not persuaded by the metaphysical approach to apologetics on behalf of Christianity: Blaise Pascal, *Pensées*, ed. and intro. A. J. Krailsheimer (Harmondsworth: Penguin, 1995).
[61]For this element in Lessing see Henry E. Allison, *Lessing and the Enlightenment* (Ann Arbor, MI: University of Michigan Press, 1966).
[62]Jonathan I. Israel, *Radical Enlightenment*; id., *Enlightenment Contested*. In the latter work, Israel argues that there were two Enlightenments: the 'radical' one where reason reigned supreme (this for him is the true version of the Enlightenment) and the 'moderate mainstream' one where reason was supplemented by faith and tradition, which was 'overwhelmingly dominant', but being compromised by faith and tradition, reason could not win the intellectual battle (pp. 10–12). He finds no trace of theism in Spinoza (p. 43). See also Anthony Pagden, *The Enlightenment and Why It Still Matters* (Oxford: Oxford University Press, 2013), a Whiggish, secularist piece of advocacy which ignores both theology and science.

spectrum of Christian theological paradigms.⁶³ It is also implausible to claim Spinoza as an atheist: he gives infinite substance – God or nature, 'nature' meaning all that is, not confined to this world – only two knowable attributes: extension and thought; but it is neither atheism nor materialism to postulate that ultimate reality *thinks*.⁶⁴ Reg Ward points out Spinoza's aversion to anthropomorphism:

> Spinoza was not in the metaphysical sense an atheist, but as an outsider he recognised that the Christian concept of God as creator and ruler of the universe differed from the metaphysical concept of an absolute, infinite, perfect, eternal and necessarily existing being ... the meaning of the world, if it had one, was not to be determined in human and personal terms. This view of course produced outraged accusations of atheism against him.⁶⁵

In parenthesis I can bring forward Thomas Hobbes as another case in point. Interpreters of Hobbes are divided on whether he should be seen as a Christian thinker or as an apostle of infidelity, though the weight of opinion is in the negative. I am with the significant minority and I have rehearsed the key arguments in my first volume on Anglican theological methodology.⁶⁶ Hobbes was a religious thinker and no mean theologian and he conformed to the Established Church while it existed. Hobbes's super-Erastianism in

---

⁶³John Robertson, *The Enlightenment: A Very Short Introduction* (Oxford: Oxford University Press, 2015), pp. 15, 18. For a sympathetic exposition of panentheism by an orthodox Christian theologian, see John Macquarrie, *In Search of Deity: An Essay in Dialectical Theism; The Gifford Lectures Delivered at the University of St Andrews in Session 1983–4* (London: SCM Press, 1984); and for a critical introduction to Macquarrie's panentheism see Michael W. Brierley, 'John Macquarrie's Panentheism', in Robert Morgan (ed.), *In Search of Humanity and Deity: A Celebration of John Macquarrie's Theology* (London: SCM Press, 2006), ch. 18; Loriliai Biernacki and Philip Clayton (eds), *Panentheism across the World's Traditions* (Oxford: Oxford University Press, 2013).
⁶⁴Benedict de Spinoza, *Ethics and On the Improvement of the Understanding*, ed. James Gutmann (New York: Hafner, 1949); Alan Donagan, 'Spinoza's Theology', in Don Garrett (ed.), *The Cambridge Companion to Spinoza* (Cambridge: Cambridge University Press, 1996), ch. 8.
⁶⁵W. Reginald Ward, *Christianity under the Ancien Régime, 1648–1789* (Cambridge: Cambridge University Press, 1999), pp. 157–8.
⁶⁶*ISOA*, pp. 175–201.

Leviathan (1651) is his theological protest against the chaos and carnage of the Civil War and early Commonwealth period and takes to an extreme the mordantly pessimistic theological anthropology of Calvinism. Hobbes's monarchical absolutism is no more extreme than the claims that Henry VIII made for himself or that Byzantine Christian emperors enjoyed, though this was not appropriate in an age when people were longing for a fresh start for the nation.[67] Hobbes's use of materialist philosophy to exegete the nature of human being and the body politic does not itself put him outside Christian theology because it does not mean that the visible world is all that exists; there are 'corporeal spirits' who are not material.

> We who are Christians acknowledge that there be angels good and evil; and that they are spirits, and that the soul of man is a spirit; and that these spirits are immortal. But, to know it, that is to say, to have natural evidence of the same: it is impossible ... But though the Scripture acknowledge spirits, yet doth it nowhere say, that they are incorporeal, meaning thereby, without dimensions and quantity.[68]

A plausible explanation of 'where Hobbes is coming from' in his political theology is that he was working within the late sixteenth- and early seventeenth-century trajectory of the Calvinist-Arminian debates on the political implications of opposed theological axioms, both in Holland and in England.[69] These thinkers, such as Hobbes, who to some seem too daring, too questioning and too subversive to be Christian, remained deeply religious – not secular and certainly not atheistical – thinkers and theologians and mostly positioned themselves within the broad stream of Christian thought and church life.

---

[67] On Henry VIII's claims see Malcolm B. Yarnell III, *Royal Priesthood in the English Reformation* (Oxford: Oxford University Press, 2013), though I do not accept all of Yarnell's conclusions.
[68] Hobbes, *Elements of Law*, p. 55, cited Richard Tuck, 'The "Christian Atheism" of Thomas Hobbes', in Hunter and Wootton (eds), *Atheism from the Reformation to the Enlightenment*, ch. 4, at p. 124. For Hobbes' theological credentials see *Leviathan*, ed. and intro. C. B. Macpherson (Harmondsworth: Penguin, 1969).
[69] A seminal statement of this interpretation is Phyllis Doyle, 'The Contemporary Background of Hobbes "State of Nature"', *Economica* 21 (1927), pp. 336–55. https://doi.org/10.2307/2548403.

The *philosophes* drew on aspects of this highly diverse sceptical tradition, especially its intellectual attitude of interrogating claims and weighing evidence. Voltaire, for whom Bayle was a model historian, quoted Aristotle that *incredulité* was the foundation of all wisdom, and recommended it for historical study, especially of ancient history.[70] In the hands of the *philosophes* the sceptical tradition took an empirical turn. Thus they drew on an intellectual heritage that has its source in ancient Greek philosophy and which influenced Christian thought at the Renaissance and then again further along the road to the Enlightenment. Christian thought tends to pass through such intellectual movements, assimilating questions and insights, rather than to steamroller over them or give them a wide berth.

Second, the *philosophes* looked back with admiration to classical civilization (which included Pyrrhonism, of course). The young Edward Gibbon, sitting among the ruins and remains of the Capitol in Rome and meditating with strong emotion his great life's work, is the paradigm of the Enlightenment's awed admiration of antiquity.[71] In spite of the complicity of some *philosophes* with the 'enlightened despots', it was the rule of law, not arbitrary absolute rule, that attracted them to ancient Rome. Cicero was on a par with Francis Bacon in their pantheon.[72] Lucretius, *De Rerum Naturae [The Nature of Things]* was popular reading among the *philosophes*; they saw Lucretius as a critical intelligence working to explain mysteries and to overcome irrational fear of the unknown.[73] Unsurprisingly, Aristotle – the empiricist and categorizer – remained a potent philosophical influence.[74] Rousseau was brought up on Plutarch, Tacitus and other Greek and Roman writers; this childhood grounding provided him with scores of historical examples for the thesis of his First Discourse that the rise of the arts and sciences

---

[70] J. H. Brumfitt, Introduction to Voltaire, *La Philosophie de l'histoire*, SVEC XXVIII (1963).
[71] Gibbon, *Autobiography*, pp. 122–4.
[72] Gay, *The Enlightenment: An Interpretation, Vol. 1, The Rise of Modern Paganism*, p. 313.
[73] Ibid., pp. 98–100.
[74] Dan Edelstein, 'The Aristotelian Enlightenment', in Anton M. Matytsin and Dan Edelstein (eds), *Let There Be Enlightenment: The Religious and Mystical Sources of Rationality* (Baltimore, MD: Johns Hopkins University Press, 2014), pp. 187–204.

had corrupted society and morals. Napoleon modelled his account of his campaigns on Julius Caesar's *Gallic Wars*. Altogether, '[t]he past – especially the classical past – was a storehouse of glorious unsurpassable achievements, especially in literature and morals, and a museum of appealing figures.'[75]

Third, they were intoxicated with the artistic and other cultural splendours of Louis XIV's France, only a century before. Voltaire designated it as one of four great ages of cultural flowering and saw it as the culmination of social progress. What did it matter to them that Louis had attempted the conquest of Europe?

But in the fourth place, even the *philosophes* were deeply indebted to earlier Christian intellectual movements and theological endeavours. This fact was pointed out by Carl Becker almost a century ago when he claimed that 'there is more of Christian philosophy in the writings of the *Philosophes* than has yet been dreamt of in our histories'.[76] More recent research has shown that the *philosophes* drew on the heated debates of Renaissance humanism and the Reformation era and, further back, the scholastic subtleties of medieval philosophical theology. And they found in those sources not only their signature metaphor of light and enlightenment, and their pivotal tactic of an appeal to reason, but also many key ideas of the Enlightenment programme and their verbal expression.[77]

Improving the human condition

Enlightenment thought, especially its philosophy of history and what we might call its eschatology, is commonly identified with belief in 'progress', however understood. As we have seen in Chapter 1 ('Engaging the Enlightenment'), the 'progressive' aspect of eighteenth-century thought does not endear the Enlightenment

---

[75]Peter Gay, *The Enlightenment: An Interpretation; Vol. 2, The Science of Freedom* (London: Weidenfeld and Nicolson, 1970), p. 92. Tacitus, the historian of prudence, rose to prominence among philosophers and historians: Peter Burke, 'A Survey of the Popularity of Ancient Historians, 1450–1700', *H&T* 5 (1966), pp. 135–52.

[76]Carl Becker, *The Heavenly City of the Eighteenth-Century Philosophers*, 2nd edn (New Haven, CT: Yale University Press, 2003 [1932]), p. 31. R. O. Rockwood (ed.), *Karl Becker's Heavenly City Revisited* (Ithaca, NY: Cornell University Press, 1958).

[77]Matytsin and Edelstein (eds), *Let There Be Enlightenment*, passim.

to some Christian writers. Lesslie Newbigin, who was intimately acquainted with mass poverty in India as Bishop of Madurai and later of Madras, saw the Enlightenment vision of progress as leading straight to the post-war British 'consumer society', which he regarded as decadent and founded on an incorrigible idolatry of created goods which were intended by God to minister to human needs and necessities, not to pander to inordinate desire and acquistiveness. Newbigin was unhappy with the idea that human beings, by their own strength and resources, could improve their situation to such an extent that they would wallow in the sort of luxury which he believed that he could see all around him when he returned to Britain in 1974. With great respect to the memory of Lesslie Newbigin, the good bishop, I think his attitude was misplaced on several counts. (He had Britain in his sights, but the discussion can be extrapolated to much of Western Europe.)

First, I do not think that the Britain of the 1970s and 1980s (Newbigin died in 1988) is correctly described as a society and culture that is primarily orientated to consumption and acquisition. It is true that there seemed to be many people at that time – and it is the case now too – who strove to find some shreds of meaning in their lives by engaging in 'retail therapy', often of the rather miserable kind of frequenting local bargain-basement supermarkets in town and city centres in their free time. But to me that is not so much a matter for moral judgement as for compassion.

Second, I think it is a mistake to imagine that a culture can be primarily obsessed with and driven by consumption. In every society, the primary motivation for mature adults – with the exception of a small minority of irresponsible persons – is the need to support their families and, to that end, their commitment to their work, the source of income.

Third, in 'Margaret Thatcher's Britain' there were large numbers of former factory workers, miners and so on, who had seen their industry destroyed and had become unemployed; they were struggling to put food on the table, not luxuriating in conspicuous consumption. The same is true now when overall living standards have risen even further: there are still many poor and struggling families and they now look to the local food bank to help them out.

Fourth, it is not correct to assimilate the Enlightenment's view of progress purely to material advancement. The lay thinkers of the Enlightenment, in all countries, whether Protestant or Roman

Catholic (the latter tending to follow some way behind the former) were fundamentally concerned with the programmatic amelioration of the living conditions of the toiling serfdom of Europe and that of those poor, struggling artisans whose economic circumstances were little better.[78] Unlike many churchmen and divines, these lay thinkers were not satisfied with charity and poor law, but sought permanent improvements. In France serfdom had been steadily reduced before the Revolution, though France still had the largest of the slave-empires in the Caribbean, which sat ill with triumphalist proclamations of *liberté, fraternité et egalité*.[79] Voltaire, Hume and Kant argued in support of slavery – sometimes Enlightenment reason was simply perverse – but Samuel Johnson was vehemently opposed to the institution of slavery, as were Montesquieu, Buffon, Burke, Ferguson, Helvétius, Condorcet, Rousseau and Herder, for example. Passionate moral abolitionism came with the English campaigners William Wilberforce, Granville Sharp, James Ramsay and Thomas Clarkson. But as McCloy points out, the *philosophes* accompanied the slogans of liberty, fraternity and equality with the ideals of reason, humanity and justice.[80] The atheistic and materialistic writers Helvétius and d'Holbach pointed out the effects of environment and circumstances on social inequality and Helvétius at least was active in seeking to improve the lot of workers on his estate. The philosophical and ethical aspiration of the *philosophes* was turned to the invention of methods and technologies for manufacture and agriculture, which we see abundantly explained, illustrated and promoted in the *Encyclopédie*, but their humanitarian ideals also had political and economic implications in terms of social justice. The eighteenth-century serious philosophers and populist prophets of progress alike were concerned with the overall enhancement of

---

[78] See Shelby T. McCloy, *The Humanitarian Movement in Eighteenth-Century France* (Louisville, KY: University of Kentucky Press, 1957) for details of the programmes and legislation. Also Gay, *The Party of Humanity*; Alan Forrest, 'Poverty', in William Doyle (ed.), *The Oxford Handbook of the Ancien Régime* (Oxford: Oxford University Press, 2012), ch. 10.
[79] See William Doyle, 'Slavery and Serfdom', in id. (ed.), *The Oxford Handbook of the Ancien Régime*, ch. 16.
[80] McCloy, *The Humanitarian Movement in Eighteenth-Century France*, p. 265. On Burke's reforming but gradualist approach see Gregory M. Collins, 'Edmund Burke on Slavery and the Slave Trade', *Slavery & Abolition: A Journal of Slave and Post-Slave Studies* 40.3 (2019), pp. 494–521.

human life in society in its moral, educational and spiritual aspects. There is more to say on this third point.

In a sort of digression within the *Decline and Fall*, Gibbon provides us with a summary of the Enlightenment belief in progress, or as he puts it, 'the improvements of society', under three aspects.[81] First, there are the achievements of persons of great talent and even genius, such as poets and philosophers, but they arise spontaneously and are not at anyone's command. Second, there are 'the benefits of law and policy, of trade and manufactures, of arts and sciences', which are 'more solid and permanent' and are the work of many, but they may be eroded by gradual decay or interrupted by warfare. Third, 'the more useful, or, at least, more necessary arts' can be carried forward, year in year out, in small communities and cottage industries, in field and farm, on land or water. Such basic skills, trades and traditions are not to be despised in this age of progress, for they enable the human race to survive from generation to generation. Writing, with all his philosophical contemporaries, against the background of the destructive and fanatical wars, on continental and British soil, of the previous century, and without foreknowledge of the imminent French Revolution, 'The Terror' and the Napoleonic Wars, let alone of course, of the unimaginable horrors and devastation of the two World Wars of the twentieth century and the accompanying Holocaust, Gibbon reflects with complacency and optimism on the future. The experience of four millennia of European civilization 'should enlarge our hopes and diminish our apprehensions'. We cannot foresee 'to what height the human species [sic] may aspire in their advancement towards perfection', but we can safely assume that no people 'will relapse into their original barbarism'. Gibbon rounds off his philosophical digression on progress thus: 'We may therefore acquiesce in the pleasing conclusion that every age of the world has increased and still increases the real wealth, the happiness, the knowledge, and perhaps the virtue, of the human race.' I like the typically Gibbonian 'perhaps'.

Belief in the innate virtue and perfectibility of human nature – precisely as a challenge to Christian theological anthropology

---

[81]Edward Gibbon, *The Decline and Fall of the Roman Empire*, abridged and intro. D. M. Low (Harmondsworth: Penguin, 1963), pp. 529–30.

and its doctrine of original sin in its Pauline, Augustinian and Calvinist form – is typically attributed to the Enlightenment, but as a generalization it is a distortion, if not a misrepresentation, of the mainstream of Enlightenment thought. The prevailing perspective of eighteenth-century philosophical anthropology was frankly morbid. Gibbon lamented that history was 'little more than the register of the crimes, follies and misfortunes of mankind'.[82] In this gloomy assessment he was echoing Voltaire, though he would not have wanted to admit it. And no-one could have taken a more jaundiced view of human nature, its stupidities, vices and crimes, as revealed in history, than Voltaire. In his view of history and progress Voltaire was indebted to the polymath Bernard de Fontenelle (though without always acknowledging it). In the light of history Fontenelle (1657–1757) viewed the future with almost unrelieved cynicism; human passions were unchanging, though reason gave some grounds for hope. But while Fontenelle scorns the follies, superstitions and crimes of humanity, Voltaire agonizes over them and pities the plight of suffering humanity.[83]

But it was an Enlightenment axiom that no absolute necessity or inevitability attached to this dismal record. Humans were not fated to be always bad; they could be taught and trained to be better. Locke's *Some Thoughts Concerning Education* (1693), which had a huge influence on Enlightenment thought, rejected the doctrine that a proclivity to do evil was a consequence of the Fall of Man and was entailed to all of Adam and Eve's descendants. (This was not a rejection of the Fall and of original sin as such, but of one aspect of the traditional dogma; Locke was refining Christian theology, not repudiating it, and building on substantial precedents, especially among the Cambridge Platonists and the Latitudinarians.) Humans were not born with an inclination to either evil or to good, according to Locke – though nine out of ten persons had an *acquired* bias towards wrong – but simply to

---

[82]Gibbon, *The Decline and Fall of the Roman Empire*, ch. 3. Cf. Voltaire, 'History Is Nothing More Than a Tableau of Crimes and Misfortunes', in *L'Ingénu* (Cork: Ligaran, 2015 [1767]), p. 61: 'Il lut des histoires, elles l'attristèrent. Le monde lui parut trop méchant et trop misérable. En effet l'histoire n'est que le tableau des crimes et des malheurs.'
[83]H. Sinn Edsall, 'The Idea of History and Progress in Fontenelle and Voltaire', *Yale Romanic Studies* (New Haven, CT) 18 (1941), pp. 163–84, at p. 166.

shun pain and seek pleasure. Locke did not mean this formula in a blatantly hedonistic sense, any more than we would moralize about a new-born baby seeking the pleasure of the breast and protesting volubly at hunger or discomfort. But the blank canvas of freshly minted humanity could be written upon indelibly by education, training and the formation of sound habits. In principle – as others, notably Hutcheson and then Helvétius, Priestley and Bentham would show – Locke had given an unintentional initial impetus to the doctrine of the indefinite moral perfectibility of human nature and social behaviour.[84]

It was Rousseau who, as so often, swam against the stream with regard to the doctrine, proclaimed by some *philosophes*, of the capacity of human nature for indefinite moral improvement and perfection. In his First Discourse, on the effect of the arts and sciences on morals, Rousseau begins by disarmingly and with ironic intention praising the 'miracles' of recent progress:

> It is a noble and beautiful spectacle to see man [*sic*] raising himself, so to speak, from nothing by his own exertions; dissipating, by the light of reason, all the thick clouds in which he was by nature enveloped; mounting above himself; soaring in thought even to the celestial regions; like the sun, encompassing with giant strides the vast extent of the universe; and, what is still grander and more wonderful, going back into himself, there to study man and get to know his own nature, his duties and his end.[85]

This 'enlightened' age, he went on, has emerged from the darkness of scholastic barbarism and ignorance.[86] But what is the result of that great escape for the quality of social intercourse? At this point, Rousseau launches into his diatribe, the thesis that 'our minds have been corrupted in proportion as the arts and sciences have improved'. '[T]he herd of men, which we call society', all conforming blindly to peer norms, speak and act falsely. 'Jealousy, suspicion, fear, coldness, reserve, hate, and fraud lie constantly concealed under that uniform and deceitful veil of politeness.' Blasphemy,

---

[84]John Passmore, *The Perfectibility of Man*, 2nd edn (London: Duckworth, 1970).
[85]Rousseau, *The Social Contract and Discourses*, ed. Cole, p. 120.
[86]Ibid.

backbiting, loss of patriotism and 'a dangerous scepticism' mark the conversation of the supposedly enlightened ones.[87]

Rousseau did not believe in the innocence or goodness of humankind under the conditions of civil society – from his own experience, he knew differently – but only in original goodness, which he found deep within his heart. In his Second Discourse, *Discours sur l'origine et les fondements de l'inégalité parmi les hommes* (1755), Rousseau's claims for the original or native goodness of humanity were confessedly grounded in introspection.[88] We cannot know what our remote forebears were like, except by finding them, as it were, living still deep within us, though buried under the corrupting accretions of centuries of so-called civilization. To effect this retrieval the roar of our passions must first be stilled to make room for inward silence (*le silence des passions*).[89] But, as F. C. Green observed, 'the passions of Jean Jacques were never silent. His whole doctrine of human natural goodness perverted by social progress was the involuntary projection on a universal scale of Rousseau's own spiritual dilemma. He had committed wicked deeds and yet was convinced of the purity of his motives. Belief in the original goodness of human nature was, therefore, for Rousseau, a vital spiritual need.'[90]

The *Confessions* are an extended and enthralling narrative apologia for the well-meaning actions of a man who felt that he had suffered too much (as he had, not least at the hands of fellow *philosophes*).[91] Such emotional dispositions as pity and sympathy, arising from the natural goodness of the heart, would soften and moderate the strength of proper and inescapable self-love, self-respect or self-esteem (*amour de soi*). At this point in Enlightenment psychology, just as in Hume, we find that the claims of passion or emotion trump the voice of reason. For Hume it meant the defeat of reason, which he could live with, but Rousseau made a positive

---

[87] Ibid., pp. 122–3.
[88] Ibid., pp. 143–229.
[89] Ibid., p. 142.
[90] F. C. Green, *Rousseau and the Idea of Progress* (Oxford: Oxford University Press, 1950 [repr. Norwood Editions, 1978]), p. 11.
[91] Jean Jacques Rousseau, *Confessions*, trans. and intro. J. M. Cohen (Harmondsworth: Penguin, 1953 [1781]). See also R. Grimsley, *Jean-Jacques Rousseau: A Study in Self-Awareness*, 2nd edn (Cardiff: University of Wales Press, 1969 [1961]).

virtue of it; for him, natural, unsullied sentiment was morally and intellectually superior to scientific reason.[92] Like Locke, he turned his moral vision – which in his case, though not in Locke's – was one of basic human innocence and goodness to serve the purpose of an educational philosophy, setting it out in the late didactic novel *Émile* (see the next chapter: 'The Enlightenment and Religion'). Rousseau was indebted to Locke's *Thoughts Concerning Education*, but Locke would not have approved of Rousseau's claim that the basic impulses of human nature were to be trusted.[93]

As for the more typical *philosophes*, they were not always blowing the trumpet of 'progress' as such because, though generally they had not developed a sophisticated theory of progress, their vision of it was comprehensive and all-pervading. Theodore Besterman, the author of the huge, definitive biography of Voltaire and the founding director of the Voltaire Foundation in Oxford, claimed that the Enlightenment had 'one outstanding characteristic which dominated it and which distinguishes it from all preceding history: the belief in progress through reason'.[94] Besterman notes that the harbinger and exemplar of the critical, investigative scholarship that typified the Enlightenment, Pierre Bayle, 'not only does not formally discuss the idea of progress, he hardly betrays any awareness of it'. Similarly, though the *Encyclopédie* does not formally discuss the idea of progress, 'the whole work is penetrated [says Besterman] by an unconscious acceptance of the notion as self-evident'.[95] Besterman goes on to say that Voltaire provides an even more striking illustration of 'the total absorption, largely by

---

[92]Green, *Rousseau and the Idea of Progress*, p. 14. On Hume's comprehensive scepticism see Basil Willey, *The Eighteenth-Century Background: Studies in the Idea of Nature in the Thought of the Period* (Harmondsworth: Peregrine, 1962 [1940]), pp. 109–32.
[93]Jean-Jacques Rousseau, *Émile*, trans. Barbara Foxley, intro. P. D. Jimack (London: Dent; New York: Dutton, 1974); John Passmore, 'The Malleability of Man in Eighteenth-Century Thought', in Wasserman (ed.), *Aspects of the Eighteenth Century*, pp. 21–46, at p. 41. See also G. Merken-Spaas, 'The Social Anthropology of Rousseau's *Émile*', *SVEC* CXXXII (1975), pp. 137–81, where the author points out that both Émile Durkheim and Claude Levi-Strauss acknowledged Rousseau as a pioneer of the modern human sciences.
[94]Theodore Besterman, 'Reason and Progress', *SVEC* XXIV (1963), pp. 27–41, at p. 28.
[95]Ibid., p. 31.

subliminal osmosis, of this revolutionary new idea'. In Voltaire's *Philosophical Dictionary* there is no article devoted to progress. 'Yet nobody could read ten consecutive pages from his pen [writes Besterman] without realizing that belief in perfectibility, or rather in meliorism, was as close to him as his skin, even in his youth.'[96] The passion to improve the wretched lot of much of humankind burned as strongly in the breast of Voltaire as it did in William Wilberforce and Anthony Ashley Cooper (Lord Shaftesbury) a generation or two later in England.

In his celebratory accounts of the French Enlightenment, Peter Gay describes it as a recovery of nerve, a surge of moral confidence that the world could be changed for the better. But Gay actually has a nuanced account of 'progress' among the *philosophes*. From the Renaissance onward a tide of hope had spread through the European intelligentsia. 'The ancients had felt helpless before the forces of nature and man's irrationality, and the philosophers of antiquity had rationalized this impotence in systems pervaded by a profound pessimism. To philosophize was to learn how to die, to study history was to trace the decline of mankind from some golden age of innocence, honour and virility.'[97] It was the 'activism' and 'practicality' of the *philosophes* that completed the great reorientation of Western thought that had been gathering strength for several centuries. It could be – and has been – claimed (notably by Karl Becker and Franco Venturi) that the philosophers' concern for the future was a secular version of Christian eschatology.[98] Personally, I do not see how that is a criticism, let alone a condemnation, of Enlightenment ameliorism, any more than it is a fault in New Testament eschatology that it is a Christianized form of late Jewish apocalyptic with its Persian influences, or a fatal flaw in Augustine's eschatology that it is tainted with the dualism of his youthful Manichaeism. For Gay, however, the resemblance between the eschatology of the Christian tradition and that of the *philosophes* is superficial: 'rhetorical rather than substantive'. It was posterity in this world, not a future life in another world,

---

[96]Ibid.
[97]Gay, *The Enlightenment: An Interpretation; Vol. 2, The Science of Freedom*, p. 84.
[98]Becker, *The Heavenly City of the Eighteenth-Century Philosophers*; Venturi, *Utopia and Reform in the Enlightenment*.

that interested them. As Diderot put it, 'What posterity is for the philosopher the other world is for the religious man.'⁹⁹

Enlightenment hopes for improvement were hard won, not a facile doctrinaire utopianism. Peter Gay, the champion among historians of the achievements of the *philosophes*, points out that the most optimistic writings on progress, those of Turgot and Condorcet, are marked not only by hope and aspiration, but also by contradiction, hesitation, pessimism and resignation.¹⁰⁰ This mood and perspective was by no means exceptional in the French Enlightenment. The *philosophes* hoped for a more beneficent future through human effort, including technology (for some, technological advancement blessed by Providence), but their hope was merely a beacon amidst the encircling gloom of history to date. In the *Discourse Préliminaire* to the *Encyclopédie*, D'Alembert spoke for the whole European Enlightenment when he stated that 'barbarism lasts for centuries and seems to be our natural element, while reason and good taste are but passing phenomena'.¹⁰¹ In the same year, 1751, Voltaire said the same thing in *Le Siècle de Louis XIV*: 'All history ... is little else than a long succession of useless cruelties ... a collection of crimes, follies and misfortunes'.¹⁰²

The rights of women

In view of the prevailing prejudice that the Enlightenment was a movement towards secularism and irreligion, it is a striking fact that some of the most able and eloquent advocates of women's entitlement to equality with men in *inter alia* education and social standing were deeply religious persons. This raises the question for me whether their sense of God, and their personal Christian piety can be detached from their proto-Enlightenment rational and ethical

---

⁹⁹Cited Gay, *The Enlightenment: An Interpretation; Vol. 2, The Science of Freedom*, p. 90.
¹⁰⁰Ibid., pp. 108, 112–22.
¹⁰¹Cited Henry Vyverberg, *Historical Pessimism in the French Enlightenment* (Cambridge, MA: Harvard University Press, 1958), p. 148.
¹⁰²Cited Charles Frankel, *The Faith of Reason: The Idea of Progress in the French Enlightenment* (New York: Octagon Books, 1969 [1948]), p. 108.

arguments and proto-Feminist demands for equality, or whether it is at least partly attributable to the fact that they had simply been reading the Gospels and had found their individual value as women cherished in the practice of prayer.

In recent years scholars have traced the origins of modern Feminist ideas and aspirations in the English language back to the upheavals of the mid-seventeenth century when the traditional landmarks were overturned in a period of political, social and religious turbulence. In Renaissance England the daughters of gentry families could expect to be schooled in the Greek and Latin classics, as well as in the Bible and supporting literature, just as their brothers were. During the Puritan and sectarian ideological ferment of the middle decades of the seventeenth century, the cultivation of women lost ground which was replaced by millenarian preaching and prophesying where women like (Lady) Eleanor Douglas and Mary Cary publically proclaimed alongside their male counterparts, the shared assumption being that the Holy Spirit was no respecter of persons. From the 1660s, the Quaker movement, led by George Fox and Margaret Fell (author of *Women's Speaking Justified, Proved and Allowed of by the Scriptures* (1666)) 'disciplined the wild individualism of Civil War prophecy and ben[t] it to a communal life and responsibility' in which the spiritual equality of women and men was affirmed as a biblical and theological principle, though the political apocalypticism inspired by the books of Daniel and Revelation, persisted.[103]

There is a truly 'apostolic succession' of women writers on philosophy and theology, including: Margaret Cavendish, Duchess of Newcastle (1623–73), 'the leading feminist humanist of the middle of the seventeenth century';[104] Damaris Cudworth, Lady Masham (1659–1708), daughter of the Cambridge Platonist Ralph

---

[103] Rosemary Radford Ruether, 'Prophets and Humanists: Types of Religious Feminism in Stuart England', *The Journal of Religion* 70.1 (1990), pp. 1–18, at p. 8. See also John Robertson, 'Women and Enlightenment: A Historiographical Conclusion', in Sarah Knott and Barbara Taylor (eds), *Women, Gender and Enlightenment* (Basingstoke: Palgrave Macmillan, 2005), pp. 692–704; Hilary Hinds, *God's Englishwomen: Seventeenth-Century Radical Sectarian Writing and Feminist Criticism* (Manchester: Manchester University Press, 1996); Margaret R. Hunt, Margaret Jacob, Phyllis Mack and Ruth Perry (eds), *Women in the Enlightenment* (New York: The Haworth Press Inc, 1984).
[104] Ruether, 'Prophets and Humanists', p. 12.

Cudworth and a philosopher, theologian and moralist, who gave a home for thirteen years at Oates Manor, Essex, to John Locke and his library, on his return from exile, and influenced his later work; Mary Astell (1666–1731); and Mary Wollstonecraft. While Cavendish was primarily a natural philosopher and metaphysician and was somewhat diffident about her religious beliefs, Damaris Cudworth and Mary Astell were fervent in Christian devotion, both writing books on the love of God. Astell was an extraordinarily intelligent, strong-minded and basically self-educated woman whose achievements are only now becoming fully known.[105] She advocated an equal (but separate and different) education for women in order to fit them for a more equal marriage. That was perhaps a limited though worthy aim, but the principle behind it was far-reaching: 'If all Men are born free, how is it that all Women are born Slaves?' she asked in the Preface to the third edition of *Some Reflections upon Marriage* (1706).[106] She discussed natural philosophy, philosophy and theology with a feminine intellectual circle in London where she founded and ran a charity school. She was confident enough to be publically critical of aspects of Locke's thought, finding his theological ethics wanting. A High Church woman, Astell had Jacobite and Nonjuring convictions, being devoted to Charles I King and Martyr, and found a patron in the Nonjuring former Archbishop of Canterbury William Sancroft. She was also supported by the exceptional cleric John Norris of Bermerton who was also a significant influence on John Wesley.

The Civil War sectaries, the Quakers, and even highly exceptional female thinkers like Mary Astell, though they challenged male superiority and dominance in the spiritual and intellectual spheres, continued to adhere to the principle of patriarchy, that is of male hegemony, in the home, in society and in the political nation. They worked with the unquestioned assumption of a divinely ordained social order. The realization

---

[105]Ruth Perry, *The Celebrated Mary Astell: An Early English Feminist* (Cambridge: Cambridge University Press, 1986); Mary Astell and John Norris, *Letters Concerning the Love of God*, ed. E. Derek Taylor and Melvyn New (Aldershot and Burlington, VT: Ashgate, 2005); Sarah Apetrei, *Women, Feminism, and Religion in Early Enlightenment England* (Cambridge: Cambridge University Press, 2010).
[106]Ellen Pollak (ed.), *A Cultural History of Women in the Age of Enlightenment, Volume 4* (London and New York: Berg, 2013), p. 5 (Pollak, Introduction).

that social order was a human construction and therefore challengeable and reformable was an achievement of the radical aspect of the Enlightenment.

The most frequently referenced intellectual giants of the Enlightenment – Spinoza and Bayle, Locke and Newton, Voltaire and Rousseau – are all male. But Mary Wollstonecraft (1759–97) was a proto-feminist philosopher and author of *A Vindication of the Rights of Men* (1790), a response to Edmund Burke's attack on the French Revolution. She attacked the eminent Burke aggressively, in a blatantly 'unfeminine' manner by the standards of the age and in a way that he had probably never been spoken to before outside of the House of Commons. She put him to shame for his sentimental defence of the executed French Queen Marie Antoinette, as though she had been a paragon of virtue. Wollstonecraft followed up with *A Vindication of the Rights of Woman* (1792). Wife of the radical secular thinker William Godwin and mother of the child who became Mary Shelley, Wollstonecraft was a radical, righteous, angry, emancipatory voice, but in no way bohemian. In her prefatory appeal to Talleyrand, she deplores the levity, neglect of domestic responsibilities, coquetry, lack of modesty and loose morals of the French women who had been liberated intellectually and morally by the *philosophes* and by the Revolution. Like Astell, Wollstonecraft linked the twin ideals of the Enlightenment: virtue and reason. '[I]t is a farce to call any being virtuous whose virtues do not result from the exercise of its own reason. This was Rousseau's opinion respecting men: I extend it to women.'[107] Her arguments are cogent, passionate and fearless. Wollstonecraft was also a God-absorbed person and thinker, albeit tinged with deism. Her *Vindication of the Rights of Woman* is set within an explicitly theistic conceptual framework; it is imbued with references to God as creator, sustainer and guide. Wollstonecraft found God all around and within: not in 'temples made with hands' (churches), but especially in creation,

---

[107] Mary Wollstonecraft, *A Vindication of the Rights of Woman, A Vindication of the Rights of Men, An Historical and Moral View of the French Revolution*, ed. Janet Todd (Oxford: Oxford University Press, 1993), p. 86. In this section Wollstonecraft takes John Milton, as well as Rousseau, to task for false and unjust notions of humanity and womanhood. In the case of Milton, it is for his portrayal of Eve in *Paradise Lost*. However, she does not take the Genesis creation story literally, but as poetry.

music and poetry – so in beauty, creativity, and the dynamic forms of life. All these spoke to her of God's love and care and of the hope of immortality.[108]

The year following the publication of Wollstonecraft's book, Olympe de Gouges (1748–93), published her manifesto *Declaration Des Droits De La Femme Et De La Citoyenne (Declaration of the Rights of Woman and the Female Citizen*, 1791).[109] Olympe demanded women's suffrage in the form of a National Assembly of 'the mothers, daughters, and sisters who together make up the female representatives of the Nation'. Appealing to 'the natural, inalienable, and sacred rights of woman ... in the presence and under the auspices of the Supreme Being', she listed seventeen 'Rights of Woman and of the Female Citizen'. First she insists (echoing Rousseau) that 'Woman is born free' and therefore has equal rights with men (I). Since 'the principle of any sovereignty essentially resides in the Nation' which comprises women and men united, woman should enjoy their share of sovereignty (III) which includes the right to share in framing legislation (VI) and to speak in public ('if woman has the right to mount the scaffold, she must equally have the right to mount the tribune' (X)). Olympe's list also includes an equal share of benefits and offices with men, corresponding to their equal taxation (XIII) and an 'inviolable and sacred' equal right to own property equally with men (XVII). She dedicated it to the queen, Marie Antoinette, but both of them were guillotined in 1793 and the manifesto came to nothing.

Within the fluid contours of radical English sectarianism, especially Quakerism, the rights of women were promoted, on theological principles, within a raft of demands for social, humanitarian, reform. As Birch puts it, 'Some of these extraordinary individuals argued for the spiritual authority of women, proposed a mandate for perpetual peace, argued for social and economic justice, racial equality and the abolition of slavery, promoted the natural sciences for the betterment of human experience, innovated

---

[108]Barbara Taylor, *Mary Wollstonecraft and the Feminist Imagination* (Cambridge: Cambridge University Press, 2003); Sylvana Tomaselli, *Wollstonecraft: Philosophy, Passion and Politics* (Princeton, NJ: Princeton University Press, 2020).
[109]Caroline Warman (ed. and trans.), *Tolerance: The Beacon of the Enlightenment* (Open Book Publishers, 2016), pp. 49–51.

in the care of the mentally ill, and promoted universal education.'[110] Birch adds that such 'enlightened critiques' were 'typically rooted in a radical moral critique' of the age, but we need to note that it was a critique based not on a notion of universal human rights applied to women, but on an ethical appropriation of the teaching and example of Jesus.[111] However, it would not be correct to see these two sources – universal human rights and gospel imperatives – as somehow alternative and opposed, but rather as convergent and congruent. The rise of individualism and with it the sense of the unbounded value placed on each person has biblical roots and is especially inculcated in the methods of Jesus' encounter with individuals, especially women, which defied the social conventions and religious taboos of the time.

The Scottish Enlightenment and the study of society

Constraints of space within this book and of the time available – as well as the fact that this is a somewhat offset sequel to my first volume on Anglican theological method – prevent me from doing anything like proper justice to the major Scottish expression of the European Enlightenment.[112] That phenomenon was not so much a theological enquiry as a contribution to the understanding of society and human social well-being and prosperity – a virtuous contribution indeed.[113] But I want to note, all too briefly, the scope, significance, merits and achievements of the Scottish Enlightenment, in laying the foundations of the modern study of humanity, civil

---

[110]Jonathan C. P. Birch, *Jesus in an Age of Enlightenment: Radical Gospels from Thomas Hobbes to Thomas Jefferson* (London: Palgrave Macmillan, 2019), p. 241.
[111]Ibid., p. 242.
[112]John Robertson, 'The Scottish Contribution to the Enlightenment', in Paul Wood (ed.), *The Scottish Enlightenment: Essays in Reinterpretation* (Woodbridge: Boydell, 2000), pp. 37–62; Hugh Trevor-Roper, 'The Scottish Enlightenment', *SVEC* 68 (1967), pp. 1635-58; Duncan Forbes, *Hume's Philosophical Politics* (Cambridge: Cambridge University Press, 1975).
[113]Gladys Bryson, *Man and God: The Scottish Enquiry of the Eighteenth Century* (Princeton, NY: Princeton University Press, 1945; repr. New York: Augustus M. Kelley, 1968).

society, political economy and the nature of the state. Such illustrious figures as David Hume (discussed later), William Robertson (ditto), Adam Smith (1723–90), John Millar, Adam Ferguson and Dugald Stewart were pioneers of the modern disciplines of sociology and political philosophy, and they were allied with the law lords Moboddo and Kames who were themselves also wide-ranging investigators, practical reformers, improvers of agriculture and public intellectuals.[114] Robertson, Ferguson (nominally) and the philosopher Thomas Reid were ministers of the Kirk. Presbyterian Christianity was the default and taken for granted context of their work. They did not need to rant about Calvinism. For example, although Reid wrote little about theology, his philosophical system is quietly but profoundly theistic (as Fergusson notes): 'in viewing the constraints of our human nature providentially. By divine design, we are equipped constitutionally to know the world and to live well in it.'[115] In keeping with the purpose of this book, I am looking at all these matters from a theological perspective and I will focus (briefly) on Smith and Ferguson.

Adam Smith

These outstanding Scottish thinkers exhibit the typical approach of the wider European Enlightenment towards religious faith in making ethical criteria the basis of their assessment of the varieties of religion. Sectarianism, 'enthusiasm', bigotry, superstition and party spirit are for them the antithesis of 'true' religion which unfailingly teaches and motivates honest, responsible citizenship and an orientation to the common good. Like Hume, Adam Smith sees the phenomenon of religion, both in history and in his own time, as dominated by the extremes of superstition and 'enthusiasm'

---

[114]Ian Simpson Ross, *The Life of Adam Smith*, 2nd edn (Oxford: Oxford University Press, 2010 [1995]); William C. Lehmann, *John Millar of Glasgow 1735–1801: His Life and Thought and His Contributions to Sociological Analysis* (Cambridge: Cambridge University Press, 1960).
[115]David Fergusson, 'Hume amongst the Theologians', in David Fergusson and Mark Elliott (eds), *The History of Scottish Theology, Volume II: From the Early Enlightenment to the Late Victorian Era* (Oxford: Oxford University Press, 2019), ch. 21, at p. 306.

(fanaticism). Smith's 'great antidote to the poison of enthusiasm and superstition', the prime forms of the abuse of religion, is not more and better theology – though he has to teach some theology – but 'science' or natural philosophy, operating by an empirical and inductive method and organized rationally.[116] As he puts it in *The Theory of Moral Sentiments* (1759):

> And wherever the natural principles of religion are not corrupted by the factious and party zeal of some worthless cabal; wherever the first duty which it requires, is to fulfil all the obligations of morality; wherever men are not taught to regard (p. 384) frivolous observances, as more immediate duties of religion, than acts of justice and beneficence; and to imagine, that by sacrifices, and ceremonies, and vain supplications, they can bargain with the Deity for fraud, and perfidy, and violence, the world undoubtedly judges right in this respect.[117]

Smith's own religious and theological opinions are elusive and continue to be the subject of conflicting interpretations.[118] He grew up in a moderate Calvinist home and was devoted to his long-lived, pious mother. But Smith's early religious impressions seem to have gradually faded in adult life as his scepticism towards Christianity apparently increased, though he was compelled to publicly adhere to Calvinist orthodoxy in order to pursue an academic career in the University of Glasgow. Smith was a past master at concealing his real opinions and making tactical evasions in print so as not to provoke Calvinist zealots and heresy-hunters, the self-appointed guardians of orthodoxy. Textual changes over successive editions of *The Wealth of Nations* (1st edition 1776; 6th edition 1789) suggest that Smith moved progressively away from 'revealed religion'

---

[116] Adam Smith, *An Inquiry into the Nature and Causes of the Wealth of Nations*, ed. Edwin Cannan, 2 vols (London: Methuen, 1904 [1776]), vol. 2, p. 281 (Bk V. ch. 1. Section III, Art.3); Bryson, *Man and God*, pp. 15–26.

[117] Cited from Adam Smith, *The Theory of Moral Sentiments*, III.5.13, by David M. Levy and Sandra J. Peart, 'Adam Smith and the State: Language and Reform', in Christopher J. Berry, Maria Pia Paganelli and Craig Smith (eds), The Oxford Handbook of Adam Smith (Oxford: Oxford University Press, 2013). See in detail Gavin Kennedy, 'Adam Smith on Religion', in id.

[118] See Paul Oslington (ed.), *Adam Smith as Theologian* (London and New York: Routledge, 2011); Eric Schliesser, *Adam Smith: Systematic Philosopher and Public Thinker* (New York: Oxford University Press, 2017).

(as divine revelation was then understood, i.e. propositionally). He is sardonic about debased religion, its beliefs and practices, but his acerbic opinions are tactfully disguised as comments on Roman Catholicism and paganism. Smith regarded hieratic institutional religion – above all in the Catholic Church – as driven by self-interest and cupidity; priests and religious were unproductive parasites. He was averse to hierarchical ecclesiastical polities and praised Presbyterianism for its more equal polity with checks and balances against the abuse of power.

However, it does seem that Smith had become highly allergic to the type of narrow, censorious and unenlightened church religion that surrounded him in the eighteenth-century Scottish Kirk. What alternative was available? Who among British divines and apologists could have offered him something better? Whether he became a deist or simply a sceptical agnostic is debatable. But neither his aspersions on superstitious and fanatical expressions of religion nor his abundant references to natural religion, providence and a supreme being make him deist, let alone an atheist, any more than Hume's or Gibbon's scepticism and revulsion at superstition and fanaticism made them atheists. In a symposium that offers a significant corrective to prevailing interpretations of Smith's religion and theology, Oslington aptly comments: 'Any interpreter who takes criticism of religious practice as evidence of a lack of faith or commitment has little experience of churches. Usually the opposite is true.'[119] Smith's rational-empirical account of religious institutions in Book V of *The Wealth of Nations*, even with its pathology of religion in the form of enthusiasm and superstition, contains no hint that this kind of scientific investigation and explanation undermines the credibility of religion. We cannot be quite sure where Smith stood theologically in the end, but his published statements do not preclude but rather suggest that he continued to hold to a theistic, essentially Christian, metaphysical framework, albeit with an increasing emphasis on rational, ethical religion.[120]

---

[119]Oslington in id. (ed.), *Adam Smith as Theologian*, p. 5.
[120]See Tom Campbell, 'Adam Smith: Methods, Morals, and Markets', in Berry, Paganelli and Smith (eds), *The Oxford Handbook of Adam Smith*, p. 570, *pace* Nicholas Phillipson, *Adam Smith: An Enlightened Life* (London: Allen Lane, 2010).

Adam Ferguson

No member of this galaxy is more impressive or actually less typical than Adam Ferguson (1723–1816), Professor of Moral Philosophy at the University of Edinburgh. What motivated Ferguson's work was the need for a political philosophy, grounded in historical research, that would secure the stability and flourishing of free, prosperous and virtuous societies in a dangerous world of autocratic rulers, their aggressive wars (typified by Frederick the Great of Prussia's military adventures) and revolutionary imperialism (embodied in Napoleon Bonaparte's wars of conquest). Ferguson traced the ups and downs ('the vicissitudes') of states in the interests of a more stable future for enlightened Europe. His *An Essay on the History of Civil Society* (1767) announced a different and arresting voice in Enlightenment historiography and political thought (i.e., political or philosophical history). Ferguson welcomed and embraced the new critical, analytical and investigative rationality of the Enlightenment as a means of combating superstitious credulity and academic obscurantism. But his admiration for some of the political-social models of antiquity, his upholding of the martial virtues and the need to defend enlightened values by force if need be, set him apart from most of his contemporaries among enlightened thinkers, including Hume, Gibbon and Burke, who all aspired to more peaceable methods of maintaining and promoting civilization.[121] In this respect, Ferguson's approach savours of nineteenth-century *Realpolitik* and is not unlike the undeceived realism of Reinhold Niebuhr's political-ethical writings in the mid-twentieth century.[122] Ferguson's three-volume work, the *History of the Progress and Termination of the Roman Republic* (1783), was a riposte to Montesquieu's optimism, sustained by faith

---

[121]Iain McDaniel, *Adam Ferguson in the Scottish Enlightenment* (Cambridge, MA: Harvard University Press, 2013), p. 2. McDaniel's otherwise very able account omits any discussion of Ferguson's relation to Christianity, the church, theology and Calvinism, except minimally and in passing. Key text: Adam Ferguson, *An Essay on the History of Civil Society*, ed. and intro. Duncan Forbes (Edinburgh: Edinburgh University Press, 1966). See also Eugene Heath and Vincenzo Merolle (eds), *Ferguson: History, Progress and Human Nature* (London: Pickering & Chatto, 2008).

[122]E.g. Reinhold Niebuhr, *Moral Man and Immoral Society: A Study in Ethics and Politics* (London: SCM Press, 1963).

in commercialism and civility, about the stability and futurity of prosperous major European states. Ferguson saw ancient Rome's transition towards military government and dictatorship as a warning, a 'signal example of the vicissitudes to which prosperous nations are exposed'.[123]

Ferguson's contribution to Enlightenment thought was a seminal, cross-bench and disruptive set of political-historical-philosophical-ethical arguments that engaged with his eminent near-contemporaries in his native Scotland (Adam Smith, John Millar), France (Montesquieu, Diderot, Rousseau) and of course England. The impact of his works is seen in the fact that they were translated, almost on publication, into several European languages. His arguments continued to reverberate well into the nineteenth century, giving stimulus and ammunition to John Adams in America and to such late-Enlightenment, proto-Romantic writers as Friedrich Schiller (1759–1805) and Johann Gottfried Herder (1744–1803) and, a generation later, Georg Wilhelm Friedrich Hegel (1770–1831) and even later John Stuart Mill (1806–73).

In this chapter on 'A Virtuous Enlightenment', I merely want to register the contribution of the Scottish (mainly Edinburgh) Enlightenment, particularly of Ferguson himself, to the enterprise of the virtuous study of a virtuous society, a moral-philosophical, if not explicitly theological, method, calling and discipline. Although, like William Robertson the historian, Ferguson was a minister of the Church of Scotland, had been a devoted and courageous military chaplain, and was regarded as orthodox in doctrine, he opted instead for an intellectual and academic life and seems to have intentionally allowed his ordained ministry to lapse. While he continued to invoke 'God', 'the Supreme Being' or 'the Almighty' in his writings, to be a communicant in the Kirk and to argue for the 'celestial' immortality of the virtuous, there is little or no trace of the direct influence of Christian doctrines in his work or of the particular Calvinistic emphases of his upbringing in a Highland presbytery.[124] Ferguson should probably be numbered among the deistic believers. The focus on virtue – more redolent of ancient

---

[123]Cited McDaniel, *Adam Ferguson in the Scottish Enlightenment*, p. 5.
[124]David Kettler, *The Social and Political Thought of Adam Ferguson* (Columbus, OH: Columbus State University Press, 1965), pp. 44–9; 171–6.

Stoicism than of Christianity – is brought out strongly in David Kettler's pioneering (1965) study of Ferguson which emphasizes his concern for the communal bonds of fellow-feeling, conviviality and mutual respect in what we would now call an organic society, which Ferguson believed was threatened by the mechanistic, proto-utilitarian, ideology of aspects of the Enlightenment. Kettler comments: 'Ferguson's concerns clearly foreshadow the problems of over-rationalization, dehumanization, atomization, alienation, and bureaucratization which have been canvassed again and again by intellectuals' in the modern era.[125] However, in the light of Ferguson's theism and good standing within the Kirk, Kettler's term for Ferguson's thought – 'secular' – is a misnomer.[126]

A more balanced view is advocated in a pair of collections of studies of Ferguson, where his emphasis on divine providence and corresponding human responsibility is brought out.[127] Ferguson does not use standard theological terminology, but there is much God-talk in his work. He is not coy about invoking God as creator and providential ruler and guide of the world. His philosophy of history and his political thought become distorted when the divine dimension is removed. His account of providence resonates with that of his fellow Moderates in the Scottish Enlightenment, particularly the historian and churchman William Robertson, and invites comparison in certain respects with Giambattista Vico's philosophy of history (which we will come to later in connection with history). Providence, for Ferguson and Vico alike, operates, not by constant miraculous interventions, but by second causes which God has designed for the smooth running of the universe and as the matrix of human effort and aspiration. Ferguson has a conviction of the reality of a progressive manifestation of divine immanence which operates silently but effectively to shape humanity to ever higher degrees of ethical, intellectual and social

---

[125] Ibid., pp. 8–9.
[126] Ibid., p. 131.
[127] Eugene Heath and Vincenzo Merolle (eds), *Adam Ferguson: History, Progress and Human Nature* (London: Pickering and Chatto, 2008), especially ch. 11: Jeng-Guo S. Chen, 'Providence and Progress: The Religious Dimension in Ferguson's Discussion of Civil Society'. See also the sequel volume: Eugene Heath and Vincenzo Merolle (eds), *Adam Ferguson: Philosophy, Politics and Society* (London: Pickering and Chatto, 2009).

perfection. One aspect of the religious and philosophical thought of the Enlightenment, that is seldom done justice to by interpreters, is its concept of the immanence, the internal presence and working, of the divine in nature, society and the human mind and heart. But we see it clearly in Spinoza (obviously), Vico, Ferguson, Rousseau, Hamann, Lessing and Herder. It belongs within the theological context of the Enlightenment.

The advancement of science

The Enlightenment's vision of what in shorthand and for the moment we can call 'progress' included the amelioration and advancement of society in manners and morals, education, religion and cultural achievement, and was by no means 'materialistic' in any reductionist sense. But in so far as it did include improvement in material security, comfort and well being, it was predicated on the advancement of science and technology, husbandry and agriculture. It is to the so-called Scientific Revolution that we now briefly turn. But if we perchance imagine that by doing so we are turning away from theological and Christian concerns to secular and materialistic ones, we are much mistaken, as we shall see.[128]

In his classic study *The Origins of Modern Science*, Herbert Butterfield claimed that the transformative effect of the scientific revolution was so momentous that historically it could be compared only to the rise of Christianity. Butterfield added that the emergence of modern science 'reduces the Renaissance and Reformation to the rank of mere episodes, mere internal displacements within the system of medieval Christendom'.[129] I am well aware that the term 'the scientific revolution' is disputed and that its very existence is

---

[128] For a concise introduction to the role of theological influences in the Scientific Revolution see Margaret J. Osler, 'Religion and the Changing Historiography of the Scientific Revolution', in Thomas Dixon, Geoffrey Cantor and Stephen Pumfrey (eds), *Science and Religion: New Historical Perspectives* (Cambridge: Cambridge University Press, 2010), ch. 4.

[129] Herbert Butterfield, *The Origins of Modern Science 1300–1800* (London: Bell, 1949), p. viii.

denied by some. But the fact is that, as Mikuláš Teich points out, during the sixteenth and seventeenth centuries in certain European countries 'a universal mode of producing natural knowledge materialised, one that did not exist anywhere before and that is still practised now'.[130] It was a nothing less than a revolution in the exploration, discovery, tabulation and practical utilization of the natural world.[131]

While the age of Enlightenment largely preceded the era of the industrial revolution, it provided the rudiments of the scientific concepts and technological tools that industrialization would require. In this respect the eighteenth century was working in the tradition and trajectory of the genius of Francis Bacon (1561–1626) and his revolutionary works of scientific method, among them *The Advancement of Learning* and the *Novum Organon (New Instrument)* and it was of course going beyond Bacon's own achievement.[132] Flatly contrary to those philosophers and theologians who have claimed that the Enlightenment repudiated all tradition, its science, like all Enlightenment thought, reached back well before Bacon, through the Reformation and the Renaissance to medieval scholastic writings and to the philosophy of the classical world.[133] This short section on the scientific enterprise of the Enlightenment will proceed very selectively by making connections between Bacon's philosophy of science and the thought and endeavours of the eighteenth century. We can note Bacon's significance and attraction for eighteenth-century scientific thought in several ways, but before that there is a preliminary point.

---

[130]Mikuláš Teich, *The Scientific Revolution Revisited* (Cambridge: Open Books, 2010), p. 83.
[131]For the background and an introduction to the theme see Butterfield, *The Origins of Modern Science 1300–1800*; E. A. Burtt, *The Metaphysical Foundations of Modern Physical Science*, 2nd edn (Mineola, NY: Dover; London: Routledge and Kegan Paul, 2003 [1932]); (London: Routledge and Kegan Paul; NY: Dover, 2003 [1932]); John Henry, *The Scientific Revolution and the Origins of Modern Science* (Basingstoke: Palgrave Macmillan, 2002 [2001; 3rd edn 2008]); Margaret C. Jacob, *The Scientific Revolution: A Brief History with Documents* (Basingstoke: Palgrave Macmillan, 2010); Lawrence M. Principe, *The Scientific Revolution: A Very Short Introduction* (Oxford: Oxford University Press, 2011).
[132]For a fuller exposition of Bacon's significance, especially for Anglican theological method, see *ISOA*, pp. 137–57.
[133]As Principe, *The Scientific Revolution*, strongly brings out.

Francis Bacon

Francis Bacon, Lord Verulam (1561–1626), was by his own account, a devout Christian, at home within the flourishing Jacobean Church of England. He was the author of prayers and sacred meditations and he translated Psalms. As his essay 'On Truth', which stands at the beginning of his collected *Essays*, makes clear, the person of Jesus Christ is the key to his search for truth.[134] Of course, this was not true for the *philosophes* – as in most cases they were deists, they had no place for Christology or the atonement – but it still obtained in England for such luminaries of scientific and philosophical method as Locke, Boyle, Newton, the clergyman Joseph Glanville and other members of the Royal Society, including several bishops.

First, the primary stated motive and purpose of Bacon's investigations was humanitarian. His aim was 'the benefit and relief of the state of man', to provide 'things useful to the future of the human race'; and, beyond this, to enhance the greatness and glory of humankind as God's custodian, so to speak, of the created order.[135] This great enterprise was not intended as a display of human arrogance and pride, or to set 'man' in the place of God, but rather to celebrate and magnify a reflected glory, one that shone in the human image of God who, as such, was mandated to take responsibility for the world and to exercise 'dominion' over all creatures (Gen. 1: 26–31). In Bacon, the philosophy of science is still emerging from alchemy and magic; Bacon has the same sense of persuading or forcing nature to yield up her secrets.[136] One part of his cultural context was the emergence of the early capitalist economy, based on financial credit; Bacon aimed to serve the requirements of the improved mechanic arts.[137] The amelioration of the struggling, suffering human condition was the purpose and

---

[134] Francis Bacon, *Essays and Colours of Good and Evil*, ed. W. Aldis Wright (London: Macmillan, 1890), p. 1.
[135] Francis Bacon, *Philosophical Works*, ed. J. M. Robertson (London: Routledge, 1905), pp. 188, 294, 300; Benjamin Farrington, *The Philosophy of Francis Bacon: An Essay on Its Development from 1603 to 1609 with New Translations of Fundamental Texts* (Liverpool: Liverpool University Press, 1964), p. 68.
[136] Rossi, *Francis Bacon: From Magic to Science*, p. 10.
[137] Edgar Zilsel, 'The Genesis of the Concept of Scientific Progress', *JHI* 6 (1945), pp. 325–49.

goal of Francis Bacon, as it was of the *philosophes* and many other eighteenth-century thinkers.

Second, although Bacon also wrote history and had a philosophy of history, he was disdainful of the past and had no use for the much lauded 'wisdom of the ancients'; he needed to begin *de novo*. Bacon treated the ancient philosophers with contempt as barren of useful results and he had no time for traditional historical methods.[138] Like Descartes after him, Bacon proceeded by – or at least purported to proceed by – setting aside received knowledge, if that is what it was, and starting with what was now to hand. 'For new discoveries must be sought from the light of nature, not fetched out of the darkness of antiquity. It matters not what has been done; our business is to see what can be done.'[139] Bacon plausibly claimed that the received tradition – basically Platonic and contemplative in character as it was – could not show one single experiment that had improved the human condition.[140]

Third, and again like Descartes, Bacon insisted that we must begin with doubt.[141] The profound difference between Descartes's method and that of Bacon lies, not in the imperatives of starting afresh and doubting and questioning what we think we already know, but precisely in where they started from. Descartes's ostensible point of departure was internal, within his thought processes; Bacon's methodological starting point was external, in what confronted him in the visible, tangible world. While Descartes went into his own mind and consciousness introspectively, thereby becoming aware of the incontrovertible fact that he was a thinking being (*cogito ergo sum*), Bacon turned outward to the phenomena of the natural world around him and did so with a new and intensive objectivity, though not without thinking (cogitating), of course. Voltaire, influenced of course by Bacon and Locke, condemned Descartes for consulting his own genius, going into his imagination, rather than trusting empirically to experience allied to mathematics. Descartes, pronounced Voltaire, had thereby delayed the progress

---

[138] On Bacon's philosophy of history see *FMHT*, pp. 68–80.
[139] Bacon, *Philosophical Works*, p. 297.
[140] Bacon, *Philosophical Works*, p. 276; Farrington, *Philosophy of Francis Bacon*, p. 85.
[141] Francis Bacon, *The Advancement of Learning* (London: Dent; New York: Dutton, 1915), p. 34.

of knowledge for half a century.[142] Locke followed in Bacon's footsteps in his empirical method, based in the first instance on sensory experience. Like Bacon, the *philosophes* prized innovation, invention and discovery.

Fourth, Bacon created a dualism of theology and science. He applied the *coup de grâce* to the process of the steady disintegration of the medieval unified worldview. He has no place for metaphysics, which in all ages has attempted to unite theology and philosophy, faith and reason. Bacon's fear was that such a synthesis of science and theology would retard the advancement of knowledge, that it would in fact freeze our understanding of the natural world at its present level, for 'every development of philosophy, every new frontier and direction, is regarded by religion with unworthy suspicion and violent contempt'.[143] Science and theology should therefore be treated separately. That judgement – which in Bacon is not intended to be hostile to religious faith – can hardly be gainsaid, even four hundred years later, as far as most religious traditions are concerned. Religious faith and practice feeds mainly, though not solely, from tradition, that is from a view of the past. (Very firmly in second place, religious faith and its intellectual exploration and articulation in theology, also draws from the anticipated future, in hope and vision.) But to the extent that religious faith feeds from new knowledge and insight, it is abundantly clear that it does so only reluctantly and after long resistance, when its rear-guard action and that of its guardians and minders has failed. The eighteenth-century *philosophes*, similarly, despaired of theology as a solution to the problems and challenges of the age and looked to science instead.

Fifth, Bacon asserted the importance of methodology. Although empirical methods had been employed sporadically in the middle ages and the sixteenth century, Bacon pioneered a new, properly scientific, method, one that was empirical, experimental, inductive and critical. While Bacon believed that his exposition of inductive logic was his greatest contribution to scientific method, he was not under the illusion that mere endless induction can prove anything: acts of discrimination, discernment and judgement are then required.

---

[142] Wade, *Intellectual Development of Voltaire*, p. 594, referencing Voltaire, *Le Siècle de Louis XIV* (1751).
[143] Farrington, *Philosophy of Francis Bacon*, p. 78.

He has, however, an over-ambitious and naively realist view of what observation of the natural world can deliver: he promises that he will 'unite you with *things themselves* in a chaste, holy and legal wedlock'.[144] Although Bacon stresses the importance of ordering and interpreting the 'facts' that he so assiduously collected, he underestimated the role of hypothesis, theoretical models, the imagination and human creativity in scientific investigation. He believed that his method left little scope for human judgement, almost guaranteeing that any fool could follow his method and obtain results.[145] Eighteenth-century thinkers could look back to Bacon as the pioneer and exemplar of the empirical, experimental, inductive and critical method – which, unlike Bacon himself, they attempted to apply to every sphere of human endeavour, including that of religion.

Sixth, Bacon articulates a remarkable eschatology – not of a 'secular' future consummation or utopia, like that of some of the *philosophes* – but a religious and Christian fusion of biblical and scientific insights which comprises his vision of the progress of knowledge and invention for the easing of the human condition. He takes his cue from such biblical prophecies as Daniel 12:4, 'Many shall run to and fro and knowledge shall increase', which he refers to the combination of scientific invention and the great contemporary voyages of discovery. He believes that the last age of the world is at hand when the people of God will enter into the promised Sabbath rest, just as the Creator rested on the seventh day of creation. Bacon believed that his method, if universally applied, would bring about the great restoration (*instauratio magna*) of creation in the state of perfection that it had enjoyed when it came forth from the hand of its Creator. As I stated in my fuller exposition of Bacon's method and its significance for historiography, 'Bacon was perhaps the first to combine a utilitarian concept of knowledge and a notion of cumulative scientific research to create a doctrine of scientific progress. It was this aspect of his thought (as well as his clear demarcation between religion and science) that commended Bacon to the Enlightenment.'[146]

---

[144]Ibid., p. 72, emphasis original.
[145]Bacon, *Philosophical Works*, p. 300.
[146]*ISOA*, p. 151.

Isaac Newton

The significance of Isaac Newton (1643–1727) for the Enlightenment – not only for its scientific achievements, but for its whole worldview – can hardly be overestimated. Many regarded his abilities and discoveries as superhuman. He acquired a godlike aura. Voltaire regarded him as the greatest man who had ever lived (though Voltaire's adulation of Locke surpassed even his ecstatic admiration of Newton; only Plato was worthy to be compared with Locke and Locke excelled even him). While Voltaire was in awe of Newton, he did not fully understand his science. Nevertheless, he popularized Newton's theories for a French audience in his *Letters Concerning the English Nation* (in French, *Lettres philosophiques*) of 1733 and the *Elements of Newton's Philosophy* of 1738). Voltaire struggled with the *Principia Mathematica*, but was irresistibly attracted to the method of observation, measurement and calculation, eschewing all speculation, and he naively imagined that that was all that was involved in scientific work. He seems to have been oblivious of Newton's sophisticated methodology, as set out in his *Regulae philosophandi* which were included in some form in all three editions of the *Principia* from 1687 (though not by that name in that edition).[147]

Being a fanatical anti-rationalist, Voltaire was perhaps inhibited from grasping that Newton also – and almost but not quite to an equal extent – needed to deploy the rational, deductive and constructive method that he owed to the tradition from Galileo to Descartes to Hobbes in order to explain, order and conceptualize his empirical findings – though he repudiated the way that Descartes and Leibniz had – in his view – abused it, with their speculative vortices (Descartes) and monadology (Leibniz). Newton was indentured to the empirical method and its rigorous disciplines; the role of mathematics in science – albeit as the divine science that revealed the mind of God – was to serve the evidence. As Burtt put it, 'for Newton, mathematics was solely a method for the solution of problems posed by sensible experience.'[148] In Enlightenment

---

[147]https://www.oxfordhandbooks.com/view/10.1093/oxfordhb/-9780199930418.001.0001/oxfordhb-9780199930418-e-4
[148]Burtt, *Metaphysical Foundations of Modern Physical Science*, p. 210.

science Newton ticked the two most important boxes: his *Principia Mathematica* was widely regarded as the paradigm and exemplar of the mathematical approach to physics, while the *Opticks* (1704) was taken as the model of experimental and observational science. So great was Newton's prestige and that of his discoveries that his methods were exported to the putative sciences of 'man', society and economics. The fact that many writers of the period saw natural philosophy *à la Newton* as the paradigm of the advancement of knowledge, and even extrapolated it in the search for the laws of social harmony, indicates that 'a revolution in the ordering of knowledge had indeed taken place'.[149]

Newton's religion has fascinated and perplexed historians. Newton was a conforming Anglican; he financially supported the distribution of Bibles to the poor and the building of new London churches. His personal beliefs were not questioned during his lifetime. The metaphysical linchpin of his cosmology was the divine ordering, sustaining and regulating of the creation. Like Descartes, Newton did not fully disentangle physics and theology as advocated by Bacon and Fontenelle. For Newton, the universe is filled with God's presence, intelligence and power. 'He is omnipresent not only *virtually* but also *substantially* ... In him all things are contained and move, but he does not act on them or they on him ... he is *always* and *everywhere* ... He is all eye, all ear, all brain, all arm, all force of sensing, of understanding, and of acting.'[150] Newton's reading of Spinoza and his interaction with Spinoza's monism is a continuing topic of academic debate.[151]

Newton was an almost lifelong, obsessive and misguided student of biblical prophecy, taking the texts mainly of Daniel and Revelation

---

[149]Cf. Henry, *The Scientific Revolution and the Origins of Modern Science*, pp. 110–12. See also Alexandre Koyré, 'The Significance of the Newtonian Synthesis', in his *Newtonian Studies* (London: Chapman Hall, 1965). There is more detail on Newton and theology in *ISOA*, pp. 275–82.

[150]Cited James Gleick, *Isaac Newton* (New York: Vintage Books, 2003), p. 108, from *Principia Mathematica* 941: *The Principia: Mathematical Principles of Natural Philosophy*, trans. I. Bernard Cohen and Anne Whitman with the assistance of Julia Budenz (Berkeley, CA: University of California Press, 1999).

[151]See Eric Schliesser, *Newton's Metaphysics: Essays* (Oxford: Oxford University Press, 2021); Howard Stein, 'Newton's Metaphysics', in I. Bernard Cohen and George E. Smith (eds), *The Cambridge Companion to Newton* (Cambridge: Cambridge University Press 2002), ch. 8.

as cryptic symbols which, if deciphered, would reveal the timing of the Second Coming of Christ. On the other hand, his theology tended to deism and he was posthumously discovered to be Socinian or non-trinitarian in his view of the godhead. Newton's christological speculations derived from an open-eyed and open-minded study of the text of the New Testament considered as empirical data. There he found insufficient evidence for the conciliar, credal doctrines of the early church. He concluded that Jesus Christ was inferior not equal to the Father and was not the eternal Son within the eternal Trinity. At this time, the so-called Athanasian Creed (*Quicunque Vult*), a convoluted explication of trinitarian and christological doctrine – its antitheses are beyond paradox – contained within the Church of England's Book of Common Prayer, was required to be said or sung liturgically at the morning or evening office on Trinity Sunday and a dozen other days of the church year. Although it was alleged to have been composed by Athanasius of Alexandria, the fourth-century champion of the divinity of Christ, it is now believed to have originated no earlier than the mid-fifth century and in Gaul. So it was neither composed by Athanasius nor is it a creed. Moreover it pronounces anathemas against anyone who does not hold its doctrine – they cannot be saved; they are damned. In as much as it revels in mysteries and condemns those who either reject or misunderstand them, it does not comport well with the main tenor of Anglican spirituality. Agitation against its compulsory use in the Church of England reached a pitch in the mid-nineteenth century, upsetting inflexible High Churchmen and Tractarians such as John Keble. It is now almost never used. Obviously, Newton could not say it.

The Newton scholar Frank Manuel concluded that Newton was a sound Anglican theist, insisting that he never held a simple mechanistic view of the universe, that he was never a partisan of pure deistic religion and that he was always a firm believer in the God of the Christian faith, but Newton's biographer Richard Westfall has challenged that view.[152] What we can say with some

---

[152]Frank Manuel, *Isaac Newton, Historian* (Cambridge, MA: Belknap Press of Harvard University Press, 1963), p. 8; id., *The Religion of Isaac Newton* (Oxford: Clarendon Press, 1974), pp. 6–7; Richard S. Westfall, 'The Changing World of the Newtonian Industry', *JHI* 37.1 (1976), pp. 175–84; id., *Never at Rest: A Biography of Isaac Newton* (Cambridge: Cambridge University Press, 1980).

assurance is that Newton was an active member of the Church of England who believed in the inspiration of Scripture and was also a theist with an inadequate or incomplete understanding of theology from a traditional or 'orthodox' point of view – like so many others! Newton's stature as the presiding genius of the European Enlightenment is hardly affected by his theological 'errors' in Christology. The fact alone of the Anglican Newton in this period proves that not even in the realm of physical science was the Enlightenment 'rationalist' or 'rationalistic', as some blinkered Christian writers would have it – except in the sense and to the extent that reason plays a vital role in every department of knowledge, whether of the sciences or of the humanities, including theology.

Voltaire's limited grasp of Newtonian science can be attributed to the fact that, as Wade puts it, for this *philosophe* 'empiricism was the opposite of imagination; observation of phenomena was the opposite of rational logic; natural science was the opposite of literary art', therefore the philosopher – who was identified with the scientist – was 'the opposite of the poet'.[153] But the fact of the matter is that Newton's beautiful intellectual universe inspired a flowering of imaginative writing, especially in poetry, as Marjorie Nicolson showed in *Newton Demands the Muse*. And as Gay has put it, Enlightenment science – which was Newtonian science – enriched poetry by 'stabilizing' the poets' philosophy, enlarging their vocabulary, and opening up hitherto unexplored regions of experience to their talents. For example, the poet James Thomson (1700–48) composed an adulatory *Poem Sacred to the Memory of Sir Isaac Newton* in the year of Newton's death (1727)[154] and Thomson's major work *The Seasons* (1726–30) has been described as 'a comprehensive celebration of the metaphysical and aesthetic virtues of the new science'.[155]

---

[153] Wade, *Intellectual Development of Voltaire*, pp. 603–4.
[154] https://quod.lib.umich.edu/e/ecco/004864236.0001.000/1:3?rgn=div1;view=fulltext
[155] Marjorie H. Nicolson, *Newton Demands the Muse* (Princeton, NJ: Princeton University Press, 1946); Gay, *The Enlightenment: An Interpretation; Vol. 2, The Science of Freedom*, p. 127; James Thomson, *The Seasons and the Castle of Indolence*, ed. James Sambrook (Oxford: Clarendon Press, 1972).

Robert Boyle

Before leaving this briefest of accounts of Enlightenment science, it is worth noting how empirical observation and reasoned construction were united and held together in the work of Robert Boyle (1627–1691). A founding council member of the Royal Society in 1663, Boyle is widely regarded as the founder of modern chemical science. He drew on and strengthened the empirical and experimental tradition stemming from Bacon, but also insisted on the reasoned analysis of sense data, confirmed by exact experiment. 'Experience', he stated, 'is but an assistant to reason, since it doth indeed supply informations to the understanding, but the understanding still remains the judge.'[156] Boyle completely accepted the mathematical metaphysics of Galileo and Descartes; mathematical and mechanical principles are 'the alphabet in which God wrote the world' and 'nature does play the mechanician'. Human beings are machines inhabited by a soul.[157] Boyle's mechanical natural philosophy did not prohibit a belief in God, any more than it did for Hobbes, though that is difficult for those not versed in the rich varieties of historical theology to grasp. Like Bacon, Boyle placed himself in the alchemical tradition, the quest for transformations of nature, but that did not prevent either of them being Christian believers.[158] As an empiricist open to rational explanations, Boyle did not dismiss apparently supernatural phenomena, such as second-sight (seeing future events before they happen) in which he took a particular interest. Like Henry More and Joseph Glanville, Boyle had a subsidiary apologetic interest in highlighting such phenomena. He (and they) wanted to prove to sceptics that, as Hamlet (Act I, Scene 5) puts it, 'There are more things in heaven and earth ... than are dreamt of in your [naturalistic] philosophy.'

Boyle was a devout Anglican; he wrote several works of theology and endowed the Boyle Lectures with their apologetical purpose devoted to the interface of Christianity and science and which

---

[156]Boyle, cited Burtt, *Metaphysical Foundations of Modern Physical Science*, p. 164.
[157]Ibid., p. 166.
[158]Lawrence M. Principe, *The Aspiring Adept: Robert Boyle and His Alchemical Quest; Including Boyle's 'Lost' Dialogue on the Transmutation of Metals* (Princeton: Princeton University Press, 1998).

continue today. His funeral eulogy was given by the outstandingly able and moderate Bishop Gilbert Burnet in a symbolic union of science, faith and church.

Toleration and the Enlightenment

Actual toleration of different religious doctrines and practices within one state was almost, but not quite, unknown before the Enlightenment. In assessing the significance of the Enlightenment for toleration we should distinguish between ideas of toleration and the implementation of toleration, between theory and practice. There were brave heralds of toleration before the Enlightenment, but they longed for what was unattainable at the time. Modern concepts of toleration and religious freedom can be traced back to the writings of radical Protestants such as Castellio, Milton and Locke. Religious toleration was not completely unprecedented nor was it unique to the Enlightenment. But in the Enlightenment theory and practice began to come together; toleration was central to the platform and programme of many Enlightenment thinkers.[159] Those scholars, especially Paul Hazard and Jonathan Israel, who hail a 'radical Enlightenment' and look particularly to Spinoza and Bayle for this, are justified in so doing, in part because these writers made a seminal contribution to the doctrine of toleration. However, not all Enlightenment thinkers were fully committed to toleration on the basis of natural right and some that were so committed held reservations about how far it should go.

---

[159] Joseph Lecler, S.J., *Toleration and the Reformation*, 2 vols (New York: Association Press, 1960); W. K. Jordan, *The Development of Religious Toleration in England* (London: Allen & Unwin, 1938); Perez Zagoria, *How the Idea of Toleration came to the West* (Princeton, NJ: Princeton University Press, 2003); John Coffey, 'Scripture and Toleration between Reformation and Enlightenment', in Elaine Glaser (ed.), *Religious Tolerance in the Atlantic World: Early Modern and Contemporary Perspectives* (Basingstoke: Palgrave Macmillan, 2014), pp. 14–40; John Christian Laursen and Cary J. Nederman (eds), *Beyond the Persecuting Society: Religious Toleration before the Enlightenment* (Philadelphia, PA: University of Pennsylvanian, 1998); Mark Goldie and Robert Wokler (eds), *The Cambridge History of Eighteenth-century Political Thought* (Cambridge: Cambridge University Press, 2006). John Milton, *Areopagitica and Other Prose Works* (London: Dent; New York: Dutton, 1927).

The freedom of belief, worship, ethical practice, public speaking and religious affiliation that we take for granted in Western democracies is a hard-won fruit of the Enlightenment. Toleration – in Spinoza's phrase *libertas philosophandi* – meant the end of practices that had cast a menacing shadow over medieval and early modern Christendom: censorship, the burning of books and of heretics, the incarceration of contrary voices, the Inquisition, the Index of Forbidden Books. Do those well-meaning but misguided writers who condemn the Enlightenment for such sins as 'rationalism' and 'secularism' wish to reinstate such horrors? They overlook the fact that the notion of toleration in the form of religious freedom is neither taught nor implied in Scripture and did not emerge from the church authorities even in the eighteenth century – quite the contrary. The Roman Catholic Church continued to condemn religious freedom until the mid-twentieth century, reversing its traditional teaching only at the Second Vatican Council (1962–5).[160]

Three pivotal assumptions that inhibited toleration prevailed in every state and every church.

- The first assumption was that only one religion or church could be true and so lead one to salvation. To be saved it was necessary to belong to the one true religion and to the one true church within it. Reformation ecclesiology had been driven initially by the quest for the 'true church', known by the marks (*notae ecclesiae*) of the true preaching of the gospel and the correct administration of the sacraments. The Catholic Church appealed to other or additional marks, quantitative (extent) and qualitative (saints) to show that it alone was the true church where salvation was to be found.[161] It followed that it was the duty of the 'orthodox', the faithful, especially those in authority, to stamp out error and to do so by any means.
- The second assumption was that, against the theological background of the Fall of Man and the resulting depravity

---

[160]See Avis, *Reconciling Theology*, ch. 3: 'Contested Legacy: Vatican II after 60 Years'.
[161]Paul Avis, *The Church in the Theology of the Reformers* (London: Marshall, Morgan & Scott, 1981; reprinted Eugene, OR: Wipf and Stock, 2002), Part 1.

of human nature, including the intellect, faith implied an ethical stance, assisted by grace, and served as an ethical indicator.[162] Did not Jesus teach that a good tree brings forth good fruit and a bad tree bad fruit and 'You will know them by their fruits' (Matt. 7:17–20)? A morally good person would naturally adhere to the true faith and only a bad person would embrace religious error. You know that a heretic is morally bad by the fact of their heresy. Divine revelation in Scripture and church doctrine was clear and understandable; to be mistaken was culpable.

- The third assumption was that to permit diversity of religious belief within a single state would lead to political and social unrest and instability, as the British Civil War and its aftermath and the religious wars on the continent of Europe had shown. The scars of both these traumas were raw. Religious commitment could not be separated from political allegiance.

So the churches clung to their monopolies and expected the state to enforce them. To teach toleration or freedom of religion was deviant, if not heretical. And the churches looked to Scripture for justification. The phrase *compelle intrare*, 'compel them to come in', from the parable in Luke 14:23, which was employed by Augustine to justify the coercion of the Donatists, had a long afterlife. Bayle's diatribe *A Philosophical Commentary on These Words of the Gospel, Luke XIV, 23: Compel Them to Come In, that My House May Be Full* (1686, 1708) is a vast portmanteau of jumbled historical examples and precedents, esoteric knowledge, logical, ethical and *ad hominem* arguments, and biblical and patristic exegesis. It may well be the longest commentary ever written on a single verse of Scripture. With this shapeless but overpowering onslaught, Bayle pulverized the received argument for religious coercion and put paid to it for ever.[163] Bayle's premises are that true religion is an inward matter, located in the heart and mind; outward

---

[162]For the theological and epistemological background see Peter Harrison, *The Fall of Man and the Foundations of Science* (Cambridge: Cambridge University Press, 2007).
[163]https://www.google.co.uk/books/edition/A_Philosophical_Commentary_on_These_Word/3Kr3g4LeFPwC?hl=en&gbpv=0 (accessed 25 January 2022).

actions alone do not constitute religion; therefore faith cannot be produced by force; so coercion and persecution are fruitless and futile. Bayle is making a distinctively Protestant argument: faith for Protestants, following St Paul's and Martin Luther's theology, is fiduciary, primarily trust in a Person and their promises, while assent to doctrinal propositions, though necessary, is secondary.[164] In the Roman Catholic tradition, however, more emphasis is placed on faith as assent to doctrines proposed on the authority of the church, though fiduciary faith is not excluded. Bayle also points out that mildness and gentleness typified the character of Christ. Here we see another typical Enlightenment appeal to the ethic of the Gospels and their portrayal of the person of Jesus.

It is striking that Bayle begins by laying down 'That the light of Nature, or the first Principles of Reason, universally receiv'd, are the genuin [sic] and original Rule of all interpretation of Scripture, especially in Matters of Practice and Morality.' Such a statement would seem to be grist to the mill of those scholars who see the origins of toleration in the 'heterodox' theology of dissident 'radical' thinkers and would be seized upon as such. But Bayle's methodological axiom about bringing all biblical interpretation to the touchstone of the light of nature or the first principles of reason is a commonplace of 'orthodox', conforming theology in this era, being stated uncontroversially by the supreme Christian apologist of the eighteenth century, Bishop Joseph Butler.[165] In response to those Christians who might take offence at the suggestion that human reason is the instrument whereby we interpret and apply the Bible, we might ask: How else could the task of biblical interpretation and its application to our questions and challenges be met, except by using our reason and moral sense? The only alternative is an official interpretation made by the naked, unsupported assertions of church authority – which were seen in the Enlightenment (and are now almost universally so seen) to lack integrity as truth until validated by reasonable thinking and ethical discernment.

No, toleration did not come from church dogma, but from the clash of church dogma in inter-religious strife. It was the irresolvable

---

[164]See Teresa Morgan, *Roman Faith and Christian Faith: Pistis and Fides in the Early Roman Empire and Early Churches* (Oxford: Oxford University Press, 2015).
[165]*ISOA*, pp. 313–16.

religious conflicts of the sixteenth and seventeenth centuries, with their accompanying violence, bloodshed and widespread destruction, that opened a window in public doctrine for those oppressed voices who were calling for toleration to be heard. In Spinoza, Bayle and Locke it was reason – albeit reason infused with the ethic of the Gospels – that forged toleration doctrine and it was the unanswerable moral case that won the day. Toleration can indeed be seen as a form of secularization in so far as it meant that the state recognized 'tolerable' religious faith and practice outside the monopolistic power of the state religion and in so doing undermined that monopoly. It is reason working through radical theology that brought toleration into the modern world.

The *philosophes* and toleration

The position of Spinoza, Bayle and Locke is secure in the pantheon of prophets of toleration, but the place of the deistic *philosophes* is disputed. Barnett claims that 'there is little evidence that in the achievement of religious toleration – the bedrock of any secularization programme – deistic radicals played any fundamental role ... On the contrary, there is evidence to indicate that religious toleration began to assert itself as an idea and a practical reality at the grass-roots level of eighteenth-century society and that the "enlightened" responded to public opinion rather than creating it.'[166]

Barnett adds: 'The dominance of the top-down model of intellectual change has prevented due recognition of the role of the wider public in the formation of the idea of religious toleration.'[167] It is true that the *philosophes* were not the only voices in favour of toleration. Ideas of greater freedom of religion were entertained by the French *parlements* also. The Jansenists, though they supported the Revocation of the Edict of Nantes in 1685, generated notions of civic rights in their own interests by claiming that members

---

[166] S. J. Barnett, *The Enlightenment and Religion: The Myths of Modernity* (Manchester, UK: Manchester University Press, 2003), p. 4.
[167] Ibid., p. 9.

of religious minorities, such as themselves, could be responsible citizens. While a growing groundswell of public opinion (of the educated classes) was essential for toleration doctrine to prevail, Barnett's disparagement of the role of the *philosophes* goes too far. Voltaire, Diderot and Rousseau, among others, articulated a vision of intellectual and religious freedom that inspired many who were not philosophers. The *philosophes* were motivated in part by an animus against the Catholic Church because it claimed to control every aspect of peoples' lives; they saw it as an incubus on the integrity of the individual and on social morals and mores.[168] They held that every person enjoyed a natural right to liberty of conscience. Their key argument is that conscience cannot be constrained or compelled.

Voltaire was enthused by the freedoms enjoyed by the English and gave a euphemistic description of it in his *Lettres philosophique* (*Letters on England*). Voltaire wrote repeatedly about toleration, but I can give only a taste. In the conclusion of his *Traité sur la tolérance* (1763), on the Calas scandal, he went beyond the mutual toleration of Christians: 'No great skill or studied eloquence is needed to prove that Christians must tolerate one another. I will go further: I say to you that we must regard all men as our brothers. What! My brother the Turk? My brother the Chinese? The Jew? The Siamese? Yes, of course; are we not all children of the same father, and creatures of the same God?'

This tiny globe, he continued, is lost in the immensity of space. Humanity is nothing in the grand scheme of creation. '[T]here may be nine hundred million little ants like us on the earth, but because only my anthill is beloved of God, all the others are an eternal abomination in his eyes. My anthill alone will be blessed, and all the others will be eternally wretched'. To spell it out like this is to see the absurdity and injustice of intolerance.[169]

Voltaire's oft-repeated battle-cry *Ecrasez l'infâme*! was intended to stir up public opinion. But his tolerant outlook was not equally distributed. His thought is disfigured by antisemitism; he remained

---

[168]Marisa Linton, 'Dissent and Toleration', in Doyle (ed.), *The Oxford Handbook of the Ancient Régime*, ch. 20, at p. 343.
[169]Voltaire, *Traité sur la tolérance* in Warman, *Tolerance*, p. 93. See also Voltaire's 'Prière à Dieu' in id., pp. 14–15.

hostile to Jews. We might note that, at this point, Voltaire's views contrast starkly with those of Lessing. As Ritchie Robertson puts it:

> One of Lessing's claims to fame is his consistent advocacy of religious toleration and in particular of equal treatment of Jews. Having exposed anti-Semitic prejudices in his early comedy *Die Juden* (The Jews), Lessing returned to the subject of toleration in *Nathan der Weise*, where once again the natural sociability of essentially good people is shown to overcome the prejudices that are encouraged by religious institutions.[170]

Diderot's pluralistic logic was devastating: 'Everywhere I hear loud accusations of heresy. The Christian is heretical in Asia, the Muslim in Europe, the Papist in London, the Calvinist in Paris, the Jansenist at the top of the rue St Jacques, the Molinist at the bottom of the faubourg Saint-Médard. What is a heretic? Is everyone heretical, or nobody?'[171]

In *Du Contrat Social* Rousseau argues that, while it is important that each citizen should have a religion that motivates them to perform their social and political duty, what they believe – the dogmas – is of no concern to the state unless it affects the community.[172] Rousseau is following Locke's *Letter Concerning Toleration* when he insists that a person's private beliefs and prayers do not fall under the legislative competence of the state. The state or the sovereign is concerned with the present life only, not with the life to come. Individuals should be free to espouse whatever religion they wish, without the state taking an interest. One is free to think and do whatever does not harm others – with one exception: professing atheists are excluded because their stance is destructive of the common good. The sovereign is responsible for the civil religion, which has tenets (but not, strictly speaking, dogmas) which are designed to ensure that one is a responsible citizen and loyal subject. Those who rebel against the state, its laws

---

[170]Ritchie Robertson, 'Preface', in id. (ed.), *Lessing and the German Enlightenment* (Oxford: Voltaire Foundation, 2013), p. xii. See the instructive comparisons of Lessing with respectively Spinoza, Locke, Bayle and Voltaire in Adam Sutcliffe, 'Lessing and the German Enlightenment', in id., pp. 205–25.
[171]Warman, *Tolerance*, p. 64.
[172]J.-J. Rousseau, *The Social Contract*, ed. Cranston, pp. 185–7.

and its civil religion, should be executed.[173] The content of the civil religion is largely ethical but it rests on a minimal theological basis comprising belief in: (a) an all-powerful and benevolent Creator who foresees events and provides for the wants of human creatures; (b) life after death, or immortality, with rewards for the just and punishments for sinners; (c) 'the sanctity of the social contract and the law' which binds the community together and so is the *sine qua non* of citizenship.

Interestingly, Rousseau adds one – and only one – 'negative dogma', namely that there should be no intolerance permitted. Intolerance, he says, belongs to the religions that he has rejected, especially that of the Roman Catholic Church. Only those religions that themselves tolerate other religions should be tolerated. Anyone who claims, 'Outside the church [in context that is, "my church"] there is no salvation', should be expelled (p. 186). Rousseau's basic tenets of civil religion invite comparison with what Immanuel Kant later believed was required by the moral law; they are also commonly found in deists from Herbert of Cherbury to Voltaire. Rousseau's ideas in *Du Contrat Social* are a refinement and in some respects a hardening of his Second Discourse, on inequality, but they are not particularly original – most of his political thought can be paralleled in the writings of the physiocrats and *philosophes* – but they are arrestingly expressed, with a directness and originality that belongs to Rousseau's unique mind and sensibility.[174]

The limits of Enlightenment toleration

However, we should not make the anachronistic mistake of equating the kind and degree of toleration that Enlightenment thinkers advocated in the late seventeenth and early eighteenth centuries

---

[173]John Hope Mason, 'At the Limits of Toleration: Rousseau and Atheism', in Ourida Mostefai and John T. Scott (eds), *Rousseau and L'Infâme: Religion, Toleration, and Fanaticism in the Age of Enlightenment* (Leiden: Brill, 2009), pp. 239–56. Mason begins by stating that Spinoza, Hobbes and Bayle 'seemed' to be advocating atheism, but he does not point out that they were in fact not atheists but theists and that the latter two were Protestant Christians.
[174]Durand Echeverria, 'The Pre-Revolutionary Influence of Rousseau's *Contrat Social*', *JHI* 33.4 (1972), pp. 543–60, at p. 559.

with twenty-first-century notions of state religious neutrality. In the era of the Enlightenment states did not for a moment entertain the very modern, or perhaps postmodern, idea that all religions – even all familiar forms of Christianity – were acceptable, let alone that they were equally valid. European regimes, including the British one, were marked by a confessional identity, allied to their state churches, though their confessional character was beginning to be whittled away even then. Toleration was a concession on the part of the state. Johnson's *Dictionary* gives just one definition of 'toleration': 'Allowance given to that which is not approved.' Toleration was grudgingly awarded when it was the only way left to hold the state together.[175] And it was selective.

Bayle went beyond what two giants of tolerationist philosophical theology, Locke and Voltaire (but not beyond Spinoza), would accept by arguing, in his *Pensées diverses sur la comète* of 1682, that a society of atheists would function as well as a society of Christians, observing the principles of honesty and civility. So why should atheists not be tolerated?[176] (Bayle disagreed with fellow Protestants Jean le Clerc on the toleration of atheists and John Milton on whether Catholics should be included.) Montesquieu and Rousseau were affronted at his impiety; for Rousseau, the two groups not to be tolerated are atheists and Roman Catholics. Here he was following Locke who was implacably opposed to both groups being admitted to the commonwealth.

Locke's was a voice of passionately cool moderation in an age of hysteria, swayed by fear and paranoia and fuelled by reports of dreams, witches, nightmares, comets, war and plague. In this frenzied climate, scapegoats were sought. Inter-confessional polemic deployed a lexicon of wild accusations: 'heretic', 'schismatic', 'libertine', 'sodomite', 'atheist'. These insults should be discounted in interpreting the literature, where a hermeneutic of suspicion is called for. In his *Letters on Toleration* (1689) Locke argued that the magistrate (ruler) should not interfere in a person's private convictions but should respect liberty of conscience. But Locke

---

[175]Barnett, *The Enlightenment and Religion*, p. 9. So also J. C. D. Clark, *English Society 1660–1832: Religion, Ideology and Politics during the Ancien Regime* [sic], 2nd edn (Cambridge: Cambridge University Press, 2000 [1985]).
[176]See Philip Stewart, 'Are Atheists Fanatics? Variations on a Theme of Locke and Bayle', in Mostefai and Scott (eds), *Rousseau and L'Infâme*, pp. 227–38.

(hypothetically) excluded atheists from toleration because he believed that they could not be trusted; the lack of an ontological religious foundation 'dissolves' all civil bonds of honesty and faithfulness, he claimed. For Locke the stern moralist, libertinage was akin to atheism; and he may have had the notorious fornicator and blasphemer the Earl of Rochester in his sights. Locke also excluded Roman Catholics (not hypothetically) from toleration on the grounds that they owed allegiance to a foreign power, the pope. Muslims were excluded for the same reason, but Jews and Quakers were included. Locke had an ecclesiological basis for his convictions: he regarded toleration as not only politically prudent but as 'the chief Characteristical Mark of the True Church'.[177] It was Christian charity that required tolerance towards those of other faiths. The persecution, torture and execution of dissidents 'upon pretence of Religion' are more contrary to the glory of God, the purity of the church and the salvation of souls than any conscientious dissent 'accompanied by Innocency of Life'.[178]

On the same lines, the English 1689 Act of Toleration was designed to include Protestant Dissenters, especially Presbyterians (of which there was reasonable hope) within the national commonwealth, though they were excluded from holding public office (until the repeal of the Test and Corporation Acts in 1828). Catholics, Jews and atheists were excluded.[179] The Toleration Act was brought in when it was clear that a comprehensive national church, which would reunite Dissenters with the Church of England, was not achievable. Comprehension had failed; toleration was second-best.[180] The compromise and pragmatic element in toleration

---

[177] Cited Nathan Guy, *Finding Locke's God: The Theological Basis of John Locke's Political Thought* (London and New York: Bloomsbury, 2019), p. 41.
[178] Cited Guy, *Finding Locke's God*, p. 42. See also: John Horton and Susan Mendus (eds), *John Locke: 'A Letter Concerning Toleration' in Focus* (London: Routledge, 1991); John Dunn, *The Political Thought of John Locke* (Cambridge: Cambridge University Press, 1969); John Marshall, *John Locke: Resistance, Religion and Responsibility* (Cambridge: Cambridge University Press, 1994); id., *John Locke, Toleration and Early Enlightenment Culture* (Cambridge: Cambridge University Press, 2006); Jeremy Waldron, *God, Locke, and Equality: Christian Foundations in Locke's Political Thought* (Cambridge: Cambridge University Press, 2002).
[179] https://www.british-history.ac.uk/statutes-realm/vol6/pp74-76 (accessed 3 March 2022).
[180] John Spurr, *The Restoration Church of England 1646–1689* (New Haven, CT: Yale University Press, 1991), pp. 376–9.

legislation aroused the wrath of principled libertarians. Goethe would later take toleration as an insult and Paine asserted that the very idea of toleration implied that 'granting' it as a *'favour'* was an act of condescension, whereas in truth freedom of conscience and its expression was a natural right, implanted in the human breast by Almighty God; the state could only *'confirm* it as a *right'*.[181]

---

[181]Ole Peter Grell and Roy Porter (eds), *Toleration in Enlightenment Europe* (Cambridge: Cambridge University Press, 2000), p. 16 (editors); J. C. D. Clark, *Thomas Paine* (Oxford: Oxford University Press, 2018), pp. 179, 337 (italics original).

4

The Enlightenment and religion

Some modern theological writers have imbibed the claim of those interpreters of the Enlightenment who usually have their own blatant secular and usually atheistic agenda that the Enlightenment was generically hostile to Christianity. Not only have these theological writers (some of them were discussed in Chapter 2) shipped this interpretation on board uncritically, but they have also shown themselves to be well behind the times in terms of Enlightenment scholarship. In the light of studies going back half a century, it is clear not only that the existential centre of gravity of the Enlightenment was not a secular, irreligious and unbelieving ideology, but also that the Enlightenment was a dominantly Christian, ecclesiastical and indeed theological movement, especially in England and Germany. The Enlightenment pervaded national life and its institutions, especially the church and the universities, in several, mainly Protestant, countries and in its general thrust was neither politically subversive nor anti-religious nor even counter-cultural.[1]

---

[1] For an insightful survey of the history in the light of the interpretative issues see Nigel Aston, *Christianity and Revolutionary Europe, 1750–1830* (Cambridge: Cambridge University Press, 2002), especially ch. 3, 'Intellectual Challenges and the Religious Response' (pp. 93–133).

Ecclesiastical Enlightenment

A major avenue for Enlightenment influence in Europe was the national church which included the ecclesiastical foundations of the universities. As Nigel Aston has nicely put it, 'Irrespective of confessional variations, every European state *c*.1700 exhibited and upheld an established church, at once a fundamental component and final sanction of its institutional life.'[2] Enlightenment agendas would have made little progress if they had not been pursued within the ecclesial structures of first Protestant and then Roman Catholic nations. The Enlightenment arose within the *ancien régime* – that was its sole and inevitable provenance – and can be seen as an internally subversive expression of the *status quo*. In no sense should the Enlightenment be viewed as a *deus ex machina*, a force operating outside the social, political and economic structures. The polity of England, post-Civil War and post-'Glorious Revolution', cannot readily be assimilated to the *ancien régime* as it subsisted in mainland Europe. J. C. D. Clark's designation of England as a 'confessional state' has value as an heuristic concept, provided we understand it of the *state* with its Anglican, monarchical and aristocratic constituents, rather than of the variegated complexion of society as whole.[3] While the Church of England subsisted within a semi-Erastian polity (the juridical dominance of the state over the church) until the twentieth century, in Roman Catholic nations the divinely anointed monarchs – not least the 'enlightened despots' (more correctly: enlightened absolute monarchs) who courted

---

[2]Nigel Aston, 'The Established Church', in William Doyle (ed.), *The Oxford Handbook of the Ancien Régime* (Oxford: Oxford University Press, 2012), ch. 17, at p. 285.

[3]Thomas Munck, 'Enlightenment', in Doyle (ed.), *The Oxford Handbook of the Ancient Régime*, ch. 25, at p. 431. J. C. D. Clark, *English Society, 1660–1832: Religion, Ideology and Politics during the Ancien Régime*, 2nd edn with slightly different title to the 1st edition of 1985 (Cambridge: Cambridge University Press, 2000). Cf. the comments of Julian Hoppit, 'Reformed and Unreformed Britain, 1689–1801', in Doyle (ed.), *The Oxford Handbook of the Ancient Régime*, ch. 29, at pp. 506ff. See also Arthur Burns and Joanna Innes (eds), *Rethinking the Age of Reform: Britain 1780–1850* (Cambridge: Cambridge University Press, 2003).

certain eminent *philosophes* – exerted 'formidable control'[4] over their established churches, while introducing significant but limited reforms, at the expense of papal authority (in some cases again until the twentieth century).

Historical scholarship has been aware of the religious and indeed Christian complexion of the Enlightenment for some time.[5] Trevor-Roper was demonstrating in the early 1960s that religion, far from being the antithesis of the Enlightenment worldview, was a direct cause of it.[6] Many dissenting and radical theological voices of the late seventeenth century – especially Hobbes, Spinoza and Bayle – are not at all irreligious, nor are they even launched on some kind of non-believing trajectory as though unbelief, even atheism, was the logical outcome of their thought, as some interpreters insist. They belong firmly within the bewilderingly broad spectrum of theological ideas that Christian history has thrown up. I argued the point in my earlier discussion of the Enlightenment (*In Search of Authority*) and it has subsequently been further vindicated (if it ever needed to be). Erdozain has recently shown that it was the bruised consciences of such figures as Spinoza, Bayle and Voltaire, and the suffering that they and those around them suffered at the hands of the church-state nexus of rigid Calvinism and/or Roman Catholicism that turned them against the embedded institutions of the church, its hierarchies, dogmas and rituals – while not driving them completely out of the orbit of Christianity.[7]

---

[4]Aston, 'The Established Church', p. 297. See H. M. Scott (ed.), *Enlightened Absolutism: Reform and Reformers in Later Eighteenth-Century Europe* (Basingstoke: Macmillan, 1990), especially the analysis of the historiography of the concept in Scott's 'Introduction'. Fritz Hartung's pamphlet, *Enlightened Despotism* (London: Routledge and Kegan Paul, for The Historical Association, 1957), regards Frederick the Great of Prussia as the first true enlightened despot and Joseph II as the most enlightened and benevolent absolute monarch. Hartung favours the term 'Enlightened Absolutism', even though some of the monarchs concerned were shamelessly despotic.
[5]Still of value as an interpretation and as a bibliography up to 1980 is Sheridan Gilley, 'Christianity and Enlightenment: An Historical Survey', *History of European Ideas* 1.2 (1981), pp. 103–21.
[6]Hugh Trevor-Roper, 'The Religious Origins of the Enlightenment', in id., *Religion, the Reformation and Social Change* (London: Macmillan, 1967), ch. 4.
[7]Dominic Erdozain, *The Soul of Doubt: The Religious Roots of Unbelief from Luther to Marx* (Oxford: Oxford University Press, 2015); cf. Anthony J. La Vopa, 'A New Intellectual History? Jonathan Israel's Enlightenment', *Historical Journal* 52 (2009), pp. 717–38 (a demolition of aspects of Israel's first two volumes: *Radical Enlightenment* (2001) and (mainly) *Enlightenment Contested* (2006)).

A forthright statement of the centrality of religion to the Enlightenment was made by the editors of a symposium on toleration more than twenty years ago. 'Religion did not merely retain a powerful presence throughout eighteenth-century Europe', the editors insisted, 'it was central to the Enlightenment project itself.'[8] They quoted Norman Hampson's blunt assertion: 'The coherence, as well as the confidence of the Enlightenment rested on religious foundations.'[9]

The thesis that the origins of Enlightenment paradigms are found within Protestantism has been seconded – in a back-handed way – by James Simpson in his *tour de force*, *Permanent Revolution*.[10] His thesis is fourfold. (i) Evangelical Protestantism was the driving force of the English Reformation. (ii) This Evangelical Protestantism was experienced by the population as unbearably oppressive in both theory and practice and could not endure unchanged. (iii) Proto-liberal ideas emerged from within Evangelical Protestantism by way of various stages of reinvention that eventually amounted to a reversal. So that (iv) by the time of the 1688 'Glorious Revolution', Arminianism had replaced Calvinism, tolerance had replaced intolerance and persecution, and aesthetic freedom had superseded iconoclasm. As Simpson likes to put it, the English Reformation had begun as an Evangelical movement driven by an unyielding belief in predestination, intolerance, stringent literalism, political quietism, and destructive iconoclasm, all brooded over by the wrath of God, while Calvinism had also denied human agency and responsibility, so inhibiting progress and innovation. Yet by 1688, this highly illiberal early modern revolution had produced the proto-Enlightenment foundations of liberalism: free will,

---

[8]Ole Peter Grell and Roy Porter (eds), *Toleration in Enlightenment Europe* (Cambridge: Cambridge University Press, 2000), p. 1. The editors introduce a note of confusion at this point (pp. 1–2). After saying that atheists certainly existed, they immediately give Voltaire as an example of someone who wanted to eradicate religion, as though he were an atheist. That is not so: Voltaire hated Roman Catholic priestcraft, dogma and persecution, but as a pious deist he had a place for religion and was far from being an atheist.
[9]Norman Hampson, *The Enlightenment: An Evaluation of Its Assumptions, Attitudes and Values* (Harmondsworth: Penguin, 1968), p. 106.
[10]James Simpson, *Permanent Revolution: The Reformation and the Illiberal Roots of Liberalism* (Cambridge, MA: Belknap Press of Harvard University Press, 2019).

liberty of conscience, religious toleration, freedom of the press and in the arts, and constitutionality in the state. Where Simpson's thesis differs from that of Trevor-Roper, Erdozain and myself, is that he posits the origins of Enlightenment paradigms not in the dissident, marginalized, persecuted, yet resilient and unbeaten intellectual heroes of radical Protestant groups and movements, especially Spinoza, La Peyrère, Locke and Bayle, but in the official mainstream of state-sponsored and state-controlled reform in England. Simpson's is a thought-provoking thesis, but I find several weaknesses and flaws in it.

First, the thesis rests on a monochrome picture of the English Reformation, which was in fact not one thing ('Evangelical Protestantism'), but a series of not straightforwardly linear, but differentiated phases. There was an early Henricean political reform (Erasmian and minimally theological), followed by a later Henricean Lutheran phase (not iconoclastic), succeeded by Edwardian Protestant theological reductionism and iconoclasm and then by a bringing the church back into balance on Elizabeth's accession. Elizabeth held in check the reforming fervour of the exiles who returned from Switzerland when Mary Tudor's persecutions were ended by her death, so that the so-called Elizabethan Settlement was neither iconoclastic nor extremely Protestant (no double predestination, for example) and promoted moderate figures such as Richard Hooker and Lancelot Andrewes. It is true that eventually militantly subversive Calvinism overthrew the proto-Anglicanism of the early Caroline divines and Archbishop William Laud, leading to the destruction of the Civil War and Commonwealth interregnum. But this episode was a rebellion against the Reformation church-state nexus, so hardly an internal evolution of Evangelical Protestantism.

Second, the picture that Simpson paints of the theology and practice of the Reformation period is a one-sided caricature. It was not always or even mainly a dismal, despair-inducing theological and moral straitjacket. Clearly many people found relief and comfort in the message of justification by grace through faith and in the more pastoral and domestic ambience of the reformed English Church. Not without reason has the Reformation been described as the liberation of the laity. Alongside that aspect, is the fact that Calvinism in no way emasculated human agency and responsibility, as the author claims. On the contrary, the Calvinistic emphasis on the sovereignty of God and on divine election spurred on and energized many a Calvinist to great feats, as any history of the Calvinist movement worldwide will show.

Third, Evangelical Protestantism was not the only religion which had gloomy and oppressive elements. Tridentine and Baroque Catholicism in France, Spain, Italy and half of Germany (to look no further) had its share of dismal, gloomy and oppressive aspects in this life and terrifying prospects in the next. The fires of hell burned equally fiercely in Catholic and in Protestant preaching and iconography. Are we to trace the emergence of French, Spanish, Italian and South German Enlightenment ideas from this source in a parallel way? If so, there is nothing distinctive or unique about Simpson's thesis.

Finally, it is another caricature to present the post-1688 religious, ecclesiastical and constitutional situation as one radiant with ideals of tolerance, liberty and constitutional government. The freedom of association and of worship granted in the Toleration Act of 1689 was significant and changed the cultural atmosphere, but the Act did not include Catholics, Unitarians, Jews or atheists. Both Catholics and Protestant Dissenters remained under serious political and social constraints and disabilities until the legislative reforms of 1828–31. In a nutshell, the evolution of early Enlightenment ideals took place within radical, displaced, Protestant groups and communities, and their philosophical dialogue partners, rather than within the ecclesiastical mainstream, which in England was not captured for the Enlightenment until the first half of the eighteenth century, by which stage Enlightenment ideas and values had become more mainstream and less marginal. Roy Porter pointed out that the aims of the Enlightenment, especially criticism, sensibility and faith in progress, 'throve in England *within* piety'.[11]

There was a credally orthodox, ecclesiastical, Protestant Enlightenment in England among Anglicans, in Scotland among Presbyterians and in Germany among Lutherans. There was a widespread, intellectually energetic Catholic Enlightenment in France (where the Jesuits were comparatively open to Enlightenment ideas, while the Jansenists were less hospitable, though strongly

---

[11] Roy Porter in Roy Porter and Mikuláš Teich (eds), *The Enlightenment in National Context* (Cambridge: Cambridge University Press, 1981), ch. 1, 'The Enlightenment in England', at p. 6.

influenced by Lockean epistemology), Germany (where the enlightened aspirations of the educated Catholic bourgeoisie and intelligentsia were eventually thwarted by ecclesiastical authority), Italy (supremely Vico) and elsewhere in Europe.[12] There was also a minority deistic Enlightenment, of various shades of unorthodoxy, in England, France, Germany and other European countries and America. Deism was sceptical of the supernatural and miraculous aspects of the Bible and the Christian tradition and was not convinced by the stock arguments of Christian apologists from miracles and from the fulfilment of prophecy. Deism fell well short of Christian belief, but deism was not irreligious or profane; it held on to belief in divine revelation of a sort and divine providence and often exhibited practices of piety after its fashion. There was also a minority atheistic Enlightenment, mainly in France among some of the *philosophes*, though most of them were deists (pre-eminently Voltaire and, in an idiosyncratic way, Rousseau). Thus there was a Protestant Enlightenment among Anglicans, Lutherans and Reformed or Calvinists, the latter particularly in the Netherlands, the home of religious refugees and exiles, primarily Huguenots after Louis XIV's Revocation of the Edict of Nantes in 1685. Christian theology and the various Christian churches of Europe operated within the 'enlightened' spirit of the age, just as they had operated and continue to operate with the spirit of other ages and cultures

---

[12] David Fergusson and Mark Elliott (eds), *The History of Scottish Theology, Volume II: From the Early Enlightenment to the Late Victorian Era* (Oxford: Oxford University Press, 2019); T. J. Reed, *Light in Germany: Scenes from an Unknown Enlightenment* (Chicago: Chicago University Press, 2015); Ulrich L. Lehner, *The Catholic Enlightenment: The Forgotten History of a Global Movement* (Oxford: Oxford University Press, 2016); Ulrich L. Lehner and Michael Printy (eds), *A Companion to the Catholic Enlightenment in Europe* (Leiden and Boston: Brill, 2010); Ulrich L. Lehner, 'Catholic Theology and the Enlightenment', in Lewis Ayres, Medi Ann Volpe and Thomas L. Humphries, Jr. (eds), *The Oxford Handbook of Catholic Theology* (Oxford: Oxford University Press, 2019), ch. 35; Michael Printy, *Enlightenment and the Creation of German Catholicism* (Cambridge: Cambridge University Press, 2009); Jeffrey D. Burson, *Rise and Fall of Theological Enlightenment: Jean Martin de Prades and Ideological Polarization in Eighteenth-Century France* (Notre Dame, IN: University of Notre Dame Press, 2010). For a clear introduction to Jansenism see Ephraim Radner, 'Early Modern Jansenism', in Ulrich L. Lehner, Richard A. Muller and A. G. Roeber (eds), *The Oxford Handbook of Early Modern Theology, 1600–1800* (Oxford: Oxford University Press, 2016), ch. 28.

across history. Christianity was within the Enlightenment and the Enlightenment was within Christianity.

Revisionist historiography

I take for convenience the philosopher R. G. Collingwood's discussion in his *The Idea of History* (1946) as epitomizing the unreconstructed view of 'the Enlightenment', that I am combating in this book, that is of an anti-religious, secular and rationalist movement of thought and action that took place outside the churches and was opposed to the churches, to the extent of seeing them as the enemy to be overthrown. Collingwood defines the Enlightenment as 'that endeavour, so characteristic of the early eighteenth century, to secularize every department of human life and thought'. It was, he adds, 'a revolt not only against the power of institutional religion but against religion as such'. So, for Collingwood, the Enlightenment stood for an attack on religious faith, on religious institutions (especially the churches and the religious orders) and on the overall influence of Christianity on Western civilization. Collingwood's view was grossly over-stated and unbalanced, but it was also fundamentally mistaken. If Collingwood were alive today, he could not credibly advance it. Symptomatically, his prejudiced view of the Enlightenment leads him to misunderstand the philosophical and theological stance of G. B. Vico, the Neapolitan genius of historical method and the father of historicism. Vico did not think, as Collingwood claims, that imaginative, poetic modes of thought were primitive in the sense of barbaric and that rational thinking as per the eighteenth century was the acme of cultural development. Collingwood misinterprets Vico as holding that it was desirable that 'a religious attitude towards life is destined to be superseded by a rational or philosophical one'.[13] Vico knew that an imaginative, empathetic indwelling of other cultures and societies was the only way to understand them. It was the avenue through which he accessed and interpreted them. If he had held the doctrines that Collingwood attributes to him, Vico could never have become

---

[13]R. G. Collingwood, *The Idea of History* (Oxford: Oxford University Press, 1946), pp. 63–71; 76–7.

one of Isaiah Berlin's intellectual heroes. Vico was loyal to the Catholic Church; he had a fundamentally Christian metaphysical theology, as we shall see when we come to discuss Enlightenment philosophy of history.

The case for the Enlightenment having a dominantly religious, Christian and ecclesiastical character has been brought forward by a number of eminent scholars during almost a century of study. As long ago as 1932 Ernst Cassirer was questioning the prevailing assumption that the Enlightenment was generally hostile to religion. When we begin to investigate this claim for ourselves, he remarks, 'we soon come to entertain the gravest doubts and reservations so far as the German and English thought of the Enlightenment is concerned'.[14] More recent studies have reinforced Cassirer's point. Ira O. Wade claimed half a century ago that the upsurge in 'philosophy' during the Enlightenment was largely motivated by a desire to strengthen religion, to compensate for the weaknesses that were becoming apparent in the traditional bases of Christian belief and thus to serve an apologetic function, Descartes himself being a prime example. Philosophy was called into action to redress the failings of an uncritical theology. Moreover, it was believed that philosophical thinking was robust enough on its own to do this.[15] In 1999 J. G. A. Pocock went further, asserting in the first volume of what became his six-volume work on Edward Gibbon, historiography and the Enlightenment, that religion was not only part of the Enlightenment, but its actual cause: the Enlightenment was 'a product of religious debate and not merely a rebellion against it'.[16] Pocock's cryptically stated and controversial thesis will be explored and tested in the course of our enquiry in this chapter.

In the same year (1999), Reginald Ward published *Christianity under the Ancien Régime, 1648–1789* (i.e. from the Peace of Westphalia to the outbreak of the French Revolution). Ward took

---

[14]Ernst Cassirer, *The Philosophy of the Enlightenment*, trans. A. Koelnn and J. P. Pettegrove (Princeton, NJ: Princeton University Press, 1951 [1932]), p. 134. See also the classic review of this work by Isaiah Berlin, *The English Historical Review* 68. 269 (October 1953), pp. 617–19.
[15]Ira O. Wade, *The Intellectual Origins of the French Enlightenment* (Princeton: Princeton University Press, 1971), p. 657.
[16]J. G. A. Pocock, *Barbarism and Religion: The Enlightenments of Edward Gibbon, 1737–1764* (Cambridge: Cambridge University Press, 1999), p. 5.

the unfashionable line that a history of Christianity in that period ought to be 'primarily a history of religious belief and experience', and that 'while not neglecting the history of the churches, [religious history] has less to do with a history of the churches than those bodies commonly claim.'[17] However, it is implausible to claim that religious belief and experience could flourish in detachment from their institutional roots, supports and expressions, especially before the impact of the secularizing tendencies of modernity.

In contrast to Ward's stance, Aston pointed in 2002 not only to the persistence of Christian belief, but to the resilience of the churches as institutions. Acknowledging that '[t]he political and intellectual challenges to Christianity between 1750 and 1830 were as acute as any since its adoption as the principal religion of the Roman Empire in the fourth century', Aston insisted that religion in the eighteenth century possessed 'a vitality and a resilience which historians have underestimated' – qualities which later 'played a key role in enabling the Churches to withstand the often traumatic experience of revolution'. Aston adds:

> It is time to insist on the underlying religiosity of eighteenth-century Europe, the deep roots of a culturally dominant Christianity that revolutionaries and republicans found impossibly hard to dislodge, and the unwillingness of the average man or woman across the continent to relinquish a belief system which conferred meaning on their lives in this world and conditionally assured them of a better one in the next.[18]

Aston goes on to state that '[i]rreligious sentiments articulated with conviction remained a rarity'. They belonged to 'a well-established libertine tradition' and were 'largely confined to the upper reaches of society and [were] seldom heard in public utterance', until towards the end of the century when open challenges to the faith, intended for wide dissemination, were on the increase. Aston notes that '[t]here is a limited sense in which such writings were sapping the

---

[17] W. Reginald Ward, *Christianity under the Ancien Régime, 1648–1789* (Cambridge: Cambridge University Press, 1999), Preface. See esp. ch. 6, 'The Enlightenment and Its Precursors'.
[18] Aston, *Christianity and Revolutionary Europe, 1750–1830*, pp. 1–2.

prevailing Christian culture', but also that their influence (except Voltaire's) was 'minimal in comparison with the omnipresence of the Church on the ground through its ministry to the mass of people'.[19] Aston reinforced this thesis in 2009 with a study of the relationship between art and religion in Enlightenment Europe, a theme that, as he noted, had been neglected by historians and cultural critics whose perception of the eighteenth century was in thrall to the prevailing ideology of the secularization narrative.[20] Aston's 2009 study brings out the fact that the quantity and quality of religious artworks that the eighteenth century produced testifies to the vitality of religious faith within European societies. The churches and their clergy acted as patrons and propagators of Enlightenment thinking. Partly through their sponsorship of artistic works, the churches served as a prime medium of the absorption of Enlightened ideas into European civilization.

At the end of her exploration of *Enlightenment Shadows* Lloyd has written of the thinkers of the Enlightenment, mainly French and German:

> The enemy they address is not religion but religious superstition. The aim was not to destroy religion but to accommodate it into a shared public space of reason. The criticisms offered of religious belief were often sardonic. Yet their target was not religion as such, but what was seen as an unholy alliance – threatening scientific knowledge and rationally based humane social policy – between superstition and state power.[21]

A major benchmark of the changing climate and revised interpretative framework of the relationship between the Enlightenment and religion was *The Cambridge History of Christianity*, vol. 7: *Enlightenment, Reawakening and Revolution, 1660–1815* (2006). This substantial volume consistently does fresh justice to the religious, Christian and ecclesiastical complexion of large swathes of the Enlightenment, not

---

[19]Ibid., p. 10.
[20]Nigel Aston, *Art and Religion in Eighteenth-Century Europe* (London: Reaktion Books, 2009).
[21]Genevieve Lloyd, *Enlightenment Shadows* (Oxford: Oxford University Press, 2013), p. 162.

only in England, Scotland, Europe and America but even further afield.[22]

Introducing his counter-cultural and against-the-tide book of 2008 *The Religious Enlightenment*, David Sorkin wrote: 'Contrary to the secular master narrative, the Enlightenment was not only compatible with religious belief but conducive to it. The Enlightenment made possible new iterations of faith. With the Enlightenment's advent, religion lost neither its place nor its authority in European society and culture. If we trace modern culture to the Enlightenment, its foundations were decidedly religious.'[23] But Sorkin, a specialist in Jewish history, takes this trend a stage further to include the Jewish Enlightenment (*Haskalah*): 'To understand the religious Enlightenment's full scope, we need to consider not just Protestantism and Catholicism but also Judaism, as well as dissenting Protestant and Catholic sects.'[24] In order to do this, Sorkin points out, theologians and their writings – Protestant, Catholic, Anglican and Jewish – must be brought fully into the Enlightenment community of scholars. 'Only by reclaiming these heretofore ostracized thinkers can we begin to replace the master narrative of a secular Enlightenment with a more historically accurate notion, complex, differentiated, and plural.'[25]

Sorkin distinguishes three parallel and co-existing versions or manifestations of the Enlightenment: first, the radical (secular, materialist, heterodox, republican); second, the moderate (espousing a deism that nevertheless held to belief in revelation, providence, divinely sanctioned morality and the immortality of the soul); and third, the overtly religious (within the churches and synagogues). Thus Sorkin detaches the religious dimension of the Enlightenment from the radical and moderate dimensions. However, Sorkin's scheme seems to me to be too tightly drawn. The three forms were not self-contained and mutually exclusive, so that religion was something apart from radical thinking and moderate deism. Religion was present in all three forms of the Enlightenment.

---

[22]Stewart J. Brown and Timothy Tackett (eds), *The Cambridge History of Christianity*, vol. 7: *Enlightenment, Reawakening and Revolution, 1660–1815* (Cambridge: Cambridge University Press, 2006).
[23]David Sorkin, *The Religious Enlightenment: Protestants, Jews, and Catholics from London to Vienna* (Princeton, NJ: Princeton University Press, 2008), p. 3.
[24]Ibid., p. 4.
[25]Ibid., p. 5.

Those who have been identified by Israel and others as radical and subversive with regard to religious belief – principally Montaigne, Charron, Spinoza and Bayle – were actually thinkers within a religious frame of mind and were patently motivated by religious convictions. There were, of course, secular, unbelieving *philosophes*, especially Diderot, Helvétius, d'Holbach and Condorcet. But those who are usually regarded as moderates – Locke and Newton in England, Voltaire and Rousseau in France, and Leibniz and Wolff in Germany – were all – let us be clear – God-obsessed thinkers.

While I wholeheartedly endorse Sorkin's conclusion that 'we should discard the facile yet tenacious notion that as a result of the Enlightenment, religion lost its power and influence in eighteenth-century society', because the religious Enlightenment 'was at the heart of the eighteenth century' and 'may have had more influential adherents and exerted more power in its day than either the moderate or the radical version of the Enlightenment', I would go beyond that tentative summary.[26] I believe that we should push the argument further and say with confidence that religious faith of one kind and degree or another, but usually Christian, permeated and dominated almost all aspects of the Enlightenment.

God and the Enlightenment

A full-scale assault on the received stereotype of the Enlightenment as an intellectual movement that was rationalist and secular, anti-Christian and anti-clerical, and as tending to liberalism and atheism – a stereotype that was popularized by Paul Hazard and which has been powerfully reinforced in recent years by Jonathan Israel and seconded by Anthony Padgen – was undertaken in the collection *God and the Enlightenment*, edited by Bulman and Ingram.[27] Bulman points out that Israel's interpretative paradigm is cited mostly by scholars who are not historians (but, it is implied, are philosophers, literary scholars or popularizers; I could add theologians). Bulman adds that 'a great deal of recent historical

---

[26]Ibid., pp. 19–20.
[27]William J. Bulman and Robert G. Ingram (eds), *God and the Enlightenment* (Oxford: Oxford University Press, 2016); page references in my main text.

scholarship suggests that we ought to discard every assumption underlying' that paradigm (p. 6). Most contributors to this volume collectively and cumulatively challenge Israel's periodization of what he regards as the real or true Enlightenment, a chronology that mysteriously excludes his founding figures, Spinoza and Bayle, from the Enlightenment itself. They were both deeply religious, albeit unorthodox and dissident thinkers, Spinoza being widely recognized as 'a God-intoxicated man'. The contributors to the Bulman-Ingram symposium show that the thinkers of the Enlightenment, far from repudiating the intellectual legacy of the Reformation and the Renaissance – the Christian humanist tradition – drew richly upon it, maintaining 'deep and persistent links' with it (p. 9).

In the realm of historical enquiry, Bulman maintains that 'there is no radical departure that can distinguish the "philosophical history" that supposedly characterized the Enlightenment use of the past from the historiography, ethnography, antiquarianism, and philology of late humanism' (p. 10). The key point being made here is that, in historical study as well as in other fields of enquiry, the emphasis was on continuity, not – as Hazard and Israel would have it – discontinuity. This claim is important because (as Bulman argues, following Pocock) as a result of the interminable and ferocious theological controversies of the sixteenth and seventeenth centuries, theology and ecclesiology had already became thoroughly historicized. Theology was now largely construed in the first place as the history of theology. One could not conduct theological debate or enquiry without first placing the issues in their historical context. Historical study became the dominant discipline among the humanities and the prime site of religious-political debate.

Again, it was not so much a liberal notion of politically neutral religious toleration, in the modern sense, that the Enlightenment promoted, but civil (or civic) religion, the politically established religion that underpinned social and political stability and virtuous citizenship (p. 24). One by one, in this symposium, the pillars of the rationalistic, subversive, libertarian, unbelieving and ungodly version of the Enlightenment are undermined. In place of the scenario, popularized with Gallic verve by Hazard and expounded with enormous energy and diligence by Israel, of a sudden, unprecedented upsurge of radical ideas that tended to secularism, rationalism, libertarianism and atheism, we have an emphasis on continuity with previous intellectual traditions and the handing on of a repertoire of concepts, models, arguments and connections that lent themselves to adaptation and development.[28]

Nevertheless, there are elements in this important collection by Ingram and Bulman that make me uneasy and leave me dissatisfied. First, there is the repeated use by Bulman, in his 'Introduction', of the phrase, with its surface plausibility, 'elite secularity' (sic; p. 19), without identification, explanation or qualification, for those groups with access to the levers of power, who sought the implementation of Enlightenment ideals of civil order, stability and peace. When we consider that almost all European states at this time were governed by sacral monarchies, underpinned by some form of the doctrine of the divine right of kings, and furthermore that even those *philosophes* – especially Diderot and Voltaire – who advised the so-called enlightened despots, were actually serving sacral monarchs who ruled by divine right, it is difficult to give much meaning to the supposed 'secularity' in practice of these 'elites'.[29] In a similar fashion, the concluding, summarizing, chapter by Van Kley refers to 'the secular state', 'secular political authority' and 'merely secular civil authority' (pp. 290–2). If the term 'secular' in these contexts is meant not in our contemporary sense of 'a God-free space', but in a more technical and semantically correct sense of 'outside the control of the churches' or more succinctly 'non-ecclesiastical', even that is claiming too much, for there was little in eighteenth-century European systems of governance that was detached or insulated from ecclesiastical influence and authority. In fact the structures of authority and governance were underpinned and legitimated by ecclesiastical authority and religious doctrine. We can make a conceptual distinction between ecclesiastical and *civil* (but not *secular*) aspects of the confessional state. But throughout the book the descriptor 'secular' has been aligned with the descriptors

---

[28] Paul Hazard, *The European Mind 1680–1715*, trans. J. Lewis May (Harmondsworth: Penguin, 1964 [1953]).

[29] Bulman also repeatedly deploys the phrase 'elite secularity' in his *Anglican Enlightenment: Orientalism, Religion and Politics in England and Its Empire, 1648–1715* (Cambridge: Cambridge University Press, 2015), pp. xiii–xiv, referencing Charles Taylor, *A Secular Age* (Cambridge, MA: Harvard University Press, 2007) and Jeffrey Stout, *Democracy and Tradition* (Princeton, NJ: Princeton University Press, 2004). For the last part of the period denoted in Bulman's title, from the union of the Scottish and English parliaments in 1707, the empire was British, not just English.

'rationalistic', 'libertarian', 'heterodox', 'unchurched', 'unbelieving', 'atheistic' and so on, and I regret to say that this is its normal context today. So what is meant by 'secular' in this work? European governments before 1789 (and in almost all cases afterwards) were none of those things. The word is out of place in any discussion of socio-political norms in the era of the Enlightenment.

Second, there is in the Bulman-Ingram work from time to time a slack use of the terms 'materialism' and 'monism', without definition, as in the reference to 'Spinoza's monist materialism' (p. 30). The interpretation of Spinoza's theology continues to be energetically debated; it is a site of impassioned exploration and contestation. Such simplistic formulae as 'monist materialism' hardly advance our understanding (I will return to Spinoza).

Third, in this volume there is the frequent cavalier deployment of the phrase *sola scriptura* as a supposedly adequate summary of the key axiom of theological method of the Reformation churches and their theologians (e.g. pp. 15, 206, 212). I regret that this assumption is a solecism that is endemic among historians whose theological education has not proceeded far enough. The main platform of the Magisterial Reformers against the Church of Rome was that Scripture alone was sufficient, not for all ecclesiastical purposes, but to show the divinely revealed way and conditions of salvation, without the accretion of human traditions and teachings (such as being in communion with the pope, auricular confession, sacramental confirmation, and various means of acquiring merit by good works). Article VI of the Thirty-nine Articles of the Church of England (1571) is a concise statement of this principle which was common to all the Reformers: 'Holy Scripture containeth all things necessary to salvation: so that whatsoever is not read therein, nor may be proved thereby, is not to be required of any man, that it should be believed as an article of the Faith, or be thought requisite or necessary to salvation.'[30] Neither Lutherans nor Anglicans held that everything that took place in the church or was done by the church had to be justified by Scripture, though the English Puritans, building on precedents in Calvinist theology, adopted that axiom

---

[30]The most convenient place to access the text of the Thirty-nine Articles of the Church of England is probably the Book of Common Prayer, 1662, where the articles are appended.

as their ideological platform in order to bolster their politically motivated bid for presbyterian church government. But this pivotal factor in the Puritan platform was comprehensively refuted by Richard Hooker in his *Of the Lawes of Ecclesiasticall Politie* at the end of the sixteenth century.[31] Reformation and post-Reformation debates between Protestants and Roman Catholics were resourced on the Protestant side not only by the Bible but by the authority of the Fathers, the councils and traditions (i.e. precedents) of the church, and by philosophical argument (reason). It is true that, as several contributors to the Ingram-Bulman collection point out, inter-confessional controversy had contributed to the turmoil of the previous era that so appalled enlightened thinkers of all stripes. But it is not the case that a principle of *sola scriptura*, as that is understood within this symposium, was the principal cause.

The final chapter also makes a number of bizarre theological statements: that Jansenism alone in the eighteenth century defended the Augustinian doctrines of predestination and efficacious grace (p. 304), when these doctrines were also very much alive in Reformed theology on the Continent and within the Church of England; that George Whitefield, a robust Calvinist, was possessed of a 'neo-Arminian religious sensibility' (p. 303); that Methodism (which was a movement within the Church of England until the end of the eighteenth century) 'challenged the Anglican establishment' (p. 308), as though it were outside of it. Most puzzling of all perhaps is the trope that begins and ends the chapter (pp. 278–9, 304) where J. S. Bach's *St Matthew Passion* is played off against Haydn's 'The Creation', the one aptly described as foregrounding sin, suffering and redemption, the other as glorying in the goodness and beauty of God's creation with never a discordant note. I doubt whether any reflective Christian, let alone a theologian, would see these two scenarios in terms of dissonance, let alone a clash of perspectives. They are not opposite poles, but are held together, as two of several generative moments, within biblical salvation history (*Heilsgeschichte*). The point of Haydn's 'The Creation', which drew on Genesis, certain Psalms and Milton's *Paradise Lost*, is that it is a poignant pre-lapsarian moment, a brief glimpse of the pristine

---

[31] For Hooker and the principles of his ecclesiology, see *AACC*, ch. 2; *ISOA*, ch. 3.

beauty and perfection of creation and of human innocence. In its liturgy the church gives praise and thanks to God for the beauty, wonder and mystery of creation and for the awesome wonder and mystery of redemption. Christ the Redeemer is also 'the first-born of all creation' (Colossians 1:15). A more generous dose of theological enlightenment would have strengthened the case – a necessary and fundamentally sound case – that this collection aims to make about the character of the Enlightenment and would have obviated an assortment of theological *faux pas*.

Reasonable religion

A significant work that I caught up with during the last lap of putting this book together is the immensely learned, massively referenced, comprehensive and at the same time quite personal interpretation of the Enlightenment by Ritchie Robertson: *The Enlightenment: The Pursuit of Happiness, 1680–1790*.[32] Robertson attempts to do justice to the religious and theological dimension of the Enlightenment, pointing out that most enlightened thinkers sought a more reasonable religion than what was currently available from the churches, rather than no religion at all. Their stress on 'reason' and the ideal of 'rationality', he explains, was largely devoted to the purification of religious belief and practice, a reform of theology and church. In the light of the evidence that I have brought forward in this chapter so far, we can say that Robertson's governing perspective on the religious dimension of the Enlightenment is now widely accepted and can be regarded as basic – but it still needs to be said and it is encouraging that the learned and prolific Robertson has reinforced the message. However, like many writers on the Enlightenment whom we have already met, or will meet, in the course of this book, Robertson is not always sure-footed in his occasional and rather compressed, theological asides in this area. This is regrettable but it was entirely preventable.

(i) For example, he states that Jesus mistakenly prophesied 'the imminent end of the world' (p. 159). This is a common

---

[32]London: Allen Lane, 2020; page references in my main text.

misconception, but any basic introduction to the New Testament would explain that Jesus foretold, not 'the end of the world', but the inauguration of a new age of freedom and justice, the coming of the kingdom or reign (*basileia*) of God, which was already being manifested in his own ministry of word and deed. To make Jesus Christ look misguided is uncalled-for.[33] (ii) Robertson also states that Arminianism included the belief that people could earn their salvation by good works (p. 164). Arminianism teaches that humans have freedom of the will to respond to the divine invitation to receive salvation. To take an example precisely from the Enlightenment, John Wesley was a fervent Arminian and produced *The Arminian Magazine* (in part to counter-act the Calvinist Methodist preacher George Whitefield). But of course Wesley preached justification by faith, a non-negotiable Protestant doctrine, not salvation by good works which is its opposite. The doctrine that virtuous human effort can lead to salvation is Pelagianism, a late fourth-century and early fifth-century heresy, combatted by Augustine of Hippo. (iii) It is a pity that, in the course of a fascinating account of the changes in the study of the Bible during the Enlightenment, the misleading slogan *sola scriptura* raises its head again (p. 183), being equated here with Protestant belief in 'the sufficiency of Scripture' (sufficient for what is not defined). I address this shibboleth, so beloved of historians who have not done all their homework, at various points in the course of the present book, so I will refrain from further comment here, except to make a very basic point. The Reformation principle of the sufficiency of Scripture referred to the final authority of the Bible with regard to the way of salvation, the essence of the gospel, against the accretions from tradition insisted on by the Roman Church. The reference was not (except for some Reformed Protestants and Puritans) to any supposed 'sufficiency' with regard to all that should be said and done in the church's worship, ministry and governance.

(iv) There are also places where Robertson over-interprets in a distorting way what he is describing in the writing of some Enlightenment thinkers. With regard to Spinoza's supposedly radical suggestion about the origins of the doctrine of the Holy

---

[33] See Paul Avis, *Jesus and the Church: The Foundation of the Church in the New Testament and Modern Theology* (London and New York: T&T Clark, 2020), ch. 2.

Spirit (p. 185): every minimally instructed Bible reader knows that the Hebrew *ruach* means wind, breath or spirit – it is a metaphor – and there is nothing inherently unorthodox in Spinoza saying that it refers to or points to 'the mind of God'. The Hebrew and Greek usages in the two Testaments provide raw material for trinitarian doctrine, which was formulated in the early centuries of the church, with the help of Greek and Latin philosophical concepts, to combat unacceptable deviations from the received 'rule of faith' (*regula fidei*), and those formulations have been – and still are – variously interpreted. (v) Lord Shaftesbury did not 'wipe away the Christian doctrine of atonement' by his ironical repudiation of the notion of the innocent suffering for the guilty (p. 221). The idea of vicarious suffering is universal in human experience and is, of course, strongly present in the New Testament, as well as in parts of the Old, where it is articulated by means of various complementary metaphors or models. However, no-one can 'wipe away the Christian doctrine of the atonement', because there is no 'Christian doctrine of atonement' as such. Notions of vicarious satisfaction (Anselm) or even penal substitution (Calvin), to which presumably Shaftesbury was alluding (and which Robertson may have well have encountered in the North of Scotland), have no credal or 'dogmatic' basis in the Christian church, though they appear in traditional liturgies. Other mainstream interpretations of the theology of reconciliation include the representation/identification account explored particularly by R. C. Moberly, the exemplarist model of Abelard, developed by Hastings Rashdall, and the *Christus Victor* theme expounded by the Swedish Lutheran theologian Gustaf Aulén.[34] Scottish theology has contributed substantially to an ethically acceptable understanding of atonement or reconciliation, especially in the work of John McLeod Campbell in the nineteenth century and D. M. Baillie, J. B. Torrance and Thomas F. Torrance in the twentieth.[35] Ethically orientated Enlightenment theology, including deistic writings, stimulated a rethinking of aspects of received Christian doctrine,

---

[34]R. C. Moberly, *Atonement and Personality* (London: John Murray, 1901); Hastings Rashdall, *The Idea of Atonement in Christian Theology, Being the Bampton Lectures for 1915* (London: Macmillan, 1919); Gustaf Aulén, *Christus Victor: An Historical Study of the Three Main Types of the Idea of the Atonement*, trans A. G. Hebert (London: SPCK, 1931 [1930]; New York: Macmillan, 1978).
[35]See also Paul Avis, *Reconciling Theology* (London: SCM Press, 2022), chs 7 and 8.

including the atonement. (vi) Finally, 'the rise of Methodism' is mentioned in passing as though it arose as an alternative to the Church of England (p. 224). It is true that Evangelical revivalism put a strain on the cohesion of the church, but there was nothing new in the church experiencing storm and stress. It probably would have been helpful to some readers to point out that the Methodist movement arose within the Church of England, largely continued within it and was led by Anglican clergymen, principally John and Charles Wesley and their one-time colleague George Whitefield. Methodism remained within the Established Church, with its members supplementing attendance at their parish church with week-night Methodist group meetings, until after the death of John Wesley in 1791, when – unnecessarily and gratuitously – it formed its own structures of ministry and oversight, becoming a separate church. But that step takes us beyond the Enlightenment era.

Jesus and the Enlightenment

It is inevitable that a study of theology and the Enlightenment should ask what was the place of Jesus of Nazareth or, as Christians would say, the Lord Jesus Christ, in the spectrum of Enlightenment religious thought and practice. The scope of the question is so wide that it is difficult to get a handle on it. It would be superfluous to show how central Jesus was to the formative figures of English culture in this period. No-one questions how precious the thought of Jesus was to William Law, Joseph Butler, Samuel Johnson or John and Charles Wesley – Enlightenment authors all. Butler was of course a bishop (Bristol, then Durham), and the same devotion to the person and work of Jesus Christ can be predicated of his fellow bishops and of the much more numerous clergy and faithful lay people of the Church of England who joined daily or weekly in the Christ-centred liturgies of the Book of Common Prayer. The same can be said (minus an episcopate) of the Reformed ministers of the Scottish, Dutch and Swiss churches and of the Lutheran clergy in Germany and (with bishops) the Nordic lands. While the Catholic Enlightenment was waxing and waning throughout Catholic lands, the mass was being offered in every parish and chapel, theology was being taught in universities, Jansenists and Jesuits were stirring up theological opinion, seminaries were functioning, religious communities were continuing, popes were being elected by conclave and generally speaking Christendom continued as before. Studies of Enlightenment culture and the place of religion within it have tended to overlook the vast submerged part of the iceberg of faith, devotion and worship in which the faithful of the various Christian traditions approached the same God through Jesus Christ in the power of the Holy Spirit.

A neglected but fruitful line of enquiry is to ask what Jesus Christ meant, if anything, to the radical edge of Enlightenment thinking, especially among those philosophers (Spinoza, Hobbes, Locke, Bayle) so admired for their supposed secularity of worldview by some interpreters of the Enlightenment. Jonathan C. P. Birch, who is well-versed in both theology and philosophy, has recently tackled this question in his impressively wide-ranging and heavily referenced work *Jesus in an Age of Enlightenment* (2019).[36] Birch summarizes:

> What this study has shown is that there were [sic] a host of philosophers, theologians, historians, and biblical critics, who were engaged with Enlightenment aims of human advancement – moral, material, and political – who thought that at least one crucial dimension of their quest for social amelioration was the determined re-examination of the historical origins and theological essence of the Christian religion.[37]

Of course, 'the historical origins and theological essence of the Christian religion' are grounded and centred on the person and work of Jesus of Nazareth, who is believed in as the Christ (Messiah), so naturally Jesus becomes the reference point of Birch's enquiry. In the course of his investigation Birch lays to rest several ghosts that haunt Enlightenment interpretation, including politely refuting key aspects of Israel's basic thesis, affirming the place of the classical and Christian humanist tradition in contributing to Enlightenment values and methods, reinstating Hobbes as a Christian and Anglican

---

[36] Jonathan C. P. Birch, *Jesus in an Age of Enlightenment: Radical Gospels from Thomas Hobbes to Thomas Jefferson* (London: Palgrave Macmillan, 2019).
[37] Ibid., conclusion.

philosopher-theologian, pointing out the significant influence of radical Protestantism on Spinoza and underlining the ethical motivation of these various tributaries of Enlightenment thought. Birch shows that the power of the Gospels in presenting the ethical and spiritual character of Jesus Christ was undimmed.

The consequences of Immanuel Kant

Immanuel Kant (1724–1804), though very far from being a typical deist, if there is such a thing, and in fact far transcending the ruck of deists in the elevation and sophistication of his philosophical explorations – famously ended his *Critique of Practical Reason* (1788) with the words, 'Two things fill the mind with ever new and increasing admiration and awe, the more often and steadily we reflect upon them: the starry heavens above me and the moral law within me.'[38] The existence of a benevolent Creator and the demands of the moral law were the twin poles of deistic belief. Of course, they are also key elements of Christian belief, but between these two poles Christianity places salvation history, the biblical witness to divine revelation, Christology and the church with its proclamation, worship and sacraments. Against that background, I will briefly explore, tentatively and as a non-expert in the demanding realm of Kantian studies, the significance of Kant within the varieties of religious belief of the Enlightenment.

As Chrisopher J. Insole has shown in *Kant and the Divine*, Kant 'explicitly distanced himself from Christianity as he would have received it'.[39] There is no point in pretending that Kant was a would-be Christian, an almost-Christian or a theologically struggling Christian. He did not cease to believe in God, but he could not accept the traditional teaching of Christianity regarding

---

[38]Cited Paul Guyer, 'Introduction: The Starry Heavens and the Moral Law', in id. (ed.), *The Cambridge Companion to Kant and Modern Philosophy* (Cambridge: Cambridge University Press, 2006), p. 1. These words are also inscribed on Kant's headstone (tombstone) in Kaliningrad.
[39]Christopher J. Insole, *Kant and the Divine: From Contemplation to the Moral Law* (Oxford: Oxford University Press, 2020), quotations from pp. 1–2, 353–4. See also id., *The Intolerable God: Kant's Theological Journey* (Grand Rapids: Eerdmans, 2015).

the connection between divine action, grace, human freedom and human happiness. It seemed to detract from or undermine what he understood of the ultimate, inescapable, human responsibility to decide and act in accordance with the moral law. For Kant, it is unacceptable to postulate God as the efficient cause of our willing and the resulting action, because it would not be fully and decisively our willing and action. God's causality, as an external factor, would take away human responsibility. But, in his mature thought, Kant also repudiates the idea that God can be the *final* cause of our moral lives, the highest good to which we are drawn and the destination towards which we travel. There can be no moral teleology external to ourselves, because that would violate our freedom – our moral responsibility – which is precisely what, for Kant, constitutes the 'inner value of the world'. Insole argues that this developed position of Kant – which is at once philosophical, theological and ethical – 'is one of the most radical things that Kant says, in relation to all the previous theology of which he would have been aware'. Although this position sounds like a solipsistic form of rational and moral autonomy, Kant wants to universalize it because he holds that 'the highest good involves our participation in a community of rational willing, where that which has unconditioned value, is the activity of rational willing itself' (p. 2). So far, Kant's stance appears to have no room for God or theism in any recognizable form.

Nevertheless, as Insole argues, Kant explicitly 'continues to believe in the uncreated highest good, who is God'. But Kant also develops the idea of 'the created highest good, which is the realm of ends, the autonomous community of harmonious and universalizable end-setting'. How does Kant connect the two: the uncreated and the created highest good(s), 'God and the ideal moral community'? Kant 'rejects the traditional account of the relationship between the uncreated and the created highest good: that the created highest good involves loving and knowing the uncreated highest good, and is, to that extent, entirely dependent upon it'. However, he continues to maintain that 'the created highest good is, in some sense, dependent upon the uncreated highest good'; but, Insole admits that he has been 'unable to find good grounds, even in Kantian terms, to sustain this claim'. Insole's own reconstruction, as I understand it, of the moral theism that he believes can be inferred from Kant's thought proceeds as follows. (a) Kant retains the idea of transcendence in that 'moral goodness is identified with a maximal state of harmonious and universalizable end-setting', one that goes beyond all individual moral achievement. (b) The dedicated moral life is a mode of participation in the transcendent (or 'noumenal') realm: 'the very activity of willing the moral law is a type of participation in the uncreated divine mind'. (c) Kant opens up an argument for the existence of the divine, or of God in some meaningful sense, not via the Christian theological categories of revelation and faithful assent, but through moral discernment, willing and action, as a form of participation in the transcendent moral realm. (d) 'This interpretation', Insole claims, 'throws a new light on Kant's conception of the Kingdom of Ends, whereby the happiness that constitutes the highest good can be construed as an enactment of divinity, through willing the moral law, rather than the contemplation of a divine being.' (e) Although, in the published work of the second half of his philosophical life, Kant had moved to a more radical and on the face of it terminal rejection of Christian belief in God, he had retained philosophically the necessity of God through a concept of participation in transcendence. (f) In conclusion, we can say that Kant offers a nuanced and sophisticated form of the moral argument for the existence of God. On this account, it is barely helpful simply to list Kant among the deists of the eighteenth century. There is as much philosophical and ethical intuition as there is Enlightenment rationality in his work. He arrives at a profound and really rather beautiful philosophical and ethical theism, albeit an attenuated one in comparison with the rich and elaborate classical Christian expositions such as those of Aquinas, Calvin or Pannenberg.

However, I will add, rather tentatively, that I think that Kant's starting point with regard to divine causation might have been different and that he could perhaps have stayed closer to 'orthodox' (difficult word though that is) Christian theism had it not been for two ideological factors in his contemporary context. First, the general Enlightenment worldview was absolutely bowled over by Isaac Newton's discoveries of the laws of nature (specifically of motion, gravitation and optics), laws which were inevitably expressed in terms of a mechanical philosophy. A major impetus and motivation of Kant's thought was to break out of this iron cage of mechanical determinism. A more emergent, organic understanding of the created order (as his contemporary and friend J. G. Hamann articulated) would have given Kant more room for manoeuvre, in terms of divine-human interaction, cooperation or influence. Second, the prevailing theological paradigm, in both the Protestant and Roman Catholic systems of the day, was of the transcendence of the Creator. The note of divine immanence, as a pervading, sustaining but not coercive presence, that we find in Luther and before him in Aquinas and Bonaventure, for example, was muted and suppressed in Lutheran scholasticism and Tridentine Roman Catholicism. I suspect that these two factors together might have eased (to put it cautiously and at its lowest) Kant's difficulties with issues of causation, which were in part a reaction against aspects of his intellectual environment.

The faith of the *philosophes*

It was in the France of the *philosophes* that eighteenth-century European thought showed itself at its most anti-clerical, anti-ecclesiastical – and in some cases outrightly anti-Christian. But that did not make it 'rationalistic', 'speculative' or 'secular', as many ill-informed Christian and other critics of the Enlightenment have alleged. Those familiar epithets are singularly inept. As Alfred Cobban insisted, 'The so-called *philosophes* were one of the most unmetaphysical schools of thinkers that has ever existed.'[40] Rather than being an upsurge of 'rationalism', the French Enlightenment was a critical challenge, based on empirical, critical enquiry, to established authority in the church and to the ideological structure that supported it. The *philosophes* were hostile not only to the secular clergy, to the Jesuits and to the privileges of the Gallican Church, but also to church dogma and doctrine and the politically enforced sanctions and persecutions that underpinned them. Peter Gay eloquently encapsulates the picture of Christianity that was held by Voltaire and his fellow *philosophes*.[41] '[L]ate in the first

---

[40]Alfred Cobban, 'The Enlightenment', in. O. Lindsay (ed.), *New Cambridge Modern History*, vol. 7, *The Old Regime, 1713–1763* (Cambridge: Cambridge University Press, 1957), p. 87.
[41]For what follows, Gay, *The Enlightenment: An Interpretation, Vol. 1, The Rise of Modern Paganism* (London: Weidenfeld and Nicolson, 1966), pp. 207–8.

century ... an insidious force began to insinuate itself into the mentality of the Roman Empire. Slyly exploiting men's fears and anxieties and offering grandiose promises of eternal salvation, Christianity gradually subverted the self-reliant paganism that had sustained the ruling classes.' For all its faults, Rome had at least attempted to build a civilization on reason and law. Then Christianity came along, 'profiting vulture-like from decay, preserving ideas that deserved to perish, and stamping out ideas that deserved to survive.' Gay continues:

> Christianity ... flourished in an age of decadence and among the lower orders, among men and women sunk in ignorance, vice and despair ... [I]t hammered out its doctrine, its discipline, and its organization amidst undignified ramblings, inane debates in endless assemblies, angry conflicts over trivial matters, mutual slanders and persecutions. Christianity claimed to bring light, hope and truth, but its central myth was incredible, its dogma a conflation of rustic superstitions, its sacred book an incoherent collection of primitive tales, its church a cohort of servile fanatics as long as they were out of power and of despotic fanatics once they had seized control.

Once the church had triumphed in the fourth century (as Gay concludes his summary of the *philosophes'* jaundiced view of *Christianity)*, it 'secured the victory of infantile credulity; one by one, the lamps of learning were put out, and for centuries darkness covered the earth'. For the *philosophes*, the Dark Ages lasted for a thousand years.

Exceptionally, the French Enlightenment had an anti-church and anti-clerical thrust. France was the only part of Europe where the dominant expression of the Enlightenment took the form of a non-Christian worldview. But does that make it secular? It could be argued that the dominant faith of the *philosophes*, that is deism, tends to postulate an epistemic distance between the world and God and thus fosters a valuation of secularity, that is of this world. In contemporary usage, 'secular' tends to refer to the world and human life without the God-factor, as a God-free reality. But that was not the position of most *philosophes*, as we shall see immediately. Some deists were devout after their fashion; Voltaire and Rousseau had a fervent faith in their different ways. Notwithstanding the impression that their propagandist trumpeting makes on us, it is among the *philosophes* that we find the strongest and most intriguing paradoxes where religion in the Enlightenment is concerned.

First, it would be a mistake to suppose that the *philosophes* imagined that they had shaken off the shackles of Christianity. They consciously continued to live, think and work within the ambit, even the matrix, of Catholic Christianity. As Peter Gay pointed out,

> Christianity had dominated their childhood; its teachings had saturated their formative years ... Many philosophes had a brother who was a priest or a sister who was a nun; many philosophes had seriously weighed a clerical career. Christianity did not retain possession of their intellects, but often it haunted them ... Their anticlerical humour has all the bitter intimacy of a family joke .... They turned against what they knew all too well.[42]

Second, the more moderate *philosophes*, led by Voltaire,[43] distanced themselves from the extreme freethinkers (*esprits forts*) who attacked not only the Roman Catholic Church's dogma and enforced authority and the Jesuits, but the Christian faith as such and conventional sexual morality. In his article of the 1730s, 'Le Philosophe', which he later revised for inclusion in the *Encyclopédie*, Voltaire dissociated himself and other moderate *philosophes* from profane and anti-Christian writers and publicists. The *esprit philosophique* that he advocated was, epistemologically, a spirit of empirical observation and, ethically, a spirit of justice; it embraced all 'true principles'. The philosopher follows reason as the Christian follows grace. The philosopher is contrasted with *les dévots* (conservative-minded religious people who opposed toleration, particularly toleration of the Huguenots), *les superstitieux* (who

---

[42]Ibid., p. 59.
[43]René Pomeau, *La religion de Voltaire* (Paris: Nizet, 1956); Theodore Besterman, *Voltaire* (Paris: Longmans, 1969).

held irrational beliefs and engaged in irrational practices) and the 'Stoics' (perhaps code for pantheists, such as Spinoza – if that is what he was).[44] For the last fifteen years of his life (from 1762), however, Voltaire raised the temperature of his attack on revealed religion, where his main targets were priestcraft and the Old Testament, to a frontal assault on Christianity as such.

Third, the deistic religion of some *philosophes* was profoundly reverential and ethical. Voltaire is the paradigm of high deism. He does not distinguish 'deism' from 'theism'. For him, religion needs only a minimum of cultus, doctrine and organization, but belief in the Supreme Being and the practice of justice and charity were essential. Nature 'herself' taught all 'men': *Adore un Dieu; sois juste, et cheris ta patrie* ('Worship God; live justly, and cherish your native land'). Voltaire may be echoing Spinoza's *Tractatus*: 'What God requires of man is obedience, and justice and charity.'[45] (Would an atheist or even a pantheist say that?) Spinoza in turn is echoing the prophet Micah in the Hebrew Bible: 'He has told you, O man, what is good; and what does the YHWH require of you but to do justice, and to love kindness, and to walk humbly with your God? (Micah 6:8). The Supreme Being rewards virtue and punishes wickedness. This is not the watchmaker-creator of the popular conception of deism, who sets the world going and then withdraws to an unconcerned distance, a passive, non-interventionist Creator. Voltaire's God watches over the world in benevolent providence.[46] Deists such as Voltaire did not entirely rule out supernatural explanations since for them the cosmos was 'suffused by the Creator with value and even a "general providence"'.[47] If there was a spectrum of views within deism, it is also true that deism itself existed on a broader spectrum

---

[44]Ira O. Wade, *The Structure and Form of the French Enlightenment*, vol. 1 (Princeton, NJ: Princeton University Press, 1977), pp. 15–17.
[45]Citations in Wade, *Structure and Form of the French Enlightenment*, vol. 1, p. 205.
[46]Voltaire, art. 'Théiste: Theist', in id., *Philosophical Dictionary*, ed. and trans. Theodore Besterman (Harmondsworth: Penguin, 1971), p. 386 & n.
[47]Lester Crocker, 'The Enlightenment: What and Who?' in J. Yolton and L. E. Brown (eds), *Studies in Eighteenth-Century Culture*, vol. 17, American Society for Eighteenth-Century Studies (East Lansin: MI: Colleagues Press; Suffolk: Boydell and Brewer, 1987), p. 340.

of eighteenth-century theological thought. As Leslie Stephen noted, 'In England, the rational Protestant could meet the deist halfway.'[48]

Fourth, not all *philosophes* persevered in the prevailing Enlightenment optimism about the state of the world and the possibility of material improvement and the prospect of attaining happiness. There is an evolution in Voltaire's own thought on this topic. Following his enforced exile in England from 1726–9, Voltaire published in 1734 his *Lettres philosophiques* (translated as *Letters on England*), including a concluding essay on Pascal's *Pensées*.[49] Voltaire claims that the Jansenist Blaise Pascal, whom he calls a *misanthrope sublime*, 'portrayed man in a hateful (*odieux*) light', as 'evil and unhappy' and that he 'vilifies the human race'. But Voltaire asserts that 'we are neither so wicked not so wretched' as Pascal depicts us. Voltaire goes on to say: 'Why make us feel disgusted with our being? Our existence is not so wretched as we are led to believe. To look on the world as a prison cell and all men as criminals is the idea of a fanatic.' On the contrary: 'To think that the world, men and animals are what they have to be in the order of Providence is, I believe, the mark of a sensible man.'[50] Voltaire took a jaundiced view of Jansenism mainly on account of its Augustinian theological tenet of the depravity of fallen human nature and denial of human free will. But in one sense Jansenism was an ally, though an historical one since its condemnation by Pope Clement XI in the Bull *Unigenitus* of 1713. Jansenism had a reforming agenda which included stripping the papacy of its temporal and some spiritual power, making the Bible and the liturgy available in the vernacular, destroying the power of the Jesuits and reforming all religious orders, and giving a voice to lay people in the affairs of the church – all of which chime with Voltaire's reforming zeal.[51] We will pursue this topic further now.

---

[48]Leslie Stephen, *History of English Thought in the Eighteenth Century* (London: Rupert Hart-Davis/Harbinger imprint, 1962 [1876]), vol. 1, p. 75.
[49]Voltaire, *Letters on England*, 'Letter 25', pp. 120–45, at p. 120. French text in Voltaire, *Lettres Philosophiques*, pp. 160–85. Blaise Pascal, *Pensées*, trans. A. J. Krailsheimer (Harmondsworth: Penguin, 1966).
[50]Voltaire, *Letters on England*, p. 125. See also Mina Waterman, *Voltaire, Pascal and Human Destiny* (New York: Octagon Books, 1971).
[51]Shaun Blanchard, *The Synod of Pistoia and Vatican II: Jansenism and the Struggle for Catholic Reform* (New York: Oxford University Press, 2020).

Enlightenment and theodicy

Voltaire's disposition to take the world and life as it is, without repining, but getting on with the job in hand, reappears at the end of *Candide*. As everyone knows, Voltaire's fervent faith in a benevolent divine providence guiding an orderly and predictable universe was rocked by the catastrophic Lisbon earthquake of 1755. Voltaire immediately poured out his distress in *le Poem sur le désastre de Lisbonne*, with the subtitle (here in English) 'an Examination of the Axiom, "All is Well"'. Voltaire took a well-merited swipe at priests and prelates who preached that the earthquake with its huge loss of life and property was a visitation of divine judgement because Lisbon must have sinned more than other cities (we might say: as though it were the Sodom and Gomorrah of eighteenth-century Europe). John Wesley was one such (though he was not targeted by Voltaire), interpreting the earthquake as God's judgement on the Inquisition and its shedding of much innocent blood in that country. But most Anglican divines of the mid-century, including Samuel Johnson (I call him a 'divine' advisedly), deplored the notion that the disaster should be attributed to divine retribution. For one thing, since Christ has borne our griefs and carried our sorrows, according to the prophet Isaiah, it was blasphemous to think that God would strike the innocent along with the guilty.[52] Voltaire's primary target, however, was the false prophets of optimism, especially the Lutheran polymath Gottfried Wilhelm von Leibniz (1646–1716), whose speculative metaphysics in his *Essais de Théodicée sur la bonté de Dieu, la liberté de l'homme et l'origine du mal* (1710) had postulated a universe in which all was for the best in the best of all possible worlds. Leibniz's formula should not be hastily dismissed as blinkered, jejune wishful thinking. God would not, or could not, have created a less than optimum world. Voltaire's admiration of Leibniz as an historian was second to none, though he would probably have struggled with some of his metaphysics. But after the trauma of the Lisbon earthquake the Leibnizian metaphysic was comprehensively discredited for him.[53]

---

[52]Nicholas Hudson, *Samuel Johnson and Eighteenth-Century Thought* (Oxford: Oxford University Press, 1988/1990), pp. 103–4.
[53]Wade, *Intellectual Development of Voltaire*, pp. 651–93.

However, it would be a mistake to think that Leibnizian optimism only began to be challenged after the 1555 Lisbon earthquake. As Caro shows in his study of the philosophical and theological debate between the publication of Leibniz's *Théodicée* and the earthquake nearly half a century later, there had been a fierce debate which can be analysed into the long-standing opposition, deriving from medieval philosophical theology, between 'voluntarists' and 'intellectualists' on the question of the divine nature and attributes.[54] Voluntarists stressed that God must be absolutely free to choose; God's will cannot be constrained by any external factor – they took ethical norms to be external to God – or God would not be God. One of the most forceful advocates of voluntarism and a fervent and prolific opponent of Leibnizian metaphysical optimism was Christian August Crusius (1715–75), a leading figure in the early German Enlightenment and an influence even on Immanuel Kant in his early thought. He believed that Leibniz and Christian Wolff (a follower of Christian Thomasius (1655–1728), an uncompromising voluntarist) denied free will in God and humans and therefore that the theodicy project was destructive of all morality and religion. The intellectualists, on the other hand, were those who insisted that canons of rationality and morality were inherent in the divine nature, not constraints imposed from 'outside'. God's actions were free because they were in conformity with God's being and were therefore also rational and ethical and could be no other. For Leibniz, God must always choose the more perfect possibility out of the infinite number of possibilities available. God's choice would be governed by two 'considerations' (and here Leibniz is again deploying medieval concepts): whatever world was simplest in general rules and at the same time richest in its variety of creaturely phenomena (the principle of plenitude).[55]

---

[54]Hernán D. Caro, *The Best of All Possible Worlds? Leibniz's Philosophical Optimism and Its Critics 1710–1755* (Leiden: Brill, 2020).
[55]Ibid., pp. 10–11. Why Caro calls Leibniz's theodicy 'rationalist' and 'rationalistic' escapes me (e.g. pp. 1, 4); of course, like all philosophy and theology (and all other intellectual disciplines), it aspires to be *rational*.

Alexander Pope and bad philosophy

A secondary target for Voltaire's outrage following the earthquake was probably the Augustan poet Alexander Pope (1688–1744), who had proclaimed in the 'First Epistle' of his *Essay on Man* (1733) that 'Whatever is, is right' (a surprising but brave faith for a suffering, persecuted Roman Catholic hunchback). Pope's *Essay* was hugely popular in Enlightenment Europe, where savants read into it a confection of humanism, deism, fatalism and even materialism, as well as optimism. Pope was branded heterodox – a compliment from some, but a condemnation from others. The Sorbonne prepared to censor the French translations (actually paraphrases). In 1748, soon after Pope's death, Julien Offray de La Mettrie, in the dedication to *L'Homme machine*, probably the most secularistic, materialistic and atheistic work any of the *philosophes*' writings, standing at the antipodes of Christian doctrine, extolled Pope's *Essay*. Voltaire initially praised Pope's *Essay on Man* as 'the most beautiful, the most useful, and the most sublime didactic poem ever written in any language', and plagiarized it in the 25th letter of his *Lettres philosophiques*, an attack on Pascal's anthropology, steeped in Augustinian and Jansenist notions of original sin, as it was, and therefore anathema to Voltaire.[56] Voltaire also drew on it in his oriental fable *Zadig* of 1747.[57] Rousseau joined in the fray, nuancing Pope's optimism in terms of his own experience of a benign and beautiful natural order ('le doux sentiment de l'existence') and, if that was not enough, a divine providence to strengthen and console. So, with reservations, Rousseau came to Pope's support, attempting to refute the charge of irreligion levelled against him. But with friends like Rousseau, who needs enemies?

Pope, far from intending to subvert the Christian faith, had an apologetic motive in this poem. He aimed to strengthen Christian belief by paraphrasing popular metaphysical nostrums in order to (echoing Milton's opening to *Paradise Lost*) 'Vindicate the Ways of

---

[56]Cited Robert Shackleton, 'Pope's Essay on Man and the French Enlightenment', in R. F. Brissenden (ed.), *Studies in the Eighteenth Century II* (Toronto: University of Toronto Press, 1973), pp. 1–16, at p. 2. Voltaire discusses the *Essay* in a variant version of the *Lettres philosophiques* dating from 1756.

[57]Voltaire, *Zadig* (ET, London: Chapman and Dodd, Abbey Classics, n.d.).

God to Man'. Pope was no supposed, stereotypical, 'Enlightenment rationalist' to be lumped with an imaginary Hobbes, Locke and the *philosophes* by those who make the same mistake as the continentals who misconstrued Pope. *Au contraire*, the poem precisely inculcates intellectual humility and awareness of our fallibility of judgement: 'In pride, in reasoning pride, our error lies;/ All quit their sphere and rush into the skies' (I, 123–4); 'Know then thyself, presume not God to scan;/ The proper study of Mankind is Man'; 'reas'ning but to err ... in endless Error hurl'd' (II, ll. 1–30). In such words Pope castigated human pride. His optimism was not so much descriptive as prescriptive. Similarly, Shaftesbury's deistic doctrines pointed to moral and aesthetic progress – improvement of the heart – not complacency, 'a guilt-soothing anondyne'. He endorsed Locke's teaching of post-mortem rewards and punishments as a motive for virtuous living.[58]

But Pope was not strong on theology or philosophy and had been led astray by the philosophical theology of William King (1650–1729), no heretic but the Archbishop of Dublin, in his *De origine mali* (*On the Origin of Evil*, 1702), translated into English by the liberal Anglican divine Edmund Law, later Bishop of Carlisle, in 1731. And Pope was further misled – probably duped – by the personal instruction of the philosophical, deistical peer Lord Bolingbroke to whom Pope dedicated the poem.[59] Warburton, Pope's patron and editor (later, like King and Law, a bishop) came to the rescue of Pope's orthodoxy in his *Vindication of Mr. Pope's Essay on Man: From the Misrepresentations of Mr de Crousaz* (1740).[60] Dr Johnson's quip to King George III that

---

[58]John Andrew Bernstein, 'Shaftesbury's Optimism and Eighteenth-Century Social Thought', in Alan Charles Kors and Paul J. Korshin (eds), *Anticipations of the Enlightenment in England, France, and Germany* (Philadelphia: University of Pennsylvania Press, 1987), ch. 4, at p. 87. Basil Willey, *The Eighteenth-Century Background: Studies on the Idea of Nature in the Thought of the Period* (Harmondsworth: Peregrine, 1962 [1940]), ch. 4.
[59]For the ideological background see Isaac Kramnick, *Bolingbroke and His Circle: The Politics of Nostalgia in the Age of Walpole* (Ithaca, NY: Cornell University Press, 1992 [1968]).
[60]William Warburton, *Vindication of Mr. Pope's Essay on Man: From the Misrepresentations of Mr de Crousaz* (1740): https://play.google.com/books/reader?id=x45bAAAAQAAJ&pg=GBS.PP1&hl=en_GB (accessed 9 March 2022).

Warburton had 'made Pope a Christian' is warranted to the extent that Warburton put the best gloss on Pope's theological crudities.[61] Warburton acknowledges the influence on Pope of Leibniz (of whom he is critical) and supports the thesis that this world is, in the divine wisdom, 'the best of all possible worlds'. But he rejects the accusation of 'Spinozism' (understood as pantheism) and insists that Pope's theodicy conforms to the teaching of the best patristic and Anglican divines, as well as standing in the estimable Platonic tradition.[62] Those who seek to paint the Enlightenment in boldly secular, rationalistic and unbelieving colours should note that the *dramatis personae* in this instructive episode were largely drawn from the Anglican episcopate, augmented by a more powerful Christian mind than any eighteenth-century bishop except Butler: Samuel Johnson.

Johnson greatly admired Pope's poetry for its gifts of invention and expression, hailing his translation of Homer's *Iliad* as the noblest form of poetry that the world had ever seen. Pope had once sought to help Johnson's career through an intermediary, so anonymously. But Johnson said contemptuously of the *Essay on Man*: '[H]e tells us much that every man knows, and much that he does not know himself' and 'Never were penury of knowledge and vulgarity of sentiment so happily disguised.'[63] Johnson discussed the controversy in print and also translated into English the 1738 attack by the French Protestant professor Jean-Pierre de Crousaz, in his *Commentaire*, on Pope's *Essay*, thereby clashing with another 'big beast' of the eighteenth-century intellectual jungle, Warburton, who had defended Pope against de Crousaz.[64] Johnson had all along disdained Leibniz's metaphysics, writing him off – absurdly – in 1773 as a 'paltry fellow'.[65] If the anti-Catholic Voltaire had a

---

[61] James Boswell, *Life of Johnson*, ed. R. W. Chapman (London: Oxford University Press, 1953), p. 382n.
[62] Alexander Pope, *Poetical Works* (London: Frederick Warne, n.d.): 'Essay on Man', pp. 193–229.
[63] Samuel Johnson, *Lives of the Poets* (London: Dent, 1925), vol. 2, p. 226.
[64] O. M. Brack, 'Samuel Johnson and the Translations of Jean Pierre de Crousaz's "Examen and Commentaire"', *Studies in Bibliography* 48 (1995), pp. 60–84.
[65] Samuel Johnson, *Journey to the Western Islands of Scotland* and James Boswell, *Journal of a Tour to the Hebrides with Samuel Johnson LL.D.*, ed. R. W. Chapman (London: Oxford University Press, 1924), p. 353.

forced conversion away from Leibnizian pan-optimism, so also did the loyal Catholic Alexander Pope, while the staunchly High Church Anglican Samuel Johnson was rendered immune to its facile temptations by bitter personal suffering. In *Rasselas* (1758) Johnson parodied the facile common coin of 'the fitness of things', 'the nature of things', 'the disposition of things' and so on, a state which was deemed to be unalterable and generally unimproveable: 'To live according to nature is to act always with due regard to the fitness arising from the relations and qualities of causes and effects; to concur with the great and unchangeable scheme of universal felicity; to cooperate with the general disposition and tendency of the present system of things.'[66] So, in Pope's words in the *Essay on Man*: 'Whatever *is*, is right.' While Voltaire's *Candide* is the product of exceptional talent, Johnson's *Rassellas* and his 1749 poem *The Vanity of Human Wishes* belong in a higher league.[67]

Voltairean pessimism

In both the Lisbon poem and the didactic novella *Candide* (1759) Voltaire depicted human life as an overall misfortune, a fate of incessant misery where suffering was prevalent and death inevitable. In *Candide* Voltaire in effect raises the question, 'If this is the best of all possible worlds, what must all the other worlds be like?' In the light of glib assumptions about the Enlightenment's supposedly rationalistic belief in inevitable progress, we should note Peter

---

[66] Samuel Johnson, *The History of Rasselas, Prince of Abissinia*, ed. Paul Goring (Harmondsworth: Penguin, 2007), ch. 22.
[67] See the extended comparisons in Mark J. Temmer, *Samuel Johnson and Three Infidels: Rousseau, Voltaire and Diderot* (Athens, GA: University of Georgia Press, 1988). See further Richard B. Schwartz, *Samuel Johnson and the Problem of Evil* (Madison, WI: University of Wisconsin Press, 1975) where Johnson's devastating review (1757) of Soame Jenyns' *A Free Enquiry into the Nature and Origin of Evil* is printed as Appendix III; Chester F. Chaplin, *The Religious Thought of Samuel Johnson* (Ann Arbor, MI: University of Michigan Press, 1968); Edward G. Andrew, *Patrons of Enlightenment* (Toronto: University of Toronto Press, 2006), ch. 8: 'Samuel Johnson and the Question of Enlightenment in England'; Willey, *The Eighteenth-Century Background*, ch. 3.

Gay's comment that 'no man, no movement committed to a theory of automatic progress could have invented such a question'.[68] In *Candide* Voltaire ridiculed the optimistic philosophy in the figure of the fatuous Pangloss, a homespun philosopher. The famous closing words of *Candide* – 'il faut cultiver son jardin' – are a combination of despair about an ultimate metaphysical explanation of the world, stoic resignation to the slings and arrows of outrageous fortune, and the morality of attending diligently to the duties that lie close at hand.[69] This muted, depressed but nevertheless dignified conclusion compares feebly with Johnson's fervent and prayerful heavenward ascent in his otherwise equally pessimistic poem 'The Vanity of Human Wishes'.[70] Rousseau could not accept Voltaire's dismal theodicy (or non-theodicy) and made that clear in his *Lettre à Voltaire sur la providence*, to which he never received an answer; but a breach between them was created, or rather widened.[71] Nevertheless, if Voltaire's deistic faith was shaken, it was not overthrown. It was indeed a matter of faith: 'the assurance of things hoped for, the conviction of things not seen', as the Epistle to the Hebrews puts it (Heb. 11:1). Gay writes of Voltaire: 'The same man who castigated life as a shipwreck and the world as a miserable pile of mud, who described history as a depressing tale and valued peaks of cultivation as rare and precious moments, also predicted a far-reaching, beneficent revolution and the inevitable triumph of philosophy, because reason, now beginning to show her strength, would ultimately prevail.'[72]

Before despising or pitying the efforts at framing a theodicy of such as Voltaire and Rousseau, Christian thinkers should immediately confess that Voltaire and his fellow deistic *philosophes* were in no worse predicament than any Christian theologian who wrestles with the unanswerable questions of theodicy. Wade comments that,

---

[68]Gay, *The Enlightenment: An Interpretation*, Vol. 2, *The Science of Freedom* (London: Weidenfeld and Nicolson, 1970), p. 105.
[69]Voltaire, *Candide*, trans. John Butt (Harmondsworth: Penguin, 1947 [1759]).
[70]Samuel Johnson, *Selected Writings*, ed. Patrick Cruttwell (Harmondsworth: Penguin, 1968), pp. 139–48.
[71]See the analysis of the arguments in John T. Scott, 'Pride and Providence: Religion in Rousseau's *Lettre à Voltaire sur la providence*', in Ourida Mostefai and John T. Scott (eds), *Rousseau and L'Infâme: Religion, Toleration, and Fanaticism in the Age of Enlightenment* (Leiden: Brill, 2009), pp. 115–35.
[72]Gay, *The Enlightenment: An Interpretation*, Vol. 2, *The Science of Freedom*, p. 105.

for the deists, 'The whole realm of evil – natural evil; positive, moral evil; metaphysical evil – became an inexplicable phenomenon in a universe filled with wonders that declared the glory of God.'[73] The same goes for Christian theists, but they have the incarnation, the cross and the resurrection of Christ to help their wavering faith, the whole panoply of which deists like Voltaire disdained. Nevertheless, *Candide* continues Voltaire's unabashed advocacy of deism. The story includes an interview with a wise old man in the realm of Eldorado. Questioned by Candide and his companions, he explains that its inhabitants worship the one God, but they do so without the aid of priests and they have never heard of monks. They do not practise petitionary prayer, but thank God unceasingly for all the blessings that they enjoy unasked.[74] The travellers wish that they could stay in this blessed land for ever.

In search of atheism

It is already clear enough that it would be an egregious error to think of the Enlightenment as essentially or generally a godless onslaught on religion. As Buckley asserted in *At the Origins of Modern Atheism* (1987), 'It would be false to tax the Enlightenment with indifference to religion. It would be more discerning to say that it was obsessed with it.'[75] But Buckley thinks that the religion of the age of Enlightenment was bad religion: failed Christian theology, or arid deism, or outright atheism. However, writing in the 1980s, he was still broadly working with an unreconstructed view of the Enlightenment, based almost exclusively on the writings of the *philosophes*, namely that a robust orthodox Christianity had

---

[73]Wade, *Structure and Form of the French Enlightenment*, Vol. 1, p. 26. See further on the Enlightenment's wrestling with theodicy Jonathan Sheehan, 'Suffering Job: Christianity beyond Metaphysics', in Bulman and Ingram (eds), *God and the Enlightenment*, ch. 7.
[74]Voltaire, *Candide*, pp. 79–80. Dominic Erdozain, *The Soul of Doubt*, pp. 132–72, has argued that Voltaire represents not an absence of Christianity, but a different, alternative, version of Christianity, one marked by and infused with compassion, mercy, justice and simplicity. I am not quite convinced, but it is a stimulating thesis.
[75]Michael J. Buckley, *At the Origins of Modern Atheism* (New Haven, CT: Yale University Press, 1987), p. 37.

given way to a generically deistic or atheistic faith, thus without divine revelation and providence or the need for churches and their worship. But here Buckley is overlooking the broad tenor of the Anglican, Dissenting Protestant, Lutheran, Calvinist (Reformed) and Catholic versions of the Enlightenment. He is also mistaken in implying that deism and atheism were allied or that the former led almost inevitably to the latter. That connection was indeed prevalent in the rather hysterical defensive writings of eighteenth-century churchmen, but it was not normally the case. Some of the most passionate and forceful attacks on atheism came from the deistic *philosophes*, notably Voltaire himself. Buckley's basic thesis is that it was the failure of Christian theology that caused the rise of atheism: 'In the absence of a rich and comprehensive Christology and a Pneumatology of religious experience Christianity entered into the defense of the existence of the Christian god [sic] without appeal to anything Christian' (p. 67). For Buckley, European religion failed through 'self-alienation' because, in its support, it appealed to external evidences and theological inferences – that is to say, natural theology – rather than to the reality of experiential, inter-personal vital religion. Thus it failed to make Jesus Christ the central and pivotal theological truth and the Holy Spirit the source of spiritual life. He ends with an appeal to Pascal, whose Jansenist theology was condemned by the pope (p. 263). It is strange to find a Roman Catholic author (namely Buckley himself) going against the teaching of his church about natural theology and the role of human reason, and a Jesuit going against the philosophical tenor of his order. Karl Barth would have been proud of him! But his account, which I find both unreliable and perverse, merely implies the truism that the eighteenth century lacked modern theology. It does not explain why atheism arose at this time, when much previous theology, whether Roman Catholic or Protestant, also on his terms lacked what he regards as essential to stave off atheism.[76] Actually, I don't think that Western theology, whether Protestant, Anglican or Roman Catholic, lacked those attributes at all.

In contrast to Buckley's dismal presentation, the truth is that though the *philosophes* in France and the radical Protestants in

---

[76]Cf. Liam Jerrold Fraser, *Atheism, Fundamentalism and the Protestant Reformation: Uncovering the Secret Sympathy* (Cambridge: Cambridge University Press, 2018).

Holland and England were anti-clerical and hostile to the church's privileges and monopolies, Enlightenment thought was not typically or generally anti-religious or anti-Christian, and certainly not atheistic, though in France it was bitterly anti-clerical. Open atheism was rare, but where it was thought to exist – or even invented for propagandist purposes – it caused intellectual and political panic. The reasons why English polemical writers decried 'atheism' remain somewhat opaque.[77] But it may well be that clever talkers ('wits') who were not thinkers or scholars and did not go into print, bandied about unbelieving, atheistic notions in London coffee-houses. We know that more intelligent minds discussed the dangerous subject in some Parisian salons, much to the disapproval of Hume, Voltaire and Rousseau. 'Atheist' began as an ill-defined insult with potentially lethal consequences. But its currency was steadily devalued over time until it could mean almost anything and therefore nothing.[78]

The accusation of 'atheism' was a common term of abuse in polemical writing and had not only theological but moral, social and political consequences. In his *Dictionary* Johnson quoted Swift's conjunction of 'w*higgism* and atheism' with approval.[79] The word 'atheist' was hurled at anyone whose ideas rocked the ideological boat and thus were deemed to threaten the security of the state and the official religious worldview that underpinned it. The devout Charron, Erasmus, Luther, Calvin and Zwingli were all accused of 'atheism' in the sixteenth century; Descartes, Spinoza, Hobbes and Bayle were prime candidates in the seventeenth. But all of these were (as it was said of Spinoza) God-intoxicated men; they lived for theology, not *atheology*. It was said that in those times two academics could not have an argument without each soon accusing the other of the twin crimes of atheism and sodomy. Febvre claimed

---

[77] Michael Hunter, *The Decline of Magic: Britain in the Enlightenment* (New Haven, CT: Yale University Press, 2020), 'Introduction: the Supernatural, Science and 'Atheism' (pp. 1–27).
[78] See Buckley, *At the Origins of Modern Atheism*, Introduction. R. R. Palmer, *Catholics and Unbelievers in Eighteenth-Century France* (Princeton, NJ: Princeton University Press, 1939).
[79] J. C. D. Clark, *Samuel Johnson: Literature, Religion and English Cultural Politics from the Restoration to Romanticism* (Cambridge: Cambridge University Press, 1994), p. 7.

that, in the seventeenth century, the charge of atheism was merely a rhetorical device for the expression of extreme disapproval – 'a kind of obscenity meant to cause a shudder in an audience of the faithful'.[80] Febvre believed that true atheism was virtually impossible in the sixteenth century; people's mental furniture could not accommodate it. But this is questionable.

We only need to recall that Thomas Aquinas, writing for thirteenth-century Christian and pagan audiences respectively, addressed the arguments of hypothetical atheists when he offered five subtle arguments in support of the existence of God, the most cogent being the arguments from a first cause, a prime mover and a non-contingent source of all contingent things, which 'everyone calls "God"'.[81] So the non-existence of God could be entertained, at least heuristically, even then; it was the common coin of medieval and early modern scholastic dialectic and disputation. Budding scholars and clergy were trained to think atheistically in order to be able to refute atheist arguments. As Kors argues, atheism did not need actual atheists in order to be recognized, challenged and refuted. The scholastic philosophical theology 'generated its own antithesis, the possibility of which it had always carried within'.[82] In the seventeenth century, after the philosophical revolution initiated by Descartes, the evidence of 'atheism' was more behavioural than cognitive, associated with unorthodox lifestyles rather than with unorthodox beliefs. Until the nineteenth century it was generally held (Bayle, with his notion of the 'virtuous atheist' being the great exception), following extensive biblical precedents, that immoral behaviour and any heresy, most of all of course explicit atheism, went hand in hand: the one entailed the other.[83] Kors's central

---

[80]Lucien Febvre, *The Problem of Unbelief in the Sixteenth Century: The Religion of Rabelais*, trans. B. Gottlieb (Cambridge, MA: Harvard University Press, 1982 [French 1942, 1947]). See the discussion of Febvre's views in Alan Charles Kors, *Atheism in France, 1650–1729. Vol. 1: The Orthodox Sources of Disbelief* (Princeton, NJ: Princeton University Press, 1990), pp. 6–9. See also the compact account in Alan Charles Kors, 'The Age of Enlightenment', in Stephen Bullivant and Michael Ruse (eds), *The Oxford Handbook of Atheism* (Oxford: Oxford University Press, 2013).
[81]Aquinas *Summa Theologiae* 1a. q.2, a.1–3; *Summa Contra Gentiles* 1. c.12. Kors, *Atheism in France*, also mentions this point: pp. 51–2.
[82]Kors, *Atheism in France*, ch. 3 and p. 379.
[83]See François Berriot, *Athéisme et athéistes au XVI siècle en France*, 2 vols (Lille: Atelier National de Reproduction des Thèses, 1977–1989 [photographic typescript]).

thesis is that it was fratricidal, internecine, theological controversy, as various philosophical-theological schools of thought demolished each other's arguments for the existence of God, that taught eighteenth-century readers the possibility of atheism.

In a theological context, the charge of 'atheism' has often been banded about carelessly and without precision. It has been aimed in a scatter-gun manner at anyone who expressed doubts about any claimed miracle, declined to take every part of the Bible literally, criticized the clergy for their moral failings, or themselves lived profligate lives. Like 'Communist' in the 1950s McCarthy era of the United States, 'atheist' in the eighteenth century was a term of indiscriminate ideological abuse. It was tinged with paranoia: nonexistent Communists/atheists were detected hiding under many a bed. Perhaps it is sufficient to remember that the early Christians were accused of being atheists. Although a lot of noise was made about 'atheism', the few actual atheists were essentially irrelevant to eighteenth-century European civilization. As Barnett puts it, 'The connections between real atheists ... and their relationship to any perceived change in eighteenth-century attitudes to religion amount to little more than the reification of ideas by historians.'[84] Roger Lund commented: 'Despite the insistence of orthodox polemicists that modern infidels – variously described as hordes, tides, shoals, herds, etc. – threatened to overwhelm the nation, one is struck by their numerical insignificance in comparison with a perceived threat assuming near-mythical proportion.'[85]

In depicting the battle against 'atheism', Reginald Ward points to the eminent Reformed divine Gisbertus Voetius (1589–1676) who gave a comprehensive eleven-point identikit of the typical atheist, as one who (I summarize) (1) denied the existence of the supernatural realm; (2) doubted Scripture and looked for contradictions in it; (3) investigated the Bible by the 'light of human history' and understanding; (4) dismissed theologians as other-worldly and partisan fantasists; (5) praised other atheists' utterances, however mediocre they may have been; (6) lived by the maxim, 'Let us eat,

---

[84] S. J. Barnett, *The Enlightenment and Religion: The Myths of Modernity* (Manchester, UK: Manchester University Press, 2003), p. 31.
[85] Roger D. Lund, 'Introduction' in id. (ed.), *The Margins of Orthodoxy: Heterodox Writing and Cultural Response, 1660–1750* (Cambridge: Cambridge University Press, 1995), p. 11.

drink and be merry, for tomorrow we die'; (7) avoided the clergy; (8) engaged in anti-religious propaganda; (9) feigned orthodoxy when necessary; (10) practised religion sparingly; and (11) behaved badly to all who wrote against atheism. Ward adds that 'to the end of the atheist controversy it remained an unsettled question whether the "atheist" philosophers of the ancient world [whose example and precedent was being invoked] simply made light of the superstition they knew or whether they really acknowledged no divinity at all'.[86] It is a striking fact that Voetius's list of atheistic attributes does not include outright denial of the existence of God. The question posed by Enlightenment theology is not so much whether God existed, as whether atheists existed. Those who assume that the Enlightenment was rife with atheism seem to have been taken in by the hysterical, paranoid rhetoric of the age. Atheists existed in the seventeenth and eighteenth centuries, but they were few. Spinoza and Bayle were not among them. Diderot, d'Holbach and La Mettrie were the atheists with the highest profile.[87]

Benedict Spinoza

At the age of twenty-three Baruch de Espinoza (1632–77) was condemned, anathematized and excommunicated for heresy from the family's Amsterdam synagogue. For the Jewish community Spinoza was already an abomination; for contemporary Calvinists he became the personification of antichrist. By the religiously minded ever since, Spinoza has generally been seen as the devil incarnate. Only Hobbes could rival Spinoza for the degree and sheer quantity of the opprobrium that was heaped upon him.[88] In his lifetime Spinoza was accused of atheism, a label that many have attempted to stick on him since then by way of either praise or blame. Along with his supposed atheism, Spinoza has also been seen as the early modern fountainhead of naturalistic materialism and

---

[86]Ward, *Christianity under the Ancien Régime*, pp. 149–50.
[87]Mark Curran, *Atheism, Religion and Enlightenment in Pre-Revolutionary Europe* (Woodbridge: The Boydell Press, 2012).
[88]Graeme Hunter, *Radical Protestantism in Spinoza's Thought* (Farnham and Burlington, VT: Ashgate, 2005), p. 182.

(contradictorily) pantheism, as well as secularism and liberalism. For some he is an intellectual and moral hero; for others an enemy of all religion, especially the two religions that he consecutively adhered to: Judaism and Christianity.[89] Spinoza cannot be both a materialist and a pantheist; he cannot be both a pantheist and an atheist. The endemic contradictions in identifying Spinoza's metaphysics and theology suggest to me that he has not been generally understood.[90] Spinoza's key category of 'substance' is not merely 'material', because in his system substance has the attribute, not only of extension, but also of thought. Purely material substances do not think. For Spinoza the one substance is also to be worshipped or adored, which hardly fits a wholly material substance. Furthermore, for Spinoza, the attributes of extension and thought are the only two knowable attributes out of an infinite number of attributes of the ultimate reality which Spinoza terms *deus sive natura* ('God or nature'). This fact suggests that within Spinoza's metaphysics there is a dimension that transcends the merely material realm. Another telling clue is the fact that Spinoza refers in the *Tractatus Theologico-Politicus* to the 'divinity' within the Hebrew Bible, a divinity that is located in the fact that the Jewish Scriptures reveal and teach true virtue.

Spinoza is numbered among the great speculative, metaphysical philosophers. Like Descartes, Hobbes, Malebranche, Leibniz and Berkeley, he sought to develop a logical, deductive system of truth, taking mathematical exactitude and certainty as his methodological model. We may note once again, in passing, that this rationalist, speculative and deductive method was disdained by the protagonists of Enlightenment thought in favour of a much more practical, empirical and experimental use of reason. So, to that extent, Spinoza cannot be claimed as a herald of the Enlightenment. Spinoza shared the concern of these rational philosophers to accommodate Christianity to the new philosophical and scientific horizons of the day. He owed much to Descartes and devoted his first book to an exposition of the French philosopher. Leibniz, 'the only living man

---

[89]Background in Steven M. Nadler, *Spinoza: A Life* (Cambridge: Cambridge University Press, 1999).
[90]John Robertson, *The Case for the Enlightenment: Scotland and Naples 1680–1760* (Cambridge: Cambridge University Press, 2005), p. 31, is one of many who refer to 'Spinoza's materialism'.

who could wholly have understood his philosophical designs',[91] was fascinated by Spinoza and travelled to The Hague at least partly to converse with him. But Spinoza's monism was of a different order to Cartesian dualism, Hobbesian mechanism and Leibnizian monadology. However, the various modes of rational theology that these thinkers represent are comprehended within Christianity, as the examples of Descartes and Malebranche (both Catholics), Hobbes (Anglican), Leibniz (Lutheran) and Berkeley (Anglican bishop) prove. But where should Spinoza be placed in relation to religion and Christianity?

The image of Spinoza as the destroyer of religion and the herald of unbelief and secularity is represented in modern times by Strauss's *Spinoza's Critique of Religion* (German original 1930), Hampshire's Penguin *Spinoza*, and the writings of Jonathan Israel which we have had cause to mention before.[92] As an example of the misguided use of the term 'atheist', as applied to Spinoza, let me mention Hampshire's verdict: Spinoza, he writes, 'was an atheist in the sense that he denied the possibility of a personal God who by an act of will created the Universe [sic]'.[93] This statement is an abuse of the language of philosophical theology. 'Atheism' refers unambiguously to the belief that there is no God. For Spinoza, God is all that is, the whole of reality (*natura*); the world is filled with God; God is all. There is no meaningful sense in which Spinoza was an atheist.

Strauss's account is useful for its exposition of Spinoza's methods of bible study and his (at the time) shocking conclusions (we will return to this aspect). However, Strauss's arresting title may not be all that it seems. By the end of the book the suspicion dawns on the reader that what Strauss means by 'the critique of religion' is actually the critical study and examination of sacred scriptures, which for Spinoza began with youthful questions about the ways that the Torah and the Talmud were taught in his synagogue. But the rigorous, scholarly study of a religion's scriptures does not normally

---

[91]Stuart Hampshire, *Spinoza* (Harmondsworth: Penguin, 1962 [1951]), p. 233.
[92]Leo Strauss, *Spinoza's Critique of Religion*, trans. E. M. Sinclair (Chicago: University of Chicago Press, 1997 [1965]). This edition includes a new 'Preface' by Strauss, dated 1962, in which he intimates that he now has some second thoughts about Spinoza and religion, though these indications remain cryptic.
[93]Hampshire, *Spinoza*, p. 53.

imply a negative overall judgement on the religion that holds those scriptures sacred, though clearly some scholars and students have lost their previous – perhaps simple or naive – faith by doing that. Within much of modern Christianity, the historical-critical study of the Bible has been taken to the heart of the academic dimension of church life, including the training of clergy and other ministers – though the gap between what is taught and learned at college and what is subsequently held forth from the pulpit is scandalously wide, even unbridgeable, in the majority of cases. It is striking that Strauss does not exclude Spinoza from Christianity, while noting that Spinoza's Christianity was one without dogmas and sacraments (we may add: just like the Quakers!). Erdozain[94] has recently gone much further in identifying Spinoza with the Christian *mythos*, pointing particularly to Spinoza's unqualified references to Jesus Christ and to his teaching of charity to all and the intellectual and ethical love of God, stripped of liturgy and ceremonial, as true Christianity. The jury is still out on the question of whether or to what extent Spinoza should be regarded as a Christian thinker. But the claim that he was a naked materialist, secularist and atheist is now firmly out of court.

Nearly a century ago Strauss perceptively noted that Spinoza was the heir of the beginnings of the historical and literal interpretation of the Bible and of other ancient texts that had been introduced into the consciousness of Europe by Renaissance humanism and by the major Protestant Reformers, who were of course humanist scholars in their own right.[95] Here Strauss points us to the context and matrix of Spinoza's (also Bayle's) radicalism with regard to theology and politics: the radical Protestant movements of Northern Europe, particularly the Netherlands, in the second half of the seventeenth century. These groups, which existed at the margins of society and sometimes 'underground', were the heirs at one remove of the bold, adventurous and creative thinking of Luther, Zwingli and Calvin. Renaissance humanists had pioneered the historical and critical study of classical, biblical and patristic texts. The Reformers' legacy was channelled to these later Protestant groups through the intellectual and spiritual trajectory of the communities of the Radical Reformation who were excluded

---

[94]Erdozain, *The Soul of Doubt*, ch. 3.
[95]Strauss, *Spinoza's Critique of Religion*, p. 251.

from the magisterial, territorial, Protestant churches and were persecuted by them. The Reformation radicals are distinguished by their untrammelled creative speculation around the Scriptures and the Christian theological tradition, their predilection for mysticism over dogma, and their demands for toleration and conscientious freedom of expression and association.

The Radical Reformation (and even aspects of the magisterial Reformation, especially Zwingli and the Swiss-German reform) was deeply influenced by Erasmian humanism. Erasmus's fertile influence continued into the next century, infusing groups of radical, disaffected Protestants, especially in the generally tolerant Netherlands where they found shelter. The Remonstrants (politicized Dutch Arminians) and the Collegiants (a network of radical anti-Calvinist believers) are described by Kołakowski in his pioneering study of radical Protestants and mystical catholics *Chrétiens sans Église* as Erasmians.[96] Significantly, Kołakowski also identifies within these groupings *chrétiens spinozistes*. The hallmarks of both Protestant and Catholic 'Christians without a church' are the conviction that each believer has the ability to discern the truth of faith for themselves and that they can hold personal communion with God without any human intermediary, be it priest or institution. The patently Erasmian characteristics of these Protestant groups include: a return to original texts, uncorrupted and uncomplicated by later official interpretations; Christian liberty grounded in free will; fearless critique of the institutional church; an inward spirituality and devotion to Christ; an international and cosmopolitan identity; and the supremacy of conscience.

There is ample evidence of Spinoza's intellectual commerce with these communities and their leading thinkers. His debt to the radical Huguenot (possibly also secret Jew) Isaac La Peyrère (1596–1676) and the irrepressible Quaker Samuel Fisher (1605–65) in biblical interpretation is sufficiently documented, though he did not follow them in their messianic eschatological dreams. The 'inner light' of mystical sectarians and Quakers merged with the 'light of reason' reverenced by the Cambridge Platonists in England

---

[96] Leszek Kołakowski, trans. from Polish (1965) by Anna Posner, *Chrétiens sans Église: la conscience religieuse et le lien confessionnel au XVIIe siècle* (Paris: Gallimard, 1987 [1969]).

and by Cartesian rationalists in France and Holland to form, in Spinoza, a contemplative yet fearless philosophical penetration of reality and of Scripture. Spinoza's thinking is 'rooted in a form of radical Protestantism indigenous to his own time' and to the methods of biblical interpretation that flourished among these radical Protestant groups.[97] In mid-life Spinoza moved to Rijnsburg (near Leiden) which was the main base of the Collegiants, a community of anti-clerical, radical Arminians or Remonstrants who had formed their own gatherings in 1620 outside the established structures.[98] Andrew C. Fix's study of the Dutch Collegiants in the Early Enlightenment is hampered by a framework that understands the trend to a more rational theology among dissident Protestants as tantamount to the secularization of their thought and also by a simplistic schema of the displacement of faith by reason in the early Enlightenment, as though faith and reason as sources of truth were intrinsically incompatible in Christianity. It is only mavericks like Tertullian, Luther (in some contexts), Kierkegaard and Barth who have claimed that.[99] Although Spinoza did not fully share their faith, certain Collegiants sheltered and supported him and, after his death in 1677 aged forty-four, they preserved, edited and published his writings. Spinoza was buried in the churchyard of the Nieuwe Kerk of The Hague. That is where I believe he belongs.

Pierre Bayle

In a recent study of French atheism, Devellennes stresses the difficulty and complexity of ascertaining Bayle's personal beliefs, since he never reveals them, though he mentions in correspondence that he

---

[97]Hunter, *Radical Protestantism in Spinoza's Thought*, pp. 5, 182. The same basic point about the radical Protestant milieu of Spinoza's thought is emphasized in Travis L. Frampton, *Spinoza and the Rise of Historical Criticism of the Bible* (London and New York: T&T Clark, 2006), especially pp. 2, 4, 22, 39–40, 73–4.

[98]Martin Mulsow and Jan Rohls (eds), *Socinianism and Arminianism: Antitrinitarians, Calvinists, and Cultural Exchange in Seventeenth-Century Europe* (Leiden: Brill, 2005). See also Lehner, Muller and Roeber (eds), *The Oxford Handbook of Early Modern Theology, 1600–1800*, including Jonathan I. Israel, ch. 37: 'Spinoza and Early Modern Theology'.

[99]Andrew C. Fix, *Prophecy and Reason: The Dutch Collegiants in the Early Enlightenment* (Princeton, NJ: Princeton University Press, 1991).

says his prayers, goes to church, and so on. Devellennes notes that Bayle has been labelled 'an atheist, an agnostic, a secularist, a fideist, a Calvinist, an Arminian, a secret Catholic, a Socinian, a Manichean, a Cartesian, an existentialist positivist, a Judaising Christian, a Judeo-Christian, or even a secret Jew' (p. 35).[100] After balancing the arguments, Devellennes decides that we should take Bayle at his word and profession: he was a rational, critical, analytical thinker – and a Christian, Protestant, Calvinist believer. It is unfortunate, however, that the title of Devellennes's study – *Positive Atheism: Bayle, Meslier, d'Holbach, Diderot* – suggests that Bayle was an atheist just like the other three names, when he was nothing of the sort and is included in Devellennes's book simply because he advocated toleration for 'virtuous' atheists. Bayle was indignant that, because he alleged that atheists existed, when some doubted it, and that they should not be persecuted for their beliefs and were capable of being responsible citizens, he himself was accused of being one. Entailed in that imposed identity was the assumption that he was an iniquitous person. Bayle pointed out that if iniquity and atheism were inseparable and conceptually convertible, and given that the world was full of bad people, the world would also be full of atheists, which was plainly not the case. Bayle's critiques were infused with ethical indignation. Although he was sceptical about almost everything, his scepticism did not run to ethics, which for him was a given. Bayle was a corrosive critic of intolerant churches, of superstition and of fanaticism, whether Calvinist or Catholic (he had experienced both), but he was no atheist. He confessed on his deathbed: 'I die a Christian philosopher, convinced and absorbed by God's goodness and mercy' ('Je meurs en Philosophe Chrétien, persuadé et pénétré des bontés et de la miséricorde de Dieu.')[101]

Bayle himself took Spinoza's doctrine as his criterion of atheism.[102] Spinoza was an atheist in Bayle's reckoning because it

---

[100]Charles Devellennes, *Positive Atheism: Bayle, Meslier, d'Holbach, Diderot* (Edinburgh: Edinburgh University Press, 2021), p. 35. See also Ruth Whelan, 'Bayle, Pierre', in Alan Charles Kors (ed.), *Encyclopedia of the Enlightenment*, 4 vols (Oxford: Oxford University Press, 2003), vol. 1, pp. 121–5.
[101]Elisabeth Labrousse, *Pierre Bayle*, 2 vols (The Hague: Nijhoff, 1963–64), vol. 1, p. 269. See also Jean Delvolvé, *Religion, Critique et Philosophie Positive chez Pierre Bayle* (Paris: Alcan, 1906; repr. New York: Burt Franklin, 1971).
[102]See Kors, *Atheism in France*, pp. 244–62.

seemed to Bayle that he equated God and the world, eliminating transcendence and negating the freedom of the Creator *vis à vis* the creation: *deus sive natura*, 'God or nature'. It is significant that Bayle, who dismissed the common accusations of atheism against many ancients and moderns, should have taken Spinoza's panentheism as his paradigm of atheism. I have already insisted that 'atheism' is a misnomer for Spinoza's doctrine. Presumably it was Bayle's Calvinism that made him allergic to any watering down of divine transcendence, sovereignty and freedom. While, for Bayle, many vagaries of religious opinion could be accommodated within the orbit of Christian belief, the transcendent sovereignty of God was non-negotiable. That is not the case today: in modern theology, ideas of emergence and process, even the image of the world as the body of God, are treated as worthy of discussion and are not dismissed out of hand.[103] A corrective move in the direction of affirming divine immanence has taken place during the past century and a half.

What might explain Bayle's eighteenth-century reputation as the scourge of Christianity? Labrousse offers at least a partial explanation.[104] The Parisian intelligentsia, the *philosophes* and their fellow-travellers, avidly reading Bayle, took him for one of themselves. Complacently regarding Paris as the centre of the universe, unaware that Bayle was not writing under the threat of censorship in the Netherlands, and ignorant of Protestant theology, they assumed that Bayle's radical Protestant stance was dissimulated to avoid censorship and prosecution. They 'studiously looked for mental reservations, innuendos or tricks' in his writings, just as they would have done in any subversive author published in France.[105] They interpreted Bayle's anti-Catholic polemic as an onslaught on the Christian faith itself – they knew no other. They took Bayle's hostile Calvinist rival Pierre Jurieu's blackening of Bayle's character

---

[103]Grace M. Jantzen, *God's World, God's Body* (London: Darton, Longman and Todd, 1984); Sallie McFague, *The Body of God: An Ecological Theology* (London: SCM Press, 1993).
[104]Elisabeth Labrousse, 'Reading Pierre Bayle in Paris', in Alan Charles Kors and Paul J. Korshin (eds), *Anticipations of the Enlightenment in England, France, and Germany* (Philadelphia: University of Pennsylvania Press, 1987), ch. 1.
[105]Ibid., p. 9.

and opinions as the truth, namely that he was a damnable apostate from the faith. To them, Bayle's moderate fideism, the leap of faith, looked like a *reductio ad absurdum* designed to discredit religion. The generally upbeat and utilitarian deism of the *philosophes*, Labrousse concludes, was 'utterly alien' to Bayle.[106] Samuel Johnson, who disdained to read the 'infidelity' of the deist Bolingbroke, had the three volumes of the second, enlarged, edition of Bayle's *Dictionnaire Historique et Critique* in his library and admired the author's learning and critical acumen. Those contemporary interpreters, notably Israel, who hail Bayle as a key figure in the (to them) welcome emergence of an unbelieving, secular civilization, fail to understand the nature of the Christian theological tradition – its protean diversity, intellectual richness and daunting complexity, shot through with passionate controversy, argument and critique regarding the sources, norms, methods and conclusions of theology, but all within the Christian world of thought! Did ever a religion provoke such a quantity and quality of internal differences?[107]

Denis Diderot

Denis Diderot (1713–84) was not a theist, nor even a deist, though he had passed through those stages. He had trained for the Catholic priesthood, so 'his anti-clerical materialism had the sharp edge of apostasy'.[108] He suffered imprisonment, at the instigation of the church authorities, for his outspoken, subversive, opinions in the *Encyclopédie*. Yet Diderot's most telling attack on the Roman Catholic Church, the novel *La Religieuse*, is delicately nuanced and in that respect it bears comparison with Gibbon's selective barbs, though the genres are completely different. *La Religieuse*, probably completed in 1780 and posthumously published in 1792, is the story of an innocent girl who is forced into a convent and tells of the

---

[106]Ibid., 'Reading Pierre Bayle in Paris', p. 15.
[107]For a defence of Bayle's Christian commitments see Erdozain, *The Soul of Doubt*, pp. 124–32.
[108]Maurice Cranston, introduction to Jean-Jacques Rousseau, *The Social Contract*, trans. Cranston (Harmondsworth: Penguin, 1968), pp. 14–15.

sadistic methods employed by the nuns to keep her there against her will. Nevertheless, in this novel the person of Jesus Christ is treated with reverence; the girl's Christian and Catholic faith survives her ordeal; her cries to God in prayer are movingly described; and she is not the only saintly person to have a part in the story. What Diderot depicts so scathingly is not what the King James Bible calls 'pure religion and undefiled' (James 1:27), but twisted, bigoted, fanatical and cruel religiosity that is the antithesis of the character of Christ – the 'abuse of Christianity', to borrow Gibbon's phrase.[109]

Rousseau and religion

Finally, we have to reckon with the very different – indeed unique – intellectual grasp and lived experience of religion by Jean-Jacques Rousseau (1712–78). Rousseau belonged for a time, just as much as Voltaire did, to the fraternity of the *philosophes*, though his role among them was primarily that of internal critic and persistent gadfly. Rousseau was involved in bitter controversies with Voltaire and others over many years on a wide range of topics, including religion and theology. If we are enquiring about the place of religion in the Enlightenment, we have to state quite emphatically that Rousseau was not only one of the most religious men of his time, but also (as McManners put it) 'the inspirational centre of the transformation of the religious consciousness of Western Europe which took place in the eighteenth century'.[110] And as Norman Hampson notes, 'Rousseau's contemporaries saw him as the evangelist of a new kind of emotional deism and many who had lost their belief in Christianity recovered a kind of religious faith as a result of his influence.'[111] In his exhaustive three-volume account of Rousseau and religion Pierre Masson ultimately presents Rousseau as the founder and high priest of a new religion of nature and the

---

[109] Denis Diderot, *The Nun*, trans. Leonard Tancock (Harmondsworth: Penguin, 1974 [1792]).
[110] John McManners, *Death and the Enlightenment* (Oxford: Oxford University Press, 1981), p. 348; cited Aston, *Christianity and Revolutionary Europe*, p. 117.
[111] Norman Hampson, *Will and Circumstance: Montesquieu, Rousseau and the French Revolution* (London: Duckworth, 1983), p. 47.

heart.[112] Although Masson overstates the case, Rousseau's life was indeed dominated by religion. His self-consciousness was permeated by religious feeling and conviction. His whole existence took the form of a religious quest as a journey towards self-understanding, existential freedom, authentic feeling and ultimate happiness, in tune with God and nature.[113] Like Spinoza, Rousseau was a 'God-intoxicated' man, but unlike the earlier Jewish philosopher, for whom God and nature were metaphysically the same thing (*deus sive natura*), Rousseau's apprehension of God was not metaphysical but experiential. For him, nature was filled with a tangible divine presence; it was the theatre of God's glory, and a source of peace, reconciliation and wholeness. One reason why other *philosophes* despised him was that he was too pious. They think, said Hume, that 'he overbounds in religion; and it is indeed remarkable that the philosopher of this age, who has been the most persecuted, is by far the most devout'.[114]

Rousseau the theologian

Rousseau not only lived out his religion and wore it on his sleeve; he also theorized about it, which makes him a theologian of sorts. As a religious thinker, Rousseau's importance is at least fourfold. First,

---

[112] Pierre Maurice Masson, *La religion de J.-J. Rousseau*, 3 vols (Paris: Hachette, 1916).

[113] As brought out in the title of Ronald Grimsley's, *Rousseau and the Religious Quest* (Oxford: Clarendon Press, 1968). Ronald Grimsley, *The Philosophy of Rousseau* (Oxford: Oxford University Press, 1973), has a chapter (6) on Rousseau's religion. I question whether this work is always reliable on the background of the *philosophes*. They are presented (p. 164) as materialists and sceptics who did not espouse even natural religion. But this stance would have been incompatible with the prevailing deism of the French Enlightenment and applies only to a minority, mainly Diderot, d'Holbach, la Mettrie, Condorcet and Helvétius. See also Ronald Grimsley, *Jean-Jacques Rousseau: A Study in Self-Awareness* (Cardiff: University of Wales Press, 1969).

[114] David Hume to Hugh Blair, 11 February 1766, *Letters of David Hume*, ed. J. Y. T. Grieg, 2 vols (Oxford: Oxford University Press, 1932), vol. 2, pp. 11–13; cited Ourida Mostefai and John T. Scott (eds), *Rousseau and L'Infâme: Religion, Toleration, and Fanaticism in the Age of Enlightenment* (Amsterdam: Rodopi, 2009), p. 14, 'Editors' Preface'.

he excoriated the superficiality and artificiality of conventional Catholic Christianity, which he saw as the inveterate tendency to domesticate the divine and to recruit divine authority to serve our convenience and advantage. This is idolatry, the making of God in our own image, which we are all prone to do, Rousseau himself being no exception! Second, he opened up new horizons in theology proper (the doctrine of God), by his rediscovery of the orthodox doctrine of divine immanence, of God's presence in nature, human community and the human heart and mind, whether suffering or delighting, as a counterbalance to an overemphasis on divine transcendence which often incubates hieratic, hierarchical and authoritarian forms of religion. Third, Rousseau provided, in his own person, experience and writings, a bridge between the Enlightenment and Romanticism, reason and feeling (see below). Finally, he become the one eighteenth-century person who most eloquently and also winsomely speaks to modern culture through his deliberately unguarded writings, especially the *Confessions*, where many of us find ourselves mesmerized by the parade of his naked humanity, raw feelings, pathetic paranoia, and desperate longing to be understood. Rousseau is the man of his age whom we know most intimately as a person and are drawn towards in empathy, notwithstanding all his manifest and admitted faults.

Rousseau and the philosophes

Rousseau found the comfortable urban ambience of the *philosophes* distasteful and unhealthy. He castigated Parisian culture (and European culture more widely) as superficial and delusory, to the detriment of nature and truth. He deplored the pampered lifestyle of those who enjoyed a privileged existence and he despised the posturing of those 'who today play the freethinker and the philosopher'.[115] Voltaire, who in fact read and annotated Rousseau's writings assiduously, reciprocated Rousseau's insults by treating

---

[115]Rousseau, *The Social Contract and Discourses*, trans. and intro. G. D. H. Cole (London: Dent; New York: Dutton, 1913), p. 118 (Preface to *A Discourse on the Moral Effects of the Arts and Sciences*).

him and his publications with contempt and ridicule. The dispute came to head with Rousseau's *Letters Written from the Mountain* of 1764.[116] But in fact Rousseau shared the core campaigning values of the *philosophes*: like them he protested against 'blind fanaticism', 'cruel superstition' and 'stupid prejudice'. Barth argues that 'it was precisely as a child of his century that [Rousseau] fought, passionately and radically, against its most typical tendencies', so that he contradicted and transcended his milieu in the very fact that he was its embodiment and fulfilment. He brought it to the point where it could transcend itself and become something else. Its trajectory, as shaped by Rousseau, was fulfilled in Romanticism, of which Goethe was for Barth the supreme embodiment.[117]

The passionate Rousseau was not attracted to Voltaire's rather cerebral brand of deism. Rousseau's own faith, which was definitely unorthodox from any standard Christian perspective, shares the fervent spiritual ethos of Christian devotion, but without its dogma, ritual and hierarchical structure.[118] However, at bottom the essential tenets of Rousseau's religion differed little from those of Voltaire and the other deistic *philosophes* and can summarized in several points. (a) Religious doctrine and the Scriptures should not be simply taken on trust, as was expected and demanded by the church at that time, but should be open to the rational and ethical criticism of reason and conscience (as Spinoza had earlier insisted). (b) The moral law is the supreme criterion of life and truth, including religious truth. The moral law is universally valid; it can be known by all humans and must be followed and obeyed. (c) Moreover, all people are capable of fulfilling the moral

---

[116] J.-J. Rousseau, *Lettres écrites de la montagne*: https://books.google.co.uk/books?id=KX4HAAAAQAAJ&printsec=frontcover#v=onepage&q&f=false. Jean-Jacques Rousseau, *Letter to Beaumont, Letters Written from the Mountain, and Related Writings*, ed. Christopher Kelly and Eve Grace, trans. Christopher Kelly and Judith R. Bush (Chicago, IL: University of Chicago Press, 2012 [2001]); Mark Hulliung, *The Autocritique of Enlightenment: Rousseau and the Philosophes* (Cambridge, MA: Harvard University Press, 1994), p. 239; Graeme Garrard, *Rousseau's Counter-Enlightenment: A Republican Critique of the Philosophes* (New York: State University of New York, 2003).
[117] Karl Barth, *Protestant Theology in the Nineteenth Century*, trans. Brian Cozens and John Bowden, Foreword Colin Gunton (London: SCM Press, 2001), ch. 5, 'Rousseau', at p. 160.
[118] Wade, *Structure and Form of the French Enlightenment*, Vol. 1, pp. 224–5.

law because human nature, which is constant at all times and places, remains fundamentally good. Thus the Christian doctrine of original sin, in its morally repugnant Augustinian form and as taught by the Catholic and Protestant churches, is to be repudiated. For Rousseau, the moral equivalent of the biblical Fall was the descent from the pure state of nature to the corrupting state of society.[119] (Barth defines Rousseau's anthropology as the apotheosis of eighteenth-century humanism.)[120] (d) It follows for Rousseau, as for the other *philosophes*, that there needed to be ideological and social space within the state for views such as his. Toleration of belief is imperative and is to be practised in a spirit of charity. It is not within the remit of the state to invigilate private beliefs. In Rousseau's personal view of Christianity, Catholic and Protestant perspectives blend, though the critical perspective is Protestant, as befits a citizen of Geneva.

Nature and the heart

Rousseau's personal religion was an ellipse with two *foci*: nature and the human heart, within both of which God is to be found and known. Indeed the two are one: the heart is but nature within and the human spirit reaching out to nature. There is no need for supernatural, propositional, revelation, mediated through the church and its teaching, for the only revelation that we need is found in God's natural creation and in the God-given centre of our emotional, moral being. True religion thus resides in the heart: *J'adore au fond de l'âme l'auteur de mon être, j'espère qu'il ne m'a pas créé pour me rendre malheureux, et ne m'imputera pas à la volonté les faiblesses de la nature* (*Lettre sur la Providence*, 1765, to Voltaire).[121] While, for Rousseau, religion resides in the heart, morality lives in the individual conscience, rather than in man-made laws embedded in political legislation, or in that mysterious entity so beloved of conventional eighteenth-century thinkers 'the nature of things'. 'Conscience! Conscience! Divine instinct, immortal voice

---

[119]Barth, *Protestant Theology in the Nineteenth Century*, p. 207.
[120]Ibid., p. 161; cf. pp. 207–8.
[121]Cited Wade, *Structure and Form of the French Enlightenment*, Vol. 1, p. 211.

from heaven; sure guide for a creature ignorant and finite indeed, yet intelligent and free; infallible judge of good and evil, making man like to God!'[122]

Rousseau's civil religion

In *Du Contrat Social*, which he eventually published in 1762 as the mere torso of an abortive *magnum opus* on *Political Institutions*, Rousseau set out his specification for a 'civil religion' which he regarded as an objective necessity for any functioning state, though it was actually not the faith of his own heart. He outlined the rudiments of a civil religion on the twin political-theology premises that (i) no state has ever existed that did not have its foundation in a religion and that (ii) any public religion that did not contribute to the stability and cohesion of society and the state was an abomination.[123] Rousseau distinguished this civil religion from the true, inward and personal religion of the heart, which was his own faith. This latter was, he claimed, 'Christianity', though 'not the Christianity of today, but that of the Gospel, which is altogether different'. 'Under this holy, sublime and true religion', he continued, 'men [sic], as children of the same God, look on all others as brothers, and the society which unites them is not even dissolved by death.' However, this private religion of the gospel, brought by Jesus as the essence of his 'spiritual kingdom on earth', is not sufficient to support civil society and the state because it lacks the vital connection to the law and constitution which is the special *caché* of civil religion. In fact, far from attaching the hearts of citizens to the state, the genuine, original form of Christianity detaches them from it, as it detaches them from all the things of this world and (Rousseau pronounces with regard to his gospel-Christianity) 'I know nothing more contrary to the social spirit.'[124] Rousseau-the-outsider's perception of what is authentic, historical Christianity is

---

[122]On conscience, Jean-Jacques Rousseau, *Profession de foi du Vicaire savoyard*, in *Émile*, trans. Barbara Foxley, intro. P. D. Jimack (London: Dent; New York: Dutton, 1974), pp. 249–54, at p. 254.
[123]Rousseau, *The Social Contract*, trans. and intro. Cranston, pp. 176–87.
[124]Ibid., pp. 182.

that it has no investment in the well-being of society, being solely concerned with the affairs of heaven, the Christian's true homeland. The Christian is indifferent, Rousseau believes, to the prosperity or even the destruction of the state. If the state prospers and flourishes, 'he hardly dares to enjoy the public happiness'; if it languishes and suffers, he blesses the hand of God that has inflicted a deserved judgement.[125] Rousseau also demarcated his concept of civil religion from the sacerdotal, hierarchical and politically ambitious form of religion, which was that of the Catholic Church in France, which Rousseau loathed and feared as much as any other *philosophe* did. Unlike the wiser and more judicious Montesquieu, Rousseau dismissed the potential of historical Christianity to contribute to social stability and moral standards.[126]

In Rousseau's view, then, neither true and sincere gospel-Christianity nor the Roman Catholic Church could minister to the well-being, safety and flourishing of society. Although Rousseau mentions that the Kings of England (he should have said 'British monarchs') have made themselves the Heads of the Church (he should have said 'Supreme Governors', which has been the case since Elizabeth I), he does not consider the merits of the Church of England as an established church with a strong, integrated civic dimension at every level of society, nor does he (here at least) refer to the Protestant churches: Lutheran in North Germany and Scandinavia and Reformed (or 'Calvinistic') in Geneva and other Swiss cantons, the Netherlands and Scotland. Rousseau praised the distinctive polity of his home city of Geneva and flattered its citizens in the 'Dedication' to his *Discourse on the Origins of Inequality* (1755) and again in a passage in *Du Contrat Social* (1762). But he did so in vain, for Geneva burned *Du Contrat Social* and *Émile* as subversive literature and issued a warrant for his arrest. Although theoretically Geneva was a republic, in practice it was, as Cranston puts it, 'a patrician gerontocracy, dominated by a few families'.[127]

---

[125]Ibid., p. 183.
[126]Hampson, *Will and Circumstance*, p. 23.
[127]Rousseau, *The Social Contract and Discourses*, trans. and intro. Cole, pp. 143–229: *A Discourse on a Subject Proposed by the Academy of Dijon: What Is the Origin of Inequality among Men, and Is It Authorized by Natural Law?*, 'Dedication', pp. 144–53. Cranston, intro. Rousseau, *The Social Contract*, p. 23.

Rousseau's profession of faith

In his *Profession de foi du Vicaire savoyard*, which Rousseau owned as his personal profession of religious faith, he takes his cue initially from Descartes's famous deduction from mental processes (*cogito ergo sum*) in Descartes's *Discours de la méthode*. 'I was in that state of doubt and uncertainty which Descartes considers essential to the search for truth.'[128] But Rousseau turns this exercise into a uniquely personal and philosophically personalist form. He follows Descartes no further than the starting point; the ethos of Descartes's method is repugnant to him. He repudiates 'all general and abstract ideas' and 'the jargon of metaphysics' which has never led to truth and involves all sorts of absurdities.[129] It is not logical deduction that appeals to him, but direct intuition of his inner being. He resolves to consult his heart and the heart's awareness of being in the world (immediate sensation): *je sens donc je suis*.[130] He has full assurance of the existence of a good and all-powerful God who has brought the world into being and now sustains and rules all things (the deistic belief in providence again). God has created human beings for goodness, freedom and happiness: 'O God of my soul ... thou hast created me in thine own image, that I may be free and good and happy like my Maker!'[131] The soul survives death (immortality again), but Rousseau has abandoned the detailed tripartite geography of medieval Christian eschatology, which is probably most familiar to us in Dante's *Divina Commedia* or Newman's *The Dream of Gerontius*.[132]

---

[128]Rousseau, *Profession de foi du Vicaire savoyard*, part IV, pp. 228–58, at p. 229. Id., *Lettres écrites de la montagne*; avec une préface de Henri Guillemin (Neuchâtel: Ides et Calendes, 1962).
[129]Rousseau, *Profession de foi du Vicaire savoyard*, p. 236.
[130]Ibid., pp. 232, 253: 'To exist is to feel.'
[131]Ibid., p. 244. In his *Lettres de la montaigne* Rousseau states that, although the basic human passion is *amour de soi*, self-love, human beings are naturally good, lovers of justice and order.
[132]Rousseau, *Profession de foi du Vicaire savoyard*, p. 246. J. H. Newman, *The Dream of Gerontius* (London: Bagster, 1908 [1865]).

Rousseau's deity remains the hidden God whom he cannot describe any further. 'I see God everywhere in his world; I feel him within myself; I behold him all around me', but 'he' eludes my understanding. However, Rousseau adds, 'the less I understand, the more I adore'.[133] Rousseau shows an affinity with the apophatic dimension of Christian theology which is profoundly mindful of all that we cannot say of God's nature and purposes. But Rousseau's apophaticism is devoid of Christianity's counter-balancing aspect – divine revelation through the history of ancient Israel, the message of the prophets, the person and work of Christ, the witness of the apostles and the ongoing presence and liturgical worship of the church.[134]

Rousseau's *Profession de foi du Vicaire savoyard*, and indeed *Émile* as a whole, was censured by the Parlement of Paris and by the Archbishop of Paris, Christophe de Beaumont. Among many scurrilous accusations, the archbishop charged Rousseau with atheism (which shows once again how loosely and carelessly that term was applied at the time). In his response, the *Letter to Beaumont*, Rousseau is respectful but merciless in exposing the archbishop's arguments as irrational, incredible and unjustified, though there is no denying that Rousseau engages in special pleading when he professes the genuineness of his Christian faith. The first part of *Letters Written from the Mountain* and the cleverly constructed *Dialogues* continue the vein of self-justification and vindication in the face of threats of persecution and the burning of his books, with the *Dialogues* particularly wrestling with the apparently insuperable problem of the reading public misunderstanding – that is, misreading – him. But perhaps they understood him all too well.[135]

---

[133]Rousseau, *Profession de foi du Vicaire savoyard*, pp. 239, 249.
[134]Geneviève Di Rosa, *Rousseau et la Bible: Pensee du religieux d'un philosophe des lumieres* (Leiden: Brill Rodopi, 2016).
[135]Rousseau, *Letter to Beaumont, Letters Written from the Mountain, and Related Writings*. Jean-Jacques Rousseau, *Rousseau, Judge of Jean-Jacques, Dialogues*, ed. Roger D. Masters and Christopher Kelly; trans. Judith R. Bush, Christopher Kelly, and Roger D. Masters (Hanover, NH: Published for Dartmouth College by University Press of New England, 1990).

Rousseau and Romanticism

It is *Émile* above all in Rousseau's *oeuvre* that has prompted speculation about Rousseau's possible influence on William Wordsworth, who after all, was drawn by admiration of the early stages of the Revolution to make his home in France for a few years as a young man and was therefore fluent in French. B. D. Sewall argued that 'The concept of an education in a natural setting, the belief in the innate goodness of man and nature, the antipathy felt towards a cosmopolitan existence, a great respect for a natural, personal religion, the importance of the senses and the conscience as a means of revealing the world's goodness, and the ability of man to choose good or evil', which we find in both Rousseau and Wordsworth, suggest at least an influence and perhaps 'a close intellectual relationship'.[136] Rousseau has often been hailed as a proto-Romantic and so he was, though it is important to insist that the connection with Romanticism does not in itself disqualify him as a member of the French Enlightenment. We are not working with a dichotomous, black-and-white, separation of 'Enlightenment reason' and 'Romantic feeling'. The Enlightenment and Romanticism were not separate, exclusively successive ideological and cultural epochs, but overlapped, each containing elements of the other. The all-too-common stereotyping and opposing of cultural paradigms, such as in 'the Enlightenment versus Romanticism' gambit, subverts genuine understanding and inhibits the historical empathy that is required for interpretation.

Rousseau's 'Romanticism' comes out strongly in the last work that he wrote, the posthumously published *Reveries of the Solitary Walker*. Here Rousseau shows his spiritual affinity with the natural world and the vitality of nature, indwelling it through what John Keats called 'negative capability', going out of oneself and entering

---

[136] B. D. Sewall, 'The Similarity between Rousseau's *Émile* and the early poetry of Wordsworth', *SVEC* CVI (1973), pp. 157–74 at p. 174. For the French connection see also Jonathan Bate, *Radical Wordsworth: The Poet who Changed the World* (New Haven, CT: Yale University Press, 2020); Russell Goulbourne and David Higgins (eds), *Jean-Jacques Rousseau and British Romanticism: Gender and Selfhood, Politics and Nation* (London and New York: Bloomsbury, 2017).

into the inner being and individuality of another person or living creature or aspect of reality.[137] Rousseau's account of his experiences is pointing towards a panentheistic religion of nature. He revels in the sheer sense of being alive. Barth captures it: 'A whole world revealed itself to him when he gazed into himself ... his own unique world, full of unique forms of truth and beauty.'[138] As he mourns the failing of his mental powers, it is pure sensation, enveloped by nature, that now alone brings him joy.[139] These sentiments, together with his references in this work and in *Confessions* to experiences of ecstasy, show Rousseau's affinity with the Romantic sensibility. The new European consciousness of which Rousseau was both source and symptom was assimilated by the churches and religious movements, including German Pietism, Anglican Tractarianism (later and indirectly) and the Catholic Church which sponsored a quieter, more reflective and more personal devotion by the end of the century, a contrast and reaction to its previous grandiose Baroque extravagances.[140] His boast in the *Confessions* that he had composed his novel *Julie: ou La Nouvelle Heloise* (1761) 'in a state of burning ecstasy' would have incurred the ridicule and contempt of more sober Enlightenment spirits. One can only imagine Johnson's scorn.[141] In any case, Johnson would have had both Rousseau and Voltaire transported to the colonies. It was 'difficult to settle the proportion of iniquity between them'. Like many subsequent observers, Johnson lumped the two together, though in reality they became not only rivals but bitter enemies. 'Infidels' was Johnson's name for the *philosophes*. Unlike Boswell

---

[137]John Keats, *Letters of John Keats*, ed. Frederick Page (London: Oxford University Press, 1954), p. 53; cf. p. 172.
[138]Barth, *Protestant Theology in the Nineteenth Century*, p. 212.
[139]Rousseau, *Reveries of the Solitary Walker*, trans. Peter France (Harmondsworth: Penguin, 1979 [1782]), pp. 89, 114–15.
[140]Aston, *Art and Religion in Eighteenth-Century Europe*, p. 47.
[141]The cross-currents in the lives and writings of Johnson, Rousseau, Voltaire and Diderot are portrayed discursively and with impressively various learning in Temmer, *Samuel Johnson and Three Infidels*. For Rousseau's interaction with England, tracked book by book, especially the reception of his *Profession de foi du Vicaire savoyard*, see Henri Roddier, *J.-J. Rousseau en Angleterre au XVIIIe Siècle: L'oevre et l'homme* (Paris: Boivin, 1950); and for Rousseau's subsequent impact in England see Jacques Voisine, *J.-J. Rousseau en Angleterre à l' Époque Romantique: Les Écrits autobiographiques et la Légende* (Paris: Didier, 1956).

the scalp-hunter, name-dropper and hero-worshipper, Johnson would not go near them, neither in London nor in Paris.[142]

Johnson and Burke, grounded as they both were in the long traditions of Christian humanism, natural law and right reason, were two of the fiercest critics in England of Rousseau and his cult. Burke early detected the consuming narcissism of Rousseau's personality, the indulgence in pure sensibility, stripped of obligation to our founders and of responsibility to posterity. He found it not winsome and intoxicating, as many did, but repugnant and toxic. Burke foresaw that if the Rousseauan cult of naked sensibility were to be widely adopted, as it was by the French Revolutionaries (the first statue to be erected by the National Assembly was of Rousseau), it would bring in its train the downfall, not only of the French monarchy but also of all the embedded institutions of the state, the church and civil society, and would lead to the Terror and the (Napoleonic) aggression.[143] McDonald argues that it was not Rousseau's political doctrines but his existential vision of the moral renovation of the individual and society that inspired the revolutionaries. As Hampson notes, 'His intentions were moral, and politics was merely the vehicle for social regeneration.'[144] Rousseau's platform or programme of emotional renewal and moral renovation vindicates Johnson's and Burke's attacks. The vision was spurious. Rousseau's narcissistic dreams and paranoid delusions made him a hero and a martyr. The self-created myth of Rousseau inspired a sentimental personality cult. The aura of Rousseau's name was invoked to justify a raft of measures that could not be justified by Rousseau's teaching.[145] The cult of Rousseau as well as selected doctrines infiltrated America also. The age of the founding fathers of the American constitution was 'the age of Enlightenment with a slight time lag. Franklin and Jefferson were

---

[142]Rousseau, *Reveries of the Solitary Walker*, p. 107; id., *Confessions*, trans. and intro. J. M. Cohen (Harmondsworth: Penguin, 1953 [1781]), p. 506.
[143]Peter J. Stanlis, *Edmund Burke: The Enlightenment and Revolution* (London and New York: Routledge, 2017 [1991]), ch. 5: 'Burke and the Sensibility of Rousseau'.
[144]Hampson, *Will and Circumstance*, p. 51.
[145]Joan McDonald, *Rousseau and the French Revolution 1762–1791* (London: The Athlone Press, 1965).

transatlantic *philosophes*.'[146] But Rousseau's influence encountered fierce resistance in America too. In particular the fact – spitefully revealed by Voltaire – that Rousseau had abandoned his offspring to an orphanage one by one after their birth discredited his claimed moral authority. As one American writer put it: 'The exposure [*sic*] of his children, by whatever sophistry it may be excused, is an indelible blot on his humanity; and invalidates all his pretensions to philanthropy.'[147]

David Hume

David Hume (1711–76) was by default a member of the Church of Scotland, which wished to disown him, twice attempting (unsuccessfully) to excommunicate him. Hume is the most brilliant British philosopher of any age. His *History of Great Britain* has the unique distinction of being the work of an eminent philosopher. As Forbes says, 'No other philosopher of Hume's stature has written a large narrative history which is a classic of historical literature.'[148] I cannot attempt here – and I make no pretence to do so – to offer a comprehensive account or assessment of the thought of David Hume or the cogency of his philosophical arguments; this is a

---

[146]Paul Merrill Spurlin, *Rousseau in America 1760–1809* (Alabama: University of Alabama Press, 1967), p. 29.
[147]Robert Fellowes, *A Picture of Christian Philosophy* (1st edn 1799), cited Spurlin, *Rousseau in America*, p. 139, n28.
[148]David Hume, *The History of Great Britain: The Reigns of James I and Charles I*, ed. and intro. Duncan Forbes (Harmondsworth: Penguin, 1970 [1754]), p. 13 (Forbes). For Hume and religious belief see: J. C. A. Gaskin, *Hume's Philosophy of Religion* (London: Macmillan, 1978), pp. 149–58; also Gaskin 'Hume on Religion', in David Fate Norton (ed.), *The Cambridge Companion to Hume* (Cambridge: Cambridge University Press, 1993); Keith E. Yandell, 'Hume on Religious Belief', in Donald W. Livingston and James T. King (eds), *Hume: A Re-evaluation* (New York: Fordham University Press, 1976); James A. Harris, *Hume: An Intellectual Biography* (Cambridge: Cambridge University Press, 2015); Paul Russell (ed.), *The Oxford Handbook of Hume* (Oxford: Oxford University Press, 2016), pts V and VI; David Fergusson, 'Hume amongst the Theologians', in David Fergusson and Mark Elliott (eds), *The History of Scottish Theology, Volume II: From the Early Enlightenment to the Late Victorian Era* (Oxford: Oxford University Press, 2019), ch. 21.

highly specialized matter to which whole scholarly careers have been devoted. I confine my discussion to the strict parameters of this study – the interface between theology and the Enlightenment – and I can do that by asking the single question, 'Where should Hume, one of the two most lethal and perhaps unanswerable British critics of Christianity in the eighteenth century – the other being Gibbon, of course – be located on the sliding scale with which we are operating: Christian-theist-deist-atheist?'[149]

Hume is the rare example of a philosopher of religion who was subjectively untouched by the power of religion and who was not able or perhaps not willing to inhabit religion empathetically. Gaskin aptly calls this Hume's 'critical aloofness' and points to his 'unusual degree of externality to religion'.[150] Boswell reported, marvelling, to Dr Johnson that Hume, on his deathbed, had faced mortality and what might lie beyond, in the presence of the eminent Presbyterian minister and historian William Robertson, with perfect calm, equanimity and even cheerfulness. Johnson, who had feared death all his life, met this account with incredulity: Hume, he pronounced, was either a liar or a madman.[151] Johnson did not regard Hume as a deist because he had heard it reported on good authority that Hume had admitted that 'he had never read the New Testament with attention'; therefore, Johnson deduced, he could not have rationally rejected it.[152] Nevertheless, for all that, Hume stands at the extreme end of the eighteenth-century spectrum of religious or non-religious opinion. However, it is important to remember that Hume not only demolished aspects of the theology of the day, but also torpedoed the much vaunted authority of reason (which he believed would always be trumped by passion) and therefore of philosophy itself. Thus Hume emerged as the nemesis of deism and Enlightenment intellectual pretensions generally, as well as of Christian claims.[153]

---

[149]Stephen Paul Foster, *Melancholy Duty: The Hume-Gibbon Attack on Christianity* (Dordrecht: Kluwer, 2010). The discussion that follows is complemented by *ISOA*, pp. 254–63.
[150]Gaskin, *Hume's Philosophy of Religion*, p. 173.
[151]Boswell, *Life of Johnson*, pp. 426, 838–9.
[152]Ibid., pp. 357, 838.
[153]David Hume, *A Dissertation on the Passions; The Natural History of Religion*, ed. Tom L. Beauchamp (Oxford: Clarendon Press, 2007). Robert Ginsberg, 'David Hume versus the Enlightenment', *SVEC* 88 (1972), pp. 599–650.

In his ethics Hume (like Bayle) is not reductionist. He does not follow Locke's *tabula rasa* or malleability doctrine, believing instead that we have certain innate moral propensities. He resists the reduction of morals to the utilitarian pleasure/pain calculus, holding that we have a 'natural instinct' to desire the punishment of our enemies for the wrong they commit and to desire the happiness of our friends as their reward for good deeds. If Hume undermined the Christian apologetic argument from miracle, which was standard at the time, he also discredited deism, which likewise had little or no place for miracles. 'While Newton seemed to draw off the veil from some of the mysteries of nature [Hume argued], he showed at the same time the imperfections of the mechanical philosophy; and thereby restored her ultimate secrets to that obscurity in which they ever did and ever will remain.'[154] So in a sense Joseph Butler, the greatest apologist, and David Hume, the greatest sceptic, were standing side by side on the point of mystery too. Hume and Butler had corresponded, the former deferring to the latter's advice at one time. We should not imagine eighteenth-century thinkers as drawn up in opposing battle-lines; there was much interaction and dialogue, though violent language was standard among many.

Chief of sceptics though he was, Hume was no atheist. Predictably, Hume was accused of being an atheist, which was (like 'Socinian') a routine insult thrown at anyone who posed a threat to the prevailing ideology. Archbishops Laud and Tillotson – two extremes – together with numerous other bishops and divines, were accused of 'Socinianism' in their time.[155] But Hume did not profess atheism – he did not deny the existence of God – because he could not quite shake off the persuasive power of the theistic argument from design, particularly from the apparent order that regulated the world.[156] Hume acknowledged the reasonableness of belief in a creator-designer of the world and did not forbear to use the word 'God' of this being. Nevertheless, this minimalist belief had no

---

[154]Cited from Hume by Ward, *Christianity under the Ancien Régime*, p. 165.
[155]Trevor-Roper, *Religion, the Reformation and Social Change*, p. 217.
[156]David Berman, *Atheism from Hobbes to Russell* (London: Routledge, 1988), pp. 101–5, tendentiously places his discussion of whether Hume doubted the existence of atheists under the heading 'Hume's atheism'. If Hume said that he knew of no atheists, he could hardly have been one himself.

religious implications for him, no consequences for faith, worship, prayer or impending death.[157]

Hume's characteristic comment that he was battling against 'Stupidity, Christianity and Ignorance' was very far from typical of British thinkers of the Enlightenment era.[158] Hume's reductionist *The Natural History of Religion* was, according to Cassirer – only slightly exaggerating – 'an isolated phenomenon in the intellectual history of the Enlightenment'.[159] The residual value, for Hume, of moderate religion regulated by the civil authority, was in inculcating and supporting moral probity, even though religion notoriously did not live up to its own precepts and typically undermined them. Hume anatomized the religious extremes of superstition and enthusiasm, the former generated by fear and anxiety, leading to the attempted propitiation of the deity; the latter arising from presumption, overconfidence and the delusion of receiving direct personal inspiration, without the mediation of priests, sacraments and church teaching.[160] In his *History*, Hume pilloried the Reformers for – having thankfully escaped from Romish superstition – plunging into fanaticism. He removed these comments in the 1759 edition. Hume originally wrote that the Reformers were 'universally inflamed with the highest ENTHUSIASM' [sic]. The Reformation was disfigured by 'the rage of dispute', combined with 'the contempt of ceremonies, and of all the external pomp and spendor [sic] of worship', combined with the spirit of 'inflexible trepidity' that would brave suffering and death, all of which ensured that, while the Protestants preached a gospel of peace, they 'carried the tumults of war, thro [sic] every part of Christendom'.[161] The passage suggests that Hume was repelled, not only by *odium theologicum*, but also by the miserable plainness and austerity of worship in the post-Reformation Kirk. Hume returns to the fray in a second passage which was also later removed. In it

---

[157]Gaskin, *Hume's Philosophy of Religion*, pp. 139–40. David Hume, *Dialogues Concerning Natural Religion*, ed. Martin Bell (Harmondsworth: Penguin, 1990 [1779]).
[158]Gay, *The Enlightenment: An Interpretation*, Vol. 1, *The Rise of Modern Paganism*, p. 20.
[159]Cassirer, *The Philosophy of the Enlightenment*, p. 182.
[160]David Hume, *Essays Moral, Political and Literary* (London: Grant Richards, 1903), Essay X: 'Of Superstition and Enthusiasm'.
[161]Hume, *The History of Great Britain*, p. 71.

he placarded the Inquisition of the Catholic Church as 'the utmost instance of human depravity' and a standing reminder of 'to what a pitch of iniquity and cruelty' humans can rise when their actions are 'covered with the sacred mantle of religion' which in its superstitious form inculcates 'blind submission ... the absolute resignation of all private judgement, reason and inquiry'.[162]

'Enthusiasm'

Jonathan Swift's *A Tale of a Tub* is often lauded as the most brilliant and devastating attack ever made on religious fanaticism or, in the language of the day, 'enthusiasm'.[163] This tale of a 'tub' (or pulpit) was several years in the making and began to circulate privately in 1697, eventually being published anonymously in 1704, with a fifth, expanded, edition in 1710 which is the one referenced here. It has 38 pages of madcap preliminary matter before the *Tale* begins. But the *Tale* itself is embedded in digressionary material and much of the actual *Tale* takes the form of digressions. In this fifth edition, Swift added explanatory footnotes, which are partly helpful in interpreting this bewildering satire, but at the same time they are fictionally attributed to various of his critics, especially William Wotton (in fact the whole work is laid at his door on the title page). The whole thing is a 'send-up', including a send-up of itself. Laurence Sterne's *Tristram Shandy* clearly had a predecessor in genre and a model half a century earlier (not that Sterne needed one). Every ingredient of the *Tale* is attended by comments that are designed to throw the reader off the scent. But scent there is, for those who manage to scramble through the dense thickets of satire, wit, slander, obscurity, obscenity, scatology and profanity. So massive is this barrage, this brain-dump from Swift's extraordinary mind and imagination, that the *Tale* was taken by many (including Queen Anne) to be an scandalous attack on Christianity, and this impression prevailed until the nineteenth century (though the

---

[162]Ibid., p. 98.
[163]Jonathan Swift, *A Tale of a Tub and Other Satires* (London: Dent; New York: Dutton, 1909).

same constituency of interpreters has – contradictorily – construed this brilliant work as a bid for preferment in the church, though Swift only needed a secure 'living' or benefice). The same potent combination of obscure learning, intellectual agility, polemical mastery and severe epistemological scepticism has allowed Pierre Charron and, even more so, Pierre Bayle to be long regarded as subverters of the Christian faith and, as we have seen, that perverse misconstrual of the evidence is advocated even today.

In fact, Swift's target is not only enthusiasm, but also superstition. The two are paired together, as satanic delusions, in Anglican polemic from this point on, if not before. The 'tale' revolves loosely around a parable of three sons or brothers: Peter (standing for the Roman Church, mired in superstition, including mercenary indulgences and the trade in relics with its ludicrous aspects); Martin (representing the reformed Church of England; it is interesting that Swift identifies the Church of England so explicitly with the Lutheran Reformation); and Jack (standing for dissenters from the established reformed churches in England and continental Europe, thus including not only Baptists, but Anabaptists; Methodism would not appear for a generation). But who is Jack? The 'third man' may be John ('Jack') Calvin, just as a footnote – possibly a spoof – indicates. Thus blinkered biblicism and predestination are two of the marks of Calvin's derogation of true religion in the *Tale*, though it is both historically and theologically completely inappropriate to link Calvin with Anabaptism or even Congregationalism (Independency), though the Presbyterian cap just about fits. But Jack of Leyden (i.e. John of Leiden, 1509–36) is also mentioned and his is a much more toxic name than Calvin's because he turned the city of Münster in Westphalia into an Anabaptist, millennialist, theocracy, abolishing property, money and monogamy, and proclaiming himself King of the New Jerusalem. The city was shortly recaptured by the prince-bishop; John and his associates were captured, tortured and executed; their remains hung in cages from the church steeple for the next half-century. If the connection is correct, Swift has gone for the kill as far as radical, subversive Protestantism is concerned. Indeed, his satire is consistently and comically lethal. Of those who reject the good and the true and turn to their opposites, he comments: '[I] have often observed with singular pleasure, that a fly driven from a honey-pot will immediately, with very good appetite, alight and finish his meal on an excrement.'[164]

While Hume – not entirely tactfully – pushed the first outburst of religious fanaticism ('enthusiasm') back to the Reformation, it was probably the frightening upsurge of untrammelled private interpretation of Scripture, and the self-styled 'prophetic' words and violent deeds that were its fruits during the mid-seventeenth-century Interregnum that were in the forefront of Swift's satire and also of Locke's attack on 'enthusiasm' a generation after the event. 'Enthusiasm', Locke wrote in the *Essay Concerning Human Understanding* (1689), is 'founded neither on reason nor divine revelation, but rises from the conceits of a warmed or overweening brain'.[165] Locke had been tutor to Anthony Ashley Cooper, who became the Third Earl of Shaftesbury (1671–1713) and one of the most influential minds of his age. Shaftesbury opened up fresh vistas of aesthetics, ethics, sentiment, theories of manners and polite society, together with the rational critique of religion, for the European Enlightenment. His *Letter Concerning Enthusiasm* (first published in 1708 and later incorporated into successive editions of his *Characteristicks of Men, Manners, Opinions, Times*, from 1711) is a sardonic, supercilious exposition of deistic religion, obliquely mocking debased theologies, belief in miracles, gullible bishops and – most concretely and topically – the charismatic convulsions of the Huguenot congregation in London, exiles since Louis XIV's Revocation of the Edict of Nantes a mere twenty years or so before Shaftesbury began to write his piece. The coupling of enthusiasm and superstition, as two sides of the same coin, that we find in Swift and later in Hume and Adam Smith, is evident here. Lord Shaftesbury's elevated, refined intellect looks down with distaste, disgust and perhaps fear at the irrational antics of both sorts of delusion. His antidote to both of them is a cultured, virtuous and rational equilibrium of mind that he whimsically calls 'Good Humour'.[166]

---

[164]Ibid., p. 131. On John of Leiden and the violent side of Anabaptism see Norman Cohn, *The Pursuit of the Millennium* (New York: Oxford University Press, 1970 [1957]).
[165]John Locke, *An Essay Concerning Human Understanding*, 2 vols (London: Dent; New York: Dutton, 1961), vol. 1, p. 290 (IV, xix, 6–7).
[166]Shaftesbury, *Letter Concerning Enthusiasm*: https://oll.libertyfund.org/title/shaftesbury-characteristicks-of-men-manners-opinions-times-3-vols (accessed 10 February 2022); Shaftesbury, *Characteristics of Men, Manners, Opinions, Times*, ed. Lawrence E. Klein (Cambridge: Cambridge University Press, 1999).

In his *Dictionary of the English Language* (1755), Johnson defined 'enthusiasm' as 'A vain belief of private revelation; a vain confidence of divine favour or communication' and cited Locke in support. 'Superstition' he defined both as 'Unnecessary fear or scruples in religion; observance of unnecessary and uncommanded rites or practices; religion without morality' (the first elements may be regretted or pitied, but the third element is damning) and as 'False religion ... false worship' (that is idolatry, which is equally damning).[167] In the same year (1655), Meric Casaubon (1599–1671) published his *Treatise Concerning Enthusiasme*, in which he explored, in the spirit of the incipient Enlightenment, the possible natural causes of 'enthusiastic' phenomena. While, in various writings, Casaubon defended the existence of witches and the reality of demonic visitations, he also explored the gradations of credulity and incredulity, seeking a basis for sound belief regarding the paranormal.[168]

Locke, Shaftesbury, Johnson and Hume were at one with Bishop Butler, as we recall from Butler's famous meeting with John Wesley in 1739 when the bishop declared, 'Sir, the pretending to extraordinary revelations and gifts of the Holy Ghost is a horrid thing, a very horrid thing.'[169] Butler was thinking of George Whitefield who had unguardedly said that God had promised to fulfil greater things in him. This kind of narcissistic delusion (colloquially, 'ego-trip'; in analytic psychology, 'psychic inflation') is a staple of charismatic Evangelical jargon today. Stolid conservatives like Johnson, arch-sceptics like Hume, churchmen like Butler and French *savants* like the encyclopaedists were agreed in their fear and detestation of enthusiasm. The article 'Fanaticism' by Alexandre Deleyre (1726–97) in the *Encyclopédie* (1756) begins: 'Fanaticism is zeal

---

[167] https://johnsonsdictionaryonline.com [viewed 16/1/2022].
[168] Meric Casaubon, *A Treatise Concerning Enthusiasme, as It Is an Effect of Nature, but Is Mistaken by Many for Either Divine Inspiration, or Diabolical Possession* (Gainesville, FL: Scholars' Facsimiles & Reprints, 1970 [1655; 2nd edn, 1656]); https://quod.lib.umich.edu/cgi/t/text/text-idx?c=eebo;idno=A35565.0001.001 (accessed 11 February 2022); ODNB, 'Casaubon, (Florence Estienne) Meric'. Lawrence E. Klein and Anthony J. La Vopa (eds), *Enthusiasm and Enlightenment in Europe, 1650–1850* (San Marino, CA: University of California Press, 1998).
[169] Joseph Butler, *Works*, ed. W. E. Gladstone, 2 vols (Oxford: Clarendon Press, 1896), vol. 2, pp. 434–7; Henry Rack, *Reasonable Enthusiast: John Wesley and the Rise of Methodism* (London: Epworth Press, 1989), p. 209; *ISOA*, pp. 316–18.

of the most blind and fervent sort. It is caused by superstition, and makes people commit ridiculous, unjust and cruel acts, not only without shame or remorse but also with a kind of delight and even a feeling of solace. Fanaticism, therefore, is simply superstition in action.'[170] Diderot pronounced that 'superstition is more harmful to God than atheism' ('la superstition est plus injurieuse à Dieu que l'athéisme').[171] Enthusiasm was the universal anathema of the era that followed the religious wars. It is distressingly ironic that such pretensions and delusions that Enlightenment Anglicans and Dissenters deplored are now a staple ingredient of conservative Evangelical piety, where the Holy Spirit is thought to speak directly to the individual, by-passing reason, learning and good counsel, and prompting decisions, directing actions and providing trivial wants for the individual believer at their instant request. I do not know of anyone in a position of authority in the church who is challenging it.

---

[170]Caroline Warman (ed. and trans.), *Tolerance: The Beacon of the Enlightenment* (Open Book Publishers, 2016), p. 39.
[171]Denis Diderot, *Pensées philosophiques*, XII, in id., *Pensées Philosophiques/ Lettre Sur Les Aveugles/Supplément Au Voyage de Bougainville* (Paris: Garnier-Flammarion, 1972 [1746]), p. 36.

5

The Anglican Enlightenment

'The Anglican Enlightenment', as a description of the unique phenomenon of the theological culture of the Church of England in the late seventeenth and the eighteenth centuries, is already current. I have already mentioned B. W. Young's pioneering retrievals of the Anglican Enlightenment. I have also used the expression in my earlier discussion of the impact of the Enlightenment on Anglican theology and church life.[1] Bulman unapologetically entitled his 2015 intellectual biography of Lancelot Addison, Dean of Lichfield and father of Joseph Addison the essayist, moralist and Christian apologist, *Anglican Enlightenment*.[2] A robust case for a real Enlightenment in England and of England as the matrix of Enlightenment ideas and values throughout Europe was made by Porter in 2000.[3] Porter's account, though weak on theology, embraces philosophy, literary culture, morals and social mores. He presents a pervasive, all-embracing English Enlightenment. It is not surprising that some historians have pointed out that an 'Anglican

---

[1] B. W. Young, *Religion and Enlightenment in Eighteenth-Century England: Theological Debate from Locke to Burke* (Oxford: Clarendon Press, 1998); ISOA, chs 7–9.
[2] William J. Bulman, *Anglican Enlightenment: Orientalism, Religion and Politics in England and Its Empire, 1648–1715* (Cambridge: Cambridge University Press, 2015). On Joseph Addison see *ISOA*, pp. 266–8.
[3] Roy Porter, *Enlightenment: Britain and the Creation of the Modern World* (London: Penguin, 2001; published in the USA as *The Creation of the Modern Mind: The Untold Story of the British Enlightenment* (New York: W. W. Norton and Company, 2000). Porter's argument is in principle in line with the earlier work of Margaret Jacob, *The Radical Enlightenment: Pantheists, Freemasons and Republicans* (London: Allen and Unwin, 1981), though without her emphasis on the cultural and intellectual margins.

Enlightenment' is an elusive entity, resisting easy detection, while other scholars have questioned whether there ever was an English Enlightenment. This historiographical puzzle lies at the heart of this chapter.

I will argue the case for an 'integrated' English Enlightenment from several angles. First, I will propose a working definition of the Enlightenment and this will be followed, second, by a short historiographical section, bringing out the reconstructed historical paradigm of the English – especially Anglican – Enlightenment. Third, I will evaluate the rise of English deism and its relationship to the received forms of Christian belief, including an assessment of the seminal deistic thought of Lord Herbert of Cherbury. This will lead me, fourth, into a brief discussion of the status of eighteenth-century atheism, real and supposed. Finally, I will present evidence from the imaginative literature of the period, namely the first English novels, for the influence and presence of Enlightenment modes of thought, showing that these thought-forms and their main protagonists were familiar to the early English novelists, were generally treated in a relaxed and unthreatened manner, and are, so to speak, taken for granted and integrated with social and intellectual norms. From these various angles, I will aim to shed some light on the intriguing nature of the Anglican Enlightenment.

An integrated Anglican Enlightenment

The problem of pinpointing the Enlightenment in England and particularly in the Church of England stems from the fact that it was more readily integrated into national cultural and religious life than elsewhere in Europe. Because the Anglican Enlightenment is pervasive, it is also elusive. Enlightenment modes of thought were absorbed by the intelligentsia of the 'establishment' – the church, the two universities and the dissenting academies. They were disseminated through novels, sermons and journalism, as well as through sophisticated philosophical and theological works. Munck's warning not to impose a binary framework on eighteenth-century culture, by means of a clear division into 'the enlightened' and 'the unenlightened', but to allow for half-digested Enlightenment paradigms among a large constituency of the 'half-enlightened', the selectively enlightened and those on the way to some kind of enlightenment, may apply particularly in England where the Enlightenment was not, on the whole, aggressive and adversarial.[4] In England the Enlightenment frame of mind came to be regarded as unexceptional, the normal way of understanding the world.

John Robertson has highlighted the paradox of an English Enlightenment that was both integral and elusive. On the one hand, he writes, the central Enlightenment commitments, 'the development of the sciences of man and of political economy, the historical investigation of the progress of society, and the critical application of ideas for human betterment to the existing social and political order ... were not at the forefront of English intellectual life between 1740 and 1780.' While each of these fields of enquiry had its devotees, 'they were not in England, as they were in France, Germany, Italy, and Scotland, the focus of concerted, systematic attention among the country's leading minds'. Robertson endorses Porter's view that in England the signals of modernity pre-empted the Enlightenment. He suggests that the most salient English contribution to the Enlightenment was made by 'the radical and unitarian [sic] minority who doubted whether liberty and the gains of commerce were quite what they seemed'. This vocal minority included Richard Price, Joseph Priestley, Jeremy Bentham, Mary Wollstonecraft and William Godwin, whose radical stance excluded them from a central role in English public life. While the role of Unitarian and dissenting ministers points to the religious and indeed Christian complexion of Enlightened thinking in England, Robertson claims that such voices 'could not make up for the absence of Enlightenment thinkers' between 1740 and 1780. 'It was an absence which left a lasting gap in the history of English intellectual and public life.'[5]

The claim that 'Enlightenment thinkers' were missing from the English cultural mainstream for almost half a century is, however, based on an over-narrow definition of the Enlightenment. While I accept the insight that Enlightenment modes of thought were

---

[4]Thomas Munck, *The Enlightenment: A Comparative Social History, 1721–1794* (London: Arnold; New York: Oxford University Press, 2000).
[5]John Robertson, *The Case for the Enlightenment: Scotland and Naples 1680–1760* (Cambridge: Cambridge University Press 2005), pp. 42–3.

integral and up to a point normative in English and Anglican intellectual circles, I dispute the inference that Robertson draws that, outside of dissenting communities, there was a vacuum of Enlightened thought between 1740 and 1780. It is true that the seminal contributions of Locke and Newton, Dryden, Clarke, Pope and Swift were made before the 1740 arbitrary watershed; but the respective impacts of Berkeley, Law, Warburton, Johnson, Butler, Wesley and Burke, to name but a few, belong wholly or mainly after 1740. They should be placed confidently within the Anglican Enlightenment. Evidently I am working with a broader, more catholic understanding of the Enlightenment than Robertson, one distinguished not only by a passion for human betterment and socioeconomic amelioration (Robertson's main criterion), but also and more fundamentally by the turn to reasoned argument, empirical evidence, experimental investigation, pragmatism, the rule of law in nature and society, toleration of divergent views, civility and sociability, and (selective) concern for the poor and uneducated.

To pre-empt a possible objection, let me add that the conservative tendency of Johnson's, Swift's and Burke's thought does not in itself exclude them from the Anglican Enlightenment, if other key criteria are met. For one thing, it does not mean that they disdained the scientific advances, most notably those of Newton and Boyle, that would tend to ameliorate the human condition and had people in awe. Johnson's respect for the new science is now well documented.[6] In connection with Johnson's – shocking to the modern mind – rejection of comprehensive religious toleration, Hudson's verdict is worth pondering. With regard to Johnson's conservatism, he writes, we should not forget 'his extraordinary willingness to promote humanitarian reform in the laws governing provision for the poor, the debtors, and capital punishment'. Hudson continues:

> [I]t was Johnson's desire for stability and order which forms the most consistent link between the various areas of his thought. He was a thinker of enormous complexity, yet everywhere he takes those positions which, in his view, best served the welfare of man and society ... Johnson's conservatism does not ordinarily reflect

---

[6]Richard B. Schwartz, *Samuel Johnson and the New Science* (Madison, WI: University of Wisconsin Press, 1971).

dogmatism or bigotry. His thought is filled with doubt concerning the ability of men to achieve a knowledge of truth or even a real 'sincerity' in their convictions. It is important to consider, however, that doubt of this sort does not necessarily cause anxiety and desperation ... It was this stabilizing resignation, rather than a desperate clinging to the need for truth, which most fully characterized Johnson's religious and moral beliefs.[7]

The Anglican Enlightenment was not only pervasive and elusive; it was also internally complex, riven with tensions and ambiguities. As Hudson writes: 'The eighteenth century has often been described as an age of reason, an age of optimism concerning the beneficence and perfection of the universal system, an age of implicit faith in the essential goodness and nobility of man.' However, 'These generalizations and others are based on an extremely limited selection of authors such as Locke, Pope, and Fielding. Another selection (such as Berkeley, Mandeville, and Swift) might lead to exactly the opposite [pessimistic] generalization'; we could add at least Johnson, Wesley and Burke.[8]

Historiographical perspectives

In England, as in (mainly) Presbyterian Scotland and (mainly) Lutheran Germany, the generality of clergy, ministers and divines regarded themselves as enlightened men of their age, fully abreast of its philosophical theories, scientific discoveries, reforming agendas and cultural creativity. The Anglican Enlightenment had a different intellectual and social profile to its continental counterparts because it was not as self-conscious about being 'enlightened' as – most notably – the *philosophes* who tended to preen themselves on this point and perhaps it understated its enlightened condition. But the Enlightenment watchwords – rational criticism, appeal to evidence, unfettered debate, emotional sensibility, human betterment, mental cultivation, sociability and civility – prevailed in England as they

---

[7]Nicholas Hudson, *Samuel Johnson and Eighteenth-Century Thought* (Oxford: Oxford University Press, 1988/1990), pp. 250–1.
[8]Ibid., p. 3.

did elsewhere in enlightened Europe.⁹ The Church of England underwent an Enlightenment in its own fashion, becoming a widely enlightened church. Enlightenment ideas equally permeated Protestant Dissent through the Academies which served as the Dissenting alternative to Oxford and Cambridge. The three most formative and seminal thinkers of the European Enlightenment's ideology were English: Bacon, Locke and Newton. England, together with the Netherlands, was the principal seedbed of Enlightenment theorizing, advancing fierce debate, intellectual experimentation and corresponding social mores. When Voltaire, who had spent three years of exile in England, wanted to disseminate enlightened ideas in philosophy, science, political reform, the theatre, literature and freedom of discussion, he pointed his French audience to England in his *Lettres Philosophiques*.¹⁰ He was not interested in the enlightened orthodox theology of the Church of England.

In his controversial revisionist study *English Society 1660–1832*, first published in 1985 and revised in 2000, J. C. D. Clark placed the Church of England, its doctrine and practice, centre stage, showing its critical involvement in the clash of ideologies of the period and bringing out the dominant nexus of church and law, to be placed alongside the already familiar historiographical combination of monarchy and parliament. 'Law and religion intertwined. Legislation on the statute book gave a clear definition of a confessional state which might still be interpreted in the language of Richard Hooker.'¹¹ The ecclesiastical-legal combination

---

⁹See a mass of evidence for this in the two ancient, Anglican, universities of England in John Gascoigne, *Cambridge in the Age of the Enlightenment: Science, Religion and Politics from the Restoration to the French Revolution* (Cambridge: Cambridge University Press, 1989) and Nigel Aston, *Enlightened Oxford: The University and the Cultural and Political Life of Eighteenth-Century Britain and Beyond* (Oxford: Oxford University Press, 2022).
¹⁰Voltaire, *Letters on England*, trans. Leonard Tancock (Harmondsworth: Penguin, 1980), p. 67. French text in Voltaire, *Lettres Philosophiques*, intro. René Pomeau (Paris: Garnier-Flammarion, 1964). For the connections between Voltaire and England see the 1,000-page study by André Michel Rousseau, *L'Angleterre et Voltaire*, *SVEC*, ed. Theodore Besterman, vols CXLV, CXLVI, CXLVII (Oxford: The Voltaire Foundation, 1976) and Norman Lewis Torrey, *Voltaire and the English Deists* (Oxford: The Marston Press, 1963 [1930]).
¹¹J. C. D. Clark, *English Society 1660–1832: Religion, Ideology and Politics during the Ancien Regime [sic]*, 2nd edn (Cambridge: Cambridge University Press, 2000 [1985]), p. 31.

was seen to provide the main bulwark against the return of the fratricidal violence and sectarian chaos of the mid-seventeenth century.[12] Clark insists that we cannot hope to understand English society during the long eighteenth century unless we take the role of the Established Church with its constitutional and legal supports seriously. He also points out that 'enlightenment' in this period was a standard term to refer to spiritual and mental illumination, not to any kind of anti-religious ideology or social secularization.[13] To give one example, plucked at random from a book that I happen to have at hand, Samuel Johnson's prayer for the new year of 1769 includes the petition, 'let my mind be more withdrawn from vanity and folly, more enlightened with the knowledge of thy will, and more invigorated with resolution to obey it'.[14] Clark insists, correctly, that in this age reason and revelation were not opposed, neither were religion and toleration. There was always a *modus vivendi*.

In a seminal review article in 2011,[15] Jeremy Gregory noted that until recently 'major eighteenth-century developments were seen in largely secular terms.' Specifically:

> The 'Glorious', American and French revolutions, for example, were all understood as purely political, economic or social events and as representing the (inevitable) triumph of secular concerns over what were regarded as the outmoded religious considerations of the past. Scholars emphasised the 'modern' constitutional and even quasi-democratic nature of these occurrences and all but ignored any religious motivations, justifications or consequences. Culturally too, developments such as the rise of the novel, the growing interest in realist and landscape painting, and musical innovations were viewed as marking a shift from an obsession

---

[12]Ibid., p. 44.
[13]Ibid., pp. 9–10.
[14]Elton Trueblood (ed.), *Doctor Johnson's Prayers* (London: SCM Press, 1947), p. 72.
[15]Jeremy Gregory, 'Religion: Faith in the Age of Reason', *Journal for Eighteenth-Century Studies* 34.4 (2011), pp. 435–43 (Special issue: 'The State of the Discipline', ed. M. O. Grenby); https://doi-org.uoelibrary.idm.oclc.org/10.1111/j.1754-0208.2011.00440.x. See also Jeremy Gregory, 'Transforming "the Age of Reason" into "an Age of Faiths"; or, Putting Religions and Beliefs (Back) into the Eighteenth Century', *Journal for Eighteenth-Century Studies* 32.3 (2009), pp. 287–306.

with religious matters to a growing preoccupation with this-worldly themes and the here-and-now.

Gregory continued:

> The neglect of religious topics by mainstream eighteenth-century historians and cultural critics in 1978 could be explained by two separate but interrelated factors. Not only was the overarching interpretative model of the century one of creeping secularisation (and even historians of religion tended to subscribe to this), but also state churches throughout eighteenth-century Europe (Catholic and Protestant alike) and their clergy were often regarded as lethargic, if not corrupt, and distanced from the bulk of their parishioners, or at best as just worldly and lacking any 'real' sense of religion, despite the efforts of insider historians to rehabilitate their reputations. Repeating some of the strictures of Voltaire and other Enlightenment figures, clergy of all denominations were frequently criticised for being spiritually moribund, pastorally somnolent and preoccupied with lining their own pockets, and were thus censured for falling short of the ideals of various religious reform movements.

The Christian and Anglican complexion of the Enlightenment in England has recently been recognized in the relevant volume of the authoritative *Oxford History of Anglicanism*, to which I now refer in support of my argument so far.[16]

A new historiographical orthodoxy

We might imagine that in the age of Enlightenment, heralded by some interpreters as a movement towards secularization and unbelief, the signs of secularization might already have been visible in the fabric of English national life, causing the marginalization of the church's ministry within society and of its principles in

---

[16] Jeremy Gregory (ed.), *The Oxford History of Anglicanism, Volume II: Establishment and Empire, 1662–1829* (Oxford: Oxford University Press, 2017); page references in my main text.

public doctrine; but that was not so – quite the reverse. The *Oxford History of Anglicanism* that covers this period shows that the Church of England continued to extend its ministry into almost all communities of the land and thereby successfully to sacralise society throughout (p. 21). The founding of the various national societies to promote religion, Christian education, virtue and good behaviour or manners and of local societies for mutual encouragement and edification (as in early Methodism, which remained within the Established Church) drew many laity into active, responsible service on behalf of the church and Christianity, as did the continuing ecclesial and moral roles of churchwardens and patrons of 'livings'. Brent Sirota has portrayed this movement of broader laicization as a further sacralization of civil society.[17] One piece of evidence – again counter-intuitive to widely received assumptions and therefore very likely to be overlooked by us – is the huge popularity and political significance of sermons, which were a major branch of literature, according to Samuel Johnson. Sermons were not only heard in church, but were bought and read voluminously, thus not only boosting the profits of publishers but also testifying to the pervasive influence of Christian ideas in the culture, notwithstanding the lower cultural role of sermons in entertainment and everyday social interaction (Chapter 15).[18]

Regrettably a few contributors to this generally admirable volume still use 'secular' in its modern sense of a social realm liberated from the authority of religion (e.g. 'Enlightenment secularism', p. 53), when what they are often referring to is the *civil but necessarily Anglican* dimension of national public life, that is the civil – not secular – aspect of a Christian nation with a state church (pp. 31, 32, 93, 273). It is encouraging to see that the current steady repositioning of Christianity generally and of Anglicanism in particular *vis-à-vis* the Enlightenment has become almost normative in this volume. As the editor, Jeremy Gregory,

---

[17]See Brent Sirota, *The Christian Monitors: The Church of England and the Age of Benevolence, 1680–1730* (New Haven, CT: Yale University Press, 2014); W. M. Jacob, *Lay People and Religion in the Early Eighteenth Century* (Cambridge: Cambridge University Press, 1996); Mark Goldie, 'Voluntary Anglicans', *The Historical Journal* 46 (2003), pp. 977–90.
[18]See further Keith A. Francis and William Gibson (eds), *The Oxford Handbook of the British Sermon 1689–1901* (Oxford: Oxford University Press, 2012).

strikingly puts it, recent revisionist writing has placed the Church of England 'in the vanguard of Enlightenment thought, deploying it in defence of, rather than against, the Church establishment' (p. 20). Gregory further notes that 'the relationship between "religious" and "enlightenment" concerns is now one of the most fruitful areas of research' (p. 19). William Jacob states in the same volume, 'In England the Enlightenment was a predominantly Christian, Anglican, and clerical phenomenon', so that 'The great majority of English clergy', far from being demoralized or detraditionalized by supposedly corrosive Enlightenment influences, 'were probably orthodox in their theological views, with high doctrines of the Church, the apostolic succession, and the sacraments' (Jacob, p. 96).[19]

A handful of bishops, most notoriously (at the time) the much 'preferred' Benjamin Hoadly (lastly Bishop of Winchester), but also Edmund Law (Carlisle) and Richard Watson (Llandaff), held ultra-low church views, tending to rationalism. They were on the left wing of the Anglican Enlightenment, the antipodes of the ultra-high ecclesiastical firebrands such as Atterbury and Sacheverell. In Gibson's view Hoadly did as much to root the Enlightenment worldview in English culture and religion as Locke and Newton.[20] Hoadley had the advantage over Locke and Newton, for unlike them, he was a preacher in the days when printed sermons were a prime means of disseminating ideas. Hoadly may also have been second only to Locke as an Enlightenment influence on the American revolution.[21] Those contemporary theological writers who carelessly scapegoat 'the Enlightenment' as responsible for all our ills, especially reductionist theology, the secularization of society and the weakness of the churches in the modern world, should take

---

[19]B. W. Young, 'Theology in the Church of England', in Gregory (ed.), *The Oxford History of Anglicanism, Volume II* (Oxford: Oxford University Press, 2017), ch. 21, comprises the theological heart of the volume.
[20]William Gibson, *Enlightenment Prelate: Benjamin Hoadly, 1676–1761* (Cambridge: James Clarke, 2004), p. 15; Guglielmo Sanna, 'How Heterodox was Benjamin Hoadly?', in William Gibson and Robert G. Ingram (eds), *Religious Identities in Britain, 1660–1832* (Farnham and Burlington, VT: Ashgate, 2005), ch. 5.
[21]Bernard Bailyn, *The Ideological Origins of the American Revolution*, 2nd edn (Cambridge, MA: The Belknap Press of Harvard University Press, 1992), pp. 37–9.

to heart the integration of Enlightenment paradigms within the eighteenth-century Church of England and its episcopate.

The sturdy orthodoxy of the 'enlightened' Church of England in this period was apparent not only in its theological literature and debates, but in its practice and life. Anyone who still pictures the eighteenth-century Church of England as devotionally torpid, liturgically drowsy, pastorally negligent and theologically arid is more than half a century behind current scholarship. Such was until recently the received impression of the Established Church in the period covered by this volume of the *Oxford History of Anglicanism*. The period begins with the Restoration of the monarchy and of the Church of England in 1660–2, reinstating the Book of Common Prayer, the Christian Year with its Feasts and Fasts, the Episcopate, functioning cathedrals and the canon law. It was 'the golden age of the Prayer Book' (p. 5). The period ends with the first radical reforms in church and state which triggered the Tractarian or Oxford Movement. The received picture of the Hanoverian Church between these two parameters, as somnolent in worship, lethargic in pastoral work, corrupt in preferment and stagnant in theology is not merely a modern canard.

During the tour of the Hebrides that Johnson undertook with Boswell in 1773, the Presbyterian parish minister of Auchinleck (the seat of Boswell's family) revealed 'a narrowness of information concerning the dignitaries of the Church of England, among whom [Boswell interjects with a view to his audience] may be found men of the greatest learning, virtue, and piety, and of a truly apostolic character'. The minister had the temerity (soon regretted, no doubt) to hold forth before Johnson of 'fat bishops and drowsy deans; and ... seemed to believe the illiberal and profane scoffings of professed satirists or vulgar railers'. As Boswell reports, 'Dr. Johnson was so highly offended, that he said to him, "Sir, you know no more of our church than a Hottentot."[22] You insulted Johnson's religion and his church at your peril, especially if you were Scottish and Presbyterian! Johnson may have protested too much. B. W. Young, who ought to know, states in this volume: 'dull, contented, unoriginal

---

[22] James Boswell in, *Johnson's Journey to the Western Islands of Scotland and Boswell's Journal of a Tour to the Hebrides with Samuel Johnson, LL.D*, ed. R. W. Chapman (London: Oxford University Press, 1924), p. 419.

men littered the higher reaches of the Church in the closing decades of the eighteenth century, probably as a greater proportion of deans and bishops than had been true in the first half' (p. 424). However, their dullness does not necessarily imply that they were not dutiful.

However, the minister of the Kirk's misconception has shown remarkable staying power. Goldie has called it 'the longest shadow in modern historiography',[23] but it bears little relation to the historical reality and is actually a polemic construction of the nineteenth century. Denigration of their forefathers and foremothers was the tendentious tactic of some Victorian Evangelicals, Tractarians and Anglo-Catholics and was an exercise in self-legitimation and self-aggrandisement. As the nineteenth century wore on, the activities of these constituencies, poles apart as they were in theology, liturgy and spirituality, often transgressed the canonical requirements of their church, especially with regard to the liturgy and the exercise of episcopal authority. In a blatant exhibition of private judgement, Evangelicals and Anglo-Catholics often chose to 'do their own thing', claiming that it was now imperative because what had gone before was so abysmal – which was in truth not the case.

A more just appreciation of the life and practice of the Established Church during this period began in small ways in the early twentieth century as historians began to chip away at the daunting edifice of disparagement and caricature. A watershed point was reached in the pioneering work of a giant among Anglican ecclesiastical historians, Norman Sykes, in his 1934 work, *Church and State in the Eighteenth Century*; and the *coup de grâce* was administered more than half a century later in the volume of essays edited by Walsh, Haydon and Taylor, *The Church of England c. 1689–c. 1833* (1993).[24] The slow-burn revolution in the historiography of the Church of England has reversed the previous interpretative paradigm; it provides the springboard for the twenty-four essays of this second volume of the *Oxford History of Anglicanism* in on almost every relevant aspect of

---

[23]Mark Goldie, 'Voluntary Anglicans', *Historical Journal* 46 (2003), pp. 977–90, at p. 988, cited Gregory, 'Introduction', in id. (ed.), *Oxford History of Anglicanism, Volume II*, p. 3.
[24]Norman Sykes, *Church and State in the Eighteenth Century* (Cambridge: Cambridge University Press, 1934); John Walsh, Colin Haydon and Stephen Taylor, *The Church of England c. 1689–c. 1833: From Toleration to Tractarianism* (Cambridge: Cambridge University Press, 1993).

the vitality of the eighteenth-century Church of England, including music, art and architecture. However, far from being excessively reactive *vis-à-vis* the tendentious paradigm of nineteenth-century historiography, the essays in this volume of the *Oxford History* are, almost without exception, balanced, judicious and tied to evidence that has been laboriously disinterred over many years. So much so, that the term 'revisionism' is now scarcely applicable; the community of historians has created a new historiographical orthodoxy for the eighteenth-century Church of England and the Enlightenment framework of ideas and values is an integral part of it. But theologians and more popular Christian writers still lag woefully behind.

Heart-felt religion within the Enlightenment

A further (and, to some people, probably surprising) aspect of Enlightenment religion in England is the dimension of 'sensibility', 'feeling' and 'the heart' in religious experience and its theological interpretation.[25] This phenomenon, which is associated with the rise of Evangelicalism and Methodism, both of them residing within the Church of England but not confined to it, looks at first sight like a reaction to what we have imagined Enlightenment reason to be like: cool, cerebral, unimpassioned. The emphasis on 'the heart', 'feeling' and 'sensibility' among mid-eighteenth-century religious writers could easily be mistaken for the first tokens of emerging

---

[25] The classic study and influential thesis is David Bebbington, *Evangelicalism in Modern Britain* (London: Routledge, 1989). See the discussion of Bebbington's account and its reception in Michael A. G. Haykin and Kenneth J. Stewart (eds), *The Emergence of Evangelicalism: Exploring Historical Continuities* (Nottingham: Apollos/Inter-Varsity Press, 2008). D. Bruce Hindmarsh, *The Evangelical Conversion Narrative: Spiritual Autobiography in Early Modern England* (Oxford: Oxford University Press, 2005) does not focus on the Enlightenment cultural context, but in one of his few references to the Enlightenment, he falls into the trap of unreconstructed stereotyping when he says that one response to the growing pluralisation of society was 'a retreat from religion altogether into secular rationalism as occurred with many Enlightenment thinkers' (p. 79). See also his later work *The Spirit of Early Evangelicalism*, discussed below.

Romanticism, where Romanticism is understood rather crudely as the ideological antithesis of the Enlightenment and as its antidote. Obviously, the rise of subjectivity, individualism and reliance on emotion has affinities with Romanticism and feeds into it. But it would be a mistake to assume that the attention paid in the early and mid-eighteenth century to heart-feelings was incompatible with the typical Enlightenment appeal to reason.

The turn to feeling that erupted in Britain, and indeed across Europe, did not contradict or supplant the established stress on reason. It was simply a different application of reason, reason with a new twist, reason looking in a fresh direction. The critically empirical reason that was at the centre of the Enlightenment mentality was now applied to inner feelings and sensory stimuli, especially those aroused by Evangelical preaching and praise. Religious 'sensations', especially in the form of the inner witness of the Holy Spirit and the sense of 'blessed assurance' of sins forgiven and therefore security of salvation, were the subject of empirical discernment. True religion was now 'experimental', that is to say experiential, evidential, capable of empirical and inductive discernment. This brand of theological epistemology was no less rational than the methods of Newtonian science, or the theological arguments of the deists as they probed and analysed the scriptural evidence for orthodox, credal, beliefs. In fact it followed the fundamental Baconian, Lockean, Newtonian inductive methodology. The typical Evangelical epistemology of religious experience manifested an attention to the evidence, collected together, critically appraised, and rationally interpreted, which was the *cachet* of the Enlightenment. Evangelical thinking was generated and shaped by Enlightenment rational paradigms, among other influences, as Bebbington has conclusively shown. He points out that the Evangelical movement, whether within the Church of England or within Dissent, was 'permeated by Enlightenment influences', noting that 'Its leaders would casually refer to the opinion of Locke as settling an issue or to his *Essay [Concerning Human Understanding]* as providing the best account of the human mind.'[26] Bebbington has conceded in the face of criticism that the observation, discernment and analysis of the sense of assurance of salvation was already strong within the Puritan spirituality of the previous century, while still maintaining

---

[26] Bebbington, *Evangelicalism in Modern Britain*, p. 57.

that it took centre stage in the rise of Evangelicalism. His basic thesis of the marriage of studied introspection with regard to spiritual assurance in this period and Enlightenment scientific paradigms has survived its challenges.[27]

Mack's fascinating study, with its arrestingly paradoxical title, of *Heart Religion in the British Enlightenment*, supplements Bebbington's thesis. She writes, in summary:

> In their receptivity to new techniques of organization and print culture, in their concern for moral and physical health, and in their passion for social justice, Methodists behaved as heirs of the Enlightenment, while in their pietism and apostolic primitivism, they were participants in then popular wave of 'heart religion' that affected Europe, the British Isles, and America, and that has often been viewed as anti-Enlightenment.[28]

She also supports Bebbington's claim that, in early Evangelicalism, spiritual experiences became a source of empirical evidence and the subject of rational investigation and assessment. She writes of John Wesley: 'As an advocate of scientific medicine and an educated citizen of the Enlightenment, he was curious about reports of strange sightings, divine dreams, trances, miracle cures, prophecies, and other supposed supernatural occurrences, but he also wanted hard evidence of their authenticity.'[29] Wesley's writings on such supposedly supernatural phenomena reveal him as 'trying to walk a fine line between the Pietist's receptivity to divine experience and the scientist's skepticism about these intangible and ultimately unverifiable events'. A weakness of Mack's presentation, however, is that she says very little about how she understands 'the Enlightenment' and what it stood for. She does not attempt to

---

[27]Michel A. G. Haykin, 'Evangelicalism and the Enlightenment: A Reassessment', in Haykin and Stewart (eds), *The Emergence of Evangelicalism: Exploring Historical Continuities* (Nottingham: Apollos/Inter-Varsity Press, 2008), ch. 2. Haykin's argument fizzles out with a *deus ex machina* appeal to the work of the Holy Spirit, which is to invoke a first cause when his job as an historian is to discover explanatory second causes.
[28]Phyllis Mack, *Heart Religion in the British Enlightenment: Gender and Emotion in Early Methodism* (Cambridge: Cambridge University Press, 2008), p. 295.
[29]Ibid., p. 223.

define either its ideological content ('Enlightenment ideals')[30] or its chronological parameters, except implicitly.

Hindmarsh reinforces the paradox of the combination of an Enlightenment scientific world view with vital Evangelical spiritual experience of the presence of God within both the human heart and the natural world:

> The evangelical devotional attitude passed over into their view of the natural world as radiant with God's presence. The God of nature and grace invited a response of 'wonder, love, and praise'; this led them to perceive God as immediately present in the material world revealed by Newtonian science and described by mechanical philosophy. This is evident in John Wesley's multifaceted interaction with science as a popular disseminator of natural knowledge, and Jonathan Edwards's probing of the meaning of the Newtonian postulates. The attitude of worship, recalling the older 'harmony of all knowledge', was manifest especially in the Wesleyan and Edwardsian view of the spiritual senses and their profound rejection of dualism.[31]

Fundamentalism and the Enlightenment

The same basic methodology, adapted to an apologetic task, continued into American fundamentalism (with British expressions also), where it tended to become legalistic, defensive, adversarial and dualistic.[32] Barr summed up its epistemology as 'empirical rationalism', by which is meant a combination of Baconian empirical

---

[30]Ibid., p. 14.
[31]Bruce Hindmarsh, *The Spirit of Early Evangelicalism: True Religion in a Modern World* (Oxford: Oxford University Press, 2017), ch. 4, abstract.
[32]James Barr, *Fundamentalism* (London: SCM Press, 1977); George M. Marsden, *Fundamentalism and American Culture: The Shaping of Twentieth Century American Evangelicalism 1870–1925* (Oxford: Oxford University Press, 1980); Mark Noll (ed.), *The Princeton Theology 1812–1921: Scripture, Science, and Theological Method from Archibald Alexander to Benjamin Breckinridge Warfield* (Grand Rapids, MI: Baker, 1983); Harriet Harris, *Fundamentalism and Evangelicals* (Oxford: Clarendon Press, 1998). J. I. Packer, *Fundamentalism and the Word of God* (London: IVF, 1958).

inductivism and the naive realism of Thomas Reid and the Scottish 'Common Sense' school of philosophy. Fundamentalism was (and is) in thrall to a spurious objectivism, that feared to admit the human, social, cultural elements in the biblical writings. 'Subjectivism' was the ultimate insult that Fundamentalists hurled at their opponents. The Bible, as a book, an artefact, was their central sacrament, 'the supreme tangible sacred reality'.[33] The Bible was treated as a completely unified, God-given, divinely inspired, textbook, a source of direct unchallengeable information about every aspect of reality. The tenet of the 'perspicuity' of Scripture, which derived ultimately from Reformation soteriology, meant that no theological education was required to understand the Bible and its way of salvation. Its data could be read off the page, indeed off any isolated verse out of context, by anyone who could read; and there was reluctance to admit even that the mere reading of it was an act of interpretation. Scripture spoke for itself and was self-interpreting; we are merely passive recipients of its message. It was also infallible and inerrant in every respect. Much intellectual energy was devoted to reconciling or harmonising 'apparent' errors and contradictions in the Bible.

In the 'Princeton School' of scholastic Reformed theology (principally A. A. Hodge, Charles Hodge, J. Gresham Machen and B. B. Warfield), the ultimately indefensible notion of inerrancy evolved into the equally untenable – indeed desperate – doctrine of the inerrancy of the (postulated) original manuscripts. The high point of this apologetic trajectory was attained in the very able apologetic writings of B. B. Warfield. His ultimate, 'knockdown' argument is that the humanly spoken or written words of the biblical authors were also, by the Bible's own testimony, the words of God and divinely inspired, which necessarily rendered them 'absolutely infallible'.[34] The criterion of infallibility – like that of 'inerrancy' which frequently accompanied it – derives indirectly from the rational empiricism of the Enlightenment which led its defenders to maintain that the truth of Scripture is not compatible with human imperfections. By contrast – an alternative which did not appeal to the Princeton School – poetic, imaginative, figurative

---

[33]Barr, *Fundamentalism*, p. 36.
[34]Benjamin Breckinridge Warfield, *The Inspiration and Authority of the Bible*, ed. Samuel G. Craig (London: Marshall, Morgan & Scott, 1951); quoted phrase from p. 422.

language is precisely mediated through human imperfections – the form and character of a passionate, suffering, longing human biography, such as that of the prophets, apostles and evangelists.

A modern expression of this stance is *Thy Word Is Truth* by Edward J. Young of Westminster Theological Seminary, Philadelphia, which was first published in 1957 and is still being promoted among those who need to grasp at straws to maintain the dogmatic faith in which they have been instructed and on which they believe their whole faith rests.[35] A precious verse in St John's Gospel (17:17 KJB), which gives the book its title, meant for Young that the empirically factual accuracy of the Bible in all respects must be defended and he engages in endless exegetical contortions to preserve that doctrine. What is 'true' must be, empirically and factually, perfectly accurate and correct. This *apriori* stance cannot be refuted by reference to any amount of empirical evidence relating to the provenance, authorship, editorial history or vicissitudes of the text of Scripture. Ingenious and far-fetched harmonization can prolong the stance indefinitely. Conservative Evangelical scholars tend to go through the motions of reviewing the whole gamut of published positions, with regard to biblical 'introduction' (provenance, date, authorship, the integrity of the book, genre, style, text), but always tend to come to the most conservative conclusions, with the earliest date and the fullest tenable view of the integrity of the book and of the text, even with a pretence of tentativeness (2 Peter 'could' have been written by the fisherman-apostle Simon Peter, but we cannot be certain). The playing of these games can continue indefinitely – until the whole mindset that clings to the empirically 'factual' perfection of the Bible as the only version of divine inspiration that is worthy of God and serviceable to human salvation, is abandoned.

In the first phase of the exit from Fundamentalism, the patently figurative genres of Scripture (especially Genesis 1–11) were taken literally (creation in 'calendar' six days). Then when the citadel of literalism began to collapse, they were grudgingly taken to be analogical (six geological ages that can be matched to the history of the earth). Then finally, the poetic, imaginative, symbolic or mythological nature of such texts was reluctantly accepted by some – but in the act of taking that step they had *de facto* escaped

---

[35] E. J. Young, *Thy Word Is Truth* (Edinburgh: Banner of Truth, n.d. [1957]).

from Fundamentalism. Enlightenment empiricism, which aspired to be open to the evidence and as a result became critical of church dogma and recognized the fallible human element in the biblical writings, had transmuted in Fundamentalism into an exaggerated form of empiricism which isolated the Bible from other sources and influences. Excessive rationalism is a fault that is often unjustly laid at the door of the Enlightenment, but it can fairly be applied to Evangelical Fundamentalism.

John Wesley and the Anglican Enlightenment

John Wesley's rational empiricism is a prime case in point. In his Oxford days, Wesley was converted, philosophically speaking, from a metaphysical or speculative to an empirical, inductive use of reason. He had deeply imbibed the writings of the Anglican philosopher John Norris (1657–1711), who has been called the last of the Cambridge Platonists. Norris, a Fellow of All Souls College, Oxford, and a country vicar, carried forward the legacy of the great 'realist' or idealist philosophers Plato and Augustine, Descartes and Malebranche. Living in the world, we are living in God, in contact with the divine. In every experience of life in the world, we touch the hem of the garment of the Creator. God is 'in' the mind, as well as 'in' the external world. So reflective (or reflexive) thought, meditating on the creation both around us and within us, can lead us up to God. For Norris, there is much in religious faith that is beyond the scope of rational enquiry; but there is also much that is simply against all reason, especially 'enthusiasm', of which the most glaring example at the time was Quakerism, against which Norris wrote.[36]

But Norris's influence on John Wesley gave way to that of Locke. Wesley immersed himself in Locke's epistemology, with its denial of innate ideas (even religious notions) and its attribution

---

[36]On Norris see https://plato.stanford.edu/archives/fall2008/entries/john-norris/. Richard Acworth, *The Philosophy of John Norris of Bemerton: 1657–1712* (New York: Olms, 1979).

of all knowledge to sensory experience, subsequently organized and interpreted by the understanding. Locke's influence on Wesley was reinforced and reshaped by the writings of Peter Browne, Bishop of Cork and Ross, who theologized on the basis of Lockean epistemology. Wesley had grown up in the heady atmosphere of Newton mania – the early Methodists were the first generation to awaken to the dawn of Newtonian discoveries – though he clearly was more at home with Newton's physics than with his mathematics.[37] Wesley's understanding of reason was not of the mathematical, logical, deductive kind, but rather of the empirical, investigative kind. Indeed Wesley's inconsistencies and contradictions amount to outright illogicality in some areas. But he was second to none in his insistence on the authority of reason, protesting on one occasion: 'It is a fundamental principle with us that to renounce reason is to renounce religion, that religion and reason go hand in hand, and that all irrational religion is false religion.'[38] But he was convinced that religious sensations were a proper, authentic material for reason to work on. Wesley's embrace of inward testimony, which is then subject to examination and assessment, does not make him any less an Enlightenment thinker, but rather confirms his status as a leading, albeit popularizing Enlightenment intellectual.

Wesley was scornful of Montesquieu, Voltaire and Rousseau and dismissed Captain James Cook's anthropological discoveries in the South Seas as fiction. But he reveals himself to be an Enlightenment intellectual in his appeal to reasoned argument, his empiricism in epistemology, his intellectual curiosity and his investigative cast of mind. In his methodistical pedagogy for his followers Wesley disseminated accounts of revelatory dreams and visitations by spirits.[39] It is clear from his *Journals* that he took such accounts at face value, posing questions about what the ghost apparently knew, and so on. He wrote books about witchcraft, not as an alien

---

[37]See Hindmarsh, *The Spirit of Early Evangelicalism*, ch. 4 for John Wesley and Newtonianism.
[38]Quoted by Bebbington, *Evangelicalism in Modern Britain*, p. 52.
[39]For examples see Mack, *Heart Religion in the British Enlightenment*.

historiographical aberration that as rational beings we should strive to understand while not believing, but as a very present reality and threat, to be taken seriously and investigated rationally.[40]

British Deism

Standing, so to speak, between ecclesiastical, supernaturalistic Christianity, in all its gradations of belief and practice – on the one hand – and freethinking, sceptical and unbelieving positions with regard to religion – on the other – there is the broad spectrum of ideas known as deism.[41] 'Deism' is the label now irreversibly attached to the bewildering range of rational theologies that were advocated across Europe in roughly the century between the mid-seventeenth and the mid-eighteenth. Deism is notoriously hard to define and the task is not made any easier by the practice of some writers of this period – notably Voltaire – of describing as 'theism' what we would regard as deism. However, that usage makes the point that deists were believers in God, creation, providence and revelation (after a fashion) and therefore stand at a remove from such materialistic, scientific, atheistical thinkers, who had no use for the benevolent, providential provision of such divinely

---

[40] Hugh Trevor-Roper, *History and the Enlightenment*, ed. John Robertson (New Haven, CT: Yale University Press, 2010), pp. x–xi (Editor's Introduction). The *Journals* are available online. I have also used the 4 vol. Everyman Library edition (London: Dent; New York: Dutton, n.d.). For John Wesley as an Enlightenment intellectual see *ISOA*, pp. 294–307.

[41] See further my introductory discussion of deism in general, of Lord Herbert of Cherbury and of John Toland in *ISOA*, pp. 282–7. I am indebted particularly to Peter Byrne, *Natural Religion and the Nature of Religion: The Legacy of Deism* (London and New York: Routledge, 1989); Isobel Rivers, *Reason, Grace and Sentiment: A Study of the Language of Religion and Ethics in England, 1660–1780*: vol. 1, *Whichcote to Wesley*; vol. 2, *Shaftesbury to Hume* (Cambridge: Cambridge University Press, 1991, 2000); Jonathan Israel, *Radical Enlightenment: Philosophy and the Making of Modernity* (Oxford: Oxford University Press, 2001), ch. 33; Henning Graf Reventlow, *The Authority of the Bible and the Rise of the Modern World* (London: SCM Press, 1984), pp. 289–334; Roland N. Stromberg, *Religious Liberalism in Eighteenth-Century England* (Oxford: Oxford University Press, 1954); Joseph Waligore, 'The Piety of the English Deists: Their Personal Relationship with an Active God', *Intellectual History Review* 22 (2012), pp. 181–97.

inscribed principles as 'the Law of Nature', 'the law of Reason', 'Natural Equity' and so on, as Diderot, d'Holbach, Helvétius and Condorcet (all French, though that philosophical tradition took a fresh, utilitarian direction in England with Bentham).[42] Pailin, in pointing out that, in the seventeenth and eighteenth centuries, 'the term "deist" was used to refer to a wide range of positions', adds: 'While modern writers may purport to define what they mean by "deist", their application of the term typically shows that it is a blanket description covering a disparate group with no discernible common creed.' Pailin quotes what Harold Hutcheson said of the so-called deists: 'if Blount, Gildon, Toland, Collins, Woolston, Tindal, Morgan, Annet and Chubb, to name the most prominent, all shared a common creed, if even a majority of these consciously took a common philosophical position, no-one to my knowledge has yet succeeded in stating that creed or position'.[43]

The European family of deists includes the usual suspects Kant, Montequieu, Voltaire, Rousseau, Shaftesbury, Bolingbroke, Gibbon, Paine and Hume (the last standing here for a galaxy of leading intellects of the Scottish Enlightenment, some of whose churchmanship shaded towards deism), distributed between Germany, France, England and Scotland.[44] Through Voltaire, the English deists exerted influence on the wider European Enlightenment, though the details are difficult to pin down because, while Voltaire read them widely, he was far from transparent in acknowledging his sources and habitually and intentionally

---

[42]Charles Taylor, *Sources of the Self: The Making of Modern Identity* (Cambridge: Cambridge University Press, 1989), ch. 19.

[43]H. R. Hutcheson, 'Lord Herbert and the Deists', *The Journal of Philosophy* XLIII (1946), pp. 219–221, cited David A. Pailin, 'Should Herbert of Cherbury be regarded as a "Deist"?' *JTS*, NS, 51.1 (April 2000), pp. 113–49, at p. 130. Henry Dodwell the younger (d. 1784) should not be confused with his father, the more famous Henry Dodwell (1641–1711), a *Nonjuror*, who led a section of the non-juring schism back into the Church of England in 1710 (*ODNB*). There was a large tribe of clerical and theological Dodwells in this period! Dodwell the deist published the enigmatic but influential work *Christianity not Founded on Argument* in 1742, a satirical send-up of William Law's semi-fideism, which some writers, including Law himself, took at face value; John Wesley was not taken in. See James C. Livingston, 'Henry Dodwell's *Christianity not Founded on Argument* Revisited', *JTS*, NS, 22.2 (1971), pp. 466–78.

[44]For Gibbon and Hume see *ISOA*, pp. 254–63. For Paine (1737–1809) see J. C. D. Clark, *Thomas Paine* (Oxford: Oxford University Press, 2018), pp. 161–3.

threw readers off the scent.[45] But the deist tribe does not include (contrary to some opinions) the two most influential thinkers of the Enlightenment in England: John Locke (1632–1704) and Isaac Newton (1643–1727). Ironically, Locke and Newton were almost deified themselves in the eighteenth century by European thinkers of all stripes; they were the brightest stars in the Enlightenment firmament. Here, having previously touched on Newton, I will focus on Locke. Suffice it to recall that Newton, though he privately advocated a less than Chalcedonian Christology (which became apparent after his death),[46] was an active, conforming Anglican, a benefactor of churches and an obsessive, lifelong (and misguided) student of biblical chronology and prophecy.[47]

John Locke's religion

Locke was a lifelong (since the Restoration of monarchy and church in 1660–2) practising lay Anglican. He was also a Christian apologist, a biblical scholar, an ethicist and a constructive political theologian. Locke was appalled at certain deistic writings and shocked beyond measure by atheism. He affirmed the supernatural dimension in Christian belief: the fulfilment of Old Testament prophecy in the coming of Christ; the miracles of Jesus' ministry; a post-mortem existence with divine judgement dispensing rewards and punishments. The labels 'rationalist', 'secularist' and 'individualist' that some writers, including Christian ones, attach to Locke are unwarranted. Such notions force Locke's thought into a Procrustian bed. When, as a youngish parish priest and aspiring theologian, I first read Locke quite extensively, I could see at once the strength of Locke's Christian commitment and that he belonged within the mainstream of Christian philosophical-theological

---

[45]Torrey, *Voltaire and the English Deists*.
[46]For the controversy that ensued, see Scott Mandelbrote, 'Newton and Eighteenth-Century Christianity', in I. Bernard Cohen and George E. Smith (eds), *The Cambridge Companion to Newton* (Cambridge: Cambridge University Press 2002), ch. 14.
[47]See also Rob Iliffe, *Priest of Nature: The Religious Worlds of Isaac Newton* (New York: Oxford University Press, 2016) and Maurice Wiles, 'Newton and the Bible', in Samuel E. Ballentine and John Barton (eds), *Language, Theology, and the Bible: Essays in Honour of James Barr* (Oxford: Clarendon Press, 1994), pp. 334–50.

traditions and within the church. The idea that Locke's overt Christianity was merely a deceptive smokescreen for a subversive secular intention is ludicrous, as well as unscholarly. This forced interpretation has been refuted by the religious and indeed theological turn in a veritable barrage of sounder Locke studies during recent decades, especially but not exclusively in the work of Dunn, Colman, Waldron, Nuovo and recently Guy and Lucci.[48] Wolterstorff, an eminent Reformed philosopher, describes Locke's philosophy of religion as 'one of the great creative achievements in the history of philosophy of religion in the West'.[49] Woltertorff regards the entire corpus of Locke's philosophy as an extended rational Christian philosophy. Lucci's recent (2021) study gives a further and irrefutable boost to the reclamation of Locke as a Christian thinker. It drives home the point that Locke's work is religious and Christian through and through. How anyone could ever have suggested otherwise, or labelled Locke as a rationalist and deist, defeats me; it merely underlines once again the ideological and tendentious nature of Enlightenment scholarship. But Lucci goes a little too far in claiming that Locke's 'theological reflections resulted in a unique version of Christianity', 'a unique, original, Scripture-based form of Protestant Christianity'.[50] Locke was indeed an eclectic, creative and courageous thinker, but the tributaries of his thought, with its bold interpretations of the Bible, can be traced to Arminian, Socininian and Latitudinarian precedents and to dialogue with eminent contemporaries, as Lucci himself shows. The

---

[48]John Dunn, *The Political Thought of John Locke: An Historical Account of the Argument of the 'Two Treatises of Government'* (Cambridge: Cambridge University Press, 1969); John Colman, *John Locke's Moral Philosophy* (Edinburgh: University of Edinburgh Press, 1983); Jeremy Waldron, *God, Locke, and Equality: Christian Foundations in Locke's Political Thought* (Cambridge: Cambridge University Press, 2002); Victor Nuovo, *Christianity, Antiquity and Enlightenment: Interpretations of Locke* (Dordrecht: Springer, 2011); id. (ed.), *John Locke: Writings on Religion* (Oxford: Oxford University Press, 2002); Nathan Guy, *Finding Locke's God: The Theological Basis of John Locke's Political Thought* (London and New York: Bloomsbury, 2019); Diego Lucci, *John Locke's Christianity* (Cambridge: Cambridge University Press, 2021).
[49]Nicholas Wolterstorff, 'Locke's Philosophy of Religion', in Vere Chappell (ed.), *The Cambridge Companion to Locke* (Cambridge: Cambridge University Press, 1994), ch. 7, at p. 172.
[50]Lucci, *John Locke's Christianity*, pp. 5, 8.

resulting mixture may well have been unique, but that can be said of almost any great thinker, so to that extent the accolade 'unique' becomes a truism.

I also regret Lucci's description of Locke's theology as 'heterodox', a term which is much in vogue among writers on early modern religious thought. While to shallow minds it may make these thinkers sound more exciting subjects of study than other, more doctrinally 'sound', scholars, it contributes nothing to our understanding of their thought or its significance. Orthodoxy and heterodoxy are not fixed quantities in the theological lexicon and have always been slippery notions. They do not place anyone on the broad and shifting spectrum of theological conviction and opinion. Writers on the history of thought who play with the term 'heterodox' seldom explain by what standard of orthodoxy, the category of 'heterodoxy' is to be defined. I regard the label as otiose and unhelpful, particularly in the case of Locke who was careful not overtly to challenge credal doctrine, but maintained a prudent reserve on trinitarian theology. As a layman, Locke was not required to subscribe the Thirty-nine Articles of Religion (which endorse the creeds as consonant with Scripture, the trinitarian articles being I and VIII). He studied at Christ Church, Oxford, from 1552, during the Interregnum, when the Church of England was in abeyance and the Puritan Independent John Owen was the Dean and head of college, so subscription to the Articles did not arise. Locke did of course participate in worship according to *The Book of Common Prayer*, after its restoration in 1662, and that liturgy is permeated by scriptural, but not speculative, trinitarian language (except for the occasionally used, so-called Athanasian Creed, the *Quicunque vult*). However, Locke's reticence on the more speculative elements of doctrine can be largely attributed to his overriding moral and practical purpose and to his sceptical sense of the limitations, the darkness, of human understanding and an ensuing principled reluctance to go beyond Scripture. Like other seventeenth-century Protestant and Anglican scholars in what many scholars have identified as the Erasmian tradition, he was sceptical about the dogmatic authority of 'antiquity' and therefore reluctant to ascribe final authority to the teachings of the early Fathers of the church. As Lucci emphasizes, Scripture itself was Locke's first and final authority.

Against the 'enthusiasts' who were carried away by their own fancies or delusions and Roman Catholics who were required to accept beliefs on the authority of their church, Locke insisted on every person's responsibility to exercise their reason in the discernment and judgement of truth.[51] It was axiomatic, for him as for Aquinas and Hooker, that God, reason and natural law were in accord. In this emphasis Locke was far from being unique among Anglican thinkers. He stood in continuity with Hooker, the members of the Tew Circle (especially Falkland, Hales and Chillingworth) the Cambridge Platonists (chiefly Cudworth) and the Latitudinarians (who included the Archbishop of Canterbury John Tillotson).[52] The axiom of the rational and ethical responsibility of every person, in matters of religious belief and practice, was echoed by Butler, William Law and Samuel Johnson, among others. Strangely, Locke's emphasis on 'rational self-responsibility' does not commend itself to the contemporary philosopher Charles Taylor. He regards it as the source of the notion of 'the punctual self' that he believes developed through the Enlightenment.[53] But this construction simply gets Locke wrong. Locke's notion of personhood was not the objectified, solitary and sealed one that Taylor imagines. Locke's vocation and life's work was to serve the stability, security and prosperity of the state, the commonwealth. While Locke certainly believed that individuals had a responsibility to make rational moral choices, he also insisted that they were not merely responsible to themselves for this, but to society and ultimately to God.

Locke's hostile contemporaries who judged him guilty of theological reductionism or worse have been followed uncritically by some modern interpreters who are evidently floundering theologically. Locke belonged within a distinct tradition of Erasmian Christian humanism: fervent in devotion, minimalist in dogma, adhering closely to the New Testament and infused with ethical passion and self-discipline (*ascesis*). Accordingly, Locke was not a dogmatist and shied away from speculative and abstract theology. He taught a practical faith and stressed that certitude was not available to us in this life; probability must be our guide. In

---

[51]John Locke, *An Essay Concerning Human Understanding*, 2 vols (London: Dent; New York: Dutton, 1961), vol. 1, pp. 279–80 (IV, xvii, 24).
[52]Further on these groups of thinkers see *AACC* and *ISOA*.
[53]Taylor, *Sources of the Self*, ch. 9, at p. 174.

The Reasonableness of Christianity he refrained from defending the contorted terminology of traditional trinitarian orthodoxy and in his *Paraphrase and Notes upon the Epistles of St Paul* he stuck to the 'plain' interpretation of the text, by-passing traditional glosses and speculations, and so achieved a striking freshness of exposition. Locke had an aversion to proof-texting for political ends and never lost sight of the ethical thrust of the Christian faith.

How did Locke, whom we sometimes see wrongly listed among the doubters and deists, respond to celebrated or notorious deistic writings? Locke was horrified by Toland's *Christianity Not Mysterious* (1695), just as he had been by aspects of Lord Herbert of Cherbury's *De Veritate* (published 1624, before Locke's birth) which, as we will see, retained a place for grace, forgiveness, worship, prayer and providence and immortality, though not for the incarnation, atonement and resurrection of Christ. In the spirit of Francis Bacon and in anticipation of the trademark Enlightenment methodology, Herbert insisted that knowledge and belief must be based upon evidence, critically examined, and that should have commended him to Locke who was no rationalist but a liberal Anglican philosopher and lay theologian. Like other moderate thinkers of the Enlightenment in France and England, Locke was also disgusted by the profane temerity of Tindal's *Christianity as Old as the Creation: Or, the Gospel, a Republication of the Religion of Nature* (1730) which in effect did away with the theological concept of divine revelation altogether while paying some lip-service to it, blatantly advocating a merely natural religion.[54] Locke was not averse to mystery and accepted the biblical revelation. In his *Essay Concerning Human Understanding* Locke had stressed the limitations of our knowledge, that probability must be our guide amid the surrounding darkness and that we have just enough light upon our path to take one step forward at a time in the ethical and spiritual life.

Those interpreters who affirm Locke's sincere Christian faith and intention, nevertheless often label him as 'heterodox' or 'heretical'. Guy's recent stout vindication of Locke as a supremely

---

[54] For an exposition of Tindal's arguments, see Leslie Stephen, *History of English Thought in the Eighteenth Century*, 2 vols (London: Rupert Hart-Davis/Harbinger imprint, 1962 [1876]), vol. 1, pp. 113–23, and for Tindal, briefly, *ODNB* (B. W. Young).

Christian political theologian is also spoiled by his swingeing designation of Locke as 'heterodox', which goes against his own argument and seems to parrot previous interpreters. Marshall too speaks of Locke's 'heterodoxy' and 'heresy'.[55] Even Clark, who is normally sure-footed in matters of theology, does the same.[56] What basis is there for such categorizing of Locke? His teaching in *The Reasonableness of Christianity* that belief in Jesus as the Messiah (the Christ, that is the promised deliverer), was sufficient for salvation has firm support in the New Testament, so he should not be criticized for that. Locke may have been drawn to a less than traditional view of trinitarian doctrine in the 1690s, but he never publically advocated or defended anything 'heterodox'. It is true that Locke's rejection of the notion of the inherited guilt of Adam's fall (one element in the received doctrine of 'Original Sin') and the 'satisfaction' version of the atonement put him out of step with certain expressions of the Book of Common Prayer (especially the 'satisfaction' language of the Prayer of Consecration in the Communion Service) and of the Thirty-nine Articles of Religion (especially Articles II and IX on Original Sin; there is no article on the atonement). It has been claimed that Locke did not deny the doctrines of original sin and the atonement, but it seems clear that he rejected certain versions of them on ethical grounds.[57] But it did not necessarily put him out of step with the New Testament. The Articles' particular version of 'Original Sin', cryptic though it is like most of the Articles, stems from St Augustine of Hippo, not from St Paul, and the satisfaction model of the atonement was classically expressed by St Anselm and reshaped into penal substitution by Calvin. Neither of these notions, nor the teaching of the everlasting punishment of the damned, which Locke also denied, is found in the creeds, so to reject them cannot, strictly speaking, be heterodox or heretical. Locke's views on these topics are within the broad range

---

[55] See further David Loewenstein and John Marshall (eds), *Heresy, Literature, and Politics in Early Modern English Culture* (Cambridge: Cambridge University Press, 2006).
[56] Guy, *Finding Locke's God*, e.g. pp. 4–5; Marshall, *John Locke*, p. xv; Clark, *English Society*, pp. 138, 328–30 (though Clark rightly sees Locke's so-called Socinianism as a position within the spectrum of the Christian tradition).
[57] W. M. Spellman, *John Locke and the Problem of Depravity* (Oxford: Clarendon Press, 1988).

of Christian debate and theological controversy, with which Locke was well acquainted through his reading, his correspondence with continental radical Protestant divines and his period of residence in the Netherlands (1683–8).

Marshall suggests that Locke's 'dissemination of religious and epistemological views corrosive of religious orthodoxy and of the political power of the priesthood was perhaps his most important contribution to the thought of the following century'.[58] Marshall's knowledge of Locke's thought in its context is possibly unrivalled, but his judgement, in those precise terms, is questionable on several grounds. (i) Whatever his personal views and private jottings may have been, Locke did not publish anything 'corrosive of religious orthodoxy'. (ii) What, in any case, was 'religious orthodoxy' (apart from its obvious reference to the trinitarian formulae of the councils of the early church) in the late seventeenth-century Church of England? It was a church that accommodated competing traditions, allowed liberty of conscience, kept definition to a minimum and existed in a permanent state of theological debate, all of which (as Marshall notes) commended it to Locke as best fitted to be the national church?[59] (iii) Locke had grown up in a Calvinist household during the Civil War and the Interregnum. Dunn stresses the continuing Calvinist influence in Locke's thought, pointing to its Protestant work ethic and concept of 'calling'. However, Locke's theology is not Calvinist – he had rejected that inheritance and held the extreme Calvinists among the Dissenters in moral contempt – though aspects of his ethics retain Calvinist influences. Locke described the turbulent state of the nation and its religious sects in those times as 'bedlam' and 'anarchy'.[60] He therefore sought a regime marked by stability, continuity and firm governance. Locke was not a politically or theologically subversive thinker. (iv) It is difficult to see how any theory of epistemology (except for a nihilistic epistemology that holds that we cannot ever know the truth – but then how could we know that either?) could negate any Christian doctrine. Christian theology has been associated with various

---

[58] Marshall, *John Locke*, p. xxi.
[59] Marshall, *John Locke*, p. 11. See further Roger D. Lund (ed.), *The Margins of Orthodoxy: Heterodox Writing and Cultural Response, 1660–1750* (Cambridge: Cambridge University Press, 1995).
[60] Marshall, *John Locke*, pp. 8, 20.

schools of epistemology through the centuries without coming to serious harm. (v) The clergy of the Church of England were not normally thought of as a collective 'priesthood' in the seventeenth and eighteenth centuries. As ministers of word and sacrament and overseers of the parish, they were (unless non-resident) integrated into the local community and assimilated to it through (normally) marriage, children, farming their glebe, performing their duties as physicians, registrars and magistrates, and even fox-hunting for some, they did not constitute a hieratic caste like the priesthood of the Roman Church. They were placed as pastors – whether good enough or not – in the midst of their people.

It was possible for 'enlightened' thinkers and publicists in England to adopt an anti-clerical animus, but that did not in itself make them 'secular', 'unbelieving' or 'heterodox'. It may have simply meant that, like Bayle and Locke himself, they were radical, sceptical, egalitarian, morally pessimistic, humanist Protestants. Nuovo's word for Locke the philosopher, 'a Christian virtuoso', seems apt. Nuovo is using 'virtuoso' in a double sense derived from Robert Boyle and his *The Christian Virtuoso* to refer not only to the elegance in conception and execution of Locke's writings, but also as a technical term, meaning one who follows an empirical or experimental and so-to-speak naturalistic method in the study of the natural world, bracketing out for that purpose any theological considerations, as pioneered by Bacon and refined by Boyle, Locke's mentor, friend and collaborator. All three sought to harmonize their scientific vocation with their religious faith and worked within a Christian theological framework.[61] Locke was not unique, but he was the greatest example and exponent to that point in time of a powerful tradition.

The 'threat' of deism questioned

Those interpretations of the Enlightenment, most notably by Margaret Jacob and Jonathan Israel, who see a powerful nexus of infidelity working at the heart of cultural change, have to reckon

---

[61]Victor Nuovo, *John Locke: The Philosopher as Christian Virtuoso* (Oxford: Clarendon Press, 2017).

with the recent challenge to the 'myth' of widespread deism. Barnett has claimed that

> The bogeyman of deism was frequently identified by clerics and protagonists of the faith, of both the orthodox and dissenting type, some of whom wished to create reputations for themselves and/or their sect by publicly appearing as stalwart defenders of 'true' Christian orthodoxy ... such ardent Christians played a major role in creating a very public antichristian bogey that did not have any substantial reality.[62]

Barnett avers that 'The deism scare proved to be one of the great and enduring European propaganda coups, the results of which, in academic terms, are still with us today.' Those historians who wished to locate the origins of secular modernity in the Enlightenment, have perpetuated the notion of a secularizing eighteenth-century international deist movement which 'never existed', according to Barnett, constituting only a small minority of even the professed enlightened ones. To view eighteenth-century Europe, he persists, 'through the prism of the deistic philosophes is simply to accept uncritically the world as the philosophes claimed they saw it'. The numbers of articulate deists were tiny, Barnett claims (though I assume that there was also a wider penumbra of reticent deists). The 'threat' of deism, like that of 'atheism' to Christian civilization was, insists Barnett, 'one of the great conservative ideological propaganda weapons of the eighteenth century'.[63]

Deists were a tiny but vocal group of writers. What did they believe and not believe? Although generalizations about deism are risky, it is possible to discern some generic features.[64] Deists believed in a Creator or Supreme Being and (usually) in the providential ordering of the world. The celebrated 'watchmaker' analogy, identified with the Anglican apologist William Paley,[65] of a Creator who set the

---

[62]S. J. Barnett, *The Enlightenment and Religion: The Myths of Modernity* (Manchester, UK: Manchester University Press, 2003), p. 5.
[63]Ibid., pp. 12–13, 16–17, 20, 68.
[64]James A. Herrick, *The Radical Rhetoric of the English Deists: The Discourse of Skepticism, 1680–1750* (Columbia, SC: University of South Carolina Press, 1997) contains some useful information, but is not a wholly reliable guide.
[65]For Paley see *ISOA*, pp. 255, 343–4.

world in motion and then left it to its own devices, to run on without divine involvement, is not applicable to most deists. They marvelled at the order, regularity and variety of the created universe. With some exceptions (notably Rousseau), the deists tended to emphasize divine transcendence more than divine immanence, but they attributed the beauty and wonder of creation to the hand of the Creator. The deistic understanding of worship was much attenuated, but some continued to commend and personally practise prayer. They often retained a truncated belief in divine revelation, Toland being – in terms of his reputation – a surprising example. Deists (especially Rousseau) tended to find God in nature, rather than in churches, though others, notably Gibbon and Voltaire (surprisingly as that may be to some) continued to attend church services (mass for Voltaire). But the deists played down the supernatural, miraculous, elements in traditional Christianity. They had no room for Chalcedonian Christology which they regarded as speculative and abstract, and were not moved by the exactions of ecclesiastical authority. They often knew their Bibles and some were formidable polemical theologians. They generally held that divine sanctions of reward or punishment after this life were attached to moral imperatives and that this conviction implied the immortality of the soul.

Reason in deism and Anglicanism

Considering that the appeal to reason is often held to be the chief identifying mark of a supposedly unbelieving and unchurched Enlightenment, it is worth underlining that eminent Anglican thinkers and writers, including Locke, Dryden, Butler, William Law, Addison, Swift, Warburton, Wesley, Johnson and Burke, all of whom adhered to the teaching of the Church of England (Dryden converted to Roman Catholicism in 1687) appealed to 'reason' in the quest for truth, just as much as the deists did. These Anglican writers invoked 'reason' as the antithesis of 'enthusiasm' and as its antidote, meaning the forces of religious fanaticism which left violence, destruction and chaos in their wake. What all British thinkers of the eighteenth century dreaded most was the irruption of the *irrational*, though there was plenty of it around, in both recent history (the British Civil War and Interregnum; the Scottish Covenanting troubles) and the present (the extreme manifestations within early Methodism). The tribunal of reason was the first line of defence against the ever-present threat of a mindless fanaticism that threatened the social, political and ecclesiastical fabric. Swift loathed Dissent more than Roman Catholicism because it had proved to be a breeding ground for 'enthusiasm' – delusions of direct private inspiration leading to religious and social chaos. Logically speaking, 'Religion being the best of things, its corruptions are likely to be the worst.'[66] It is against this backdrop that Swift apostrophized the Church of England as 'the most perfect of all others in discipline and doctrine'.[67] Johnson, with his endemic fear of insanity, clung to religion and reason together, pronouncing that 'religion ... [was] the highest Exercise of Reason'.[68] Like Locke in the *Enquiry Concerning Human Understanding* and Butler in *The Analogy of Religion, Natural and Revealed* (1736), Johnson held that 'Reason has its proper task assigned to it: that of judging, not of things revealed, but of the reality of revelation.'[69]

But for Locke, Butler, Johnson, Wesley and Burke 'reason' was not the arrogant, *apriori* kind of reason espoused by the more aggressive deistic philosophers of their day, such as Bolingbroke, but a God-given faculty of discernment and judgement, grounded in a grasp of proportionality and the virtue of prudence. Reason for them was informed by the wisdom drawn from human social experience and lessons learnt over time, Hooker being the great Anglican exponent of this classical Anglican quality of mind.[70] Johnson and Burke

---

[66]Jonathan Swift, *A Tale of a Tub and Other Satires* (London: Dent; New York: Dutton, 1909), p. 13. Victoria Glendinning, *Jonathan Swift* (London: Hutchinson, 1998), pp. 187–91.
[67]Swift, *A Tale of a Tub and Other Satires*, p. 12.
[68]Cited Edward G. Andrew, *Patrons of Enlightenment* (Toronto: University of Toronto Press, 2006), p. 157, from Hester Lynch Thrale, *Thraliana: The Diary of Mrs. Hester Lynch Thrale*, vol. 1, ed. Katherine C. Balderson (Oxford: Clarendon Press, 1951), p. 183.
[69]Cited Hudson, *Samuel Johnson and Eighteenth-Century Thought*, pp. 19–20, from Johnson, *Lives of the Poets*. I have not succeeded in verifying the reference.
[70]Peter J. Stanlis, *Edmund Burke: The Enlightenment and Revolution* (London and New York: Routledge, 2017 [1991]), *passim* and especially ch. 4: 'Burke and the Rationalism of the Enlightenment'. As will be clear from the whole of the present work, I do not agree with Stanlis that the Enlightenment as such was particularly characterized by an appeal to 'rationalism' in the sense of a speculative, Cartesian reason; I think that phase belongs to the pre-Enlightenment period; but it is partly a matter of definition.

were in tune with the turn to Lockean empiricism in eighteenth-century epistemology and the scientific method of Boyle and Newton. Johnson said that he had a lifelong respect for any one who 'added one useful Experiment to natural Knowledge'.[71] John Wesley undertook experiments in electricity and medicine. Burke, in a life of ceaseless controversy, deployed a supremely practical and pragmatic rationality, though one infused with the high, inflexible principles of justice, equity and compassion. So invoking the authority of reason was not an identifying mark unique to either deists or unbelievers; it was endemic and across the board. These Anglican writers were all *rational* thinkers – obviously they could not think without being rational – but they were not *rationalistic*, which would imply that their own or others' reasoning powers were their sole authority. On the contrary, they were immersed in Scripture, the Book of Common Prayer, the liturgical round of the Christian Year and the broader ecumenical streams of the Christian tradition both before and beyond 'Anglicanism' and were poised in the classical, humanist trajectory of intellectual Christianity.[72]

Charles Taylor on deism and the 'secular age'

Charles Taylor's discussion of the brand of rational theology which we know as deism, in his *A Secular Age* (2007), is aptly entitled 'Providential Deism'.[73] In terms of our investigation, it is a strength

---

[71] Cited from Johnson, *The Idler*, no. 88, 22 December 1759, by Stanlis, *Edmund Burke: The Enlightenment and Revolution*, p. 133.
[72] See further Paul Fussell, *The Rhetorical World of Augustan Humanism: Ethics and Imagery from Swift to Burke* (Oxford: Clarendon Press, 1965). Fussell's subjects are Swift, Pope, Johnson, Reynolds, Gibbon and Burke, of whom, for him, Johnson is the greatest. There is much more to his account than rhetoric, as his list of twelve attributes of classical humanism in chapter 1 shows, including metaphysics, literature, anthropology, ethics, theology, politics, criticism. The major early modern influences on the Augustan classical humanists are identified by Fussell as Hooker (*Of the Lawes of Ecclesiasticall Politie*), Shakespeare (*Hamlet* and *King Lear*) and Milton (*Paradise Lost*).
[73] Charles Taylor, *A Secular Age* (Cambridge, MA: The Belknap Press of Harvard University Press, 2007), ch. 6; page references in my main text.

of Taylor's genealogy of secularism that he attempts to do justice to the phase of deistic religion. However, the title of his key chapter, which is also his operative concept, is a little puzzling. Was there any form of deism that was not 'providential'? Belief in a benevolent divine providence – albeit a general providence or guiding hand, rather than a process of continuous, particular, and even miraculous interventions, which is how providence was popularly viewed – was intrinsic to deism. Deists were sceptical about supernatural interventions, but otherwise they usually retained much of the Christian belief in a benevolent divine providence, making for justice and human flourishing.

If there is one image of deism that lingers in the semi-popular mind, it is the 'clock-maker' analogy of a Creator who, as it were, wound up the universe in the beginning and set it going, but thereafter refrained from interfering with its running. The image was common coin in the eighteenth century, but it is associated indelibly with William Paley's natural theology. It was intended as a fully Christian analogy. Paley (1743–1805) was a priest and an archdeacon in the Church of England and said the creed twice a day. Paley was no deist and certainly did not deny the loving providential care and succour of 'the God and Father of our Lord Jesus Christ'. His use of the clock-maker image reflects the all-conquering influence of the 'Newtonian universe', which was assimilated to the mechanical philosophy and the laws of motion. In Paley's hands, it is an apologetic tactic of his *Natural Theology or Evidences of the Existence and Attributes of the Deity* (1802), and as such not too much should be read into it.[74] Deism was intrinsically 'providential' and Taylor's rather tautologous term at least emphasizes that fact. However, I think Taylor is mistaken in interpreting deistic 'providence' as merely 'God's plan for us' which we apprehend by reason and are ethically motivated (or not) to follow (pp. 223–4). Deistic providence is a guiding hand, fostering and rewarding virtue, protecting against evil and punishing evil-doers.

Along with what he dubs a 'hollowed-out' notion of providence, Taylor places what he believes to be the deists' rejection of divine

---

[74]William Paley, *Natural Theology or Evidences of the Existence and Attributes of the Deity*; the *Works of William Paley*, D.D. (London, 1825). Cf. *A View of the Evidences of Christianity*, ed. Canon Birks (London: Religious Tract Society, n.d.). See in summary, ISOA, p. 343.

revelation in favour of an appeal to reason alone. The deistic religion based on nature or reason 'doesn't need revelation', he avers (p. 292). But some major deistic writers do have a place for revelation: they reinterpret, rather than reject the concept. Taylor seems to think that reason and revelation are incompatible and that reason plays little or no part in the Christian understanding of revelation. But this is not so; it has never normally been the case and certainly was not held to be so by the Anglican divines of the Enlightenment era.

I also find Taylor's view of Anglican religion in this period constricted and lacking in nuance. He cites, as a criticism, the Archbishop of Canterbury, John Tillotson (1630–94) teaching that a religious life is the way to true happiness and that it is to our advantage to be religious (pp. 225–6). It is true that churchmen of this era played up the moral dimension of Christianity as a life of virtue and constantly drummed home the importance of duty. But it does not follow that, in Enlightenment Anglicanism, 'Religion is narrowed to moralism', as Taylor asserts (p. 225). That the Christian path is the way to true and eternal happiness, to beatitude, is a perennial trope in Scripture, Christian preaching and theology and probably no-one has insisted upon it more strongly than St Thomas Aquinas (as Taylor surely knows). But Taylor does contribute a necessary corrective when he argues that it was not merely the progress and prestige of science and rational enquiry that turned some members of European elites against orthodox Christianity, but also and perhaps more so, it was moral revulsion against the prevailing juridical and penal concepts of the doctrines of original sin and the atonement, combined with vengeful notions of hellfire in the afterlife (pp. 262–4), that were common to Catholic, Protestant and Anglican traditions. These teachings prevailed from medieval times through the Reformation and Counter-Reformations to the nineteenth century and even beyond. At this point, it was conscience, rather than pure reason, that rebelled.

The deists' objections and achievements

What interests me most of all about the deists is what motivated them to depart from Christian orthodoxy and the sacramental life of the church. What made late seventeenth- and early eighteenth-century people into deists? In a previous discussion,[75] I outlined three fronts on which deistic writers attacked Christianity and the Church. I will now summarize, comment on and expand these points.[76]

First, with regard to the basic truth of the Christian faith, certain deistic writers employed the philosophical argument from probability. They called into question the frequently claimed 'proofs' for Christianity from alleged miracles, whether biblical or ecclesiastical, that is to say the miracles of Jesus, the apostles and the saints. These Enlightenment figures regarded miracle-claims as contrary to the standards of probability that we rely on in everyday life in assessing evidence. Hume provides the most uncompromising statement of this argument in his essay, incorporated into *An Enquiry Concerning Human Understanding* (1748).[77] Diderot (though latterly not a deist but a materialist) remarked that even if it were unanimously reported that a dead man had come back to life in a nearby town, he would not believe it. The evidence for claimed miracles demanded a degree of probability that could never be met. The improbability of an event that defied the known laws of nature outweighed any appeal to historical 'evidence' in principle.

Second, the deists held ethical objections to Christianity. They found plenty of material in the Bible that deserved to be disqualified, on moral grounds, as divine revelation. Theologians of all stripes at this time assumed a propositional understanding of revelation as essentially the communication of information, whatever spiritual, mystical and experiential aspects were attached to it. They lacked a concept of the gradual unfolding and progression of revelation and of the development of doctrine. Theology obviously had not achieved the understanding, such as modern theologians work with in their various ways, of the human, cultural mediation of divine revelation through the minds of the biblical writers or (which amount to much the same thing) a way of distinguishing the actual text of Scripture from the revelation of God that it conveys, attests or witnesses to. Divine revelation and the Bible were equated; they were synonymous for both Protestants and Catholics (though the

---

[75]*ISOA*, p. 282.
[76]See Byrne, *Natural Religion*, especially ch. 4.
[77]William L. Vanderburgh, *David Hume on Miracles, Evidence, and Probability* (Lanham, MD: Lexington Books, 2019).

Council of Trent had made room for revelation to be contained also in church tradition). Moreover, in spite of the impact of humanist methods of documentary study that stemmed from the Renaissance and had deeply influenced the Protestant Reformers, the church's scholars, especially in the Catholic Church, had not done justice to the human element in Scripture, to the mediation of divine revelation through the minds, hearts, lives and contexts of the biblical writers. To compound these weaknesses – as they now appear to us – biblical interpreters had also put the Old Testament very much on a par with the New Testament, reconciling the two by means of often far-fetched figurative interpretation. Deistic Enlightenment thinkers particularly challenged, on ethical grounds, the moral worthiness of many of the miracles contained in the Bible, even some of those attributed to Jesus, alleging that they did not reflect the justice and universal benevolence that everyone attributes to God, the Creator or the Supreme Being. As Byrne states the ethical objection: miracles, far from supporting the authority of Scripture, become reasons for distrusting Scripture; 'not indications of divine warrant but of human error, superstition, and enthusiasm'.[78] We should not overlook the fact that, before modern times, doctrinal deviance was deemed morally culpable by theologians. It took a bad person to believe wrongly. Heterodoxy was an indicator of sinfulness. Superstition was not regarded as the quaint residue of charming folklore, and 'enthusiasm' was the prevailing technical term for the sort of crazed fanaticism that had contributed to the European religious wars and powered the morally, socially and politically disruptive agitation of the sects, especially in seventeenth-century Britain.

Third, English deistic writers, not least the influential and elegant Shaftesbury, developed the rudiments of an historical and critical approach to the Bible. We will return to this topic in a broader context in the chapter on Enlightenment historiography and the Bible.

Fourth, there is no evading the fact that deists tended to ridicule aspects of the history of Christianity – there was plenty of ammunition there – together with certain bizarre aspects of the Bible in the days before the rise of the historical-critical method of

---

[78]Byrne, *Natural Religion*, p. 100.

biblical interpretation and the more subtle understanding of genre that informs modern biblical study. Their ridicule provoked William Blake's devastating poetic riposte some decades later:

> Mock on, mock on, Voltaire, Rousseau:
> Mock on, mock on: 'tis all in vain!
> You throw the sand against the wind,
> And the wind blows it back again.
> And every sand becomes a Gem,
> Reflected in the beam divine;
> Blown back they blind the mocking Eye,
> But still in Israel's paths they shine.[79]

Although deistic writers had a field day poking fun at Christian (and other) claims of miracles and other supernatural phenomena, they also raised serious questions that philosophers and theologians have wrestled with – rather inconclusively – ever since. Hume's critique of the credibility (more than the impossibility) of reported miracles triggered 'a tidal wave of responses'.[80] Although his arguments have been challenged, not least on technical philosophical grounds, they nevertheless tend to leave a nagging sense in the minds of the majority of those people who have considered the matter that miracle claims, whether biblical or ecclesiastical, should be treated as open to question and with at least caution and at most scepticism.

The apologists for orthodox belief were naturally hampered, just as their deistic opponents were, by pre-critical views of the biblical material, its formation and transmission, including little awareness of genre. The churchly defenders' arguments tended to exhibit a naive evidentialism: bringing forth the apostolic testimony from the New Testament, taken at face value and supported by reference to biblical miracles and claims of fulfilled prophecy. For example: if the apostles had not been speaking the truth about the resurrection of Jesus they would not have been granted the gift of tongues

---

[79]William Blake, *The Complete Poems*, ed. Alicia Ostriker (Harmondsworth: Penguin, 1977), p. 494.
[80]Timothy McGrew, 'Miracles', *The Stanford Encyclopedia of Philosophy* (Spring 2019 edn), Edward N. Zalta (ed.), 3:3: https://plato.stanford.edu/archives/spr2019/entries/miracles/.

on the Day of Pentecost! How is that for a circular argument? Enlightenment writers on both sides of the debate demanded evidence and sought to evaluate it rationally, but they lacked the tools to do so adequately.[81]

Middleton and miracles

The most devastating attack on ecclesiastical miracles came from the pen of Conyers Middleton (1683–1750) in his *A Free Inquiry into the Miraculous Powers, which are Supposed to Have Subsisted in the Christian Church, from the Earliest Ages through several successive Centuries* (1749), preceded by his hard-hitting *Introductory Discourse*.[82] Middleton was no infidel or deist, but a highly gifted, acutely critical, but incorrigibly quarrelsome clergyman of the Established Church, whose invective displayed the open wounds caused by lack of recognition, through preferment in the church, of his exceptional intellectual and polemical gifts. Middleton anticipated that he would stir up a hornets' nest with this diatribe. In the event, he needed all his resilience to withstand the attacks that his work provoked. While defending the veracity of the miracle accounts of the Gospels, Middleton exposed the credulity, superstition and fraudulent intent of the early Fathers with regard to miraculous happenings, many of which he held up as bizarre and absurd. He had Roman Catholic apologetic, official and unofficial, in his sights. It was a stock argument, in support of the claim that Rome was the (one and only) true church, that the miraculous, in the form of signs and wonders, healings, exorcisms and resurrections, had continued within it without ceasing since apostolic times. The tricks of medieval 'monkery' had been exposed at the Reformation and thereafter Anglican divines normally held that miracles had ceased after the conversion of the Roman Empire to Christianity in the third century. Middleton, however, was not satisfied with that half-way house and targeted the miraculous

---

[81]See Herrick, *The Radical Rhetoric of the English Deists*, for the arguments of the orthodox.
[82]https://play.google.com/books/reader?id=tXFPAAAAYAAJ&pg=GBS.PR34&hl=en_GB (accessed 30 December 2021).

claims of the pre-Nicene period also, holding them up as examples of fraud, fable and credulity. He noted that the first generation after the apostles, that of the Apostolic Fathers, was not given to claiming miracles.

Leslie Stephen judged that Middleton was 'more open to the charge of insidious hostility to Christianity than such writers as Tindal and Collins; for, whilst expressing sentiments almost identical with those of the deists, he retained ecclesiastical preferment to the end of his life'. Stephen also made an unwarranted extrapolation from the critique of miracle claims – in the process somewhat endorsing the mostly hysterical attacks on Middleton at the time – when he alleged that Middleton made a 'covert assault upon the orthodox dogmas'.[83] The standard line among historians is that Middleton was an unbeliever, to be aligned with the more destructive deists and freethinkers, and therefore a traitor in the ranks of the clergy, a fifth-columnist. But, as Young comments, proponents of a secular, as opposed to a clerical, Enlightenment in England, are bound to have trouble with the fact that Middleton was a priest.[84]

To attack the credibility of ecclesiastical miracles is no indication of hostility to Christianity and it does not touch dogma. Such questioning cannot in itself be 'heterodox', another redolent but essentially vacuous term beloved of historians of the period, because to question the alleged miracles of the saints has nothing to say about the creeds, which are the key or possibly the only test of orthodoxy. Orthodoxy is about correct profession of faith; its scope should not be extended to intentions, research methods or effects. Middleton did not deny miracles in principle, only certain claimed miracles that did not meet his rational historical criteria.

---

[83]Stephen, *History of English Thought in the Eighteenth Century*, vol. 1, pp. 213–30, at pp. 214, 227.

[84]Young, 'Theology in the Church of England', pp. 407–8; id., 'Conyers Middleton: The Historical Consequences of Heterodoxy', in Sarah Mortimer and John Robertson (eds), *The Intellectual Consequences of Religious Heterodoxy 1600–1750* (Leiden: Brill, 2012), pp. 235–65; Hugh Trevor-Roper, 'From Deism to History: Conyers Middleton' in id., *History and Enlightenment*, ed. John Robertson (New Haven, CT: Yale University Press, 2010), pp. 71–119; Robert G. Ingram, 'The Weight of Historical Evidence: Conyers Middleton and the Eighteenth-Century Miracles Debate', in Robert D. Cornwall and William Gibson (eds), *Religion, Politics and Dissent 1660–1832: Essays in Honour of James E. Bradley* (Farnham: Ashgate, 2010), pp. 85–109.

The fact that his opponents charged him with intending to discredit all miracles – miracles as such, and even the Gospel miracles – is not relevant to Middleton's profession of faith, as required by subscription to the church's formularies. Orthodoxy exists only in relation to heterodoxy and vice versa, but these terms and the conceptions that they represent are continually circling around each other in the history of theology and the church. They feed on one another and devour one another. They were certainly banded about freely within the Church of England in our period. But 'heterodox' was a term of abuse and reprobation flung at those who challenged received notions – rather like 'atheist' when atheists were few or none (the earliest British thinker to admit to being an atheist was Matthew Turner in 1782), or 'Socinian' for the many divines who advanced the role of reason in religion. As Pocock has suggested with reference to such polemics, you cannot have 'orthodoxy' unless you can discuss its content, debating its centre and boundaries. But then it has become a matter of opinion (*doxa*) and everything is 'up for grabs'.[85] The language of violent polemic of a past age does not provide suitable criteria for historical judgements today.

Middleton was no deist, nor freethinker, but a turbulent priest with an incisive intellect and a grasp of the cogent criteria for historical evidence. He aligned himself with the rational, low-church Bishop Hoadly who was a star of the episcopal bench, though suspect to many. The debates that Middleton and Hoadly stirred up were internal to Christianity and the church. As Leslie Stephen himself pointed out, the authority of the church Fathers had already been attacked by such Protestant controversialists as the Huguenot Jean Daillé (1594–1670) in France. I might add Chillingworth in England who deconstructed the Fathers and their councils and is an obvious predecessor of Middleton in scepticism. Like Chillingworth, Middleton was a *sola scriptura* Protestant, but with a strong injection of anti-clericalism and of resentment against those less able clerks who enjoyed comfortable preferment – he could not abide authority in high places. The spirit of historical scepticism, applied to tradition, was of course supremely exemplified in the radical Protestant pedant and polemicist Pierre Bayle, but is

---

[85] J. G. A. Pocock, 'Within the Margins: The Definition of Orthodoxy', in Lund (ed.), *The Margins of Orthodoxy*, ch. 1.

also apparent in Erasmus, the loyal Catholic of the Reformation era whom Gibbon dubbed 'the father of rational theology'.

As a licensed Clerk in Holy Orders, Middleton would have been required to lead or at least join in Morning and Evening Prayer and the eucharistic liturgy of the Church of England and therein to say the Apostles', Nicene and (at that time) so-called Athanasian Creeds. A strange kind of infidelity (though not without precedent)! What was particularly challenging to the *status quo* in Middleton was his application of the first principles of historical enquiry, the rational investigation of evidence, which raised the debate to a higher level where his numerous assailants (including heavyweights such as Wesley, Warburton and Thomas Sherlock) found him practically invulnerable. Less than a century later, when J. H. Newman and his disciples uncritically celebrated medieval miracles in the Tractarian series *Lives of the English Saints*, with the rationale that they were 'history' and 'fact', he caused alarm among other Tractarians and High Churchmen (W. E. Gladstone for one). The miracle tales were met with derision by Broad Church Anglicans who read the great German historians and were among the leading exponents of historical criticism of their time.[86] Middleton had contributed at long range to the slow and often reluctant enlightenment of Anglican theological method in the realm of history. But now let us return to the alleged deists.

Lord Herbert of Cherbury

Lord Herbert of Cherbury (1582–1648), the elder brother of the priest-poet George Herbert, has been widely identified both as a deist himself and as 'the father of English deism'. But is his thought correctly described as deistic?[87] At the end of his *De Veritate* ('On

---

[86]Stewart J. Brown, Peter B. Nockles and James Pereiro (eds), *The Oxford Handbook of the Oxford Movement* (Oxford: Oxford University Press, 2017), pp. 120–1 (James Pereiro).
[87]This discussion of Herbert of Cherbury is concerned only with his relation to deism and to the dawning of the Enlightenment. I will be referencing David A. Pailin, 'Should Herbert of Cherbury be regarded as a "Deist"?', which I was not aware of when I composed my previous brief account in *ISOA*, pp. 284–5. I am also

Truth', 1624) Herbert puts forward five 'Common Notions regarding Religion': (1) 'There is a Supreme God.' (2) 'This Sovereign Deity ought to be Worshipped.' (3) 'The connection of Virtue with Piety ... is and always has been held to be, the most important part of religious practice.' (4) 'The minds of men have always been filled with horror for their wickedness. Their vices and crimes have been obvious to them. They must be expiated by repentance.' (5) 'There is Reward or Punishment after this life.' Herbert holds that these 'notions' or, as we might say, 'religious convictions', are both universal to humanity and also innate in the mind or consciousness – a dual claim that Locke later challenged on both counts.[88] So we might note in passing, first, that Herbert anticipates the Enlightenment in assuming, on the basis of little knowledge of other global cultures, the universality of the principles and values that he himself holds dear; and second, that, in maintaining that there were quite detailed innate ideas, so not derived from experience of the world, especially sensory experience, he is not representative of Enlightenment thought, which was essentially experiential and empirical.

In the *De Veritate* Herbert also proposes four tests of the validity of revelation, four epistemic conditions that need to be met before a doctrine could be accepted as a revealed truth.[89] First, the revelation must have been received in response to proper invocations of the divine: 'we must employ prayers, vows, faith and every faculty which can be used to invoke particular and general providence'. Second, the revelation must have been given directly

---

drawing on: Herbert of Cherbury, *The Life of Lord Herbert of Cherbury, Written by Himself and Continued until His Death* (London: Cassell, 1893); id., *De Veritate*, trans. Meyrick H. Carré (Bristol: University of Bristol Press, J. W. Arrowsmith, 1937; facsimile reprint: Thoemmes Continuum, 1999), esp. pp. 291, 308–15; R. D. Bedford, *The Defence of Truth: Herbert of Cherbury and the Seventeenth Century* (Manchester: Manchester University Press, 1979); Richard H. Popkin, *The History of Scepticism: From Savonarola to Bayle*, 2nd edn (Oxford: Oxford University Press, 2003 [1960]); Peter Harrison, *'Religion' and the Religions in the English Enlightenment* (Cambridge: Cambridge University Press, 1990); Byrne, *Natural Religion and the Nature of Religion*.

[88] John Locke, *An Essay Concerning Human Understanding*, vol. 1, pp. 36–43 (I, iii, 15–27).

[89] The summary that follows is adapted from Pailin, 'Should Herbert of Cherbury be regarded as a "Deist"?', p. 139.

to an individual. What others tell us has been revealed should not be regarded as revelation but as 'tradition or history' and so subject to somewhat different criteria of validity. As tradition or history, its truth 'depends upon him who recounts it, its foundations lie outside us' and therefore it does not have for us the character of revealed truth but 'is, so far as we are concerned, mere possibility'. Third, the purported revelation should recommend what is good. A purported revelation is shown to be a wicked temptation if it be contrary to our moral understanding or is contrary to the 'dogmas' that have been 'fully sanctioned by the authority of the true Catholic Church' (the dogmas, that is, that are contained in and follow from the Common Notions of Religion). The fourth condition of a genuine revelation is that it should be accompanied by a sense of 'the breath of the Divine Spirit' (*afflatum Divini Numinis sentias*). It is this experiential testimony that enables us to distinguish between a revelation, as an imparting of truth from 'without us', and an inner effect of a faculty of truth within us, and so to separate authentic acts of divine revelation from natural disclosure-events. If these four conditions are satisfied, we must, according to Herbert, 'recognize with reverence the good will of God' in making known to us what 'surpasses human understanding'. In so far as every Christian theologian – and every reflective, Bible-reading Christian, for that matter – operates, even implicitly, certain criteria in evaluating what is of God and what is of human invention or delusion, Herbert's criteria are unobjectionable; in fact they are spot-on.

If we draw up a rough calculus, we can say that Herbert is a Christian believer in several respects: he finds the Bible to be a source of inspiration and comfort; he believes in prayer, angels, signs and special providences (he claims to have experienced signs and providences); he affirms that it is our duty as creatures to worship the Creator and that a virtuous life is the best part of worship; he teaches that we should repent of our sins and that there will be post-mortem rewards and punishments for virtue and vice respectively. But on the other hand, Herbert falls seriously and decisively short of Christianity in that he studiously declines to mention the incarnation and atoning death of Jesus Christ; moreover, the salvific sacraments of the church have no place in his theological scheme.

Herbert's attacks on all forms of ecclesiastical authority that demand unquestioning consent and obedience and on Calvinistic doctrines of predestination and election do not, of course, disqualify him as a Christian. For him, God is the God of all humankind equally. He was opposed on moral grounds to all narrow, chauvinistic notions of God, revelation and salvation. And as Pailin remarks, Herbert was 'deeply suspicious of claims to divinely sanctioned authority in religious matters. He considered that religious beliefs and practices had been widely corrupted by priestcraft'.[90] He staked the claim of the laity (*laici*) to engage in theology and to follow their own moral and rational judgement. Neither does his insistence that all claims to revelation and all church dogmas should be brought to the bar of reason and the moral conscience in itself call in question his possible Christian allegiance. Bishop Butler says much the same in his *Analogy of Religion*, the most powerful and effective work of apologetics of the eighteenth century, and in this Butler is merely representative of the mainstream of Anglican thought in the period. Herbert's *De Veritate* ('On Truth', 1624) is a pioneering essay in epistemology in which he seeks a path to truth between the Scylla of dogmatic certainty, as evinced by the churches, and the Charybdis of scepticism or Pyrrhonism, which had a wide appeal even among Christian apologists (especially Pierre Charron, d. 1603) at the time. Herbert's invocation of the authority of reason takes its place between these two extremes. However, he is not correctly described as a 'rationalist'; reason is not the dominant factor in his scheme. That position is held by the initiative of the Creator in implanting the 'Common Notions regarding Religion' into the human mind.

To round off this brief discussion of Herbert, we need to return to the question, Should Herbert be considered a deist? And if not, what is his relation to deism and the varieties of religious conviction within the Enlightenment? Pailin's assessment that Herbert was 'an independent thinker who relished his freedom', rather than an identifiable deist, is worth pondering. Herbert's conviction of the active presence of God, the immortality of the soul, rewards and punishments after this life, the reality of divine revelation, and the effectiveness of prayer 'distinguish his thought from many of the characteristics alleged to be distinctively "deistic"' (as Pailin points out). On the other hand, as Pailin puts it, 'his reliance on the touchstone of the common notions supposedly perceivable by every human being, his criteria for authenticating claims to revelation, his

---

[90]Pailin, 'Should Herbert of Cherbury Be Regarded as a "Deist"?', p. 132.

severe criticisms of priestcraft, together with his views on salvation, the Bible and history[,] show that his independence made him an uncongenial thinker to those who upheld beliefs that they regarded as traditionally orthodox.' Altogether, I am persuaded by Pailin's conclusion:

> Since, however, the notion of 'deism' is unclear, since Herbert flourished decades before the disparate group of thinkers identified by [John] Leland [1696–1766] as the 'deistical writers' came to the fore, since Herbert did not hold many of what are supposed to be typical views of the 'deists', and since to call him a 'deist' (and even more 'the father of deism') is to give a misleading impression of many of his views, it is arguably best to reject the description. He was a liberal thinker in religious matters who, like many liberal theologians then and since, has suffered from a characterization that encourages others to ignore his ideas rather than to take them with due seriousness.[91]

To pigeon-hole Lord Herbert of Cherbury as 'a deist' – to lump this luminous, reverent thinker with such variously egregious, scurrilous and profane writers as Blount, Tindal, Woolston, Chubb and Collins – is to reduce his spiritual and intellectual stature and to diminish his significance in the history of English religious thought.

John Toland

Should John Toland (1670–1722) be included in any list of English deists? Toland was a feisty, boisterous and elusive Irishman with a finger in several pies.[92] Toland's most famous or infamous work *Christianity Not Mysterious: A Treatise Shewing That There Is*

---

[91]Pailin, 'Should Herbert of Cherbury Be Regarded as a "Deist"?', pp. 147–8.
[92]Robert E. Sullivan, *John Toland and the Deist Controversy: A Study in Adaptations* (Cambridge, MA: Harvard University Press, 1982); Stephen H. Daniel, *John Toland: His Methods, Manners, and Mind* (Kingston, Ontario: McGill-Queen's University Press, 1984); Justin A. I. Champion, *Republican Learning: John Toland and the Crisis of Christian Culture, 1696–1722* (Manchester: Manchester University Press, 2003); *ODNB* (Stephen H. Daniel); *ISOA*, pp. 285–7.

Nothing in the Gospel Contrary to Reason, nor above It: and That No Christian Doctrine Can Be Properly Call'd a Mystery (1696) was an important influence on Voltaire.[93] As I have previously written, I rate him as a serious, though somewhat maverick, religious thinker and one who stands both within the parameters of Christianity and within the church in some sense (as he insists). Toland himself refused the label 'deist' and although it seems that he was a member of a Unitarian congregation within pan-Presbyterianism, he repudiated the charge of Socinianism. His relationship to other currents of thought is difficult to pin down. Sullivan writes: 'In his critique of Christian orthodoxy, Toland systematically developed arguments which Socinians had broached and Anglican rationalists were to accommodate.'[94] The difficulty of pigeon-holing Tolland bears out Sullivan's conclusion that 'The continued use of deism as a category requires that it be divested of excessive analytical pretensions and treated as a flexible verbal convention.'[95] In this assessment, I am taking into account particularly his biblical centre of gravity, his affirmation of divine revelation and his apologetic motive (albeit misguidedly executed), even though his exposition is very far from Christ-centred. The title, subtitle and contents of Toland's *Christianity Not Mysterious* comprise a crass antithesis of the essence of Christianity. The 'mystery' of God's purpose and plan of salvation, now made known in Jesus Christ, is a key theme in the Pauline Epistles and mystery has been a central theme of modern theology in all Christian traditions. What is not mysterious, Toland rashly assumes, is the realm of reason, defined by the Cartesian canons of clear and distinct ideas. But, as all Enlightenment theologians insisted, the Christian gospel could not be contrary to reason, so for Toland it must consist of ideas that are clear and distinct (the Cartesian criteria of truth). God would not require

---

[93] John Toland, *Christianity Not Mysterious: A Treatise Shewing That There Is Nothing in the Gospel Contrary to Reason, nor Above It: And That No Christian Doctrine Can Be Properly Call'd a Mystery*, facsimile edition with an introduction and textual notes by G. Gawlick (Stuttgart-Bad Cannstatt: Friedrich Fromann Verlag, 1964); P. McGuinness, A. Harrison and R. Kearney (eds), *John Toland's Christianity not Mysterious: Texts, Associated Works and Critical Essays* (Dublin: Lilliput Press, 1997); the accompanying essays are slight.
[94] Sullivan, *John Toland and the Deist Controversy*, p. 275.
[95] Ibid.

us to assent to what was beyond our understanding and what remained a mystery would be unintelligible to us anyway. Toland's thesis 'Christianity not mysterious' was subsequently refuted by Butler in *The Analogy of Religion, Natural and Revealed*, where Butler showed that Christianity was indeed essentially mysterious to us, but no more so than the natural creation itself, as the deists themselves understood it. Rather daringly citing Origen, Butler pointed out that, if we believe God to be the author of both Scripture and nature, we should not be surprised to find in Scripture the same kind of difficulties that arise in the study of the natural world. Whoever is led to repudiate the divine origin of the Bible, should on the same grounds, reject the creation of the world by God. Yet, for the deists, God, creation and nature, permeated by reason and synonymous with reason, was the centre of their faith.[96]

The Enlightenment in the early English novel

My first encounter with the imaginative literature of the English Enlightenment was at the age of nine, in the form of a Christmas present from my parents. I probably do not need to say that this was *The Adventures of Robinson Crusoe* (in a children's edition with thirty vivid colour plates, which have lived in my memory ever since).[97] I struggled a bit with Daniel Defoe's

---

[96]Joseph Butler, *The Analogy of Religion, Natural and Revealed to the Constitution and Course of Nature, to Which Are Added, Two Brief Dissertations: On Personal Identity, and on The Nature of Virtue; and Fifteen Sermons* (London: Bell, 1889 [1736]). Leslie Stephen strongly brings out this point in his extended discussion of Butler: Stephen, *History of English Thought in the Eighteenth Century*, vol. 1, pp. 235–61, at p. 245. On Butler see also ISOA, pp. 307–26.
[97]Daniel Defoe, *The Adventures of Robinson Crusoe*, with 30 Colour Plates by A. E. Jackson (London: Ward, Lock & Co., Limited, n.d. [1719]); I still have the book. I have not been able to familiarize myself with the wealth of secondary literature, in books and articles, on the early English novel. I have used as background mainly the standard works: E. M. Forster, *Aspects of the Novel* (Harmondsworth: Penguin, 1962 [1927]); Richard Church, *The Growth of the English Novel* (London: Methuen, 1951) and Ian Watt, *The Rise of the Novel: Studies in Defoe, Richardson and Fielding* (London: Hogarth Press, 1987 [1957]).

early eighteenth-century prose, but I was enthralled by the uncompromising realistic narrative, stamped with circumstantial verisimilitude, at which he excelled, which I now recognize as a fictional expression of Lockean empiricism. Like many a child – and even adult – reader, I *was* Crusoe on the island, building with great ingenuity an impregnable fortress-house to keep potential attackers at bay. And I was Crusoe as he stared, 'thunderstruck', at the single naked footstep in the sand and marvelled at what it might mean. Crusoe is the universal, the representative, human being, resilient in adversity. But what did puzzle me most at the time was the word 'Providence' which I had never come across before. After reading of several occasions in which Crusoe trusted to 'Providence' to see him through, or gave thanks to 'Providence' for deliverance and sustenance, I began to understand its meaning. Naturally, I had no idea of the slightly cool deistic overtones of the word – Crusoe himself was fervent enough in using it, unsurprisingly in the circumstances. But I took it as a reverential word for God and fitted it into my childish religious faith. Many years later, I discovered (through Isaiah Berlin) the Neapolitan philosopher of history Giambattista Vico (1668–1744) and his work of genius, the *Scienza Nuova*, where the theological concept of Providence is pivotal (as will be explained in the next chapter).

Raised a Presbyterian Dissenter, the adult Daniel Defoe (d. 1731) was a man who skirmished the margins of society and, without seeming particularly devout himself, championed with his powerful pen the rights of dissenting minorities. Defoe's philosophy of life held together religious faith and ethical integrity, twin marks of the Christian Enlightenment. Writing about the funeral of John Churchill, Duke of Marlborough, the saviour of his nation and of much of Europe from the aggressive wars of Louis XIV, Defoe states that the business of great men is 'to add virtue and piety to their glory, which alone will pass them into Eternity, and make them truly immortal ... What is glory without virtue? A great man without religion is no more than a great beast without a soul.'[98] Invocations of 'Providence' notwithstanding, religious faith and practice are but faintly present in *Robinson Crusoe*, an 'impotence' that Watt attributes to the secularizing effect of Puritanism on the

---

[98]Cited Watt, *The Rise of the Novel*, p. 78.

socio-economic nexus of society,[99] which remains dominant in the novel, by virtue of the vacuum created by its absence.

Many years later, I tried to read *Moll Flanders*, which appeared three years after *Crusoe*, but I struggled to finish it. I looked in vain for any sense of serious moral purpose, or shall I say guiding Providence, in that chaotic, nihilistic narrative. As often as not, Moll gets away with her misdemeanours and lives to practise further variations on the theme of her heedless, headlong love life mingled with petty crime – though quite uncharacteristically she is penitent at her life's end.[100] E. M. Forster comments on Defoe's underworld characters: 'Their innate goodness is always flourishing despite the author's better judgement' and he describes Moll and her associates as 'sensible good-hearted rogues' who 'make no fuss' about their setbacks.[101] Defoe was overfond of Moll and there may have been reasons in his life for that. But whether his narratives were truly novels in the modern sense is much debated. Walter Scott did not include him in his *Lives of the Novelists*. I think they do not quite merit the name. They have consummate realism, vividness and life-likeness, combined with slick narrative pace. But do they have rounded characterization and the moral seriousness that comes from gifted psychological insight into individual motivation and social relations, on the part of the author, or are they a kind of literary facsimile of life?

The first true novel in English (albeit in the epistolary form) is generally thought to be Samuel Richardson's *Pamela*.[102] But Henry Fielding (1707–54) was treading on his heels. Fielding's *Shamela* (published over a pseudonym the year after *Pamela*) was a parody, mockery and bawdy 'send-up' of Richardson's concoction of titillation, suspense and sententious puritan morality, which was all smothered in an infinitely dissected and brilliantly executed anatomy of human psychology, feeling and 'sensibility' amid a welter of domestic trivia.[103] Pamela is also Joseph Andrew's sister in Fielding's

---

[99]Watt, *The Rise of the Novel*, pp. 80–5.
[100]Daniel Defoe, *The Fortunes and Misfortunes of the Famous Moll Flanders* (Oxford: Oxford University Press, 1971 [1722]).
[101]Forster, *Aspects of the Novel*, pp. 64, 66.
[102]Samuel Richardson, *Pamela; or, Virtue Rewarded* (Harmondsworth: Penguin, 1980 [1740]).
[103]Henry Fielding, *An Apology for the Life of Mrs. Shamela Andrews* (Oxford: Oxford University Press, 1981 [1741], with *Joseph Andrews*).

eponymous novel; Lord and Lady Booby and Parson Williams also figure in both stories. Fielding does not let Richardson go easily. E. M. Foster nicely says of *Joseph Andrews* and its successors: 'Its author begins by playing the fool in a Richardsonian world, and ends by being serious in a world of his own – the world of Tom Jones and Amelia'; they are rounded, fully human characters.[104] Samuel Johnson, a proponent of Richardson (who was a friend and benefactor) against Fielding, pronounced that there was 'more knowledge of the human heart in one letter of Richardson's than in all *Tom Jones*' and that Richardson had 'dived into the recesses of the human heart', while Fielding had been content with the externals of character.[105] There is some truth in this judgement, though it does not effect our final assessment of their respective merits or greatness. Fielding's novels are narratives of action, amid the bustle and sometimes chaos of eighteenth-century English wayfaring life and London society, high and low, while Richardson's are mainly narratives of enclosed psychological processes.

Literature, empiricism and the Enlightenment

My introduction to English novels (properly speaking) of the Enlightenment was Fielding's comic epic *Tom Jones* (1749), which was a set text at school. Henry Fielding repeatedly insists that his novels are 'histories' or 'true histories'; that is to say, true to life, unvarnished narrative portrayals, in all their immediacy, of (on the one hand) rough social mores and human turpitude (and on the other) of virtue and innocence triumphant after many vicissitudes and poignant portrayals of redeeming human love. In his preface to *Joseph Andrews* (1742) – surely one of the most enjoyable of all novels – Fielding states that 'everything is copied from the book of nature, and scarce a character or action produced which

---

[104]Forster, *Aspects of the Novel*, p. 125.
[105]Cited Watt, *The Rise of the Novel*, p. 261.

I have not taken from my own observations and experience'.[106] As Saintsbury says, 'For the very first time in English prose fiction every character is alive, every incident is capable of having happened.'[107] Fielding was tolerant of and (often) compassionate towards many of the multifarious expressions of human frailty, but never towards hypocrisy, cruelty, brutality and corruption.

In *Joseph Andrews* a moral and religious framework controls the story. In *Jonathan Wild* (1743),[108] however, Fielding – who had been a tearaway in his younger days – seems to revel in 'wildness' while exposing, in a vein of consistent and olympian irony, a pervasive climate of brutality, hypocrisy and corruption, which is a signature theme of all his works. *Jonathan Wild* is not a pure novel but is half biography of the notorious highwayman of that name, who was hung at Tyburn in 1725, and half romance.

Defoe's mundane factuality and physical concreteness strike the Enlightenment note of empirical observation, investigation and description. There is something of this in Smollett, whose prose (as Church suggests) is marked by 'a firmness of touch and attack'; it is 'terse' and 'uncompromising'; it confronts the reader fair and square.[109] There is nothing fuzzy or indefinite in him. The same highly particular attention to the empirical facts on the ground (or in his case, in the air, in the trees, or on the water) is brought to perfection in Gilbert White's *The Natural History of Selborne*. Obviously this is not a novel, but it has an assured place in the classics of the English Enlightenment, the date of its publication being particularly poignant: 1789.[110] White should never be patronized as a rustic amateur; he represents a high point of self-conscious Enlightenment epistemology and sensibility, applied directly to nature, both wild and cultivated. The selection of his

---

[106] Henry Fielding, *The History of the Adventures of Joseph Andrews and His Friend Mr. Abraham Adams*, intro. George Saintsbury (London: Dent; New York: Dutton, 1910 [1742]), p. xxxii.
[107] Fielding, *Joseph Andrews*, p. xxi.
[108] Henry Fielding, *The History of the Life of the Late Mr Jonathan Wild the Great*, ed. and intro. George Saintsbury, *The Works of Henry Fielding*, ed. George Saintsbury, 12 vols, vol. 10 (London: Dent, 1893).
[109] Church, *The Growth of the English Novel*, pp. 83–4.
[110] Gilbert White, *The Natural History of Selborne in the Country of Southampton* (London: Oxford University Press, 1937 [1789]); page references in my main text.

poems, added from manuscripts in the second edition of 1813, while rather stiltedly emulating earlier eighteenth-century models ('in lone sequestered nook,/ Where skirting woods imbrown the dimpling brook'; 'love-sick turtles [doves] breathe their amorous pain'), also contain intimations of Romanticism and the Gothic ('Wildly majestic'; 'Romantic spot'; the ruined convent from which 'the cowl'd spectre' issues forth at night; '[land]scapes, grotesque and wild') (pp. 3–8).

Gilbert White's systematic record-keeping, his correspondence with fellow naturalists in different parts of the country, and his reading of English and French works of natural history mark him as an Enlightenment philosopher (in the eighteenth-century sense). He identifies with those 'philosophers investigating the works of nature' (p. 82). He urges that botanists – normally, as notes, amateur and dilettante – should 'study plants philosophically' and 'investigate the laws of vegetation' (p. 226). He applauds improvements in husbandry, agriculture and communications, highlighting wild Ireland and the Scottish Highlands as subjects for research (pp. 114–15). He is touched with complacency about technological progress, claiming that agriculture has 'arrived at such a pitch of perfection' that no-one need resort to salted meat in Winter (p. 218). He partly quotes (p. 227), without naming him, Swift's *Gulliver's Travels* where the King of Brobdingnag gives his 'opinion, that whoever could make two ears of corn, or two blades of grass to grow upon a spot of ground where only one grew before, would deserve better of mankind, and do more essential service to his country, than the whole race of politicians put together.'[111] White notes with satisfaction the virtual eradication of leprosy in England (pp. 216–17). True, he loves to regale the bizarre, such as the quack who swallowed a live toad to impress his potential customers (p. 59); but prodigies are documented and mysteries explained. He warns against superstition and the propensity of the country folk to be deceived and to deceive (p. 67). White's Enlightenment credentials are also apparent in his incredulity with regard to witchcraft (p. 202). But he is also a default Anglican, and

---

[111] Jonathan Swift, *Gulliver's Travels*, ed. Peter Dixon and John Chalker, intro. Michael Foot (Harmondsworth: Penguin, 1967 [1726]), ch. 7: 'A Voyage to Brobdingnag', at p. 176.

quotes Scripture routinely. The tinges of deism in his expressions are typical of his age. He often invokes (e.g. p. 67) both the title and spirit of John Ray's *The Wisdom of God Manifested in the Works of the Creation* (1691) and speaks of 'the GOD of NATURE' (p. 78, capitals original).

Key Enlightenment themes in the early English novel

In Fielding, Sterne, Smollett and Goldsmith, we find several Enlightenment hot topics, all aspects of the authors' enlightened drive for reform in the church, the law, prisons and the medical profession, while in Richardson we have a smothering moralistic puritanism, married to salacious temptations, with minimal social agenda. Watt draws attention to Richardson's typical ethical vocabulary: virtue, propriety, decency, modesty, delicacy, purity, which all have individualistic sexual connotations. Prudery and prurience combine in *Pamela* to constitute the 'immitigable vulgarity of the book's moral texture', as Watt finely puts it.[112] The fact that the ethical horizon is mainly contracted and compressed to the 'indoors' arena in Richardson suggests that he had taken shelter within domesticity from the social, political and theological challenges of the Enlightenment. Here are the themes that stand out for me, in the novels, selected by ethical, social and theological criteria.

1. *The state of the clerical profession.* Parson Adams in *Joseph Andrews* is one of the few worthy and loveable – as well as learned – clerics in the early English novels, but he is representative of the fate of poor and insecure unbeneficed clergy; his cassock is in tatters and he is forced to sell some precious classics to buy food. Lazy, hypocritical and mercenary clergy abound in Fielding and Smollett.[113] The exceptions in Fielding are not only Adams but also

---

[112]Watt, *The Rise of the Novel*, pp. 157, 171.
[113]Tobias Smollett, *Roderick Random* (London: Dent; New York: Dutton, n.d. [1748]).

the Reverend 'Doctor Harrison' in *Amelia*, who rescues Booth and Amelia from prison and penury and saves their marriage, all the while catechizing them with wholesome Anglican divinity and theological ethics. Oliver Goldsmith (1728–74) offers a deceptively charming example of the humble, scholarly and dutiful priest in *The Vicar of Wakefield* (1766, though written in 1762). Here we find the narrator's claim – surely tongue-in-cheek, as the immediate context is the quality of a gooseberry wine! – to have written 'with the veracity of an historian'; also the idiom of the age in references to 'Providence'.

2. Unworthy clergy and other professionals. In *Joseph Andrews* Adams shares the pittance in his pocket with a fellow-traveller who picks his pocket and turns out to be a Roman Catholic priest.[114] Roderick Random encounters a vicar and curate who are as bad as each other, the one, who has two good livings, regularly gets his housekeeper with child, the other being a bawdy card-sharp – and nothing unusual about either, apparently.[115] In Sterne we have the nameless and hapless curate who, in haste because the infant might not live, misnames Tristram Shandy at his baptism[116] (alongside the much mocked, incompetent Roman Catholic physician and male midwife Dr Slop who makes ludicrous attempts throughout to defend the Roman religion). We have seen how the historiography of the Hanoverian Church of England has been turned around during the past century, to bring out the energy, dedication, application and learning of the 'inferior' clergy and the bishops. But here is a contra-indication. In the first English novels the clergy are generally pilloried as ignorant, bigoted and neglectful of their duties, a disgrace to their cloth. Not least among them is the boorish (!) pig-farming Parson Trulliber in *Joseph Andrews*, though he is only one of a rogues gallery in the early English novel of clerics who betray their calling.

---

[114]Fielding, *Joseph Andrews*, pp. 188–9.
[115]Smollett, *Roderick Random*, pp. 46–8.
[116]Laurence Sterne, *The Life and Opinions of Tristram Shandy, Gentleman* (London: Dent; New York: Dutton, n.d.), p. 209.

As a footnote, I include the ironic reversal of confessional doctrines when Roderick Random is 'catechized' by the bigoted, ignorant ship's captain. When Random is asked to make the sign of the cross, the captain takes it as conclusive proof that he is a Protestant! And when Random says that he deplores the doctrine of 'transubstantiation' and 'a real presence', Oakum declares that he always suspected that he was a Roman Catholic! This makes uncomfortable reading for a theologian![117]

3. *Urging social reform.* A century before Dickens and his lurid descriptions of debtors' prisons, Fielding was holding up London's prisons as the epitome of barbarism, squalor and corruption, especially in his last and most serious novel *Amelia*.[118] In fact officialdom as such – from the rural magistrate Justice Thrasher to the gaoler of the anti-hero Booth – is unsparingly portrayed as incompetent, venal and corrupt. Towards the end of his life Fielding was engaged in reforming the policing arrangements (we cannot say 'system') of London. While Fielding – both as narrator and through his characters – consistently upholds the dignity of the clerical order, the same cannot be said of the legal or medical professions, for lawyers are often exposed, not only in Fielding but in his peers, as ignorant, mercenary and fraudulent, while physicians are revealed as ignorant, boorish, grasping and corrupt quacks, ripe for regulation (not least the panel of naval surgeons and later 'Doctor Mackshane', the ship's surgeon, in *Roderick Random*).[119]

4. *Against 'enthusiasm' and in favour of early Christian simplicity and purity.* In *Joseph Andrews*, Barnabas the bookseller, whom Adams is seeking to interest in publishing his sermons, calculates the comparative commercial value of sermons versus plays, pronouncing, 'I would as soon print one of [George] Whitefield's [sermons] as any farce whatever.' The bookseller continues: 'Whoever prints such

---

[117] Smollett, *Roderick Random*, p. 175.
[118] Henry Fielding, *Amelia*, ed. David Blewett (Harmondsworth: Penguin, 1987 [1751]).
[119] Smollett, *Roderick Random*, pp. 33ff, 174f.

heterodox stuff ought to be hanged ... He [Whitefield] would reduce us to the example of the primitive ages, forsooth! and would insinuate to the people that a clergyman ought to be always preaching and praying. He pretends to understand the Scripture literally; and would make mankind believe that the poverty and low estate [of] the Church in its infancy ... was to be preserved in her ... established state.' The principles of notorious deists and freethinkers could not do as much harm as Whitefield and his followers, Barnabas concludes.[120] Adams responds that he once wished Whitefield well, but turned against him 'when he began to call nonsense and enthusiasm to his aid, and set up the detestable doctrine of faith against good works, I was his friend no longer; for surely that doctrine was coined in hell; and one would think none but the devil himself could have the confidence to preach it.'[121]

5. *Subverting a caricatured Enlightenment 'reason' that is divorced from ethics.* In *Tom Jones* the tutor Square, who is a philosopher of little brain, invokes the Enlightenment clichés of 'the unalterable rule of right, and the eternal fitness of things', which Johnson mocked in *Rasselas*. But Square is eclipsed in Fielding's satire by the bigoted parson Thwackum who gives us the much quoted but self-condemning definition of 'religion': 'When I mention religion, I mean the Christian religion; and not only the Christian religion, but the Protestant religion; and not only the Protestant religion, but the Church of England.'[122] It doesn't get much more delicious than that. But a scene in *Joseph Andrews* raises the spectre of atheism. Joseph falls in with a set of habitual revellers who, in the manner of the London coffee-houses and other hostelries gather to imbibe and discuss. Their conversation 'rolled on the deepest points

---

[120]Fielding, *Joseph Andrews*, p. 54.
[121]Ibid., p. 55. The whole passage is not be missed, with its indirect allusions to the low-church sacramental teaching of Benjamin Hoadly (praised by Adams who is evidently inclined to Latitudinarianism) and to Hobbes's *Leviathan*, linked by the bookseller to the Koran and to radical deism (Thomas Woolston)! (though, of course, the bookseller has not read a word of any of these works).
[122]Henry Fielding, *Tom Jones* (Ware: Wordsworth, 1992), p. 77.

of philosophy'. As Joseph recounts: 'These gentlemen were engaged in a search after truth, in the pursuit of which they threw aside all the prejudices of education, and governed themselves only by the infallible guide of human reason. This great guide, after having shown them the falsehood of that very ancient but simple tenet, that there is such a being as a Deity ... helped them to establish in his stead a certain rule of right, by adhering to which they all arrived at the utmost purity of morals.'[123] The innocent Joseph is soon, though reluctantly, undeceived by the less than virtuous behaviour of individual members of the club. For the equally innocent Parson Adams (as for his age), good morals and right belief are inseparably connected. 'The first care I always take is of a boy's morals; I had rather he should be a blockhead than an atheist or a presbyterian'![124] But there is a right use and right kind of reason: Adams teaches Joseph that, in times of affliction, 'it is the business of a man and a Christian to summon Reason ... to his aid.' Why? '[S]he will presently teach him patience and submission', in other words, the virtues.[125]

6. *Airing Enlightenment ideas, debates and names.* Fielding, Sterne and Goldsmith, together with Smollett to some extent, show themselves to be Enlightenment intellectuals (but that did not stop them writing sermons). Fielding devotes the first chapter of each book of *Tom Jones* to an apologia for his method (i.e. it is a 'history' and inculcates virtue to the virtuous; what may seem low or disreputable is in the mind of the reader) and to miscellaneous philosophical and literary reflections Many names are dropped: the devout and ascetic Locke and the notorious libertine and blasphemer John Wilmot Earl of Rochester are mentioned in close proximity, followed later by Swift and Garrick, Pope and Shaftesbury, Warburton and Hogarth, among many non-contemporary authors, such

---

[123] Fielding, *Joseph Andrews*, p. 163.
[124] Ibid., p. 178.
[125] Ibid., p. 207.

as Shakespeare, Cervantes and Moliere, together with the classics in which Fielding was well versed.[126] In *Amelia* he adds Bishop Gilbert Burnet, the Puritan Bible commentator Matthew Poole, the excellent sermons of Isaac Barrow and Robert South (the latter not by name) and the notorious Bernard Mandeville; Hogarth and Handel reappear; Swift, Cervantes and Pope share a paragraph. Eventually Isaac Newton makes his inevitable appearance and even Pierre Bayle pops up.[127] Smollett's *Roderick Random* introduces *en route* Shaftesbury, Tindal (the militant deist), Hobbes and the company of 'Freethinkers'.[128] *The Vicar of Wakefield*, which could be mistaken at first sight for an innocent idyll of clerical life, contains much intellectual content. Goldsmith introduces Richard Hooker and Bishop John Jewel, Lord Falkland, William Whiston and Alexander Pope. There is much discussion of Enlightenment notions, including reason, virtue and 'Natural Law', together with the late-Enlightenment concepts of sensibility and imagination.[129] In Fielding we come across those familiar Enlightenment circumlocutions for God: 'the Deity', 'the Supreme Being', 'the Almighty', 'the Highest', 'our great Creator' and of course 'Providence'.

The Enlightenment in *Tristram Shandy*

In further support of my thesis that the Anglican Enlightenment was integrated into eighteenth-century English culture, without the ideological friction that pertained in other nations, I now bring forward the case of Laurence Sterne (1759–67) and *Tristram Shandy*. Obviously, I fully recognize that it stands unique in the annals of English literature up to the twentieth century, as a work of fiction unlike any other until we reach James Joyce (whom Church

---

[126]Fielding, *Tom Jones*, Bk I, pp. 98, 100, 195, 243; Bk II, pp. 155, 200.
[127]Fielding, *Amelia*, pp. 256, 329, 397, 398, 427, 514, 522.
[128]Smollett, *Roderick Random*, p. 122.
[129]Oliver Goldsmith, *The Vicar of Wakefield* (London and Edinburgh: Thomas Nelson, n.d.), pp. 6, 7, 19, 105, 173.

calls Sterne's 'disciple') and *Ulysses*, and is not typical of the early English novel.[130] In *Tristram Shandy* Sterne alludes frequently, but on the whole glancingly, to various iconic figures of the English and European Enlightenments.[131] His manner is playful and never solemn or deferential, as though to say: 'Here's that Mr. Locke again; we all know him, don't we, but let's not get too excited about it.' Sterne was a beneficed clergyman of the Church of England; he preached in churches bursting at the seams and published seven volumes of sermons under the Shakespearean name 'Mr. Yorick' (which is also the name of the parish priest in this bewildering and disconcerting novel, packed with extreme whimsicality). In the face of the basic Enlightenment paradigm of uniformitarianism, Sterne is an advocate of diversitarianism, individuality, originality, difference and strangeness. He takes nothing seriously or conventionally, not even birth and death, and we cannot take ourselves seriously when reading him (or attempting to do so).

While keeping his readers guessing and scratching their heads in puzzlement, he slyly deconstructs some Enlightenment shibboleths and he toys with some great names of the Enlightenment. The names include (again, I spare the reader most of the page references; others are included in the text): Erasmus, Luther, Rabelais, Montaigne, 'my beloved Cervantes' and *Don Quixote*, Francis Bacon (Lord Verulam), Descartes, Casaubon and Scaliger (and miscellaneous humanists, real and possibly fictional), Malebranche, George Whitefield, Voltaire (by mention of *Candide*) and Rousseau. Locke is in a category of his own, receiving multiple mentions, not all respectful: he appears in a sentence along with 'farting and hickuping'. But we also have 'the sagacious Locke' and Locke's *Essay Concerning Human Understanding*, which Sterne calls 'a history book ... of what passes in a man's own mind' (p. 62), adding, 'many ... quote the book, who have not read it – and many have read it who understand it not' (p. 62). The Enlightenment nostrum, '[R]eason in scientifick research', is given its due (p. 4), as are the Enlightenment's hierarchy

---

[130]James Joyce, *Ulysses*, ed. Jeri Johnson (Oxford: Oxford University Press, 1993); Church, *The Growth of the English Novel*, p. 92.
[131]Cf. Alice Green Fredman, *Diderot and Sterne* (New York: Columbia University Press, 1955), an enlightening compare-and-contrast exercise; Diderot borrowed from Sterne in *Jacques the Fatalist*, trans. Michael Henry, intro. Martin Hall (Harmondsworth: Penguin, 1986).

of authorities: 'Tis contrary to the law of nature ... to reason ... to the GOSPEL' (p. 386, capitals original). The deity is called, in deistic fashion, 'the supreme Maker and first Designer of all things' (p. 171).

Conclusion

By collating the allusions to Enlightenment ideas and writers in the works of four early English novelists, we have, I believe, been able to establish certain conclusions which support the central claim of this chapter devoted to the Anglican Enlightenment. It is implicit in some leading authorities on the English Enlightenment, especially Pocock, Porter and Young, and is made explicit in the present work, that in England and especially in the Church of England, the Enlightenment was more or less smoothly integrated with dominant cultural norms, intellectual trends and social mores. In Fielding, Sterne, Smollett and Goldsmith, the key Enlightenment paradigms, intellectual, ethical and theological, are presented, expounded and sometimes quizzically observed. Four interlinked conclusions emerge. (i) The early English novel inhabits a Christian and ecclesiastical universe. (ii) Its authors are usually theologically literate as well as culturally accomplished. (iii) They exhibit a reforming agenda with regard to the clergy, lawyers and physicians. (iv) Enlightenment paradigms are embedded in the narrative and dialogue of these novels. I will expand briefly on these points, taken together, to give a rounded picture.

The early English novel is permeated with a Christian theological and ethical worldview. Their authors at simply at home in it. Sterne was a serving Anglican cleric; when he wrote about parsons and parishioners, theology and philosophy, he did so from the inside. The title of Goldsmith's most famous and much loved work *The Vicar of Wakefield* speaks for itself. But it is much more than a gentle, naive and touching story; it is in fact studded with allusions and discussions of Enlightenment philosophical, theological and ethical questions. But what of Henry Fielding? His novels are earthy in places. *Tom Jones* was judged by some early critics as a bawdy romp (e.g. Walter Scott was a little reserved in his appreciation of Fielding's work on ethical grounds, though he owed much to Fielding, and ultimately defends him)[132] and so it is, in part. But Fielding aims to be true to life and to nature and therefore he must do justice to both flesh and spirit. Indeed, he was a man of flesh and spirit himself. But he was also a highly cultured person. He knew the Greek and Latin classics, the Bible, published sermons (especially those of Isaac Barrow), and the lineaments of Enlightenment thought. He had a layman's theology and writes as a Christian and as a reformed character – if *Amelia* is a clue, redeemed by marital love – and committed in his turn to social and legal reform. Fielding was no eighteenth-century dilettante; he was active in practical reforming initiatives, grappling particularly with the challenges of crime and policing in London. Altogether, the handling of Enlightenment ideas, challenges and personages in these novels is relaxed and unthreatened. Unlike the situation in France, Germany, Italy and the Netherlands, Enlightenment principles are treated in a non-polemical way and are not presented as a cause of conflict and division. In the Church of England the Enlightenment appears to have been more seamlessly integrated than elsewhere.

---

[132] Sir Walter Scott, *The Lives of the Novelists* (London: Dent; New York: Dutton, 1910), pp. 46–70, especially pp. 56, 64, 66–7.

6

Enlightenment history and the Bible

Why include a chapter on historiography and the philosophy of history in a book that sets out to examine the Enlightenment's theological dimension and its reception and interpretation? I will suggest several reasons why the present chapter is relevant and necessary, beginning with some basic comments on the inextricable connection between theology and history. I intentionally approach the subject from the standpoint of hermeneutics in the sense of a method of empathetic understanding of the constellation of texts, persons and events in the past, leading to explanatory hypotheses. This was not generally the approach or method of Enlightenment historians and philosophers of history (with the exceptions of Spinoza, Vico, Lessing and later Herder – who actually weight down the scales in quality, if not quantity). Enlightenment historians, notably the big four Voltaire, Hume, Gibbon and Robertson, were committed to the ethical and rational adjudication of the historical personages, events and cultural epochs, that came within their purview, by the canons of their own Enlightenment ideology. They rushed to judgement. But, as Karl Barth, who knew the Enlightenment better than most theologians, pointed out, we are 'not called to hold the Last Judgement on one another'. Such is not the purpose of our work as scholars: 'History writing cannot be a proclamation of judgement.'[1] So it follows that the study of

---

[1] Karl Barth, *Protestant Theology in the Nineteenth Century*, trans. Brian Cozens and John Bowden, Foreword Colin Gunton (London: SCM Press, 2001), p. 9.

the theology in history writing and philosophy of history must be: first, hermeneutical (an exercise in empathetic understanding, as in Vico); then explanatory (working with the questions 'Why?' and 'How?', as well as 'What?' and 'Who?'); and only finally, though inescapably, ethical, which means not pretending that good and evil do not matter in the history of the human race (here the shade of Lord Acton hovers over us, castigating us if we dodge the ethical challenge).[2]

Why Enlightenment historiography?

(a) The most basic point is that no theological enquiry can exclude an historical referent without collapsing. Historical study is an essential and integral part of the theological curriculum. The historical dimension of the capacious discipline of Christian theology takes various forms: historical theology (the study of theologies of the past in their contexts), ecclesiastical history (study of the church in history) and historical-critical study of the Bible (the origins, transmission, editorial processes, genre, authorship and purpose of the biblical literature). There is no avoiding the historical pathway to theological understanding and there is no substitute for it, though it is not the only pathway to that goal and is not sufficient in itself. So an enquiry into the historiography and philosophy of history of the Enlightenment era is crucial to any understanding of the theological content and theological significance of the Enlightenment.

(b) Second, history is the inescapable milieu and environment of all life and thought, including work in theology and philosophy and the practice of historical research itself. As Blondel insisted in *History and Dogma*, 'One can do nothing without history and nothing against it.'[3] In the Judaeo-Christian tradition, historicity

---

[2]A key resource for the study of Enlightenment historiography is Sophie Bourgault and Robert Sparling (eds), *A Companion to Enlightenment Historiography* (Leiden: Brill, 2013).
[3]Maurice Blondel, *The Letter on Apologetics* and *History and Dogma*, trans. and intro. Alexander Dru and Illtyd Trethowan (Grand Rapids, MI: Eerdmans, 1994), p. 232.

is an inescapable ingredient of religious faith and religious community. But history is also the source of the permanent state of crisis and *angst* of modern theology since the Enlightenment. The contingent nature and ceaseless flow of events in time, coupled with the uncertain status of our knowledge of them, together seem to make them an unstable basis for Christian truth. As we shall note in its place, a major figure of the German, Lutheran, Enlightenment, Gotthold Ephraim Lessing, posed the deeply troubling theological dilemma: How can the contingent, human, events of history display or manifest the eternal truths of (divine) reason? We will come to Lessing's statement of the problem and his solution. It is an appropriate and necessary response to the human reality of theological knowledge and belief – grounded in the reception, appropriation and interpretation of divine revelation – that the theological questions that arise from the Enlightenment should be examined within the framework of historical theory. Historical study includes the historiography and the philosophy of history of the period that is the subject of research, that is to say the character and rationale of the historical writing and the framework of meaning and interpretation within which it is being pursued.

(c) Third, we need to put the record straight regarding the contribution of Enlightenment historians and philosophers of history, which was considerable. We have already seen (Chapter 3, 'A Virtuous Enlightenment'), that Paul Hazard, possibly the most widely read, semi-popular interpreter of Enlightenment thought, falsely claimed that the Enlightenment – even the French Enlightenment, which was his main concern – was dismissive of tradition and that it set out to make a clean break and a fresh start. By the same token Hazard claimed that the Enlightenment had no use for history. 'In their inmost consciousness', he asserted, 'men [*sic*] had come to look on history as a broken reed.' Moreover, 'The very notion of historicity was tending to disappear ... Henceforth all the alluring visions lay in front.'[4] On the contrary, as Cobban insists, history came second only to science in the Enlightenment's hierarchy of

---

[4] Paul Hazard, *The European Mind 1680–1715*, trans. J. Lewis May (Harmondsworth: Penguin, 1964 [1953]; French, *La Crise de la conscience européenne*, 1935), p. 47.

intellectual disciplines.⁵ The truth of the matter is that the 'alluring visions', as Hazard calls them, of a future in which benevolent, non-tyrannical government and technological innovation had reduced human misery, granted toleration, provided education and enabled the arts to flourish, were resourced and inspired by the achievements of classical antiquity and of the Renaissance (Voltaire added the reign of Louis XIV). However, Enlightenment historiography was not motivated by humanist self-aggrandisement, as some Christian – even theological – critics seem to suspect. It was ethically motivated to a significant degree, as well as being driven by the thirst for knowledge and understanding of what had hitherto remained simply unknown or had been misinterpreted because evidence and explanation had been distorted by ecclesiastical authority. However, Enlightenment historians did not aspire to the unattainable objectivity of a Ranke, namely to show events as they really happened at the time; that was not their motive. They had an agenda: to spread intellectual, moral, social and political 'enlightenment' in all areas of knowledge and practice. Cassirer points out that the common notion that the eighteenth century had no sense of history is 'directly and convincingly contradicted by a glance at the development of religious thought', which is precisely what we have been doing.⁶

(d) Fourth, we cannot hope to understand the theological dimension of the Enlightenment unless we take into account the historiographical context because theology itself became historicized in the late seventeenth and the eighteenth centuries.⁷ This development constituted a radical transformation of theological method, one that is now accepted and practised almost universally. In modernity, almost the first pair of spectacles through which theological questions and debates have been viewed are the historical ones. The second half of the seventeenth century and

---

⁵Alfred Cobban, 'The Enlightenment', in *New Cambridge Modern History*, vol. 7, *The Old Regime, 1713–1763*, ed. J. O. Lindsay (Cambridge: Cambridge University Press, 1957), p. 93.
⁶Ernst Cassirer, *The Philosophy of the Enlightenment*, trans. C. A. Koelln and J. P. Pettegrove (Princeton, NJ: Princeton University Press, 1951 [1932]), p. 182; cf. p. 197.
⁷J. G. A. Pocock, 'Historiography and Enlightenment: A View of Their History', *Modern Intellectual History* 5 (2008), pp. 83–96.

the whole of the eighteenth saw the beginnings of the historical movement which would reach fruition in the nineteenth. This was the era of the historicizing of all branches of thought, including theology. That is not to deny, but rather to affirm, that there were outstanding earlier precedents, Valla, Erasmus and Hooker among them. Historicized theology is the alternative and only acceptable approach for modernity to scholastic theology, which typically goes about its work by comparing and evaluating written authorities, without asking about what their provenance, context and transmission can tell us about their validity. Today we begin by asking, 'How trustworthy are the sources?' The fundamental question of trust, which is a hermeneutic of restoration, reception and appropriation, contains within it several subsidiary questions: 'Where did these sources come from and why did they emerge? What factors shaped these sources to make them what they are? What other potential sources were suppressed in order that these might survive? How have they been interpreted by others both previously and recently?' Whatever we believe to be knowledge, in any discipline, must undergo a process of historical scrutiny and interrogation along these lines; theology is no exception. Historical scrutiny and interrogation includes critical evaluation both of the available evidence and of the interpretations of it, ancient and modern, that are on offer. But the historical-critical method should eventuate in and lead up to historical reconstruction, as far as that is possible long after the events that the sources describe. And such reconstruction forms an essential preliminary stage in overall theological and ultimately doctrinal construction, where the biblical, historical, systematic and philosophical-ethical aspects of theology all have their part to play.

(e) Fifth, we need to do justice to the Enlightenment background of the concept of development, which is now second nature to an historian. It was the achievement of nineteenth-century historians and historical philosophers to make the category of development the key heuristic concept of historical interpretation. But the seeds and the first shoots of the development of development are found in Enlightenment history. It did not quite attain to the empathetic historical vision of historicism, but it began the transition from the uniformitarian framework, within which certain periods were held to exhibit the ideal values of enlightened civilization (or civilization *per se*), to a sense of historical process within which there was necessarily change and development. Montesquieu's grasp of the integrated, organic nature of a society, the subsequent broadening out of historical enquiry to include social, economic, moral and cultural aspects (crudely in Voltaire, more sophisticatedly in the Scottish school), coupled with a belief in progress in all these areas, facilitated this movement. Historicism as a method stands for more than 'a sense of history' and of 'the pastness of the past', though these notions are elements within it. The nub of historicism is that an understanding of historical phenomena – which itself cannot be attained without an imaginative, empathetic penetration of historical events – requires a grasp of their place within an unfolding process of development.[8]

(f) Sixth, we should be aware that the historians and historical philosophers of the Enlightenment era were a mixture of Christian believers, Protestant and Catholic, lay and clerical, as well as sceptical deists. That mixture of historical minds further undermines the still widespread assumption of the anti-Christian animus of Enlightenment thought (see 'Enlightenment historians and Christianity', below).

(g) Lastly, we should connect the nascent scientific work on the Bible in this period with Enlightenment history. The Enlightenment's study of the Bible was carried forward by broadly historical methods, including philology (the study of the history of words within a language), the study of ancient Oriental languages that are relevant to the Bible, and – for the first time – the comparative study of religion. It was mainly by historical research and enquiry that biblical study was progressed. In the Enlightenment we see the pioneering efforts of scholars who began to apply the historical-critical methods to the Bible – methods that are now standard for all students of the Bible except fundamentalists. The critical-historical method is certainly not the only valid or fruitful method of biblical research and needs to be supplemented by hermeneutical and exegetical work, but biblical research and understanding would be ham-strung without it. The historicization of biblical study began at this time with Spinoza, Richard Simon, Hobbes, Locke, Isaac

---

[8] Maurice Mandelbaum, *History, Man and Reason: A Study in Nineteenth-Century Thought* (Baltimore, MD: Johns Hopkins University Press, 1971), pp. 42–54. Friedrich Meinecke, *Historism* [sic]: *The Rise of a New Historical Outlook*, trans. J. E. Anderson (London: Routledge and Kegan Paul, 1972).

La Peyrère, Jean Le Clerc, Lessing and Johann David Michaelis, all Christian scholars bar Spinoza. We will return to biblical study in the Enlightenment era with reference especially to Spinoza and Lessing (having already touched on Hobbes and discussed Locke more substantially elsewhere) and we will conclude with a reflection on the relation of history and faith.

Philosophical history

Here I am aiming to identify what was distinctive or innovative – whether good or bad – in the conceptual framework and methodological axioms of the historical thought of the Enlightenment. I will be touching on its historiography (historical writing) and its philosophy of history (frameworks of meaning and purpose in history) and looking for their theological implications. In this vast and specialized field, I can only scratch the surface, but I aim to bring out what is relevant to my present enquiry. A prefatory caveat is that the originality of Enlightenment historians should not be exaggerated. Those interpreters who either praise or condemn the Enlightenment for supposedly abandoning tradition and starting *de novo*, are bound to marvel disproportionately at its achievements in historical study. Nadel points out that even major interpreters like Cassirer and Meinecke 'cited as new and revolutionary certain ideas put forward by men like Bayle and Hume which, in fact, were merely paraphrases or quotations from the classics, drearily familiar to any educated person living between the renaissance [*sic*] and the nineteenth century'.[9] A choice instance is the intentionally didactic purpose of historical writing; the doctrine that 'history is philosophy teaching by examples' (Bolingbroke) is traceable back to Pseudo-Dionysius of Halicarnassus, who himself attributed it (in substance, though not in words) to Thucydides.[10]

Enlightenment historiography went beyond the accumulation of facts or sheer erudition, in which the seventeenth century had excelled,

---

[9]George H. Nadel, 'Philosophy of History before Historicism', *H&T* III. 3 (1964), pp. 291–315, at p. 292. Cf. Cassirer, *The Philosophy of the Enlightenment*; Meinecke, *Historism*.
[10]Nadel, 'Philosophy of History before Historicism', p. 301 & n.

and beyond narrative technique and mastery of style, both which are evident in the histories of Machiavelli and Guicciardini, which the *philosophes* admired as models. What Enlightenment historians achieved was a principled conceptual or ideological standpoint – 'philosophical history'. Pocock points out that *'philosophie'* and 'philosophy' in this period 'very often denoted a fixed determination to have nothing to do with epistemology [or] metaphysics'.[11] So philosophical history was reflective history, history evaluated, called to account and related critically to the historians' worldview, in their case that of the Enlightenment, understood as normative European civilization. So Hume could crow: 'this is the historical Age and this the historical nation' (i.e. Scotland).[12] They did not claim that their method was unprecedented. Gibbon accorded the Roman historian Tacitus the title 'philosophical historian' as 'the first of historians who applied the science of philosophy to the study of facts'.[13] To be a philosophical historian did not mean that one had to pontificate at every turn, like Voltaire, or engage in wishful thinking about the remote past, like Rousseau. One could be more subtle and therefore more effective – indeed lethal. Gay writes of Gibbon: 'It is as a philosophical historian that Gibbon establishes his presence in every sentence of his history; he rarely steps out on stage to speak a line in the first person, but his firm management of the pace, his value-charged epithets, his psychological and sociological pronouncements alert the reader to the philosopher's mind beneath the narrative surface.'[14]

Under the influence of Bacon's inductive methodology and Newton's law-based theories, Enlightenment history was reaching towards history as a science, slowly leaving exemplarist history behind. In order to achieve a scientific form of historiography, the elements of erudition, narrative and an explanatory intention

---

[11]Pocock, *Barbarism and Religion, Volume Two: Narratives of Civil Government* (Cambridge: Cambridge University Press, 1999), p. 177.
[12]Cited from *The Letters of David Hume*, ed. J. Y. T. Greig, 2 vols (Oxford: Oxford University Press, 1932), vol. 2, p. 230, by Simon Kow, 'Politics and Culture in Hume's *History of England*', in Bourgault and Sparling (eds), *A Companion to Enlightenment Historiography*, ch. 2, at p. 65.
[13]Peter Gay, *Style in History* (London: Jonathan Cape, 1975 [1974]), citing Gibbon, *Essai sur l'étude de la littérature* and *Decline and Fall*.
[14]Gay, *Style in History*, p. 49.

needed to be brought together. Philosophical history meant history explored without resort to theological explanation and occult causes such as divine providence, the fulfilment of prophecy and miraculous interventions. The analysis of causation was a critical component of philosophical history and by causation the historians and philosophers meant secondary causation within the mundane nexus, not transcendent, teleological causation, which was not visible or accessible to historical research. Hence the complementary term 'Theoretical or Conjectural History', coined by Dugald Stewart (1753–1828) which does better justice to the role of hypotheses and hidden factors and acknowledges gaps in our knowledge, but perhaps does not do full justice to the reflective element implied in 'philosophical history'. So Enlightenment historians, especially Hume and Gibbon, describe developments as taking place 'insensibly', that is unperceived at the time – working secretly, so to speak – but evident with benefit of hindsight to the historian.[15]

Hume is notorious for his theoretical deconstruction of rational causation: in principle, anything could be the cause of anything, for all we know. We cannot see causation at work. Yet, as a philosophical historian, Hume cannot avoid making causality a major theme. In his essay 'On the Rise and Progress of the Arts and Sciences', he examines in detail the causative effect of particular national polities or constitutional arrangements, for good or ill, on how the arts and sciences fare.[16] William Robertson is regarded as the first global historian because he reached beyond Europe to America and India. John Wesley condemned him for not tracing the hand of providence in human affairs when he discussed causation. But in Robertson, this omission represented not a secularizing impulse, but a scientific one. He was a son of the manse, studied divinity at Edinburgh, served as minister of a rural parish for fourteen years, was made a chaplain to the King, became Principal of the University of Edinburgh (1762–93) and Moderator of the General Assembly of the Church of Scotland (1763). His credentials as a Christian scholar are impeccable and he was theologically competent and perceptive too,

---

[15] James Noggle, *Unfelt: The Language of Affect in the British Enlightenment* (Ithaca, NY: Cornell University Press, 2020), ch. III: 'Historiography'.
[16] David Hume, *Essays, Moral, Political and Literary* (London: Grant Richards, 1903), pp. 112–38.

anticipating Lessing's concept of gradually unfolding progressive revelation by twenty years.[17] He is the only one of the three great British historians of his time who came to history through theology (though one could say that Gibbon's historical perspective was filtered through theology, while Hume came to history partly as an allergic reaction to theology).[18] Although he did not overtly preach in his histories – he saved that for the pulpit where he could be fervent – Robertson had a didactic purpose: 'History should be a teacher of wisdom for the benefit of statesmen and philosophers', which is reminiscent of Bolingbroke's oft-quoted dictum, 'History is philosophy teaching by examples.' But Robertson's biblical, providential framework, allied to moderate Presbyterianism, is generally tacitly (and sometimes explicitly) present and discernible in his histories. John Wesley wanted Robertson to wear his Protestant's heart on his historian's sleeve; but for Robertson that was not the method of scientific history.

The equivalent of 'philosophical history' in Lutheran Germany was 'pragmatic history'. It presupposed the Leibnizian principle that all the events in the world are internally interconnected. According to the prolific historian and philosopher of history Johann Christoph Gatterer (1727–99), 'The highest degree of pragmatism in [the writing of] history would be the portrayal of the general connections of things in the world (*nexus rerum universalis*).' Pragmatic history is one that 'unearths the causes and effects of important events', he wrote, seeking 'to develop ... the whole system of causes and effects, of means and intentions'.[19] Although the goal was to seize immanent, not transcendent, causation, the spiritual realm was not excluded. Both scientific or empirical and poetic or intuitive modes of thought were needed in order to grasp the human as well as the mechanical aspects of history. It is the poetic genius that effects spiritual change. The character of a people or nation is revealed in

---

[17]Ritchie Robertson: *The Enlightenment: The Pursuit of Happiness, 1680–1790* (London: Allen Lane, 2020), p. 165.
[18]Stewart J. Brown (ed.), *William Robertson and the Expansion of Empire* (Cambridge: Cambridge University Press, 1997); Jeffrey Smitten, 'William Robertson: The Minister as Historian', in Bourgault and Sparling (eds), *A Companion to Enlightenment Historiography*, ch. 3; *ODNB* (Smitten).
[19]Cited P. H. Reill, *The German Enlightenment and the Rise of Historicism* (Berkeley, CA: University of California Press, 1975), pp. 40, 42.

their sacred and poetic writings. Reill finds an incipient historicism already in the *Aufklärung* that leads to Johann Gottfried Herder (1744–1803).[20]

To be 'philosophical' in the eighteenth century also meant a disposition to engage in free, open and 'polite' discussion and debate (in the coffee houses of London and the *salons* of Paris, as well as in books, journals and epistolary correspondence), without appeal to knock-down arguments drawn from divine revelation in Scripture and ecclesiastical authority and without religious fervour ('enthusiasm') and eschewing the *odium theologicum* of the recent past. It is noteworthy that the promoters of this usage of 'philosophical' in England included Anglican writers such as Locke and Addison).[21]

In striving for a more scientific, explanatory method, eighteenth-century historians brought together three principles: (i) the idea of the progress of civilization; (ii) a concept of the organic nature of society; and (iii) a doctrinaire notion of uniformity of human nature.[22] I will briefly recapitulate on the first before saying a little more on the second and third.

(i) *Progress*

The overarching notion of progress has already been discussed (Chapter 3), so it will be sufficient here to remind ourselves that there was a strong humanitarian element to the idea of progress as expressed by the *philosophes*, coupled with belief in technological innovation (the *Encyclopédie*), economic enhancement and agricultural reform (Turgot) to make life safer, easier and more productive, coupled with improvements in urban civility and the arts.[23] However, in

---

[20]Reill, *The German Enlightenment and the Rise of Historicism*, p. 218. See also Ulrich Muhlack, 'German Enlightenment Historiography and the Rise of Historicism', in Bourgault and Sparling (eds), *A Companion to Enlightenment Historiography*, ch. 8.
[21]J. G. A. Pocock, *Barbarism and Religion, Volume Two: Narratives of Civil Government*, pp. 18–19.
[22]Hugh Trevor-Roper, 'The Historical Philosophy of the Enlightenment', in id., *History and the Enlightenment*, ed. John Robertson (New Haven, CT: Yale University Press, 2010), pp. 1–16 [first published *SVEC* XXII (1963), pp. 1667–87].
[23]N. Suckling, 'The Enlightenment and the Idea of Progress', *SVEC* LVIII (1967), pp. 1461–80.

adopting a view of progress grounded in rational and mechanical principles, the *philosophes* were moving away from the presiding spirit of Enlightenment historiography, Montesquieu's *The Spirit of the Laws*, with its deep respect and appreciation for the integrity and internal dynamics of a given society. Progress rested on the stability that pan-European trade brought to a continent that had been ravaged by war in the two previous centuries. 'Commercial society' was a unifying and stabilizing factor. 'Civil history', combined with economic theory, generated the collateral discipline of Political Economy, which flourished in the latter part of our period.[24]

(ii) *Organic society*

The concept of the organic nature of a society contributed to the unity of historical knowledge. Montesquieu (*D'l'Esprit des lois*), Voltaire (*Essai sur les moeurs*) and Gibbon (*Essai sur l'étude de la littérature*) pioneered the idea of a comprehensive historical account of society or civilization as a whole. Montesquieu's governing theory was that every society is a 'spiritual union' (*union d'esprit*) within which a common character or 'universal soul' becomes formed, which generates its effects from age to age, both being changed itself and causing change.[25] Montesquieu was far from unique in comparing the development of a society to that of an individual – it is a timeless trope. Pascal had used it – he is a pioneer of the parallel of culture or spirit between the individual and society. Both have their *suise d'idees* and their *manière de penser totale*; both pass through all the stages of life.[26] Hume was directly inspired by Montesquieu to devote himself to his historical labours and in his history and his essays he too is reaching for a more organic understanding of society, no longer as a congeries of autonomous individual actors, but as a complex of interdependent lives and

---

[24]On the concepts of progress and development, see Frank E. Manuel, *Shapes of Philosophical History* (London: Allen & Unwin, 1965; reprinted Aldershot: Gregg Revivals, 1993).

[25]Montesquieu, *On Politics* (fragment), cited Henry Vyverberg, *Historical Pessimism in the French Enlightenment* (Cambridge, MA: Harvard University Press, 1958), pp. 161–2.

[26]Meinecke, *Historism*, p. 140.

relationships.[27] Voltaire and Gibbon were profoundly influenced too. Rousseau's 'general will' (*volonté generale*) resonates with Montesquieu's notion of the 'spiritual union' of a society, as does Burke's conceptuality of the identity and integrity of a people or nation from one generation to another. Notwithstanding his antipathy to the *philosophes*, Burke regarded Montesquieu as an immortal genius. Voltaire's *moeurs* became a substantive concept in Enlightenment historiography, a new genre of 'manners' or human behaviour within society.

However, for most Enlightenment historians, their idea of the 'whole' was selective and arbitrary. They were not interested in chronicling the less worthy or less admirable aspects of how people lived in the past – the chaos, cruelty and superstition that typified most human lives. Gibbon alone dealt intentionally with 'barbarism' (more primitive, violent and culturally unrefined societies), which for other historians of the time was deserving only of contempt and avoidance. He deplored the way that eighteenth-century historians had over-intellectualized history by portraying human beings as rational, calculating beings. By trying to do honour to the intellect, they had often done little honour to the heart. Gibbon combined the vast learning of the seventeenth-century *érudits* with the typical moralizing, generalizing approach of the 'philosophic' historians of the Enlightenment and thus set a new standard for historiography, adding also superlative skill in narrative technique and style.[28] Gibbon shared Voltaire's hatred of superstition, intolerance and cruelty, and had the same faith in reason, but he did not condone Voltaire's contempt for learned detail, and was contemptuous of Voltaire as an historian for this fault among others. Gibbon learned from Bayle 'to blend malice with erudition', Bayle being a master of both.[29] The great names of the Scottish Enlightenment – Hutcheson, Hume, Ferguson, Robertson, Smith and Millar – excelled in the study of the social behaviour of humankind. They moved beyond

---

[27] George H. Sabine, 'Hume's Contribution to the Historical Method', *The Philosophical Review* 15 (1906), pp. 17–38.
[28] Pocock, *Barbarism and Religion, Volume Two: Narratives of Civil Government*, pp. 4–5.
[29] Arnaldo Momigliano, 'Gibbon's Contribution to Historical Method', in id., *Studies in Historiography* (London: Weidenfeld & Nicolson, 1966), pp. 40–55, at p. 43.

psychological analysis of individuals to the proto-sociological study of societies as wholes, and from the study of individual morality or virtue to the moral character of society and the overall ethical dispositions of nations. In 1818 John Millar said of the new study of societies that Montesquieu was the Bacon and Adam Smith was the Newton; he did not mention Voltaire.[30] It is as though 'civil history' replaced ecclesiastical history for the Enlightenment.[31]

(iii) *Uniformitarianism*

It was the unexamined presupposition – in effect a dogma – of Enlightenment historians, swayed by Newton's law-based physics, that human nature was uniform and unvarying in all times, places and cultures. This assumption is pervasive; it underpinned their attempts to venture beyond the history of Europe to embrace other continents and cultures. It was the methodological unifying factor. It alone made the scientific historical enterprise possible.[32] Given that nature, including human nature, was equated with reason and reason was the same in all mankind, it is not surprising to find Hume asserting that reason was 'grounded in the nature of things, eternal and unyielding'.[33] Within the uniformity of human nature lay the uniformity of human reason.[34] We might imagine that the cult of primitivism bucked the trend and countered the stress on uniformity. However, the philosophers of the Enlightenment 'knew' (and Rousseau 'knew' best of all) that primitive 'man' was the same as themselves, though unencumbered with the corruptions and complications of civilization and religion. So primitivism was also rationalistically uniformitarian. In Tindal's *Christianity as Old as the Creation, or the Gospel a Republication of the*

---

[30]Trevor-Roper, 'The Scottish Enlightenment', in John Robertson (ed.), *History and the Enlightenment* (New Haven, CT: Yale University Press, 2010), pp. 17–33.
[31]Pocock, *Barbarism and Religion, Volume Two: Narratives of Civil Government*, p. 12.
[32]S. K. Wertz, 'Hume, History and Human Nature', *JHI* XXXVI (1975), pp. 481–96, at p. 491.
[33]Cited Meinecke, *Historism*, p. 157, from David Hume's *Enquiry Concerning the Principles of Morals*.
[34]A. O. Lovejoy, *Essays in the History of Ideas* (Baltimore, MD: Johns Hopkins University Press, 1948), p. 80.

Religion of Nature (1730) the tropes of nature, reason, theism, creation, primitivism and the gospel are wrapped up together.[35] History could only instruct on the premise that human nature, its motives, values and judgements – even its intellectual frailty and moral weaknesses – were ever the same. So Bolingbroke could say that history is philosophy teaching by examples because 'Such is the imperfection of human understanding, such is the frail temper of our minds, that abstract or general propositions, though ever so true, appear obscure or doubtful to us very often, till they are explained by examples.'[36] History embodies universal truths and we can learn them there. The moral value of history diminished as post-Enlightenment, proto-Romantic historical relativism began to bite into uniformitarianism.

Hume psychologizes human nature and therefore history. Meinecke says (for effect) that Hume's historical work was 'nothing more nor less than applied psychology'.[37] For him, the passions, emotions and instincts were more powerful than reason; even these irrational impulses, which were equally part of human nature, operated according to unvarying psychological laws in any society. Hume is speaking for the Enlightenment when, sounding like a parody of himself, he announces: if you want to understand the ancient Greeks and Romans, all you need to do is to study the French and English, because:

> It is universally acknowledged, that there is a great uniformity among the actions of men, in all nations and ages, and that human nature remains the same, in its principles and operations. The same motives always produce the same actions: The same events

---

[35]Ibid., pp. 86–8.
[36]Cited J. W. Johnson, *The Formation of English Neo-Classical Thought* (Princeton, NJ: Princeton University Press, 1967), p. 33, from Henry St. John, Viscount Bolingbroke, *Letters on the Study and Use of History*. Johnson's ch. 2, 'The Role of Historiography', vindicates the centrality of neo-classicism in English eighteenth-century literature and thought.
[37]Meinecke, *Historism*, p. 165. But see the qualification of Hume's alleged uniformitarianism in Wertz, 'Hume, History and Human Nature'. On the ideological interactions between national consciousness and cosmopolitan aspirations in Enlightenment historians, which must surely be relevant to their default uniformitarianism, see Karen O'Brien, *Narratives of Enlightenment: Cosmopolitan History from Voltaire to Gibbon* (Cambridge: Cambridge University Press, 1997).

follow from the same causes ... Mankind are so much the same, in all times and places, that history informs us of nothing new or strange in this particular. Its chief use is only to discover [i.e. reveal] the constant and universal principles of human nature.[38]

Hume played off reason and passion against each other; they were polarities, though passion always trumped reason and Hume thought it right that it should. Hume's psychological dichotomy points to the fact that the philosophers of the Enlightenment were thwarted in their attempts at historical understanding for lack of an adequate psychological theory or model in which reason on the one hand and passion, emotion and imagination, on the other, could work together in an integrated way, not as mutually exclusive but as mutually constitutive, in the form of a passionate reason and a reasonable passion. This psychological dichotomy excluded vast realms of historical evidence – legend, myth, fable, symbol – from their purview and was of a piece with their disdain and distrust of metaphorical, mythopoeic and generally figurative language. Eighteenth-century writers from Locke to Hume were swayed by a scheme of the evolution of language from the primitive grunts of the first humans, through increasingly complex sentence structures, to the refined language of philosophy. 'Clear and distinct ideas' was the ideal inherited from Descartes. There was a steady movement towards greater abstraction. Turgot was 'led by his worship of reason to prefer the purest mathematical abstraction over all other forms of knowledge and to look upon the metaphors and images ... as a sort of baby-talk'.[39] (Voltaire being an extreme example.)[40] William Robertson reinforces the connection between nature and uniform humanity when he says, 'A human being as originally shaped by the hand of nature is everywhere the same.'[41]

---

[38] David Hume, *An Enquiry Concerning Human Understanding*, VIII, part 1: https://davidhume.org/texts/e/8 (accessed 18 February 2022).
[39] Frank E. Manuel, *The Prophets of Paris* (Cambridge, MA: Harvard University Press, 1962), p. 32.
[40] Hayden White, *Metahistory: The Historical Imagination in Nineteenth-Century Europe* (Baltimore, MD: Johns Hopkins University Press, 1973), pp. 45–80. See Voltaire, *Philosophical Dictionary*, ed. and trans. Theodore Besterman (Harmondsworth: Penguin, 1971), art. 'Metaphor'.
[41] Cited White, *Metahistory*, p. 197.

The equivalent in law of the uniformity of human nature is the equality of all persons. An equality of rights was enshrined in the French and American revolutionary constitutions. But a reversal took place in France under the impact of the terrible events as the revolution unfolded. Burke attributed the Terror to the egalitarian ideology of the *philosophes*: the anchor points of hierarchy, deference and 'prescription' had been swept away and there were no more boundaries.[42]

Enlightenment historians and Christianity

How did the great historians of the Enlightenment depict Christianity and the Christian church? Voltaire dismissed all theology both as meaningless in itself and as generative of insoluble disputes which undermined civil order and hampered commercial enterprise, which were the necessary conditions of the flourishing of the arts. How could Voltaire even begin to do justice to the Christian centuries when he found Dante' *La Divina Commedia* 'bizarre', took Pascal as his fanatical adversary, and dismissed theological controversialists as blind madmen? Voltaire was no atheist, but rather a convinced deist. His deistic faith needed no historical institutions to sustain it; so he did not see the need of churches. Voltaire's prejudice against religion generally and his particular antipathy to historical Christianity, was not confined to the Catholic Church; it extended also to the Protestant Reformation. Prejudice warped his historical writing. He could not bring himself to recognize the sincere religious convictions and motives behind the Reformation, insisting on regarding it as a secular event. Neither could he overcome his suspicion of theologians as a breed, especially those that had previously been monks or friars, such as Martin Luther. Although Voltaire lived for many years at Ferney, near Geneva, the city of Calvin, he hated the French Reformer, particularly because he had been party to the execution of Servetus. (Voltaire cannot be criticized for that!) On the other hand, Voltaire's attitude towards

---

[42]Frank E. Manuel, 'From Equality to Organicism', *JHI* XVII.1 (1956), pp. 54–69.

the Church of England became more positive over time, though it was partly the church's Erastianism, or subservience to the state, that commended it to him.[43]

Gibbon and Robertson despised Voltaire as an historian because of his slapdash method with sources and failure to acknowledge them. 'When he treats of a distant period', Gibbon confided to his journal, 'he is not a man to turn over musty monkish writers to instruct himself. He follows some compilation, varnishes it over with the magick of his style, and produces a most agreeable, superficial, inacurate [sic] performance.'[44] In Gibbon's view, Voltaire did not contribute to the public commonwealth of historical scholarship. Gibbon further detested Voltaire because he was blatantly in thrall to an ideology – hatred of the Catholic Church. In Gibbon's eyes – and he had briefly converted to Roman Catholicism in his youth – this made Voltaire a religious bigot.[45] Gibbon has the reputation of sneering at Christianity, but his portrayal is much more nuanced than that, as we have seen. Hume, like Voltaire, regards theological language as virtually meaningless and is allergic to religion as such, treating it as an inveterate 'social pathology'. For example, Hume claims that the British Civil War was unnecessary and was the product of religious fanaticism and bigotry. So his history will have to be a critical account of the natural and civil dimensions of the human mind through time.[46] For Hume, history – not theology – provided the empirical raw material for the study of human nature and so for the task of philosophy. 'It is not simply that the philosopher abstracts from history the universal principles of human nature, but rather that the history of humanity ... is constitutive of the knowledge of humanity.'[47] And this knowledge can be put to use for the future well-being of humankind.

---

[43]Graham Gargett, *Voltaire and Protestantism* (Oxford: Voltaire Foundation, 1980).
[44]Cited from Gibbon's *Journal* by Robert Mankin, 'Edward Gibbon: Historian in Space', in Bourgault and Sparling (eds), *A Companion to Enlightenment Historiography*, ch. 1, at pp. 32–3.
[45]Edward Gibbon, *The Decline and Fall of the Roman Empire*, abridged and intro. D. M. Low (Harmondsworth: Penguin, 1963), VI, ch. 67, n.13.
[46]Pocock, *Barbarism and Religion, Volume Two: Narratives of Civil Government*, p. 193.
[47]Kow, 'Politics and Culture in Hume's *History of England*', p. 69.

Gibbon was indebted to Hume for sound advice (just as Hume himself was indebted to Butler), including persuading him to write the *Decline and Fall* in English, rather than in French like his youthful *Essai sur l'étude de la littérature*.[48] Gibbon held Hume the historian in awe for his easy, polished, lapidary, ironical style – not at all like Gibbon's unmistakably portentous, sententious and symmetrical prose. As Trevor-Roper says, Hume's 'faultless ironic style struck despair into the heart of Gibbon'.[49] Nevertheless, Gibbon disparaged Hume's *History* as '*Ingenious but superficial*'.[50] Gibbon acknowledged the role of Hume and Robertson in the birth of British philosophic history and that, in doing so, they had helped to cure the 'British disease': a state of continual ideological-theological turbulence, perpetuating political faction, economic distress and social unrest.[51] After these prefatory indications, we now continue to explore the Enlightenment historians' relationship to Christianity and Christian theology through a series of case studies.

Voltaire as historian

(a) Voltaire drew back from attempting an analysis of the motives of historical actors because he felt that he did not have enough knowledge or psychological insight.[52] He shied away with aversion from the irrational and unpredictable.[53] He mostly aimed at a straightforward narrative of events (accompanied by moral

---

[48]Edward Gibbon, *Essai sur l'étude de la littérature: A Critical Edition*, ed. Robert Mankin (Oxford: Voltaire Foundation, 2010).
[49]Trevor-Roper, 'David Hume, Historian', in id., *History and the Enlightenment*, pp. 120–8.
[50]Cited Mankin, 'Edward Gibbon: Historian in Space', p. 32, n.17 (Gibbon's italics).
[51]Pocock, *Barbarism and Religion, Volume Two: Narratives of Civil Government*, pp. 174–5.
[52]Sylvia Vance, 'History as Dramatic Reinforcement: Voltaire's Use of History in Four Tragedies set in the Middle Ages', *SVEC* CL (1976), pp. 7–31.
[53]On the irrational and Enlightenment history see Hayden White, 'The Irrational and the Problem of Historical Knowledge in the Enlightenment', in H. E. Pagliaro (ed.), *Irrationalism in the Eighteenth Century* (Cleveland, OH: Press of Case Western Reserve University, 1972).

judgements), but as Cobban notes, the narrative method, far from enabling Voltaire to avoid preconceived prejudices, merely enabled him to take them for granted.[54]

(b) Voltaire was intent on charting the progress of civilization, so he intentionally embraces a method of radical selectivity. The historical record itself is selective; it keeps no account of times of peace and tranquillity, but narrates only 'a long succession of useless cruelties'; it is 'a collection of crimes, follies and misfortunes'. The historian is therefore fully justified in being selective: not every happening is worth writing about. In his history of the age of Louis XIV, Voltaire announced, he would confine himself to what was deserving of the attention of posterity and had a didactic value in terms of polite manners, love of virtue and the flourishing of the arts.[55] As he tellingly put it: 'If you have nothing else to say but that one barbarian succeeded another barbarian on the banks of the Oxus and the Iaxantes, where is your public usefulness?'[56]

(c) Voltaire's mental attitude as an historian was juridical, passing sentence on moral and aesthetic grounds. He sits in judgement on the past, denouncing abuses, condemning cruelty, castigating intolerance and despising lack of civility and refinement. In this, Voltaire was most representative of the Enlightenment. As Meinecke wrote, the Enlightenment subjected 'the whole historical scene to its own standards with a sovereign certainty of touch. Never had there been an age that looked back on the past with such an autonomous attitude and with such complete self-assurance.'[57] Meinecke adds of Voltaire, 'he wanted to write the universal pre-history of the French bourgeoisie'.[58] Notwithstanding Voltaire's historical pessimism, the fact that he believes that he can do this implies a belief in rational progress and a liberation from past errors, crimes and crudities. The present age was the criterion and standpoint. The course of

---

[54] Cobban, 'The Enlightenment', p. 93.
[55] Voltaire, introduction to *The Age of Louis XIV*, in Fritz Stern (ed.), *The Varieties of History: From Voltaire to the Present*, 2nd edn (London: Macmillan, 1970 [1956]), pp. 40–4. See also Charles Frankel, *The Faith of Reason: The Idea of Progress in the French Enlightenment* (New York: Octagon Books, 1969 [1948]), pp. 108, 110.
[56] Voltaire, art. 'Histoire' in the *Encyclopédie*, in N. N. Schargo, *History in the Encyclopédie* (New York: Columbia University Press, 1947), p. 35.
[57] Meinecke, *Historism*, p. 55.
[58] Ibid., p. 57.

European history showed 'the extinction, the renaissance and the progress of the human mind', how it has progressed from a state of 'barbaric rusticity' to the 'refinement' of the present age. The 'savage times' recorded in Julius Caesar's account of ancient Gaul were 'a disgrace to nature'. The early Middle Ages were no more worthy of the historian's attention than the doings of wolves and bears. It was necessary to know something of it in order to scorn it.[59] The age of Louis XIV, on the other hand, he judged 'the most enlightened century that ever was'.[60] Montesquieu spitefully commented that, just as the monks had written for *la gloire de leur ordre*, so Voltaire wrote for the glory of his *couvent* (the 'convent' of the *philosophes*)![61]

(d) G. P. Gooch, the historian and historian of historiography stated, à-*propos* Voltaire's *Essai sur les Moeurs*, that the historiography of the Enlightenment 'put an end to the era of mere compilation' and 'widened the scope of history from a record of events to a survey of civilization'.[62] (Montesquieu had already pioneered this approach.) Voltaire wanted to know how people lived in the good times. His target was the history of the human mind, heart and cultural experience, not the history of mere 'facts', which he knew to be usually distorted in the record. Michelet later described the ideal of historical science as *la resurrection de la vie intégrale*.

(e) Like other Enlightenment writers, Voltaire, assumes the uniformity of human nature. In conclusion to the *Essai sur les moeurs* he lays down that everything which pertains intimately to human nature is much the same from one end of the world to the other, but everything which depends on custom is different. The empire of custom is broader than the empire of nature. Nature spreads unity, human custom promotes diversity. So, while human nature is unvarying, everyone is shaped (*formé*) by the age they live in.

---

[59]G. P. Gooch, *History and Historians in the Nineteenth Century* (London: Longmans, Green, 1928), p. 11; id., 'Voltaire as Historian', in id., *Catherine the Great and Other Studies* (London: Longmans, Green, 1954), pp. 199–274.
[60]Voltaire, introduction to *The Age of Louis XIV* in Stern (ed.), *The Varieties of History*, pp. 40–4.
[61]Cited J. H. Brumfitt, 'History and Propaganda in Voltaire', *SVEC* XXIV (1963), pp. 271–87, at p. 271.
[62]Gooch, *History and Historians in the Nineteenth Century*, p. 8.

Fontenelle, the progenitor of many Enlightenment ideas and attitudes and a secular 'godfather' to the *philosophes*, second only to Bayle, was a prime architect of the idea of progress.[63] But his *Dialogues des morts* assumes that human nature is essentially unchanging; he not only has Erasmus conversing with the Emperor Charles V, but Montaigne talking with Socrates, and so on. Fontenelle was not able to reconcile the two principles of progress and uniformity, any more than Voltaire was.[64] Following Montesquieu, Voltaire allows for the influence of material and natural factors in the shaping of experience, but although he was a devotee of Locke's epistemology, he does not see that Locke's principle that human nature is formed by experience points to a greater degree of historical relativism. Rather, he extrapolates from the physical laws of his other great English hero, Newton, in holding (as Brumfitt puts it) that 'The laws of human conduct are as immutable as the laws of gravity.'[65] Voltaire reveals the weakness of his historical sense in the way that he assimilates resistant esoteric material to the canons of the French Enlightenment.

> He sees the pure flame of natural religion behind every form of primitive cult, and discovers the philosophe [*sic*] beneath the robes of the Chinese mandarin or the Indian Brahman. He attaches universal validity to the beliefs and standards of his own time, and searches for their equivalent throughout the world with little concern for national and racial variations. He is much less concerned with oriental architecture or Islamic poetry than with showing that both Chinese and Mohammedans are really tolerant deists.[66]

(f) To what extent does Voltaire accommodate a principle of historical relativism? He will not entertain a relativism of truth,

---

[63] Haydn Mason, *Pierre Bayle and Voltaire* (London: Oxford University Press, 1963).
[64] J. H. Brumfitt, *Voltaire: Historian* (Oxford: Oxford University Press, 1958), p. 36. My copy of Bernard le Bovier de Fontenelle's *Les nouveaux Dialogues des Morts anciens* was published in 1724 in Paris and has been passed down through my mother's family (Le Loup). The original complete set was published in 1683 in Amsterdam.
[65] Ibid., p. 103.
[66] Ibid., p. 77.

but he allows for a relativism of context. In order to understand the persons and events within specific historical periods, they must be viewed in their relation to time and place, the conditions and circumstances in which they were placed. Voltaire exhibits this key axiom of the historical movement. Montesquieu had begun to lay the foundation. Flint claimed that Montesquieu won over educated Europe to the principle of historical relativism.[67] If circumstances vary but human nature is everywhere the same, the changing historical context becomes merely a stage-set for thoughts and actions that are essentially independent of it.

(g) Voltaire, the great advocate of toleration was in practice intolerant of those who challenged him, especially about religion. He was unwilling to accept the sincerity of other perspectives, tending to accuse his interlocutors of hypocrisy. Voltaire was a campaigner, a fighter, and his lack of historical and contemporary empathy was perhaps a function of his calling. As Brumfitt puts it: 'Not only is he unwilling to admire, say, a Gothic cathedral, but he really cannot believe that the people of the thirteenth century could have been so foolish as to do so.'[68]

(h) Voltaire did not specifically acknowledge his authorities. Gibbon despised him for this unscholarly trait and Robertson gave it as a reason for not citing Voltaire in his own histories.

(i) What Gay wrote of Enlightenment history – that it was 'rationalist in sensibility, partisan in purpose, careless in detail, hasty in judgement, unfair in characterization, and deficient in empathy, wilful, sectarian, even vicious', but nevertheless imparted enduring validity to the discipline of history and took the first steps towards a scientific history of culture – applies to Voltaire.[69] He contributed to the modern sense that the study of history must include the totality of past experience. In spite of his limitations as an historian, he aspires to narrate *l'histoire de l'esprit humain* and then adds to this the realms of social, economic and cultural developments. His significance and (we may say) greatness as

---

[67] Robert Flint, *Historical Philosophy in France*, French *Belgium and Switzerland* (Edinburgh: Blackwood; New York: Charles Scribner's Sons, 1893), p. 279.
[68] Brumfitt, *Voltaire: Historian*, p. 102.
[69] Peter Gay, *The Enlightenment: An Interpretation, Vol. 1: The Rise of Modern Paganism* (London: Weidenfeld and Nicolson, 1966), p. 59.

an historian lies in the fact that he aims to embrace the mental, spiritual and material aspects of human history. I take the question of anachronism separately.

Anachronism

Voltaire frequently falls into anachronism and in this he is typical of Enlightenment historians. Their historiographical failure follows from the judgemental stance that they adopted, informed by Enlightenment criteria. Voltaire condemns the Pharaohs for diverting resources to building the pyramids, 'products of despotism, vanity, servitude and superstition', instead of using those resources for digging irrigation channels. Recognizing that the hope of immortality is barely glimpsed in the Hebrew Bible, Voltaire pronounces that Moses should have taught life after death as a deterrent against crime.[70] Hume dismissed the events of Anglo-Saxon England as 'a battle of kites and crows'.[71] A series of barbarous ages gave way at last to the dawn of civility and science in the reign of Henry VIII. There is nothing to learn from the Middle Ages; we may study them merely to satisfy our curiosity. The main use of historical study for Hume is 'only to discover the constant and universal principles of human nature by showing men in all varieties of circumstances and situations'.[72] As Black points out, this model excludes the possibility of irrational or aberrant motives and actions. He attributes this deficiency to Hume's 'false mechanical psychology'. His characters are not real people, but 'a dexterously poised, mechanically sustained assemblage of divergent, disconnected or conflicting qualities'.[73] Robertson had done more research on the Middle Ages than had Hume, but he viewed the centuries before the Emperor Charles V (the history of whose reign he had written) as marked by 'confusion and barbarism',

---

[70]Cited from *Essai sur les Moeurs* in Jerome Rosenthal, 'Voltaire's Philosophy of History', *JHI* XVI.2 (1955), pp. 151–78, at p. 156.
[71]Gooch, *History and Historians in the Nineteenth Century*, p. 11.
[72]Cited J. B. Black, *The Art of History: A Study of Four Great Historians of the Eighteenth Century* (London: Methuen, 1926), p. 98.
[73]Ibid., p. 101.

which at that point (the early sixteenth century) had given way to order, regularity and refinement. Robertson could not cope with the extreme manifestations of humanity. He dismissed St Ignatius Loyola, the founder of the missionary Society of Jesus, with the words, 'The wild adventures and visionary schemes in which his enthusiasm [sic] engaged him ... are unworthy of notice in history.'[74] Bolingbroke, who had a huge influence on Voltaire, conceded that to be entirely ignorant would be shameful, so a temperate curiosity may be indulged. But to seek to be learned about preceding ages was 'a ridiculous affectation in any man who wishes to be useful to the present age'.[75] Diderot, with his more supple mind, warned against the trap of anachronism, condemning those who criticize Homer for the excesses of his gods and the coarseness of his heroes. 'Homer had to represent an Ajax and a Hector, not a courtier of Versailles or St James.'[76]

Edward Gibbon

It would be risky – though not stupid – to suggest that Gibbon was a Christian; but it will surprise some to learn that he was a regular churchgoer, often attending divine service twice on a Sunday and paying special attention to the sermon, notebook in hand. What preacher would not be grateful – albeit with great trepidation – to have such an attentive and intelligent auditor?[77] Edward Gibbon (1737–94) was a cradle Anglican who in his youth converted to Roman Catholicism and later converted back again before adopting a cool, sceptical and ethical form of

---

[74]Cited ibid., p. 131.
[75]Henry St John, Lord Viscount Bolingbroke, *Letters on the Study and the Use of History*, Letter VI: http://www.eliohs.unifi.it/testi/700/bolingbroke/letterVI.htm (accessed 16 February 2022).
[76]Cited Schargo, *History in the Encyclopédie*, p. 39.
[77]On Gibbon and the Christian faith and church see Shelby T. McCloy, *Gibbon's Antagonism to Christianity* (London: Williams & Norgate, 1933); B. W. Young, '"Scepticism in Excess": Gibbon and Eighteenth-century Christianity', *The Historical Journal* 41.1 (1998), pp. 179–99. David Dillon Smith, 'Gibbon in Church', *JEH* 35.3 (1984), pp. 450–63; Paul Turnbull, 'The Supposed Infidelity of Edward Gibbon', *The Historical Journal* 25.1 (1982), pp. 23–42.

deism, infused with the critical element of radical Protestantism and bitterly disdainful of the Catholic Church as it appeared in patristic and medieval history.

Although Gibbon's *The Decline and Fall of the Roman Empire*, a work beyond compare in historiography, has been judged by many at the time and since to have a destructive intention with regard to Christianity, it was a work of such sublime calibre, historically and stylistically, that Gibbon was neither persecuted nor excluded by the English establishment. Gibbon is a professed, accomplished and unrivalled 'philosophical' historian, that is to say a historian who is not content to offer what aspires to be a mere chronological record or narrative (the forte of the Annalists), but who excels in wide-ranging documentary research, incisive analysis and magisterial ethical and rational judgement. Gibbon was attacked by various critics (mainly clergymen), but he brushed off their criticisms and triumphed over them in his *Vindication* (1779), commenting crushingly in his *Memoirs*, 'A victory over such antagonists was sufficient humiliation.'[78]

Those readers of Gibbon who do not over-react to his aspersions on the church in history cannot fail to be impressed by his moderation, restraint and dignified posture as an historian. J. W. Johnson describes the *Decline and Fall of the Roman Empire* as 'perhaps the most complete statement of the Neo-Classical world-view'. Johnson adds: 'If the Gibbonian synthesis is not a total one, it encompasses most of the aspects of eighteenth century classicism.'[79] And Pocock, noting that, in J. H. Newman's judgment (no less) the greatest narrative history in English was Gibbon's *Decline and Fall*, points out that Gibbon's sources were drawn from writers across the essentially orthodox Christian traditions. Gibbon admired 'the Jansenist Tillemont, the Gallican Fleury, the Remonstrant Le Clerc, the Huguenot Beausobre and the Lutheran Mosheim a great deal more than he did the Unitarian Priestley, whose *History of the Corruptions of Christianity* told essentially the same story as his own but led it to radical and millenarian conclusions where

---

[78] Edward Gibbon, *Autobiography* (London: Dent; New York: Dutton, 1911), p. 151.
[79] Johnson, *The Formation of English Neo-Classical Thought*, p. xix; see also Arnaldo A Momigliano, *Classical Foundations of Modern Historiography* (Berkeley, CA: University of California Press, 1990).

his were skeptical and conservative.'[80] Gibbon was repelled, not by the sincere devotion of the generality of Christian people, not by the holiness of the saints (though repelled by the masochistic austerities of some), but by the morbidity, superstition, abuses and cruelty that have been inculcated and practised by the priesthood of the church and indeed by the sacred hierarchies of all religious institutions throughout the centuries. So what should we make of what is probably Gibbon's most celebrated barbed comment about Christianity, his boast that, in *The Decline and Fall*, he had traced 'the triumph of barbarism and religion' over a noble Roman civilization?[81]

This resonant phrase (borrowed and translated by Gibbon from Voltaire) does not mean quite what many readers assume. Gibbon was not equating Christianity with barbarism or implying that religion was barbaric. His assessment of Christianity is far from monochromely negative. Surprising as it may seem to some, his scattered comments on Christianity in the *Decline and Fall* cumulatively amount to a discriminating and nuanced assessment. Monks, ascetics, fanatics and corrupt, avaricious ecclesiastics are his *bêtes noires*. Saintly persons and capable church administrators are treated with respect and appreciation. The order, learning, education and respect for the individual that the early church introduced into a largely savage world, are given their due. Jesus Christ is never mocked. In one telling phrase, Gibbon modifies what he is saying to make it clear that his target is not Christianity *tout court*, but 'the abuse of Christianity'. In the same passage as that telling phrase, Gibbon speaks of 'the benevolent temper of the Gospel' and of 'the pure and genuine influence of Christianity'.[82] Gibbon's critique of the excesses of early Christianity are fair comment. 'Who can deny', I previously asked, 'the elements of credulity, fanaticism,

---

[80]Pocock, 'Within the Margins: The Definition of Orthodoxy', in Roger D. Lund (ed.), *The Margins of Orthodoxy: Heterodox Writing and Cultural Response, 1660–1750* (Cambridge: Cambridge University Press, 1995), ch. 1, at pp. 51–2.
[81]Gibbon, *The Decline and Fall of the Roman Empire*; id., *The Decline and Fall of the Roman Empire and Other Selections from the Writings of Edward Gibbon*, ed. H. R. Trevor-Roper (New York: Washington Square Press, 1963; London: New English Library, 1966).
[82]Edward Gibbon, *The Decline and Fall of the Roman Empire*, ed. Low, pp. 525–6.

intolerance, self-harm and anti-civil behaviour on the part of the early Christians?' I noted that 'Gibbon took it as his "melancholy duty" as an impartial historian to describe "the inevitable mixture of error and corruption" which an originally pure Christianity had "contracted in a long residence upon earth, among a weak and degenerate race of beings"'. I added that 'Gibbon's hatred of inhumanity, cruelty, bigotry, irrationality and mindless fervour goes a considerable way to explaining his authorial stance.'[83] So it would seem that the famous phrase, 'the triumph of barbarism and religion', was the portentous, ironical Gibbonian way of referring to the historical events of the invasions of the Roman Empire by the pagan German tribes and the rise of the institutional Christian church, which he regarded as a mixed blessing.[84] We should not forget that Gibbon had repudiated in disgust the brief sojourn of his youth in the Roman Church and that his place of residence, both immediately after his conversion to Rome and in later life was the Swiss, Protestant, city of Lausanne. There is a radical Protestant streak in Gibbon, as there is in Bayle, Locke, Toland, Conyers Middleton and others, even including Spinoza. Gibbon's cool and minimalist deistic religion was shot through with scepticism, anti-dogmatism and anticlericalism. He intentionally reserved his position and left unanswerable questions for his admirers and interpreters to puzzle over.

Rousseau and history

I begin this brief notice of Jean-Jacques Rousseau's significance for Enlightenment history with a selection of assessments by historians. It was Ernst Troeltsch's view that, by placing human consciousness at the centre of thought, Descartes and Cartesianism gave an initial impetus to the rise of the historical movement and that this impetus was strengthened by Rousseau (to whom his own self-consciousness

---

[83]For Gibbon and religion, with references to primary and secondary sources, see *ISOA*, pp. 254–8; quotations from p. 258, citing Gibbon, *Decline and Fall*, ed. Low, p. 143.
[84]Black, *The Art of History*, p. 170.

was ultimately all that mattered).⁸⁵ At one time, Troeltsch regarded Voltaire as the founder of the philosophy of history (Voltaire had a claim as he coined the term as the title of his pseudonymous tractate *La Philosophie de l'histoire* in 1765), but Troeltsch later revised his judgement in favour of Rousseau. According to Troeltsch, Rousseau 'gave the strongest impetus to modern philosophy of history' in both 'the Anglo-French positivist' branch and the German speculative branch. Rousseau's influence on historical thought was further enhanced by the French Revolution which, for Troeltsch, 'seemed to spring out of Rousseau's ideas'.⁸⁶

Similarly to Troeltsch, Karl Barth recognized that actual historical humanity is not visible in Rousseau's purportedly historical work. But Barth believed that what Rousseau had contributed to historical thought was to lift up the problem of human being, the 'anthropological' question.⁸⁷ I might add that it was precisely Rousseau's achievement in highlighting the question of philosophical and theological anthropology and treating them empirically – even though the data of Rousseau's empirical world were found largely in his own existence and self-consciousness – that constitutes his significance for the historical movement.

Along similar lines, Gossman claimed that, by his attention to the human condition over time, Rousseau showed an 'acute awareness of history as the mode of being of all things'. One of the most distinguishing features of Rousseau's writings, for Gossman, is 'the discovery and application of an historical method of analysis'. Rousseau evinces 'deep pessimism' about history, but finds wholeness or a sense of totality in nature, within which he includes original human nature, uncorrupted by civilization. So, if Gossman is right, rather than being seen as a prime witness to a Romantic escape from history into nature, Rousseau should be regarded as a prophet of historical thinking.⁸⁸

---

⁸⁵Robert J. Rubanowice, 'Ernst Troeltsch's History of the Philosophy of History', *Journal of the History of Philosophy* XIV.1 (1976), pp. 79–95, at p. 85.
⁸⁶Ibid., p. 87.
⁸⁷Barth, *Protestant Theology in the Nineteenth Century*, ch. 5, 'Rousseau', especially p. 205.
⁸⁸Lionel Gossman, 'Time and History in Rousseau', *SVEC* XXX (1964), pp. 311–49.

Gossman's view is supported by Mandelbaum who notes that the most radical and influential of the voices that challenged the canons of judgement of Enlightenment thought – especially the criteria of universal rationality, uniformitarianism and the progress of civilization – was Rousseau's. Mandelbaum then points out that 'Whereas the Enlightenment had considered those forms of thought, feeling and social cohesiveness which characterized the lives of "simpler" people as vestiges of a primitive state of society which was being gradually overcome', Rousseau's influence affirmed the necessity and moral worth of precisely those elements within the fabric of social life at all times, thus focusing the attention of historians upon them.[89]

When we turn to examine Rousseau's use of history, we might conclude that the character of his political writings, especially the Second Discourse, *On the Origin and Foundation of the Inequality of Mankind* and *The Social Contract*, militates against claims for his historical sensibility. When Rousseau speaks about the 'state of nature', which he contrasts with the state of 'civil society', he does not have any specific historical period in mind and is not claiming that the state of nature existed in such and such a time and place. The state of nature is a construct, extrapolated from Rousseau's belief in the contingent, precarious and above all morally imperfect status of civil society. With regard to the Second Discourse, it is ironic and confusing that in an essay on 'origins' and 'the foundation', Rousseau explicitly disclaims any historical basis for his argument. His antithesis of humankind in a state of nature and humankind in civil society is grounded in an existential, not an historical, contrast. Rousseau is saying with Hamlet, 'Look here upon th's picture, and on this.'[90] Rousseau speaks like the theologians when they described the perfections of Adam before and after the Fall of Man. 'Instead of a being, acting constantly from fixed and invariable principles, instead of that celestial and majestic simplicity, impressed upon it by its divine Author, we find it only the frightful contrast of passion mistaking itself for reason, and of understanding grown delirious.'[91] We cannot know what laws or

---

[89]Mandelbaum, *History, Man and Reason*, p. 55.
[90]William Shakespeare, *Hamlet*, III.iv.63.
[91]Jean-Jacques Rousseau, *The Social Contract and Discourses*, trans. and intro. G. D. H. Cole (London: Dent; Dutton: New York, 1913), p. 154 (Preface).

constitution are best for humankind until we rediscover the 'natural law', grounded in the 'original' nature of humankind. However, if we throw aside scientific treatises and instead 'contemplate the first and most simple operations of the human soul', we can discern two principles, both 'prior to reason': the one a concern with ourselves, our own welfare and preservation, and the other a concern with our fellow human when suffering. As well as a proper, inevitable self-love (*amour soi*), there is a sympathy and compassion for anyone like ourselves, who is in pain.[92] This compassion extends, with moderation, to animals. Rousseau is in broad agreement with David Hume on the point of innate sympathy and compassion for our fellows. Rousseau's idiosyncratic version of history is what he calls 'hypothetical history'.[93] However, in the second part of this *Discourse* Rousseau expatiates at length and in considerable circumstantial detail on what life was like, physically and socially, for 'the first man', as though giving an historical account based on evidence – which of course he was not in a position to do, as he had previously confessed.[94]

Rousseau's admission that he is not dealing in history, but in types or principles, lends credence to those who have accused *The Social Contract* of excessive abstraction and idealism, even utopianism – *Utopia* (the title of Thomas More's classic political satire, published in Latin in 1516 and translated into English in 1551)[95] meaning of course 'no place'. However, Echeverria has argued that the idealism and abstraction of *The Social Contract* have been exaggerated and that Rousseau 'was as much a political relativist as Montesquieu and that he was as much convinced that a given system of government could function successfully only in a certain peculiar geographical, historical and social environment.'[96] In Book III, chapters 8 and 9, of *The Social Contract* Rousseau insists, appropriately invoking Montesquieu, that the type of good

---

[92]Ibid., pp. 157–8; cf. p. 182.
[93]Ibid., p. 159.
[94]Cf. A. O. Aldridge, 'The State of Nature: An Undiscovered Country in the History of Ideas', *SVEC* XCVIII (1972), pp. 7–26.
[95]Thomas More, *Utopia* (London: Dent; Dutton: New York, 1910).
[96]Durand Echeverria, 'The Pre-Revolutionary Influence of Rousseau's *Contrat Social*', *JHI* XXXIII.4 (1972), pp. 543–60, at p. 544.

government must be suited to the conditions in which it is to function; there is no 'absolute' formula for good government; it is an 'indeterminate' concept, dependent on circumstances.[97]

G. B. Vico

Giambattista Vico (1668–1744) is not a household name like Voltaire and Rousseau, Johnson and Gibbon, Kant and Lessing, though he deserves to be. Philosopher, rhetorician, jurist and historian, Vico is the brightest star of the Italian Enlightenment, even though the effect of his work was to demolish several pillars of the standard Enlightenment conceptual framework. Brought up in poverty and married to an illiterate wife who bore him eight children, isolated academically and socially in his lifetime, the astonishing fertility and penetration of Vico's thought and his huge significance for the philosophy of history were belatedly recognized in the late twentieth century. The modern reception of Vico's thought was helped by translations of his *Scieza Nuovo* (*New Science*) and his *Autobiography* into English and by Isaiah Berlin's enthusiastic promotion (recycled in various formats) of Vico as battling heroically 'against the current', that is the current of Enlightenment 'rationalism' and uniformitarianism.[98] Vico historicized thought itself, even his own thought. For my purposes, I will pinpoint two aspects of Vico's thought: his method and his metaphysic.

---

[97] Rousseau, *The Social Contract*, trans. and intro. Maurice Cranston (Harmondsworth: Penguin, 1968), pp. 124–30; id., *Lettres écrites de la montagne*; avec une préface de Henri Guillemin (Neuchâtel: Ides et Calendes, 1962); Alfred Cobban, *Rousseau and the Modern State*, 2nd edn (London: Allen & Unwin, 1964 [1934]); Charles Edwyn Vaughan, *The Political Writings of Jean-Jacques Rousseau*, [in French] 2 vols (Cambridge: Cambridge University Press, 1915; reduced photographic reprint, Oxford: Blackwell, 1962).
[98] G. B. Vico, *Autobiography*, trans. M. H. Fisch and T. G. Bergin (Ithaca, NY: Cornell University Press, 1944); id., *The New Science of Giambattista Vico*, trans. T. G. Bergin and M. H. Fisch (Ithaca, NY: Cornell University Press, 1970 [1948]); Isaiah Berlin, *Against the Current: Essays in the History of Ideas*, ed. Henry Hardy, intro. Roger Hausheer (Oxford: Oxford University Press, 1981); id., *Vico and Herder: Two Studies in the History of Ideas* (London: Hogarth Press, 1976); id., *Three Critics of the Enlightenment: Vico, Hamann, Herder* (Princeton, NJ: Princeton University Press, 2013).

But, first, I have to insert a brief personal caveat. In my early foray into historiography *Foundations of Modern Historical Thought*, influenced by the tendentious perspectives of Paul Hazard and Peter Gay, I tended to identify the Enlightenment with the eccentric French version, the ideology of the *philosophes*, and consequentially I designated Vico a pre-Enlightenment thinker.[99] In the present study I am obviously working with a broader and more hospitable and variegated understanding of the scope of the Enlightenment. I have already argued that we falsify the Enlightenment unless we can accommodate its internal critics, notably Hume, Rousseau, Burke and Herder, as well as Vico, within it. They were certainly not typical (though what and who can safely be called 'typical' of the Enlightenment?), but they were genuine members of that great cultural movement, working within its ideological paradigms, and saw themselves as such. I regret that, in the present work, I have had to draw the line before Herder.

(a) Vico is important for his historical method. The Neapolitan philosopher is deservedly regarded as the progenitor of historicism, as it came to fruition in the nineteenth century, in the sense of the method of empathetic indwelling of past persons, events and cultures. Vico's innovative method pivots on his (variously stated) axiomatic insight, which he discovered before embarking on the *New Science*: *verum ipsum factum* or *verum et factum convertuntur*: the true and the made are interchangeable. We can understand the historical human world because it is a human product. As Vico puts it, the world of civil society has been made by men [*sic*], therefore it necessarily reflects the modifications of the human mind. As we approach a society distant in time, such as the Homeric heroic type, we can have confidence that by an act of arduous study in the spirit of self-abnegating empathy, we will eventually be enabled to enter into and understand it. Vico is frank about the agonizing imaginative effort that his approach demands.

---

[99]*FMHT*, ch. 6, especially pp. 158–61. In addition to the works listed there, I now recommend Karl Löwith, *Meaning in History* (Chicago, IL: University of Chicago Press, 1949), 'Vico'; and Donald Phillip Verene, *Vico's Science of Imagination* (Ithaca, NY: Cornell University Press, 1981) and id., 'Giambattista Vico's New Science of the Common Nature of the Nations', in Bourgault and Sparling (eds), *A Companion to Enlightenment Historiography*, ch. 7.

(b) The metaphysical framework of Vico's interpretation of history is a theological one and will take a little longer to explain as it has been misinterpreted and distorted by some scholars. The linchpin of his philosophy of history is a belief in benevolent, purposeful, divine providence, working in a hidden way through contingent second causes for the good of humankind. Vico even came to believe that his grievous, corrupt academic marginalization and isolation in Naples was turned by providence to good in that it enabled him to devote himself to working out and writing up his *Scieza Nuovo*. But Vico's theological concept of the secret but effective working of divine providence – which alone gives his system coherence – is misunderstood, overlooked or downplayed in some influential treatments of Vico's thought. Against all the evidence of his *New Science* and the testimony of his *Autobiography*, some scholars make Vico out to be an exponent of a secular philosophy of history, sometimes also outrageously interpreting his professions of faith as a cover or smokescreen to avoid censorship or persecution.

I endorse Vaughan's judgement, in an older study, that 'Providence is the single most important element in the *New Science*.'[100] But Vaughan is mistaken in opposing Vico's conception of 'divine providence' to the Christian understanding of providence (for example in Augustine or Aquinas) which (according to Vaughan) emphasizes the direct, personal guidance of human affairs by God in order to lead humankind back to God and is therefore incompatible with an affirmation that events happen through necessary natural causes and are devoid of any transcendent purpose.[101] For the Enlightenment, nature and reason were synonymous realities and were manifestations of the mind and purpose of the Creator. When we read the words 'rational' and 'natural' in Vico or other thinkers, we should not assume that God is excluded. Vaughan holds that Spinoza is the most important single influence on Vico and that both philosophers deliberately sought to reduce divine providence to natural necessity. However, Vaughan (who wrote half a century ago) is working with a superseded and unreconstructed interpretation of Spinoza as a mere naturalist or pantheist for

---

[100] Frederick Vaughan, *The Political Philosophy of Giambattista Vico* (The Hague: Martinus Nijhoff, 1972), p. 38.
[101] Ibid., pp. 38–45.

whom the term *deus sive natura* in effect meant nature without God. By contrast, I interpret both Spinoza and Vico as proponents of a radical theology of divine immanence. There is little doubt of the influence of Spinoza on Vico, but it was in the direction of an immanent world-historical process infused with divine presence and action, not in the direction of secular rationalism.[102]

Vaughan goes further in claiming that 'Vico clearly intended to undermine the Bible', just as (so Vaughan claims) Spinoza 'discredits the Bible completely'.[103] These statements are either meaningless, like claiming to 'undermine' or 'discredit' Shakespeare's plays, or they are false in any case because both Spinoza and Vico work with the Bible, interpret the Bible and incorporate it as a building block of their philosophy. However, if Vaughan means – as seems to be the case as we read on – that both writers exposed the human, social, imaginative and anthropomorphic complexion of the biblical writings, especially the Old Testament or Hebrew Bible, then they importantly anticipated and pioneered some aspects of the modern, uncontroversial, methods of biblical study which has been accomplished without 'undermining' or 'discrediting' the Bible.

In his impressive study *The Case for the Enlightenment: Scotland and Naples 1680–1760*, John Robertson brings out the biblical basis of Vico's concept of divine providence, but he seems not to recognize Vico as a Christian philosopher, loyal to the Catholic Church.[104] However, it is significant that, in Vico's use of Scripture, which he integrates into his narrative, he accepts the church's teaching, at that time, of the literal truth of the Bible and so stands apart from the (as it happens, deeply religious) Enlightenment pioneers of biblical criticism: Spinoza, Simon, Le Clerc and La Peyrère. The difference is most apparent in Vico's docile acceptance of the chronology of Genesis and of the historical nature of the mythical proto-history of the first eleven chapters, including Noah's flood. Moreover, Robertson's depictions of the thought of Hobbes, Spinoza and Bayle (three of Vico's targets) do not do justice to the theistic and Protestant-Christian elements in their thought, partly because he

---

[102] James C. Morrison, 'Vico and Spinoza', *JHI* XLI.1 (1980), pp. 49–68. Vaughan, *The Political Philosophy of Giambattista Vico*.
[103] Vaughan, *The Political Philosophy of Giambattista Vico*, p. 46.
[104] John Robertson, *The Case for the Enlightenment: Scotland and Naples 1680–1760* (Cambridge: Cambridge University Press, 2005).

does not ostensibly engage with the extensive discussions of these matters in significant secondary studies. In his ample exposition of Vico's thought, Robertson does not explicitly show why Vico should be taken as a representative of the European Enlightenment and therefore deserve his key place in Robertson's book. He finally locates Vico as a figure of the Pre-Enlightenment, which strangely seems to go against his announced thesis. Similarly, Jonathan Israel perversely lumps together Hobbes, Spinoza, Bayle and Vico as heroic founders of a secular modern worldview, when none of them was in any meaningful sense a secular thinker; quite the reverse: they were all religious believers and obsessed by theology.[105]

Robertson is the co-editor, with Sarah Mortimer, of the revisionist symposium *The Intellectual Consequences of Religious Heterodoxy, c. 1600–1750* – a serious bid to reinstate the religious and Christian (albeit so-called heterodox) context of radical Enlightenment thought.[106] Robertson's credentials as an exponent of the Enlightenment are second to none, even though I cannot agree with all of his interpretations. Mortimer is an acknowledged expert on Socinianism, which commendably she has brought in from the cold.[107] Her exposition in this volume of the thought of Faustus Socinus in relation to Grotius and Crell, on the subject of human and divine justice and their implications for the main lines of the Christian theology of the atonement and the forgiveness of sins, is a model of cogency and lucidity. However, I am uncomfortable with the undefined and unqualified use of the term 'heterodox' in this volume, in spite of the editors' inevitably broad-brush account, in their introduction, of the development of 'orthodoxy' and 'heterodoxy' through Christian history.[108] Equally troubling is

---

[105] Jonathan Israel, *Radical Enlightenment: Philosophy and the Making of Modernity* (Oxford: Oxford University Press, 2001).
[106] Sarah Mortimer and John Robertson (eds), *The Intellectual Consequences of Religious Heterodoxy, c. 1600–1750* (Leiden: Brill, 2012).
[107] Sarah Mortimer, *Reason and Religion in the English Revolution: The Challenge of Socinianism* (Cambridge: Cambridge University Press, 2010).
[108] The terms 'orthodoxy' and 'heterodoxy' need to be related to the formation of the theological concept of heresy; for the historical hinterland see A. P. Roach and J. Simpson, *Heresy and the Making of European Culture: Medieval and Modern Perspectives* (Farnham: Ashgate, 2013); for the immediately pre-Enlightenment period in England see David Loewenstein and John Marshall (eds), *Heresy in*

the curt dismissal, at the conclusion of the editors' introduction, of the Christian and Catholic tenor of Vico's philosophy of history. Vico is placed with Hobbes and Spinoza as a genuinely religious thinker who nevertheless was not aiming to articulate a Christian system, but merely a 'civil' history (like his fellow-citizen the ill-fated Giannone's civil histories of Naples) and for whose thought the person of Christ had little or no significance.[109] At this point I need to register dissent.

To note the 'civil' character of human institutions, as Vico does, is not to exclude the operation of 'grace' (the editors' chosen term for a transcendent divine dimension) from human life on this earth. Vico himself makes his intention clear when, in the *New Science*, he contextualizes 'civil' in the expression 'a rational civil theology of divine providence'. Civil is not 'secular' in the modern sense of the word, which is how it is used in the book under discussion. The civil and the spiritual are twin perspectives. For example, Richard Hooker, a pre-Enlightenment thinker, but a profound influence on Locke and Burke, for example, insisted that the church of Christ was simultaneously a 'politic society' and a 'mystical body'.[110] A governing paradigm of Pocock's historiography (as we have noted previously) is the tension between two ecclesiological truths: that the church is by definition, both the historical institution, derived from the apostles, and the place of the presence of Christ on earth. In Christian ecclesiology, to maintain both the civil and the spiritual dimensions is not to postulate an irreconcilable dualism but to state the inevitable tension in which we live, individually and socially, as beings who are both material and spiritual. The presence of 'grace' should not be understood as postulating a series of discrete divine interventions or incursions into the causal nexus of the world. The mystery of divine-human interaction and cooperation cannot

---

Literature and Politics in Early Modern English Culture (Cambridge: Cambridge University Press, 2006) and David Loewenstein, *Treacherous Faith: the Specter of Heresy in Early Modern English Literature and Culture* (Oxford: Oxford University Press, 2013).
[109]Mortimer and Robertson (eds), *The Intellectual Consequences of Religious Heterodoxy*, p. 38.
[110]See W. D. J. Cargill Thompson, 'The Philosopher of the "Politic Society": Richard Hooker as a Political Thinker', in W. Speed Hill (ed.), *Studies in Richard Hooker: Essays Preliminary to an Edition of his Works* (Cleveland, OH: Case Western Reserve University Press, 1972), ch. 1.

be reduced in such a crude fashion and rarely if ever has been in philosophical theology. I do not believe that any Christian theologian has ever denied the reality of natural, secondary causes. While natural causes are necessarily respected and affirmed, they are also held to be the site of constant divine sustaining and guiding power, within what today we might call an open system. Vico saw the operation of divine providence as veiled and mysterious, awesome and benevolent, hidden and indefeasible. But it was divine providence, operating in history, that made possible responsible human action, guided by sound judgement, the virtue of prudence. *Providentia* and *prudentia* went hand in hand and both belonged in the realm of grace.[111]

Equally perplexing and unsatisfactory is the dichotomy employed in the Robertson-Mortimer volume between 'nature' and 'revelation' and the claim that the prevailing Aristotelian-Scholastic theological framework was shaken when 'nature' and 'revelation' came apart (so it is alleged) in early modern thought. This way of putting it confuses and conflates some stock pairs of concepts in theology: 'nature and grace', 'reason and revelation' (I could add, relevantly, immanence and transcendence). But it is important to grasp that these hoary polarities are not set in antithesis, as some historians and philosophers seem to assume, but are interrelated, complementary and mutually illuminating. It is not that affirming natural law undermines divine law or that a new focus on nature excludes grace or that the advent of biblical criticism undermines revelation. All such matters have been continually – and sometimes successfully – negotiated in the history of Christian theology for the sake of the coherence and credibility of Christian belief.

Pioneers of biblical criticism

The origins of modern scientific biblical research are to be found in a range of sources – Protestant and Catholic, deistic and Jewish – in the early or pre-Enlightenment.[112] Deistic writers in

---

[111] Verene, 'Giambattista Vico's New Science of the Common Nature of the Nations', p. 246.
[112] General: Klaus Scholder, *The Birth of Modern Critical Theology: Origins and Problems of Biblical Criticism in the Seventeenth Century*, trans. John Bowden (London: SCM Press, 1990 [1966]); Henning Graf Reventlow, *The Authority of the*

France, Germany and Britain, not least the elegant and influential Shaftesbury, contributed significantly – from whatever motives – to the development of an historical and critical approach to the Bible.[113] They built especially on the earlier work of Spinoza (no deist, of course), mainly on the Hebrew Bible, and the French Oratorian priest Richard Simon (1638–1712) on both Testaments. But first I will make some comments on selected recent studies in this area, of varying usefulness.

1. Jonathan Sheehan, *The Enlightenment Bible: Translation, Scholarship, Culture* (2007). The title notwithstanding, Sheehan's work is not centred on the chronological period of the Enlightenment, but places the Bible, as a cultural artefact and ideological totem, within the trajectory of secularization as an aspect of the modernization of Western civilization. He seems to regard the progressive undermining and downgrading of the Bible as an authoritative sacred text as inevitable and thus has a teleological axe to grind.[114]

2. Michael C. Legaspi, *The Death of Scripture and the Rise of Biblical Studies* (2010). Legaspi follows in the wake of Sheehan and sets out to show that the Bible as an authoritative ecclesial text failed and became moribund as a result of internecine theological conflict from the Reformation onwards and was superseded by the academic or scientific study of the biblical literature which (he claims) has in turn secured a place for the Bible in modernity. Although he provides a useful intellectual biography of the biblical scholar and Hebraist Johann David Michaelis (1717–91) in the context of the Göttingen school, Legaspi's

---

Bible and the Rise of the Modern World, trans. John Bowden (London: SCM Press, 1984); Euan Cameron (ed.), *The New Cambridge History of the Bible. Volume 3, From 1450 to 1750* (Cambridge: Cambridge University Press, 2015); Kevin Killeen, Helen Smith and Rachel Willie (eds), *The Oxford Handbook of the Bible in Early Modern England, c. 1530–1700* (Oxford: Oxford University Press, 2015), Part II: Scholarship; Peter Harrison, *The Bible, Protestantism, and the Rise of Natural Science* (Cambridge: Cambridge University Press, 1998).

[113]On Shaftesbury's biblical comments see Reventlow, *Authority of the Bible*, pp. 308–21.

[114]Jonathan Sheehan, *The Enlightenment Bible: Translation, Scholarship, Culture* (Princeton, NJ: Princeton University Press, 2007).

argument seems to pivot on the false antithesis of the ecclesial validity of sacred Scripture versus the Bible as object of academic enquiry. He plays off the traditional appeal of Scripture against the growing attraction of the Greek and Roman classics to seventeenth-century scholars in a way that is challenged by the tradition of Christian classical humanism (of which we have seen ample evidence in earlier chapters). Sometimes his rhetoric is misplaced, as when he claims that the Bible had become 'opaque' as a result of Christian divisions, when the problem was in the minds of its users.[115]

3. Nicholas Hardy, *Criticism and Confession: The Bible in the Seventeenth Century Republic of Letters* (2017). This immensely learned work challenges the premises occupied by Sheehan and Legaspi. Hardy shows that the scholarly study of the Bible by such humanist luminaries as Joseph Scaliger, Isaac Casaubon, John Selden, Hugo Grotius and Louis Cappel (and later Richard Simon and Jean Le Clerc and others) was in no way ironically detached from inter-confessional and even intra-confessional debate and polemic, in some idealized ivory-tower 'republic of letters', as imagined by other writers on the topic, but was confessionally positioned, providing ammunition for fierce theological argument, as it always had done and has done, though not at the expense of the Bible's continuing validity as a spiritual and moral resource.[116]

4. Gerard Reedy, S.J., *The Bible and Reason: Anglicans and Scripture in Late Seventeenth-Century England* (1985). Reedy's older work mainly concerns the interpretation of the Bible, rather than the wider and more fundamental investigative aspects of biblical scholarship, and is obviously confined to Church of England divines and philosophers. Reedy, interestingly writing as a Roman Catholic, soundly refutes the common notion that Anglican divinity in the

---

[115]Michael C. Legaspi, *The Death of Scripture and the Rise of Biblical Studies* (Oxford: Oxford University Press, 2010).
[116]Nicholas Hardy, *Criticism and Confession: The Bible in the Seventeenth Century Republic of Letters* (Oxford: Oxford University Press, 2017).

late seventeenth century was rationalistic, pointing out that all biblical study and interpretation is rational. He warns against the simplistic but prevalent opposition, among non-theological commentators, between reason and revelation. It is refreshing to find such elementary but ubiquitous errors summarily dispatched. Unfortunately, Reedy succumbs to the equally common and spurious notion that, as a reformed church, the Church of England held to the principle of *sola scriptura* (a post-Reformation shibboleth embraced by the Swiss Reformed and the English Puritans). Reedy also labels Hobbes and Spinoza secular philosophers rather than religious thinkers – 'secular' being a designation that is correct in only a very restricted, technical sense.[117]

5. The 'accessible' broad survey *God's Last Words: Reading the English Bible from the Reformation to Fundamentalism* by David S. Katz[118] falls into the same trap as Reedy (and many others) in assuming that the slogan *sola scriptura* defined the confessional position of the Reformation churches with regard to the authority of Scripture.[119] The phrase 'God's Last Words' is meant to underline his claim that Protestants believed that God had ceased to communicate with humankind after the completion of the biblical canon; divine revelation became entombed in the text. But this is a caricature. For the Reformers, divine revelation, inscribed in Scripture, was living and dynamic; its trajectory continued through the proclamation of the gospel, which for Luther was primarily an oral event. Katz's stance on *sola scriptura* enables him (and others) to adopt a slightly superior and patronizing tone when discussing pre-critical methods of biblical study. But the premise is false. The phrase is a post-Reformation polemical

---

[117]Gerard Reedy, S. J., *The Bible and Reason: Anglicans and Scripture in Late Seventeenth-Century England* (Philadelphia, PA: University of Pennsylvania Press, 2016 [1985]). Reedy's work can be supplemented by Joel C. Weinsheimer, *Eighteenth-Century Hermeneutics: Philosophy of Interpretation in England from Locke to Burke* (New Haven, CT: Yale University Press, 1993).
[118]David S. Katz, *God's Last Words: Reading the English Bible from the Reformation to Fundamentalism* (New Haven, CT: Yale University Press, 2004).
[119]Ibid., e.g. pp. x, 19, 74, 80, 313.

slogan. Although, as mentioned immediately above, the Swiss Reformation and the Reformed churches elsewhere who adhered to that form of Protestantism purported to take Scripture as the touchstone of all to be said and done in the church and this remained a mark of puritanism thereafter,[120] the Lutheran and Anglican churches did not. The Lutherans continued the use of liturgy, vestments, ceremonial, music and images in worship and accepted episcopacy in governance. The Church of England continued the use of liturgy, reduced ceremonial and vestments, priesthood, episcopacy and canon law. Richard Hooker (d. 1600) argued effectively against the legalistic Puritan scruple and made a case for the church to make reasoned adaptations of practice in the light of what is fitting, where God had not made permanently binding laws to the contrary. For Lutherans and Anglicans alike there was a recognized area of *adiaphora* (things that did not make a difference to salvation). 'Scripture alone' came into play in a specified area; it was the touchstone of doctrinal faith, of what was necessary to salvation. This was a polemical stance against Rome and against Rome's insistence that communion with the pope, sacramental confession and sacramental confirmation were necessary to salvation and that meritorious works such as pilgrimages, donations and mortification of the flesh could obtain remission of time in purgatory.[121] Moreover, no major Reformer

---

[120] Carl S. Trueman's article 'Scripture and Exegesis in Early Modern Reformed Theology', in Ulrich L. Lehner, Richard A. Muller and A. G. Roeber (eds), *The Oxford Handbook of Early Modern Theology, 1600–1800* (Oxford: Oxford University Press, 2016), ch. 12, provides a clear exposition of the subject without deploying *sola scriptura* at any point! Regrettably, not all contributors to the *Handbook* are as assured (e.g. p. 26) and there are several sloppy uses of the phrase.

[121] See Article VI of the Thirty-nine Articles. See further *AACC*, chs 1 and 2; *ISOA*, chs 1–3. Katz's treatment of Fundamentalism belies his title, as he gives only a couple of pages to the subject, mainly on 'The Fundamentals', a series of pamphlets published in the USA between 1910 and 1915, adding brief comments on the century since then. His discussion of the impact of Darwin's theory of evolution (ch. 8) does not mention the innovative Anglican approach of Charles Gore and the symposium *Lux Mundi* (1889) in taking the evolutionary paradigm to the heart of biblical interpretation. When he does mention Gore and company, in another context, he thinks they were Roman Catholics!

attempted to argue a theological case from Scripture only. Alongside fevered biblical exposition, there was a veritable Reformation industry of research into patristic theology and the history of ecumenical councils, the results being mobilized in inter-confessional polemics. Anyone who comments on Reformation theology should know this.

Spinoza and the Hebrew Bible

Here I will focus on Spinoza's biblical work (mainly found in his *Tractatus Theologico-Politicus*),[122] having already looked at his theology and metaphysics in Chapter 4. In understanding him – a challenge that has defeated many interpreters – in addition to the standard work by Reventlow, the studies of Strauss and Frampton are useful, while that of Preuss deserves to be challenged in places, while a recent symposium from Italy *Philosophers and the Bible*,[123] proves to be a mixed blessing. I will comment briefly on all these interpretations.

(1) In his work *Spinoza's Critique of Religion*, a work whose origins go back to the 1930s,[124] Strauss perceptively notes that Spinoza applied to the Hebrew Bible the interpretative methods, primarily literal and historical, of the humanists and the Reformers and did so more radically than they (p. 251). Spinoza discerned the 'vulgarity' of biblical discourse, its contextual, human, antiquated mindset (*antiqui vulgi praeiudicia*) and its total lack of a 'scientific' outlook (pp. 254, 303–4). He postulated an epistemic distance between the world of the biblical text and his own *sitz im leben*. But Strauss also recognized that, for Spinoza, a purely rational

---

[122]Spinoza, *The Chief Works*, trans. and intro. R. H. M. Elwes (New York: Dover Publications, 1951), vol. 1, *Political Treatise* and *Theologico-Political Treatise*; Susan James, *Spinoza on Philosophy, Religion, and Politics: The Theologico-Political Treatise* (Oxford: Oxford University Press, 2012).
[123]Antonella del Prete, Anna Lisa Schino and Pina Totaro (eds), *Philosophers and the Bible: The Debate on Sacred Scripture in Early Modern Thought* (Leiden: Brill, 2022).
[124]Leo Strauss, *Spinoza's Critique of Religion*, trans. E. M. Sinclair (Chicago, IL: University of Chicago Press, 1997 [1965]), with a new 'Preface' (1962); page references in my main text.

hermeneutic was not sufficient; one needed to be open also to the moral or ethical content of Scripture, which was its true message and one of abiding and universal import. In face of the intolerant and persecuting spirit of his times, Spinoza sees Scripture as a document that evinces a humane, gentle and conciliatory temper (pp. 258, 260). Although the Hebrew language and its idioms are marked by plasticity and ambiguity, the moral truth stands out clearly and teaches all that is needed for a life of piety (p. 261). Ever one to bring unchallengeable authorities crashing down, in this case the rigidities of Calvinist Protestantism and the Catholic Church, Spinoza shows why Moses could not have written the Pentatech, David all the Psalms and Isaiah all of the book that bears his name. The letter kills, but the spirit gives life.

(2) With the help of *Philosophers and the Bible*, I can add to Strauss's account the fact that, for Spinoza, the (Hebrew) Bible should be allowed to interpret itself; its Hebrew language, grammar and idioms, in the context of its history, when they are all mastered, will reveal the true meaning of the text. As Totaro points out, Spinoza has his own version of the much misunderstood Protestant slogan *sola scriptura*; for him it means that the original text, outwith scribal glosses, forced harmonization and authoritarian dogma, will reveal its meaning and import, which he found to be ethical and existential, as well as metaphysically generative.[125] However, I need to place a health warning on Diego Donna's chapter, 'Hermeneutics and Conflict: Spinoza and the Downfall of Exegetical Interpretation', in the same volume, which seems to argue that Spinoza's method evacuated the Bible of all valid 'exegetical' or theological meaning, or even of all meaning. Donna takes as his starting point, uncritically, Jonathan Israel's claim (with which, in its general thrust, we are already wearisomely familiar) that Spinoza's *Theological-Political Treatise* reduces theology to philosophy and faith to reason (Donna, p. 91).[126] I hope it has become abundantly clear in the present work (and the point will be reinforced as we move to a conclusion) that there is no inherent contradiction

---

[125] Pina Totaro, 'More on Spinoza and the Authorship of the Pentateuch', in del Prete, Schino and Totaro (eds), *Philosophers and the Bible*, ch. 2.
[126] Diego Donna, 'Hermeneutics and Conflict: Spinoza and the Downfall of Exegetical Interpretation', in del Prete, Schino and Totaro (eds), *Philosophers and the Bible*, ch. 5.

between theology and philosophy or between faith and reason. Far from it; they are always interdependent and mutually constitutive, both for theologians and for philosophers. It is a concocted problem, a completely fake issue. It is gratifying to be able to conclude this brief and selective excursus into the symposium *Philosophers and the Bible* by recommending Giovanni Licata's chapter which draws out the biblical (Old Testament) and radical Protestant sources of Spinoza's key concept of the divine – and at the same time 'natural' or 'rational', as for all Enlightenment thought – law inscribed on the human mind and heart.[127]

(3) Some aspects of Frampton's account of Spinoza have not won support, but his work is of value in several respects. (a) With Strauss, he traces the rise of biblical criticism back to the humanism of the Renaissance and consequently to the Protestant Reformers who had challenged traditional authority in several spheres. (b) As I have done, he sets Spinoza in the context of the radical Protestant freethinking community of mid-seventeenth-century Amsterdam and shows his debt to earlier Protestant writers, especially Isaac La Peyrère and Samuel Fisher. (c) Like Strauss, he brings out the way that Spinoza separates the superseded Hebrew worldview and cosmology from the enduring spiritual and moral meaning of Scripture. However, I think that Frampton is mistaken in dubbing Spinoza's thought a 'rationalistic system' and stating that he rejected religious faith.[128] Instead, I would describe Spinoza's metaphysics as primarily biblical and mystical and his religious faith as (in his own words) 'the intellectual love of God (*amor dei intellectualis*)', a concept that has precedents not only in Plato and Aristotle, but also in medieval scholastic theology, principally that of Thomas Aquinas, where the pure intellectual contemplation of the divine perfections is the height of blessedness.

(4) Preus argues that in the *Tractatus Theologico-Politicus* (1670) Spinoza set out to demolish the Hebrew Scriptures of his own community as a source of theological truth in order to make way for purely political and secular authority. But this thesis invites

---

[127]Giovanni Licata, '"The Law Inscribed in the Mind": On the meaning of a Biblical Image in Spinoza's Theological-Political Treatise', in del Prete, Schino and Totaro (eds), *Philosophers and the Bible*, ch. 11.
[128]Travis L. Frampton, *Spinoza and the Rise of Historical Criticism* (London and New York: T&T Clark, 2006), pp. 17, 75.

several objections. (a) Spinoza does not intend to eliminate the Hebrew Scriptures as a source of theological truth, but understands that theological truth in the sense of ethics and inward piety. (b) In an age when a purely secular state was inconceivable, what theological foundations was political authority deemed to depend on, if not the existing Judeo-Christian and ecclesiastical one? You could not separate the two.[129] (c) Spinoza did not need to demolish the Jewish Scriptures in order to make way for something else. The Hebrew Bible was treasured by a small and politically insignificant community in Amsterdam. Spinoza had been expelled long before he published the *Tractatus Theologico-Politicus* in 1670.

Spinoza's biblical findings aided the researches of the Catholic priest Richard Simon. His motive was not, as many suspected, to be subversive of Catholic orthodoxy, but defensive and apologetic. By showing the critical limitations of the biblical literature, he aimed to undermine the Protestant appeal to the primacy of Scripture and particularly the post-Reformation shibboleth of *sola scriptura*. Although he was hostile to Spinoza's metaphysical system, Simon acknowledged Spinoza's pioneering work in his own *The Critical History of the Old Testament*, published eight years after Spinoza's *Tractatus Theologico-Politicus*.[130]

Deism and the Bible

Voltaire, the most prominent and provocative critic of biblical history and theology and one of the least empathetic, was also profoundly influenced by Spinoza's approach in the *Tractatus* of treating the Hebrew Scriptures, considered as a cultural artefact, by the same methods as one would treat natural phenomena, namely by the law-based methods of Newtonian physical science. Voltaire's method

---

[129] J. Samuel Preus, *Spinoza and the Irrelevance of Biblical Authority* (New York: Cambridge University Press, 2001). See also Richard H. Popkin, 'Spinoza and Biblical Scholarship', in Don Garrett (ed.), *The Cambridge Companion to Spinoza* (Cambridge: Cambridge University Press, 1996).
[130] Richard Simon, *A Critical History of the Old Testament: Written Originally in French by Father Simon ... and since Translated into English by a Person of Quality. Histoire Critique du Vieux Testament* (London: Walter Davis, 1682).

was excessively literalistic, parodistic and prosaic. He had no sense of genre, especially of the figurative, the poetic and the mythical, in the Bible. He waged war on the Old Testament. While Luther had sat light to the Old Testament considered as 'law' (though finding the 'promise' and the gospel hidden within it), and had insisted, 'God did not bring us [Christians] out of Egypt', Calvin tended to set the two Testaments side by side as of equal value and authority, like the two breasts of mother's milk. This reckless stance set up an 'aunt sally' for target practice and invited the swinging attacks of such as Voltaire in the eighteenth century and Richard Dawkins in the twentieth. (I should add that the deists and freethinkers by no means confined their attacks to the Old Testament; some sayings and some miracles of Jesus were not spared.)

Deistic writers began to bring out the human and historically contingent character of the biblical literature, treating it in the first instance just as they would approach any other collection of ancient texts. They despised the traditional figurative ways (the medieval fourfold exegesis) of softening the morally or intellectually unacceptable aspects of the Bible by allegorizing or 'spiritualising' the letter of Scripture. In line from the Renaissance humanists and the Protestant Reformers, the deists prioritized the literal sense of the biblical text, as did Spinoza himself. By so doing, they in principle called into question the stock proofs of Christian apologetics from the claimed fulfilment of Old Testament prophecy in the New, but the effect took time to work through. Dr Johnson was certainly not alone among the orthodox intelligentsia in continuing to maintain that it was inconceivable that anyone could be a sincere atheist when the proofs of Christianity were so compelling. However, while the deistic critique was largely external to the churches and generically hostile to clerical authority, the substance and methodological core of it was gradually and painfully absorbed through literary media into the mainstream theology of the churches, though this osmosis did not – and still does not – usually affect their official claims. The historical-critical method of interpreting both the Bible and the ancient records of church history is now universally approved by the major churches and is practised almost universally by scholars. It is no accident that the traditional arguments for the truth of Christianity from miracles and fulfilled prophecy have disappeared from contemporary apologetics, with the exception of fundamentalist literature.

Gotthold Ephraim Lessing

Gotthold Ephraim Lessing (1729–81), the most impressive and versatile figure of the German Enlightenment, opens a new perspective on the question of the significance of history (focused on the Bible as an historical text or artefact) for religious faith. Lessing was deeply imbued with Lutheran worship, theology and piety and with the powerful legacy of Martin Luther, the creator of the German Bible. Lessing engaged with this tradition dialectically in his theological speculations; he wrestled with it and did not abandon it, though he also drew on the theologically deviant ideas of Spinoza, Leibniz and Voltaire among others. Lessing approaches theological questions by the complementary routes of history and philosophy. He was acutely aware of the Achilles Heel of Christianity as an historical religion based on sacred texts: the protracted and sporadic process of the formation of the New Testament Canon and the diverse ways that its first interpreters, the early Fathers, understood it. He was unpersuaded by the current standard apologetic appeal to miracles, such as the Israelites' crossing of the Red Sea and even the resurrection of Christ, in support of the truth of Christianity. He was warm towards Jews and Judaism, about which he wrote two plays, one of his closest interlocutors being the wise, peaceable and virtuous Jewish philosopher Moses Mendelssohn (1729–86). Lessing insisted that the letter is not the spirit and the Bible is not the whole of religion. Luther has freed us from the yoke of tradition, but (he asks) who will free us from the yoke of the letter? Lessing appeals to the 'inner truth' (*die innere Wahrheit*) of the Christian religion. He is reaching for a participatory, experiential, performative and practical conception of revelation, not one that consists of the communication of propositional information and requires its passive reception. God has not revealed 'himself' in a way that can be appropriated in a purely theoretical, objective and as it were disinterested manner, but only in a way that involves a transforming encounter of the whole person and life with what – or rather who – is revealed. Lessing is not the founder of a theological system or style or tradition of Christian piety; he remains a pioneer and a catalyst in relation to the daunting questions of the relation between faith and history, revelation and reason, that we continue to wrestle with today.

Lessing's published religious views are expressed obliquely, sometimes ironically, and in riddles and parables, which his opponents (especially the senior Lutheran pastor Johann Melchior Goeze, whom Lessing accused of 'Bibliolatry') found infuriating. Lessing's theological views are framed as questions and tentative answers, or as a dialogue. They are constructed *ad hominem* and do not necessarily represent the full scope of his own convictions. They should not be taken literally or at face value. Lessing is always thinking and speaking in the interrogative mode. His supposed death-bed confession to Jacobi that he was a Spinozist at heart remains opaque and raises more questions than it answers, the most basic question being: To which aspect or aspects of Spinoza's thought was he referring?

Lessing was committed to an unending quest, not to a set of definitive solutions. For him, the journey not the arrival mattered. He believed that, contrary to what much religion teaches, we do not have the final truth; but if we pursue truth with a pure heart we have integrity. Ultimate truth is eschatological and lies beyond any of the positive religions, including Christianity, at least in its present form (though Lessing professed himself a faithful member of the Lutheran Church). Lessing throve on disagreement, perplexity and questioning. He probed to the limit, fearlessly. Goethe pointed out that 'In keeping with his polemical nature, Lessing was most at home in the region of contradictions and doubts.'[131] Lessing had an antithetical, contrarian and some would say perverse spirit. He instinctively sided with the weaker argument in a debate or with the underdog in an unequal relationship. He was constitutionally averse to triumphalism and dogmatism. 'The more insistently a person wanted to prove Christianity to me, the more doubtful I became. The more willfully and triumphantly another sought to trample it completely underfoot, the more inclined I felt to uphold it, at least in my heart.'[132]

---

[131] J. W. von Goethe, conversation with Eckermann, 11 April 1827, cited and translated by H. B. Nisbet in Ritchie Robertson (ed.), *Lessing and the German Enlightenment* (Oxford: Voltaire Foundation, 2013), p. 8 and n.15.
[132] Cited from Lessing, *Bibliolatrie*, by Toshimasa Yasukata, *Lessing's Philosophy of Religion and the German Enlightenment* (Oxford: Oxford University Press, 2003), p. 9.

Lessing was dismissive of both English deism and German theological rationalism (Neologism) in their attempts to iron out and explain away the miraculous and the overtly supernatural in the biblical revelation. He regarded the solution that they proposed as worse than the problem that it was meant to solve. Their unhistorical approach discredited their claims. While Lessing attacked rationalistic or Socinian interpretations, he regarded orthodox Lutheran theology, in its scholastic mode, as pitiful. It may have been 'false' overall, he said, but it was not half as much 'a patchwork of bunglers and half-philosophers' as the rationalistic alternative.[133] Thus Lessing saw himself as fighting a theological battle on two fronts (*der theologische Zweifrontenkampf*) against both a rigid Lutheran orthodoxy and an unhistorical, rationalistic Neologism. Like almost all thinkers of the Enlightenment, he was implacably opposed to atheism. But Lessing remained coy about his deepest convictions, setting up a smoke-screen to avoid censorship and censure by the Lutheran Church and the Duke of Brunswick, whose librarian he was (it ultimately failed). He practised a prudent reserve which still partly conceals his ultimate convictions from us.

Faith and history

Lessing was a capable student of the Scriptures and his Gospel-criticism was often superior to that of his opponents. He did not accept that the biblical writers, even of the New Testament, had been supernaturally preserved from making mistakes. He wrote about the four Evangelists as 'merely human historians' and argued that the Bible should be studied as one would study any other classical text. He held, in opposition to the claimed finality of the church, that biblical interpretations must remain provisional because there were many angles of interpretation. 'Everyone has his

---

[133] G. E. Lessing, *Lessing's Theological Writings*, ed., trans. and intro. Henry Chadwick (London: Adam & Charles Black, 1956), p. 13. See also Gotthold Ephraim Lessing, *Philosophical and Theological Writings*, trans. and ed. H. B. Nisbet (Cambridge: Cambridge University Press, 2005). A definitive study is Hugh Barr Nisbet, *Gotthold Ephraim Lessing: His Life, Works, and Thought* (Oxford: Oxford University Press, 2013).

own hermeneutics. Which of them is true? Are they all true? Or is none of them true? And this thing, this wretched, irksome thing, is to be the test of inner truth! Then what would its test be?'[134]

In 1774, Lessing began to publish in instalments what he entitled the *Wolfenbüttel Fragments* from the unpublished voluminous writings of Hermann Samuel Reimarus which were radically subversive of standard pre-critical understandings of the New Testament.[135] For Reimarus, Jesus was a teacher of rational, ethical and practical religion, but who had embraced the Jewish expectation of a political Messiah who would deliver the nation from foreign oppression. His doctrine had undergone a process of deliberate mystification by his followers after his tragic death on the cross. Lessing made no apology for publishing the fragments, stating (tongue in cheek, for sure) that any 'enlightened' Christian should be able to cope with their challenge – adding that, while theologians might be embarrassed by them, ordinary believers would be unaffected, for they would know the joy and comfort of the Christian faith in their hearts. His reasons for putting these incendiary documents into the public domain must remain speculative, but it is likely that it was his dialectical mind and method that motivated Lessing. He hoped that by a process of disputation and debate, for and against, he and his church might move a little nearer to the truth. He may have also wanted to provoke the Neologists (the rationalistic theologians), whom he scorned, and flush them out by ventilating a theology more radical, challenging and rationalistic than their own.[136]

In viewing the orthodox Lutheran theologians as fools and the rationalist Neologians as theologically corrupt, Lessing distanced himself from the rationalistic element in the *Aufklärung* and so moved beyond the intellectual framework of the early German Enlightenment. Though he was a man of many parts, Lessing was – perhaps primarily – a gifted poet and a dramatist of genius. It is the poetic, not the empirical or analytical, that leads to truth. He stands on the verge of the transition to Romanticism and the religion located in the heart and the imagination. I think that, if he had

---

[134] Cited and translated by H. B. Nisbet in Robertson (ed.), *Lessing and the German Enlightenment*, p. 9 & n. 17. See further in the same volume Christoph Bultmann, 'Lessing and the Bible', pp. 245–62.
[135] Nisbet, *Gotthold Ephraim Lessing*, ch. 18, for a detailed account.
[136] Ibid., p. 547.

known it, he would have embraced S. T. Coleridge's notion of 'that willing suspension of disbelief for the moment, which constitutes poetic faith'.[137]

Lessing's most disruptive contribution to the Enlightenment's philosophies of history concerns the distinction between the contingent truths of history and the universal truths of reason (a distinction previously employed by Spinoza and Leibniz) and the epistemological impossibility of crossing from the first to the second. This is Lessing's famous 'broad, ugly ditch' (*der garstige breite Graben*) that he could find no way to cross. Lessing addresses the challenge in the tract *On the Proof of the Spirit and of Power* (*Über den Beweis des Geistes und der Kraft*, 1777), echoing St Paul in 1 Corinthians 2:4 'my speech and my message were not in plausible words of wisdom, but in demonstration of the Spirit and power'. For Lessing, the two realms of reality are divorced and need somehow to be brought together again. The problem is that the accidental (contingent, particular) truths of history cannot (in the nature of the case) ever serve as a proof of the necessary truths of reason (that are valid for all times and places): *zufällige Geschichtswahrheiten können der Beweis von notwendigen Vernunftswahrheiten nie werden*. There are two weaknesses in the historical approach to religious truth; Lessing's ditch is double-dug, both temporal and metaphysical.

(i) Historical events in the remote past are uncertain because we learn of them from fallible human testimony, rather than from our own first-hand experience. The fulfilment of a prophecy that I myself experience is one thing; a fulfilment that is reported to me is another. An alleged fulfilment is not a fulfilment for me. Similarly, a miracle that I personally witness and can in principle verify is one thing; but a miracle that happened in the past and that others spoke of at the time is another. 'I live in the eighteenth century, in which miracles no longer happen. A reported miracle is not a miracle for me.'[138] The reports may be as reliable as historical reports ever can be, but that is not enough to secure our assent. The temporal lapse

---

[137]Samuel Taylor Coleridge, *Biographia Literaria or Biographical Sketches of My Literary Life and Opinions*, ed. George Watson (London: Dent; New York: Dutton, 1965), p. 169 (ch. XIV).
[138]Lessing, *On the Proof of the Spirit and of Power*, in Chadwick (ed.), *Lessing's Theological Writings*, pp. 51–2.

between the alleged miraculous event and my reception of it by distant report can never be bridged.

(ii) The second weakness in the historical approach to religious truth is that, like all empirical phenomena, historical events are 'accidental', that is to say contingent or not necessary, and are causally relative to all other events. They might not have happened at all, or they might easily have turned out differently. The universal truths of reason, on the other hand, are metaphysical (above the physical realm), and so are universally and eternally true. Because they refer to the ultimate reality that grounds all experienced reality, they are always and everywhere the same. The narratives of the Bible, including the Synoptic Gospels, belong in the first category as reported historical events; the theological truths of faith and the principles of ethics belong in the second, the realm of metaphysics. It is this metaphysical problem that, even more than the temporal one, forms 'the ugly, broad ditch, which I cannot get across, however hard I try'.[139] After Lessing, Fichte pronounced, 'Only the metaphysical can save, never the historical.'[140] Lessing was raising the question whether historical events can be *vehicles* of theological truths. About a century later Blondel posed the same dilemma: 'the Christian facts do not, by common consent, suffice for Christian beliefs; how then can one pass from the former to the latter?' and how is it possible 'to extract faith in the invisible supernatural from visible events?'[141]

A challenge from Hamann

Once again J. G. Hamann provides a foil to Enlightenment assumptions. Although Hamann admired Lessing, he rejected the notion that there was a gulf between fact and meaning, history and reason, event and interpretation. For him they are a unity in tension; the temporal realm, which is the sphere of divine action, unites both. The standpoint from which we survey the past – the present moment – is not separate from the past, but constituted by

---

[139] Ibid., p. 55.
[140] Cited Chadwick in ibid., p. 32.
[141] Blondel, *The Letter on Apologetics* and *History and Dogma*, p. 233.

it, while also looking to the fulfilment of God's scriptural promises in the future, eschatologically. So for Hamann there can be no division between temporal facts and eternal truths. God is present and at work in history, as in nature and art and the human spirit. But God's involvement in the world is always indirect, veiled or hidden. Echoing Luther's concept of the hidden God, which itself is drawn from Isaiah (45:15: 'Verily thou art a God that hidest thyself, O God of Israel, the Saviour', KJB), Hamann postulates a divine presence *incognito*. The divine is 'manifest' in signs, symbols and ciphers. To affirm this manifestation is paradoxical, but to the eyes of faith, taught by Scripture, it is real and inescapable. The 'Word made flesh' (John 1:14) refers supremely to the Incarnation, but it also a universal truth, applying to all that is. Creation is permeated by the Word, which is 'made flesh' in history, art and human life. Hamann also scorned Lessing's concept of the progressive divine education of the human race (*deus paedagogus*), to which we turn next. For Hamann, revelation was always 'full-on' and 'non-stop', not released in drips and drabs, as though the revealing God were holding back the full truth.[142]

Revelation as the education of the human race

As he struggled with the problem of faith and history, Lessing developed in the one hundred cryptic propositions of *Die Erziehung des Menschengeschlechts*, the theological conception of the progressive education of the human race. Ideas of historical change and of progression were already current and were given with the ideas of 'Renaissance' and 'Reformation'. Indeed, the images of rebirth and reform are perennial tropes. Lessing applies them to the

---

[142]Ronald Gregor Smith, *J. G. Hamann 1730–1788: A Study in Christian Existence; With Selections from His Writings* (London: Collins, 1960), pp. 89–102.Gordon E. Michalson, Jr., *Lessing's 'Ugly Ditch': A Study of Theology and History* (University Park, PA: Pennsylvania State University Press, 1985) does not find Lessings 'ditch' a problem. Michalson believes that the problematic rests on a pernicious academicizing of Christian theology according to secular canons. We can dispose of the ditch if we ditch critical history!

progressive human reception of divine truth or revelation, by analogy with the Baconian vision of ever-increasing scientific understanding of the world. To take that approach was necessarily to challenge the basic Enlightenment tenet of the uniformity of human nature throughout history and across societies. The well-worn theological trope of divine 'accommodation' to human weakness had already been put to work by the Anglican Edmund Law who argued that all human ideas about religion were 'proportionable' to our way of life and our operative understanding of the world.[143] Lessing teases from various angles the notion of an unfolding divine revelation coupled with unfailing divine providence, so that revelation is adapted and attuned to the human capacity to receive it at any one time or stage of development.[144]

Lessing seems ambivalent and conflicted about this text, fragmentary and interrogative as it is. Nevertheless, there it is, for us to ponder and puzzle over! The patristic scholar Henry Chadwick points out that, in his exploration of the idea of progressive revelation, Lessing was influenced by the Christian Platonism of Alexandria in the time of Clement and Origen with its positive engagement with classical culture and its apologetic intention to commend the Christian faith to enquirers and doubters. The notion of the history of the human race as an educative process, combined with the idea of divine accommodation to human weakness and ignorance, was common coin in enlightened Protestant thought. What Lessing adds to a well-winnowed trope is the idea of the continual development and gradual strengthening of the human capacity to reason.[145] He has arrived at the concept of progressive revelation. I see this as a step in the right direction in the Christian understanding of divine revelation. But progressive revelation is a two-edged sword. Is revelation to be viewed as progressive in the purposes of God because God, the author of revelation, holds back

---

[143]R. S. Crane, 'Anglican Apologetics and the Idea of Progress', *Modern Philology* 31 (1934), pp. 273–306, 349–82.
[144]*The Education of the Human Race*, in Chadwick, op. cit., pp. 82–98. See further Nisbet, *Gotthold Ephraim Lessing*, pp. 571–84; David Hill, 'Enlightenment as a Historical Process: Ernst und Falk and Die Erziehung des Menschengeschlechts', in Robertson (ed.), *Lessing and the German Enlightenment*, pp. 227–44.
[145]Yasukata, *Lessing's Philosophy of Religion and the German Enlightenment*, pp. 97–8.

all that God has in store to be revealed until humans are able to receive it and therefore releases it in instalments (transcendently or objectively progressive)? Or is revelation progressive within the human subjective perception and appropriation of it because of the incorrigible human tendency to distort and corrupt divine truth, as revealed, and even to claim as revelation what, on ethical or other grounds, cannot be accepted as coming from a divine source (immanently or subjectively progressive)? Or both at once?

And if, as Lessing claims, truths derived from revelation, when fully assimilated into our thinking, have now become truths of reason, has he effectively dissolved the concept of revelation and made it redundant?[146] As we follow Lessing, do we reach a point where revelation is no longer needed? I think Lessing is justified in proposing that revelation becomes transposed into reason because this has to happen in order for it to be assimilated and put to use by us. We are motivated to live and act for the common good only on the basis of ethical or value principles that we have made fully our own (autonomy), not on the basis of principles that we feel are being imposed on us from outside (heteronomy), even though a devout person will continue to recognize and acknowledge the ultimate source of those principles in God (theonomy). A further question is whether there is ambiguity in Lessing's account of revelation: is he slipping back into a basically propositional account of revelation, or is he holding consistently to a relational, ethical and even mystical one?[147]

While modern sources for the idea of the progressive education of the human race have been identified, the ultimate source is in both Testaments of the Bible. The prophet Hosea is overtly pedagogical: 'When Israel was a child, I loved him ... it was I who taught Ephraim to walk, I took them up in my arms ... I led them with cords of human kindness, with bands of love. I was to them like those who lift infants to their cheeks. I bent down to them and fed them' (Hos. 11:1–4). Isaiah 49:15 pictures Israel as a baby at the breast: 'Can a woman forget her nursing child, or show no

---

[146]Cf. ibid., p. 116.
[147]Further on revelation see Balázs M. Mezei, Francesca Aran Murphy, and Kenneth Oakes (eds), *The Oxford Handbook of Divine Revelation* (Oxford: Oxford University Press, 2021), including Paul Avis, 'Revelation, Epistemology, and Authority' (ch. 12).

compassion for the child of her womb? Even these may forget, yet I will not forget you.' The idea of stages of revelation is prominent in the New Testament. Paul contrasts the dispensation of the Mosaic law with the dispensation of the gospel of Christ and links them in historical and theological sequence: 'the law was our pedagogue to bring us to Christ' (Gal. 3.24). Under the law, the heirs of God's promises remained under guardians and trustees until the date set by 'the father' for their majority or coming of age. While we were minors, we were enslaved to the rudiments of the world. 'But when the fullness of time had come, God sent his Son, born of a woman, born under the law, in order to redeem those who were under the law, so that we might receive adoption as children' (Gal. 4:1–5). And in the Epistle to the Hebrews we have a crisp statement of this idea: 'Long ago God spoke to our ancestors in many and various ways by the prophets, but in these last days he has spoken to us by a Son' (Heb. 1:1–2). The concept of staged revelation occurs most explicitly in the Prologue to John's Gospel: 'The law indeed was given through Moses; grace and truth came through Jesus Christ' (John 1:17). Promise and fulfilment, preparation and inheritance – so a kind of progression in the reception of divine revelation – are twin themes in much biblical literature.

In Lessing's hands, revelation is no longer the once-for-all deliverance of a body of propositional truths, but a pedagogical process in which one perspective is corrected, augmented and eventually superseded by another. As Lessing puts it: 'What education is to the individual, revelation is to the human race.'[148] What is revealed in this process of education or 'enlightenment' (*Aufklärung* occurs three times in this brief essay) are truths of reason (that is to say, abiding or eternal truths about reality which in principle and perhaps in fact could be attained by human reason) which stand above the constantly changing scene of earthly events and shape them. But what is the connection, the hinge, between the two? How do they interact?

Lessing was able to formulate the conception of *The Education of the Human Race*, with its twin *foci* of revelation and providence, because – influenced by Spinoza and Leibniz – he was working with a different theological paradigm to the one that prevailed

---

[148] Chadwick (ed.), *Lessing's Theological Writings*, p. 82.

in Lutheran orthodoxy. Lessing owed his high view of divine immanence to Spinoza and probably tended towards Spinoza's monism of substance (which I have argued elsewhere in this book, is in no way equivalent to atheism, nor even necessarily to pantheism, but approximates to panentheism). Spinoza the Jew also stressed the need to enter into the worldview and linguistic idioms of the ancient Hebrews and held a doctrine of divine accommodation to human weakness. And Lessing owed his paradigm of unfolding process to Leibniz, especially the latter's *Monadology* (1714) with its motifs of continuity, evolution by degrees and harmony between any particular event (the microcosm) and the total process (the macrocosm). Liebniz worked within the metaphysical framework of the gradual human ascent to a rational worldview, an approximation to the divine nature.[149] For Lessing, the essence of the Christian faith was at the same time rational, ethical and poetical.

The nature of faith

In the final analysis, Lessing was not interested in mere historical verification, but in the spiritual, experiential fruits of divine revelation. His strategic move was not only to loosen the connection between the truth or validity of Christian faith and its putative historical basis, but actually to detach them from each other. For Lessing, claimed historical events may suggest religious truth or represent it as it were in a parable or symbol, but they can never legitimate it. The truths of reason, which are properly the truths of revelation, must stand forth in their own light. As a biblical scholar, Lessing held that the discrepancies between the various Gospels and the many struggling attempts to reconcile or harmonize them are irrelevant to faith; the effort is futile. It is the Christianity which we feel to be true and in which we feel blessed that is the real faith. As Coleridge (d. 1834) protested in his posthumously published *Confessions of an Inquiring Spirit*, proofs and 'evidences' were futile and wearisome. It is 'what finds me' at the deepest level of my

---

[149]White, *Metahistory*, p. 61.

being that counts and reveals itself as a manifestation of the power of the Spirit. Then I have the evidence within myself.[150]

For Lessing, the central dogmas of the Christian faith in its Lutheran form – the biblical Word, the sacrament of the Lord's Table, the Trinity, the Incarnation, the atonement, justification by faith – are not irrational, superstitious accretions to original Christianity, as the Neologists held, but obscure, historically conditioned, symbolic expressions of ultimate truths that lie just beyond our ken. Allison states: 'Lessing begins by maintaining the orthodox position against rationalistic objections, and ends by so transforming the orthodox doctrine that the result is more radical than the objections themselves.'[151] There has been a suspicion that, for Lessing, 'revelation' is a prudent diplomatic metaphor for a purely natural phenomenon, that of the gradual ascent of human reason. Without a doctrine of divine transcendence, what meaning has 'revelation'? The truth seems to be that human reason is also a divine gift, so that revelation is not opposed to reason. They are two ways of looking at the same reality.

It is precisely Lessing's sense of the severe evidential limitations of what can be disinterred from the past that shows his historical consciousness and acumen. He contributes to the philosophy of history by his holistic awareness of historical process and within it the unfolding of a divine purpose. Looked at in one way, that purpose is one of education; looked at in another way, it is one of revelation. An immanent divine presence, that 'rolls through all things' (as Wordsworth would later put it) gives history its integrity and autonomy.[152] There is an eschatological quality to Lessing's theology: the perfect religion, which is natural and rational (though not naturalistic or rationalistic), is the goal towards which human

---

[150]Samuel Taylor Coleridge, *Confessions of an Inquiring Spirit*, Collected Works, ed. Kathleen Coburn (Princeton, NJ: Princeton University Press; London: Routledge, 1976–).
[151]Henry E. Allison, *Lessing and the Enlightenment* (Ann Arbor, MI: University of Michigan Press, 1966), pp. 100, 163.
[152]William Wordsworth, 'Lines Composed a Few Miles above Tintern Abbey, On Revisiting the Banks of the Wye during a Tour. July 13, 1798'. For the whole poem see https://www.poetryfoundation.org/poems/45527/lines-composed-a-few-miles-above-tintern-abbey-on-revisiting-the-banks-of-the-wye-during-a-tour-july-13-1798 (accessed 17 February 2022).

consciousness is being drawn by the alluring power of a benevolent providence, though that goal remains a transcendent horizon, a limit situation.[153]

Lessing: A tentative assessment

By way of a very preliminary evaluation of Lessings pioneering contribution to the problems of faith and history, I have to say, first, that I find his dichotomy between historical events and ultimate truths – though it should give us serious pause for thought – too hard-drawn, too absolute and that in two ways. (i) With regard to the events: they are made by personal agents who have reasons for their actions, even if the results do not turn out exactly as intended. Any historical research worth its salt – that is not merely a positivistic accumulation of data, of naively supposed 'facts' – aims to penetrate behind the outward manifestation of an event to the inner motivation of the actors involved in it. The 'inwardness' of any event is the thinking, willing and feeling that was going on in the mind and heart of the agent. Historical investigation, as Vico pioneered it and Collingwood later expounded it, aims to think the thoughts of historical agents after them by a process of delicate, self-effacing empathy and artistic or imaginative reconstruction, on the basis of the evidence available. Active agency and creative mind are present in every event and our interpretations needs to account for that fact. (ii) With regard to the metaphysical truths of reason, we have to recognize that they are not timeless, but are both historically conditioned and metaphorically, analogically and poetically expressed. So, first, these rational truths do not exist in an ahistorical vacuum, but are constructed in human minds with words and concepts that are formed from historical components, which are the thoughts (conveyed by the writings) of those who wrestled with such ideas in the past. There is thus an historical dimension to all our thinking, feeling and experiencing of the world (theology being no exception). Second, the metaphysical truths of reason transcend our grasp; they are metaphorically or figuratively

---

[153]Allison, *Lessing and the Enlightenment*, p. 134.

expressed. They are obscure and veiled to our finite minds, so they can be stated by us only in metaphorical, symbolic and poetical language. Metaphysics is metaphorical. But this characteristic is not confined to metaphysics; it also resonates with the creative impulse behind and within historical events. So we have to reckon with the truth that the problematic of historical action and the problematic of rational enquiry into those actions – two exercises of thought with the same focus but separated in time – are both infused with the poetic, imaginative and intuitive dimension of human intellection.[154]

It seems to me that the ditch between the contingent events of history and the eternal truths of reason is not as absolute as Lessing, in his provocative way, tries to make out. There is some traffic across the ditch and it is two-way. A 'leap of faith' is still required, but it is not an irrational leap; it is a calculated act of connecting the one with the other on the basis of creative, poetical intuition. Once again, this is not simply or exclusively a theological problem. All enquiry, however empirically based, requires an

---

[154] R. G. Collingwood, *The Idea of History* (Oxford: Oxford University Press, 1946), esp. pp. 214ff; id., *Autobiography* (London: Oxford University Press, 1939), *passim*; a powerfully direct statement. A classic discussion of the relation between history and faith is Van A. Harvey, *The Historian and the Believer* (London: SCM Press, 1967 [1966]). I am aware that some philosophers of history reject the Vichean, Collingwoodian ideal of reliving or rethinking past actions and the thought and motives that supposedly lay behind them; e.g., classically, Patrick Gardiner, *The Nature of Historical Explanation* (Oxford: Oxford University Press, 1952), pp. 47–51, 128ff. Gardiner takes exception to Collingwood's inside-outside metaphor, preferring to ask 'What?' and then 'Why?'. He also finds the approach 'misleading' because it implies that history is an esoteric study of mysterious 'mental agencies'. I think Gardiner 'doth protest too much'. When we ask the question 'Why?', we are immediately plunged into difficult but unavoidable questions of provenance, psychology and motivation. Croce proposed that the historian 'lives again in imagination individuals and events'. See also Patrick Gardiner, 'Historical Understanding and the Empiricist Tradition', in Bernard Williams and Alan Montefiore (eds), *British Analytical Philosophy* (London: Routledge and Kegan Paul, 1966), pp. 267–84; id., 'The Concept of Man as Presupposed by the Historical Studies', in Godfrey N. A. Vesey (ed.), *The Proper Study of Man*, Royal Institute of Philosophy Lectures, IV, 1969–1970 (London: Macmillan, 1971). Gardiner notes that the 'Covering Law' approach to history assumes the Enlightenment paradigm of the uniformity of human nature by analogy with the phenomena that are studied by the natural sciences.

exercise of empathetic understanding of its object, followed by an intuitive leap to an explanatory theory. This active, exploratory element of scientific discovery is now widely recognized and can be conclusively demonstrated. The pathway to making cogent sense of the relationship between the unreliability of historical reportage, including in the Bible, and theologically coherent Christian beliefs is to recognize (as Augustine, Hamann and Blake, among others, suggest in so many words) that God's creative, revelatory and redemptive work is aptly likened to the work of a poet and that Jesus and the apostles were, in their way, artists. In its form and content, its beauty and glory, the Christian gospel is a work of art. The divine creativity is poetic – what else could it be? While mere historical events alone, as fallibly reported but with whatever wealth of circumstantial detail, cannot either help or harm us, the divine revelation that shines through them to the eyes of faith, addressed to the human imagination and responded to by the whole person within the community of faith, is transformative and life-giving.[155]

---

[155]See Paul Avis, *God and the Creative Imagination: Metaphor, Symbol and Myth in Religion and Theology* (London and New York: Routledge, 1999).

7

The Enlightenment in the frame of Christian theology

In this concluding chapter my aim is to discuss the continuing significance, meaning and value of the Enlightenment in the perspective of Christian theology. I will attempt this, all too briefly, in just two ways. I will look first at the phrase 'coming of age', in the sense of thinking for oneself and taking one's share of responsibility for the world, which Immanuel Kant used to sum up the import of the Enlightenment (*Aufklärung*). I will link this Enlightenment motif with the biblical, Pauline, use of the expression and with Dietrich Bonhoeffer's intriguing use of it in his jottings from his prison cell. But I will add a caveat. Then I will round off the book by drawing out – inevitably selectively – the symbolism of light and enlightenment in the Bible and in the church's liturgy and in Christian spirituality. I will bring out the truth that enlightenment is the key religious (especially Jewish and Christian) symbol and remains potent.

Coming of age

'Coming of age' refers to the age of majority, the age of maturity and discretion, the age at which we take responsibility for matters that previously others took responsibility for on our behalf. Immanuel Kant chose this expression to define the essence of the *Aufklärung*. The radical philosophical element of the Enlightenment claimed the expression 'coming of age' for a (supposedly) new and bold collective sense of self-reliant individual and collective autonomy. It was a sense of intellectual and moral freedom and self-confidence that involved rejecting the existing unchallengeable ecclesiastical authority which claimed to be the sole divinely appointed guardian and divinely authorized interpreter of divinely revealed truth. The phrase 'coming of age' had been used by St Paul, and would be picked up again by Dietrich Bonhoeffer in his final theological explorations from prison. So the idea of a 'coming of age' has cropped up in three very different watershed or 'axial' eras of Western intellectual history: first, in Paul's struggle to interpret the significance of the coming of Christ in relation to God's previous dealings with Israel through the law; second, as a watchword and almost battlecry of the eighteenth-century *Aufklärung*; and third, during the darkest night of deliberate wholesale evil deeds that possibly the world has ever known to this day, where it is laden with ghastly irony. The first and third of these authors (Paul and Bonhoeffer) gave their lives for their convictions.

I am using the phrase 'coming of age' in the sense of *accepting responsibility for one's beliefs and actions*. I trust that this sense will be found unobjectionable, even by those who take a jaundiced view of the Enlightenment, for the simple reason that to take personal responsibility for our beliefs and actions is precisely what we are bound to do in the pluralistic world in which we live, where personal choice is pervasive and unavoidable.[1] In advanced economies there has never been as much choice available as now, far more than anyone needs to enjoy 'the good life'. The permutations within product lines and retail outlets are theoretically endless. I do not find even ostensibly counter-cultural Christians, who affect to despise the culture of late modernity, objecting to having to make choices, great or small, in their local supermarket.

The notion of a 'coming of age' is found in many cultures and has often been favoured by anthropologists as a subject for field research.[2] Perhaps it attracts them by its combination of the strange

---

[1] The imperative of personal choice with regard to belief as an aspect of modernity is strongly brought out by Charles Taylor in *A Secular Age* (Cambridge, MA: The Belknap Press of Harvard University Press, 2007).
[2] A classic is, of course, Margaret Mead, *Coming of Age in Samoa: A Study of Adolescence and Sex in Primitive Society* (Harmondsworth: Penguin, 1943 [1928]).

and the familiar, the weird and the readily explicable, and by the transition from innocence to responsibility. Rites for the coming of age normally take place at the time of puberty or a little later. They are bracketed in time as sacred, liminal moments, in which the ordinary 'hastening on' momentum of life is suspended. They are marked by certain rituals, some private and some public, and are followed by the acceptance of new responsibilities by the initiate.[3] Modern societies retain the notion of a watershed moment in growing up, a transition from childhood to adulthood. So 'coming of age' lingers on in the form of – for example – the age at which one can qualify for a driving licence, the legal age of sexual consent and of marriage, eligibility to vote in elections, and the church's sacrament of confirmation. St Paul adapts the idea to illustrate the new transformative dispensation that has been ushered in by the coming of Christ. Immanuel Kant used it to define the essence of the Enlightenment, and Dietrich Bonhoeffer wrestled with it in his prison cell.

Coming of age in salvation history

'Coming of age' is one of a cluster of metaphors that St Paul uses in a rather convoluted, rabbinic style of argument in his Epistle to the Galatians. Paul has set out to draw the Jewish Christians of Galatia away from seeking salvation or justification through observance of the Jewish law and back to the liberty that they have in Christ, according to his gospel (Gal. 1:6–9; 3:1–5; 3:1–15). In Galatians 3:10 to 4:7 Paul runs rapidly through a gamut of images to highlight the contrast between the old order under the oppressive Jewish law and the new order of Christian liberty. He starts with the metaphor of a curse: as Christians we are delivered from the curse of the law by Christ who became a curse for us (3:10–14).

---

[3]On liminality see A. Van Gennep, *The Rites of Passage* (London: Routledge and Kegan Paul, 1960); Victor Turner, *The Ritual Process* (London: Routledge and Kegan Paul; Chicago: Aldine Press, 1969). For an application of liminality to the sacramental ministry of the church see also Paul Avis, *A Church Drawing Near: Spirituality and Mission in a Post-Christian Culture* (London: T&T Clark, 2003), ch. 6: 'Transformations of Being'.

Paul then moves to the contrast between the giving of the law to Moses and the fulfilment of the covenant of promise, first made to Abraham, in Christ (3:15-18). The next metaphor is one of release from prison: imprisonment under the law and freedom from imprisonment through Christ (3:22–23). This suggests to Paul that the law was like a tutor, mentor or pedagogue (NRSV: 'disciplinarian'; παιδαγωγός, *paidagōgós*), training us up and leading us to Christ (3:24–26). This image in turn prompts Paul to a further comparison: without Christ, we were like a minor who, while the heir to the property, is subject to guardians and trustees until his or her coming of age. Therefore (claims Paul in a another semantic leap) our status was no better than that of slaves; we were slaves to the elements or rudiments (NRSV: 'spirits') of the world (τά στοιχεία του κόσμου, *ta stoicheia tou kosmou*).[4] To indicate the idea of a coming of age Paul uses two expressions: 'until the date set by the father' (4:2) and 'when the fullness of time had come' (4:4; τὸ πλήρωμα τοῦ χρόνου, *to pleroma tou chronou*). There is another transition at this point, from minor/slave to child/heir, albeit an adopted child and heir. The word 'adopted', rather than born into God's family, seems incongruous and a little deflating. But Paul seems to grasp at it because he lacks the alternative: born into God's family. While he employs the extended metaphor of dying and being raised with Christ (Rom. 6:1–11; Gal. 2:19–20) and has the metaphor of the new creation (2 Cor. 5:17), he does not have the precise metaphor of new birth, of sacramental regeneration, that we find explicitly elsewhere in the New Testament (Jn 3:1–8; 1 Jn 5:18; 1 Pet. 1:3; 2:2), though there is hint of it in Gal. 4:29: 'born according to the Spirit'. Paul's argument may bounce around a bit, but his central affirmation in this passage is that, at God's right time, God sent God's Son, born of a woman, born under the dispensation of law (there is no definite article here in the Greek), in order to ransom from slavery those who were enslaved to the elemental powers of the cosmos, and so were ruled by ignorance and fear, in order that they might become children of God (4:4–5). So, for Paul, 'coming of

---

[4] On the vexed question of the meaning of this expression in Paul, see the review of interpretations in Dieter T. Roth, 'What ἐν τῷ κόσμῳ are the στοιχεία του κόσμου?' *Herv. teol. Stud.* 70.1 (Pretoria, South Africa) January 2014: http://www.scielo.org.za/scielo.php?script=sci_arttext&pid=S0259-94222014000100036.

age' refers to a critical point in salvation history (*Heilsgeschichte*), the outworking of God's saving purposes in history, especially in the history of the people of Israel.

'Coming of age' in the Enlightenment

Immanuel Kant (1724–1804) used the image of coming of age to capture the essence of the Enlightenment. Addressing the question, 'What Is Enlightenment [*Aufklärung*]?', in 1784, Kant asserts that 'Enlightenment is man's emergence [*der Ausgang des Menschen*] from his self-incurred immaturity (*Unmündigkeit*).' *Unmündigkeit* is literally dumbness, so a state of dependency on others and of not being able to speak for oneself. Kant understands *Unmündigkeit* as 'the inability to use one's own understanding without the guidance of another'. For Kant, this state is not due to lack of intelligence or education, but is caused by lack of confidence, loss of nerve. 'This immaturity is self-incurred if its cause is not lack of understanding, but lack of resolution and courage to use it without the guidance of another.' The motto of Enlightenment is, therefore, Kant proposes, in the words of the Roman poet Horace, *Sapere aude!* 'Have the courage to use your own understanding'.[5] On all sides, Kant complained, he could hear the command, 'Don't argue!'. 'The officer says, Don't argue, get on parade! The tax official: Don't argue, pay! The clergyman, Don't argue, believe!'[6] Religious immaturity, Kant continued, was 'the most pernicious and dishonourable of all'; 'dogmas and formulas' were 'the ball and chain' of this permanent state of immaturity.[7] *Selbsdenken* – thinking for oneself instead of

---

[5]Immanuel Kant, 'An Answer to the Question, What Is Enlightenment?' (*Beantwortung der Frage: Was ist Aufklärung?*), in Immanuel Kant, *Kant's Political Writings*, ed. H. B. Nisbet, trans. H. Reiss (Cambridge: Cambridge University Press, 1970), pp. 54–60, at p. 54. The essay is also found, along with others on the same or a similar theme, in James Schmidt (ed.), *What Is Enlightenment? Eighteenth-Century Answers and Twentieth-Century Questions* (Berkeley, CA: University of California Press, 1996). See also T. J. Reed, *Light in Germany: Scenes from an Unknown Enlightenment* (Chicago: The University of Chicago Press, 2015), ch. 1.
[6]Kant, 'An Answer to the Question, What Is Enlightenment?' ed. Nisbet, p. 55.
[7]Ibid., pp. 54–5, 59.

blindly accepting traditional authority – was a watchword of the *Aufklärung*. Wilhelm Dilthey, almost certainly with Kant's dictum in mind, later said that Lessing was *der erste ganz mündige Mensch*, the first fully mature human being.[8] In the same vein as Kant but taking the argument to its logical conclusion, Friedrich Nietzsche would claim that the word 'God' was 'fundamentally even a crude *prohibition* to us', meaning, 'You shall not think!'[9] Kant did not claim in this essay that German civilization had attained such maturity, only that it was on the way to doing so.

A little later (1790) Kant touched on this theme again in a digression within his *Critique of Judgement*, where he offers three 'maxims of common ["not cultivated"] human understanding'.[10] (i) Think for yourself, 'non-passively', which Kant calls 'unprejudiced thought'. (ii) Think from the universal standpoint, the *sensus communis*. In other words, put yourself in the position of others. Kant calls this 'enlarged thought' and regards it as the essence of judgement. Here Kant makes the transition from the individual to the collective basis of understanding. (iii) Think consistently. Kant regards 'consistent thought' as the essence of rationality. To absorb current prejudices uncritically or 'passively' is to give way to the 'heteronomy of reason'. The greatest of such prejudices is superstition. 'Emancipation from superstition is called *enlightenment*', he pronounces. Enlightenment of the understanding resides in critical detachment from prevailing prejudices and this is a standpoint of reason that only the individual can perform. So, in spite of his injunction to step into the shoes of others – an injunction to practise empathetic identification with the other – Kant ends by affirming the autonomy or sovereignty of one's own reason. Ultimately, others cannot make your judgements

---

[8] Wilhelm Dilthey, *Das Erlebnis und die Dichtung: Lessing-Goethe-Novalis-Hölderlin*, 16th edn (Göttingen: Vandenhoeck & Ruprecht, 1985), p. 107, cited Toshimasa Yasukata, *Lessing's Philosophy of Religion and the German Enlightenment* (Oxford: Oxford University Press, 2003), p. 3.
[9] Friedrich Nietzsche, *Ecce Homo*, trans. Walter Kaufman (Harmondsworth: Penguin, 1979), p. 51 (italics original); also cited – translated slightly different – by Walter Kaufman, *Nietzsche: Philosopher, Psychologist, Antichrist* (Princeton, NJ: Princeton University Press, 1968 [1950]), p. 101.
[10] Immanuel Kant, *The Critique of Judgement*, trans. J. C. Meredith (Oxford: Clarendon Press, 1952), Book II, Part I, Sec. 40, pp. 152–3.

or decisions for you and that, for the Enlightenment, as for all modernity, is self-evident.[11] Kant's immaturity/maturity trope is a metaphor of intellectual, moral and emotional growth and development; it is orientated to the future. As his essay 'Idea for a Universal History with a Cosmopolitan Purpose' further exemplifies,[12] Kant's vision of the dawning and spread of enlightenment was a kind of intellectual eschatology. But what is particularly significant here and throughout the eighteenth-century fixation on the spread of knowledge as enlightenment is that the *parousia* is not awaited passively in hope and expectation, to be received from divine intervention, as in Christian eschatology, but is to be activated and undertaken by human agency – and this is a moral imperative.[13]

Kant and J. G. Hamann were both citizens of Königsberg in Northern Germany and were friends. Kant helped and supported Hamann. They read each other's work, though Kant pleaded with Hamann not to write so obscurely. But Hamann came to regard the Kant of the critical philosophy as a false prophet, offering cold and illusory oracles, like the Aurora Borealis (Northern Lights). He scorned Kant's notion of 'pure reason' (as in the *Critique of Pure Reason*). There is no 'pure' reason because reason is not autonomous but rests on other sources of truth. It is constituted by language which itself is formed by symbols and transmitted by tradition.[14] In particular, Hamann looked askance at Kant's promotion, in 'What is Enlightenment [*Aufklärung*]?', of individual autonomy, liberation from tradition, and standing on one's own two feet intellectually and ethically. For Hamann biblical revelation and the Christian

---

[11]Confusingly, Kant also calls this last stance, in the English translation, a 'merely negative attitude', meaning negative towards superstition as the worst form of prejudice.
[12]Also in Reiss (ed.), *Kant's Political Writings*.
[13]See further Genevieve Lloyd, *Enlightenment Shadows* (Oxford: Oxford University Press, 2013), pp. 10–13. Michel Foucault, 'What Is Enlightenment? (Was ist Aufklärung)', takes Kant's injunction as a jumping off point for seeing the 'enlightenment' [*sic*] as an 'ethos' that critiques the present and every other age: Catherine Porter (trans.), in Paul Rabinow (ed.), *The Foucault Reader*, New York: Pantheon Books, 1984, pp. 32–50.
[14]Ronald Gregor Smith, *J. G. Hamann 1730–1788: A Study in Christian Existence; with Selections from His Writings* (London: Collins, 1960), p. 87.

tradition were the twin sources of true illumination. They were to be apprehended not literally and prosaically, but imaginatively, in a poetic mode, for God creates and communicates poetically.[15] He anticipated Schleiermacher (who, it seems, had not read him) in underlining our absolute dependence on the life, the presence and the wisdom of God.[16] He offered – if one could understand it – a radical, mystical, poetical and biblical alternative to Kant's *Aufklärung*: the way of Christian discipleship and devotion to Jesus Christ.[17]

Dietrich Bonhoeffer and a world come of age

In his letters from his prison cell in June and July 1944, Bonhoeffer echoed, almost certainly consciously, what Kant had written about the Enlightenment as the mature exercise of autonomy on the part of a world that needed to accept responsibility for itself.[18] His fragmentary jottings, smuggled out of prison, have intrigued and puzzled scholars ever since they saw the light of day after the war. Bonhoeffer believed that he saw around him a 'world come of age', a world that had attained self-confidence, in which God and religion

---

[15]For this pathway into faith and theology see Paul Avis, *God and the Creative Imagination: Metaphor, Symbol and Myth in Religion and Theology* (London and New York: Routledge, 1999).
[16]Smith, *J. G. Hamann*, p. 58.
[17]Isaiah Berlin, *The Magus of the North: J. G. Hamann and the Origins of Modern Irrationalism*, ed. Henry Hardy (London: John Murray, 1993), pp. 107–9; Smith, *J. G. Hamann*, p. 58.
[18]Dietrich Bonhoeffer, *Letters and Papers from Prison*, ed. Eberhard Bethge (London: SCM Press, 1971), pp. 324–63; page references in my main text. See the reflections on this theme in Ronald Gregor Smith (ed. and intro.), *World Come of Age: A Symposium on Dietrich Bonhoeffer* (London: Collins, 1967). My copy is inscribed by Bonhoeffer's twin sister Sabine (Leibholz). On Gregor Smith see David Fergusson and Mark W. Elliott (eds), *The History of Scottish Theology, Volume III: The Long Twentieth Century* (Oxford: Oxford University Press, 2019), ch. 16 (George Pattison).

seemed superfluous (p. 326). He saw in fact a 'godless' world. Yet, for Bonhoeffer, God was still present – and all the more present – in passive or suffering presence at the heart of this-worldly reality. God was teaching humankind to stand on its own feet and to take responsibility for its actions. Very possibly, this thought was aided, if not actually suggested, by the fact that Bonhoeffer had been compelled by his conscience to renounce the apolitical Lutheran quietism in which he had been brought up, with its dualism of Luther's Two Kingdoms doctrine (*Zwei-Reiche-Lehre*)[19] and to become implicated in the resistance movement to Adolf Hitler and the Nazi regime, which culminated in the assassination attempt of 20 July 1944. Bonhoeffer was forced to get his pure Lutheran pastor's hands politically dirty. By his cryptic phrase 'religionless Christianity', Bonhoeffer seems to mean a non-dualist faith, an integrated practice of discipleship, in which God is not defined in contrast or opposition to the world, primarily as transcendent, but is discovered at its heart, immanently, though unrecognized, so anonymously. 'Before God and with God we live without God' (p. 360). (I think that Hamann's version would have been: 'Before God and with God we live within God.')

The Enlightenment, Bonhoffer seems to be saying, has relentlessly reduced and circumscribed the sphere of God's activity in the world, when that activity is understood in a traditional, dualistic way, as the action of a transcendent *deus ex machina*. We do not need to invoke God as an explanatory hypothesis for how the world works. Secondary causation is sufficient for all our purposes – except for the 'ultimate questions' that revolve around guilt and death, where God, the church and pastors are still needed (p. 326). A stopgap God is invoked only in those areas that have not yet become enlightened by the advance of science and technology. The church has attempted to fight a rear-guard action against the encroaching enlightenment, Bonhoeffer believes, imaging that by doing so it will manage to preserve the sphere of divine action. But 'The attack by Christian apologetic on the adulthood of the world I consider to be

---

[19]Explication with references of Luther's Two-Kingdoms theology in Paul Avis, *Beyond the Reformation? Authority, Unity and Primacy in the Conciliar Tradition* (London and New York: T&T Clark, 2006), pp. 111–13.

in the first place pointless, in the second place ignoble, and in the third place unchristian' (p. 327).

> Pointless, because it looks to me like an attempt to put a grown-up man back into adolescence, i.e. to make him dependent on things on which he is, in fact, no longer dependent, and thrusting him into problems that are, in fact, no longer problems to him any more. Ignoble, because it amounts to an attempt to exploit man's weakness for purposes that are alien to him and to which he has not freely assented. Unchristian, because it confuses Christ with one particular stage in man's religiousness, i.e. with a human law. (p. 327)

In these preliminary thoughts from prison, Bonhoeffer was coming to the realization that Christianity and the church should come to terms with the Enlightenment and the progress of rational mastery of the world through technology. It should cease to fight blindly against it and instead it should shoulder the responsibilities and dilemmas of modernity in which we address most of our problems as though God does not exist (*etsi deus non daretur*).

The freedom to think things out for oneself, the freedom to investigate, even in the face of the prohibitions and threats of powerful, privileged authority in church and state, and to speak and act upon them, was the main platform of the European Enlightenment. No-one could stop a person thinking. So this freedom meant: (a) having the liberty to research, speak and write, to make public one's private thoughts, when the threat of censorship was removed; (b) enjoying legal toleration of opinion, when the fear of persecution was removed; (c) exercising the right to challenge injustice, privilege and the abuse of power in high places, once the threat of the Bastille (for the *philosophes*) was removed. With these liberties, which should be seen as responsibilities, European civilization came of age. In Peter Gay's phrase, the Enlightenment was a 'recovery of nerve' on the part of European civilization after all the strife, turmoil, destruction and mass death that the religious and dynastic wars of the previous century (especially the Thirty-Years' War in which between five and eight million persons had perished), had brought about. The churches and the unresolvable clash of Roman Catholic and Protestant confessional identities had imposed bloody conflicts on Europe. Now it was time to see whether an appeal to reason, rather than to dogma, could do better. Reason would not only explode superstition and expose corruption and deceit; it had the power to shape a better world for all humankind.[20]

Clearly, there is nothing in the vision and programme of the Enlightenment in these particular terms that is inherently incompatible with Christianity. The patent fact that the three basic freedoms that I have mentioned – freedom of speech and publication, legal toleration of political, religious and philosophical convictions, and the right to challenge injustice – would be owned and supported by almost all Christians in the world today shows how far we have all imbibed Enlightenment assumptions. We are all children of the Enlightenment. It has made the world we live in possible. I do not like to see the Enlightenment and its legacy demonized wholesale and treated as the scapegoat for all our problems, especially by Christian writers.

Nemesis of the *philosophes'* faith?

However, in the light of Kant's and Bonhoeffer's affirmations of a world come of age, we should look critically at the *philosophes'* vaunting of individual intellectual and moral autonomy. The sinister side of the *philosophes'* challenge to the supposedly unchallengeable authority of the *Ancien Régime* is the assumption of the self-sufficiency of the individual mind, an almost godlike autonomy. The typical liberated thinker of the French Enlightenment was the master of his fate, the captain of his soul. He would not bow the knee to any human institution that claimed divine sanction – though Voltaire was happy to court Frederick II ('the Great') of Prussia and Diderot Catherine ('the Great') of Russia who reigned over states that were upheld by ecclesiastical structures of authority and ideology, Protestant and Orthodox, respectively. The deistic religion of a truly enlightened person was one of meditation, not supplication. Very few of the *philosophes* were atheists – the most notorious being Baron d'Holbach – and generally they were sincere in their deistic faith. But Paul Ricoeur argues that the *philosophes'*

---

[20]Ernst Cassirer, *The Philosophy of the Enlightenment* (Princeton: Princeton University Press, 1951), p. 13.

idealistic concept of the imperial human consciousness is *implicitly* atheistic because, at its root, it is opposed to the characteristic posture of religion, which is one of dependence.

We recall that, in the next generation, Friedrich Schleiermacher found the essence of religion in an existential attitude of absolute dependence upon God. We know that we owe our existence in the world to Another and depend upon that Creator-power to uphold us and the world at all times. The religious attitude is the opposite of autonomous; in a spirit of reverence it acknowledges a source of our being that is both transcendent and immanent. For Schleiermacher, Christian faith does not dispense with the sense of absolute dependence – rather it reinforces it – but it gives it fresh content and shapes it to the redemption accomplished through the life and work of Jesus Christ, which for Schleiermacher is the essence of Christianity, building on the essence of religion.[21]

Paul Ricoeur endorses Schleiermacher's insight. Religion, Ricoeur insists, avows the disposition of passivity and receptivity in human existence: we receive our being as a gift.[22] I think that Schleiermacher and Ricoeur grasped the vital truth of the nature of faith. It is an essential mark of the religious attitude – I could say, the life of faith – to acknowledge one's dependence on a source of life that is (in Matthew Arnold's varied phraseology) 'the not ourselves that makes for righteousness' and is indeed infinitely greater in creative power, justice and holiness than ourselves.[23] In Christian theology this insight is developed into the concept of the power and presence of the Triune Creator-Redeemer-Sanctifier. However, while I support Ricoeur's insight in principle, I do not fully agree with his blanket judgement on the French Enlightenment. I sense that some at least of the *philosophes* had an awareness of their existence as a gift, an endowment and a responsibility. I think that could be said of Voltaire and Rousseau, though obviously they responded to it in very different ways. However, it does not follow that this thought of dependence and gift was in the forefront of their minds

---

[21] F. D. E. Schleiermacher, *The Christian Faith*, trans. H. R. Macintosh and J. S. Stewart (Edinburgh: T&T Clark, 1928).
[22] Paul Ricoeur, *Lectures on Ideology and Utopia*, ed. G. H. Taylor (New York: Columbia University Press, 1986), p. 32.
[23] Matthew Arnold, *Literature & Dogma: An Essay Towards a Better Apprehension of the Bible*, 2nd edn (London: Smith, Elder, & Co., 1873), p. 83; cf. p. 75.

at all times, any more than it is for religious persons today. So who among us Christians is in a position to cast the first stone at those eighteenth-century persons who sometimes forgot that they were at every moment of their lives and in every atom of them totally dependent upon God (John 8:7)?

Enlightenment as spiritual metaphor

Although its origins are in antiquity and indeed prehistory, the image of the dawning of the light after deep darkness was proudly adopted in much eighteenth-century thought. The metaphor of the *lumen naturale* (the natural light) had been revived in the sixteenth century by the Spanish humanist Joannes Vives in his *De disciplinis* (1531) and employed by the Spanish, Jewish philosopher Francisco Sanches (1551–1623), before Descartes (d. 1650) claimed – implausibly as it turned out – to have conducted his famous thought-experience *solo lumine naturali* (by the natural light alone).[24] The metaphor underwent ethical intensification in the Enlightenment, becoming a crusading banner and battle-cry. The darkness in question was the darkness of ignorance and superstition, of authoritarianism and censorship by church and state, of unquestioned tradition and of unchallengeable dogma. Conversely, the light that was now shining was the light of truth attained by enquiry, experiment, criticism, unfettered debate and a free press. Natural science was the bringer of enlightenment. The poet Alexander Pope's proposed epitaph for Isaac Newton captures this sense of science as revelation: 'Nature and nature's laws lay hid in night. God said, Let Newton be, and all was light.'[25] Pope was neither sceptic nor rationalist, but a loyal Roman Catholic, albeit a confused one. His couplet is not a blasphemous quip, but an intentional echo and adaptation of Genesis 1:3: 'And God said, "Let there be light": and there was light' (KJB). Pope here depicts God as

---

[24]John Cottingham, *Cartesian Reflections: Essays on Descartes's Philosophy* (Oxford: Oxford University Press, 2008), pp. 58, 68. See further Anton M. Matytsin and Dan Edelstein (eds), *Let There Be Enlightenment: The Religious and Mystical Sources of Rationality* (Baltimore, MD: Johns Hopkins University Press, 2014).
[25]Alexander Pope, *Poetical Works* (London: Frederick Warne, n.d.), p. 371.

creating Isaac Newton as a gift to the world and to science. When Denis Diderot drew up his prospectus for the *philosophes'* multi-volume reference work of useful knowledge in the sciences, arts and crafts, the *Encyclopédie*, he spoke of the general enlightenment that had already spread throughout French society.[26] The *philosophes* congratulated themselves that they lived in *le siècle des Lumières* and in an enlightened age (*siècle éclairé*).

The German equivalent term *Aufklärung* was in common use by the 1780s. The image of enlightenment was often recruited to gloss the meaning of Christianity. Thus G. E. Lessing wrote: 'The ultimate purpose of Christianity is not our salvation, which may come how it will, but our salvation by means of our enlightenment.' Lessing added: 'This enlightenment is necessary, not merely as a condition of our salvation, but as an ingredient in which, in the last analysis, our entire salvation consists.'[27]

Light is a universal symbol of truth, goodness, justice and love. I take merely three examples, spread over twenty-five centuries. (i) In the India of the fifth century BC, Siddhartha attained *bodhi*, that is knowledge, wisdom or mental enlightenment, and so became the *Buddha*. Buddhism remains a pathway to spiritual enlightenment. (ii) In the mid-seventeenth century, John Milton, lamenting his blindness, the loss of his outward vision of all beautiful things and the 'human face divine' of loved ones, at the beginning of Book III of *Paradise Lost*, invokes the light that the Creator first called into being: 'Hail, holy Light, offspring of heaven first-born! ... Bright effluence of bright essence increate!' Then he prays for inward illumination and enlightenment: 'So much the rather though, Celestial Light,/ Shine inward, and the mind through all her powers/ Irradiate; there plant eyes; all mist from thence/ Purge and disperse, that I may see and tell/ Of things invisible to mortal sight.'[28] (iii) The Statue of Liberty, the gigantic neoclassical sculpture in New York's harbour, holds aloft the torch of truth in her right

---

[26] Denis Diderot, 'Prospectus'. https://play.google.com/books/reader?id=f5hpq-X0GdOUC&pg=GBS.PA2&hl=en_GB (accessed 5 March 2022).
[27] Henry E. Allison, *Lessing and the Enlightenment* (Ann Arbor, MI: University of Michigan Press, 1966), p. 66.
[28] John Milton, *The English Poems of John Milton*, ed. H. C. Beeching (London: Oxford University Press, 1913), p. 163 (Bk III, ll. 1–6, 44, 51–5).

hand. The sculpture's full title is 'Liberty Enlightening the World' (in the French of its designer, Frédéric Auguste Bartholdi, *La Liberté éclairant le monde*).

Movements and moments of intellectual, moral and spiritual renewal or revelation have always drawn to themselves the language of illumination or enlightenment, taking their cue from the diurnal sequence of day and night, dawn breaking and dusk gathering, sunrise and sunset. During the past century, the feminist movement, the racial equality movement and the environmental protection movement have brought their own forms of enlightenment. Their work is not complete and they need to continue to shine their spotlight on the dark shadows of prejudice, inequality and exploitation.

Enlightenment in the Bible

Light is also the primary Christian symbol. The Bible contains a superabundance of enlightenment imagery, beginning with the creation of light by the word and command of God. In Haydn's oratorio of 1797–8, *The Creation* (*Die Schöpfung*) the recital of 'Let there be light' calls forth an electrifying sound-burst. Alexander Pope alluded to it in his putative epitaph for Isaac Newton. But we should read on in Genesis: 'And God saw that the light was good; and God separated the light from the darkness. And God called the light Day, and the darkness he called Night' (Gen. 1:1–5a). Light is created by God and given by God to the world. Light and darkness, good and evil have been demarcated by the Creator.

The Psalms, the prayers of the Jewish and Christian churches, are filled with light-imagery. Psalm 36:9 brings together, in mutually informing Hebrew parallelism, the images of 'life' and 'light' in a way that we find later in the Johannine literature of the New Testament: 'For with you is the fountain of life; in your light we see light.' God is not only the source of light – spiritual and intellectual illumination – but also the one who bestows it upon God's people, so that they may see clearly. Again we have, 'The LORD is my light' (Ps. 27:1), which became the motto of the University of Oxford more than four centuries ago: *Dominus illuminatio mea*. In this verse, the convention of Hebrew parallelism shows that light and salvation are equated: 'The LORD is my light and my salvation.' Then Psalm 43:3 takes light as the image of divine truth which is given for our guidance: 'O send out your light and your truth; let them lead me.' Psalm 118:27, with its ritual and sacrificial context, suggests that the prayer for light has been heard: 'God is the Lord who hath showed us light' (BCP).

The Book of Proverbs depicts the light of divine Wisdom shining in the depths of the human spirit, seeking out all that needs to be cleansed and purified: 'The human spirit is the lamp of the LORD, searching every innermost part' (Prov. 20:27). This text resonates with the teaching of the Cambridge Platonists of the seventeenth-century Church of England that divinely imparted reason is 'the candle of the Lord' (as the verse is translated in the KJB) in humankind; it was their favourite Old Testament text. They may also have been influenced by Psalm 18:28 in the KJB: 'Thou also shalt light my candle: the Lord my God shall make my darkness to be light.' For these Anglican Platonists the biblical image of 'the candle of the Lord' united the intellectual and moral dimensions of spiritual discernment. Reason and conscience went together and the practice of the virtues was necessary in order to see the light.[29]

In the New Testament, the birth of Christ is heralded by the shining of a star and the infant Jesus is hailed as 'a light of revelation for the Gentiles' (Lk 2:32). In the Prologue of the Fourth Gospel, the 'life' that is inherent in the eternal Logos (Word), as it permeates the creation, becomes as 'the light of all people'. The light continues to shine in the darkness of the world and the darkness has not overwhelmed it. In the incarnation, 'the true light that enlightens everyone (ὁ φωτίζει πάντα ἄνθρωπον) was coming into the world' (Jn 1:3b–5, 9, 14). No wonder that Karl Rahner, SJ, said that he would be willing to die for the truth of the Johannine Prologue: 'I can accept the words of the Johannine prologue with a faith so steadfast that I am ready to die for it. These words will always be accepted as a real and vital foundation of my own theology. With joyous abandon born of firm faith I can let myself be overwhelmed by the bright darkness of

---

[29]*ISOA*, pp. 171–5 (with bibliography); William Cecil de Pauley, *The Candle of the Lord: Studies in the Cambridge Platonists* (London: SPCK, 1937; repr. Freeport, NY: Books for Libraries Press, 1970).

God's revelation.'[30] The Christ of John's Gospel proclaims, 'I am the light of the world. Whoever follows me will never walk in darkness, but will have the light of life' (Jn 8:12). In the early fifteenth century Thomas à Kempis took this text as the epigraph or starting point of his *De Imitatione Christi* (*The Imitation of Christ*), a timeless handbook of devotion and discipleship, commenting: 'With these words Christ counsels us to follow his life and way if we desire true enlightenment (*si volumus veraciter illuminari*) and freedom from all blindness of heart.'[31] With the breathtaking audacity of the Christian revelation, the First Epistle of John names the divine nature as 'light', but also as 'light' and 'love' together (1 Jn 1:5; 4:8, 16), so that, in the Johannine literature, taken as a whole, the divine reality is named as a trinity of life, light and love. Here we behold the beauty of the New Testament revelation displayed.

From the first, the Apostle Paul deploys the metaphor of light for Christ, the gospel and the Christian. In the earliest of his surviving epistles, he addresses the Thessalonians believers as 'children of light and children of the day' (1 Thess. 5:5). In 2 Cor. 4:4 Paul speaks of 'the light (*photismon*) of the gospel of the glory of Christ' (2 Cor. 4:4), so that the light of the ascended and glorified Lord Jesus Christ fills the gospel message and radiates from it in the preaching of Paul and of the whole church. In Ephesians 1:18, Paul or 'Paul' prays that 'the eyes of the heart' of the Ephesian Christians may be 'enlightened' (πεφωτισμένους). Paul has been given the commission and privilege 'to enlighten [*phōtizein*] everyone' with respect to God's secret plan of salvation (Eph. 3:9; literally, 'the economy of the mystery').[32] The proclamation of the gospel of Christ spreads enlightenment throughout the world.

---

[30]Karl Rahner, SJ, *Theological Investigations*, vol. 21, trans. Hugh M. Riley (New York: Crossroad; London: Darton, Longman & Todd, 1988), p. 222.
[31]Thomas à Kempis, *The Imitation of Christ*, trans. Leo Sherley-Price (Harmondsworth: Penguin, 1952), p. 27. Cf. the prayer in Bk 3, ch. 23: 'O merciful Jesus, send the brightness of your light into my mind, and banish all darkness from the sanctuary of my heart' (p. 125).
[32]Eph. 3:9 has a divergent manuscript tradition; either stand-alone φωτίσαι, 'illuminate', 'bring to light', or φωτίσαι πάντας, 'enlighten all people'. See the weighing of the alternatives in Ernest Best, *Ephesians*, ICC (London and New York: T&T Clark, 1998), p. 319. Best reads φωτίσαι πάντας, as does John Muddiman, *The Epistle to the Ephesians*, Black's New Testament Commentaries, gen. ed., Morna D. Hooker (London and New York: Continuum, 2001), pp. 158–9.

The author of Ephesians (whether Paul or 'Paul') also quotes, as though referring to a recognized authority, what seems to be an early Christian hymn or, more probably, a piece of a baptismal liturgy (enlightenment was a metaphor for baptism in early Christianity, being so used by, for example, Justin Martyr and Clement of Alexandria, though it may not be coincidental that both of these writers engaged with an apologetic intent with the thought and culture of their day with which the metaphor of enlightenment would have resonated): 'Sleeper, awake! Rise from the dead, and Christ will shine upon you' (5:14). This precious fragment in Ephesians also echoes such Old Testament texts as Isa. 60:1, 'Arise, shine, for your light has come. And the glory of the LORD has risen upon you', and Mal. 4:2: 'But for you who revere my name, the sun of righteousness shall rise, with healing in its wings.' But here it is Christ, who has the light of eternal life within himself, who calls the catechumen to wake and arise from the death of sin and alienation from God, and be bathed in his light in baptism. In this verse, as Markus Barth puts it, 'Enlightenment *is* resurrection'.[33]

In Hebrews it is almost certainly baptism that is described as 'enlightenment' with reference to certain apostates: 'those who have once been enlightened (φωτισθέντας), who have tasted the heavenly gift, and have shared in the Holy Spirit, and have tasted the goodness of the word of God and the powers of the age to come, and then have fallen away' (Heb. 6:4–6; cf. 10:32, 'after you had been enlightened (φωτισθέντες)'). Continual rays of divine enlightenment are promised to faithful Christians 'until the day dawns and the morning star arises in your hearts' (2 Pet. 1:19). The Epistle of James has a beautiful ascription to God, 'the Father of lights, with whom there is no variation or shadow due to change' (Jas. 1:17). The last book of the Bible pictures the heavenly city, the Bride of the Lamb, as filled with the light of God's presence: 'the city has no need of sun or moon to shine on it, for the glory of God

---

[33]Markus Barth, *Ephesians 4–6: A New Translation with Introduction and Commentary*, The Anchor Bible (Garden City, NY: Doubleday, 1974), pp. 574–7; 598–603, at p. 598. He expounds the New Testament symbolism of light as having a five-fold significance: intellectual, ontological, ethical, existential and cultic. On this text see also Andrew T. Lincoln, *Ephesians*, Word Biblical Commentary (Dallas, TX: Word Books, 1990), pp. 331–3, 496–500.

is its light, and its lamp is the Lamb' (Rev. 21:23). In the biblical revelation, God is the fount of life, love and light; the source of all the light we have or need.

Enlightenment in the liturgy

The Epiphany or 'The Manifestation of Christ to the Gentiles' (BCP) forms a link between the biblical narrative and the church's cycle of worship. The Epiphany season begins with the story of the Gentile Magi journeying from a far country and guided by a moving star, to seek 'the King of the Jews' and pay him homage (Matt. 2:1–12). But the liturgical season continues through the Baptism of Christ and the revelation of his messiahship given through a voice from heaven (Mark 1:9–11; Matt. 3:13–17; Luke 3:21–22). Epiphany then continues through the Marriage at Cana when, in a miracle of transformation – water into wine – Jesus reveals or manifests his glory and enables his disciples to believe in him (ἐφανέρωσεν τὴν δόξαν αὐτοῦ, καὶ ἐπίστευσαν εἰς αὐτὸν οἱ μαθηταὶ αὐτοῦ). It is John's Epiphany (Jn 2:1–11). In a late letter of the New Testament both the first appearing of Jesus Christ and his final manifestation in glory are described as his 'epiphany' (ἐπιφάνεια; Tit. 2:11, 13).

Throughout its history, the Christian church has prayed for divine illumination or enlightenment. Since well before the Reformation the English Church has prayed the tender collect 'For Aid against all Perils', originally at Compline in the Sarum liturgies, then at Evening Prayer, and from the First Prayer Book of Archbishop Thomas Cranmer in 1549 onwards: 'Lighten our darkness, we beseech thee, O Lord; and by thy great mercy defend us from all perils and dangers of this night; for the love of thy only Son, our Saviour, Jesus Christ. Amen.' Similarly, the Prayer Book Collect for Whitsunday (now designated Pentecost), which comes from the Gregorian Sacramentary, speaks of God sending the 'light' of the Holy Spirit to 'teach the hearts' of God's 'faithful people', endowing them with 'a right judgement in all things'.[34] The

---

[34] I am grateful to Dr Bridget Nichols for advice on the provenance of these Collects; see also Bridget Nichols (ed.), *The Collect in the Churches of the Reformation* (London: SCM Press, 2010).

Book of Common Prayer Collect for St John the Evangelist's day (27 December) originated in the Verona Sacramentary, but was altered for the 1662 BCP to emphasize the theme of light: 'Merciful Lord, we beseech thee to cast thy bright beams of light upon thy Church, that it being enlightened by the doctrine of thy blessed Apostle and Evangelist Saint John may so walk in the light of thy truth, that it may at length attain to the light of everlasting life; though Jesus Christ our Lord. *Amen.*' The church's liturgy teaches us that the church does not complacently view itself as already filled with light and as having all the light that it needs, but rather as standing in need of continual divine enlightenment.

Reform and Enlightenment

As we would expect, the imagery of light was claimed by the Reformation. The motto of John Calvin's Reformation city of Geneva, inscribed on its coinage, was *Post tenebras lux*, 'After darkness light'. The protagonists and publicists of the Enlightenment, particularly the *philosophes*, applied the same sentiment to their own age and work. For reasons that I hope I have adequately explained in this book, I do see a credible parallel between movements of reform and renewal in the Christian church, whether it be the various monastic reform initiatives and the Franciscan movement in the middle ages, or the Conciliar Movement of the early fifteenth-century, or the sixteenth-century Reformation, on the one hand, and the work of Enlightenment scholars and writers in the late seventeenth and early eighteenth centuries. I have not attempted to conceal that there was much that was wrong with the Enlightenment – self-seeking, spiritual pride, hypocrisy, arrogance, wrong-headedness – but all that has to be applied to the church too.

Light is and always has been the primary symbol of the Christian revelation. Light describes the nature of God and the character of divine revelation; it is the attribute of the gospel and of the mission of the church. How painfully ironic is it, then, and how unbearably tragic, that a major tendency within the European Enlightenment saw the Christian church as standing in the way of the light of knowledge and truth, even regarding it as the abode of darkness – the darkness of superstition, ignorance and bigotry, of the suppression of enquiry and debate, the darkness of censorship, persecution and violence. How ironic that the radical, disaffected and wounded Christian, semi-Christian and ex-Christian critics of the oppressive church-state nexus, such as Spinoza, Bayle, Locke, Voltaire, Diderot and Rousseau, could have turned the cry of the Jewish church to God in Psalm 74:20, 'Have respect unto the covenant: for the dark places of the world are full of the habitations of cruelty' (KJB) against the church itself.

BIBLIOGRAPHY

à Kempis, Thomas, *The Imitation of Christ*, trans. Leo Sherley-Price (Harmondsworth: Penguin, 1952).
Acworth, Richard, *The Philosophy of John Norris of Bemerton: 1657–1712* (New York: Olms, 1979).
Adams, Nicholas, George Pattison and Graham Ward (eds), *The Oxford Handbook of Theology and Modern European Thought* (Oxford: Oxford University Press, 2013).
Aldridge, A. O., 'The State of Nature: An Undiscovered Country in the History of Ideas', *SVEC* XCVIII (1972), pp. 7–26.
Alexander, James, 'Radical, Sceptical and Liberal Enlightenment', *Journal of the Philosophy of History* 14 (2020), pp. 257–83.
Allison, Henry E., *Lessing and the Enlightenment* (Ann Arbor, MI: University of Michigan Press, 1966).
Andrew, Edward G., *Patrons of Enlightenment* (Toronto: University of Toronto Press, 2006).
Apetrei, Sarah, *Women, Feminism, and Religion in Early Enlightenment England* (Cambridge: Cambridge University Press, 2010).
Armenteros, Carolina and Richard A. Lebrun (eds), *Joseph de Maistre and the Legacy of Enlightenment* (Oxford: Voltaire Foundation, 2011).
Arnold, Matthew, *Literature & Dogma: An Essay towards a Better Apprehension of the Bible*, 2nd edn (London: Smith, Elder, & Co., 1873).
Astell, Mary and John Norris, *Letters Concerning the Love of God*, ed. E. Derek Taylor and Melvyn New (Aldershot and Burlington, VT: Ashgate, 2005).
Aston, Nigel, *Christianity and Revolutionary Europe, 1750–1830* (Cambridge: Cambridge University Press, 2002).
Aston, Nigel, *The French Revolution, 1789–1804: Authority, Liberty, and the Search for Stability* (Basingstoke: Palgrave Macmillan, 2004).
Aston, Nigel, *Art and Religion in Eighteenth-Century Europe* (London: Reaktion Books, 2009).
Aston, Nigel, 'The Established Church', in William Doyle (ed.), *The Oxford Handbook of the Ancien Régime*, ch. 17.

Aston, Nigel, *Enlightened Oxford: The University and the Cultural and Political Life of Eighteenth-Century Britain and beyond* (Oxford: Oxford University Press, 2022).

Augustine, *The City of God*, ed. David Knowles; trans. Henry Bettenson (Harmondsworth: Penguin, 1972).

Aulén, Gustaf, *Christus Victor: An Historical Study of the Three Main Types of the Idea of the Atonement*, trans A. G. Hebert (London: SPCK, 1931 [1930]; New York: Macmillan, 1978).

Avis, Paul, *Ecumenical Theology and the Elusiveness of Doctrine* (London: SPCK, 1986).

Avis, Paul (ed.), *The History of Christian Theology, Volume 1: The Science of Theology* (Basingstoke: Marshall Pickering; Grand Rapids, MI: Eerdmans, 1986).

Avis, Paul, *God and the Creative Imagination: Metaphor, Symbol and Myth in Religion and Theology* (London and New York: Routledge, 1999).

Avis, Paul, *The Church in the Theology of the Reformers* (London: Marshall, Morgan & Scott, 1981; repr. Eugene, OR: Wipf and Stock, 2002).

Avis, Paul, *Anglicanism and the Christian Church: Theological Resources in Historical Perspective*, 2nd edn (London and New York: T&T Clark, 2002).

Avis, Paul, *A Church Drawing Near: Spirituality and Mission in a Post-Christian Culture* (London: T&T Clark, 2003).

Avis, Paul, *Beyond the Reformation? Authority, Unity and Primacy in the Conciliar Tradition* (London and New York: T&T Clark, 2006).

Avis, Paul, *In Search of Authority: Anglican Theological Method from the Reformation to the Enlightenment* (London and New York: T&T Clark, 2014).

Avis, Paul, *Foundations of Modern Historical Thought: From Machiavelli to Vico*, 2nd edn (London and New York: Routledge, 2016 [1986]).

Avis, Paul, *Jesus and the Church: The Foundation of the Church in the New Testament and Modern Theology* (London and New York: T&T Clark, 2020).

Avis, Paul, 'Towards a Richer Appreciation of the Oxford Movement', *Ecclesiology* 16.2 (2020), pp. 243–53.

Avis, Paul, 'Revelation, Epistemology, and Authority', in Mezei, Murphy, and Oakes (eds), *The Oxford Handbook of Divine Revelation* (Oxford: Oxford University Press, 2021), ch. 12.

Avis, Paul, 'Overcoming "The Church as Counter-Sign of the Kingdom"', in Mark D. Chapman and Vladimir Latinovic (eds), *Changing the Church: Transformations of Christian Belief, Practice, and Life* (Cham, Switzerland: Palgrave Macmillan, 2021), pp. 243–9.

Avis, Paul, *Reconciling Theology* (London: SCM Press, 2022).
Ayres, Lewis, Medi Ann Volpe and Thomas L. Humphries, Jr, (eds) *The Oxford Handbook of Catholic Theology* (Oxford: Oxford University Press, 2019).
Babbitt, Irving, *Rousseau and Romanticism*, intro. Claes G. Ryn (New Brunswick, NJ: Transaction Publishers, 1991 [1919]).
Bacon, Francis, *Essays and Colours of Good and Evil*, ed. W. Aldis Wright (London: Macmillan, 1890).
Bacon, Francis, *Philosophical Works*, ed. J. M. Robertson (London: Routledge, 1905).
Bacon, Francis, *The Advancement of Learning* (London: Dent; New York: Dutton, 1915).
Bailyn, Bernard, *The Ideological Origins of the American Revolution*, 2nd edn (Cambridge, MA: The Belknap Press of Harvard University Press, 1992).
Ballentine, Samuel E. and John Barton (eds), *Language, Theology, and the Bible: Essays in Honour of James Barr* (Oxford: Clarendon Press, 1994).
Barnett, S. J., *The Enlightenment and Religion: The Myths of Modernity* (Manchester, UK: Manchester University Press, 2003).
Barr, James, *Fundamentalism* (London: SCM Press, 1977).
Barth, Karl, *Protestant Theology in the Nineteenth Century*, trans. Brian Cozens and John Bowden, Foreword Colin Gunton (London: SCM Press, 2001).
Barth, Karl, *Wolfgang Amadeus Mozart*, trans. Clarence K. Pott, foreword John Updike (Eugene, OR: Wipf and Stock, 2003).
Barth, Markus, *Ephesians 4–6: A New Translation with Introduction and Commentary*, The Anchor Bible (Garden City, NY: Doubleday, 1974).
Bate, Jonathan, *Radical Wordsworth: The Poet who Changed the World* (New Haven, CT: Yale University Press, 2020).
Bayle, Pierre, *Dictionnaire historique et critique*, ed. Alain Niderst (Paris: Éditions Sociales, 1974).
Bayle, Pierre, *A Philosophical Commentary on These Words of the Gospel, Luke XIV, 23: Compel Them to Come in, That My House May be Full* (1686, 1708): https://www.google.co.uk/books/edition/A_Philosophical_Commentary_on_These_Word/3Kr3g4LeFPwC?hl=en&gbpv=0
Bebbington, David, *Evangelicalism in Modern Britain* (London: Routledge, 1989).
Becker, Carl, *The Heavenly City of the Eighteenth-Century Philosophers*, 2nd edn (New Haven, CT: Yale University Press, 2003 [1932]).

Bedford, R. D., *The Defence of Truth: Herbert of Cherbury and the Seventeenth Century* (Manchester: Manchester University Press, 1979).
Beiser, Frederick C., *The Sovereignty of Reason: The Defense of Rationality in the Early English Enlightenment* (Princeton, NJ: Princeton University Press, 1996).
Berlin, Isaiah, review of Cassirer, *The Philosophy of the Enlightenment*, *The English Historical Review* 68. 269 (October 1953), pp. 617–9.
Berlin, Isaiah, *Vico and Herder: Two Studies in the History of Ideas* (London: Hogarth Press, 1976).
Berlin, Isaiah, *Against the Current: Essays in the History of Ideas*, ed. Henry Hardy, intro. Roger Hausheer (Oxford: Oxford University Press, 1981).
Berlin, Isaiah, *The Magus of the North: J. G. Hamann and the Origins of Modern Irrationalism* (London: John Murray, 1993).
Berlin, Isaiah, *The Roots of Romanticism: The A. W. Mellon Lectures in the Fine Arts, 1965, the National Gallery of Art, Washington, DC*, ed. Henry Hardy (London: Pimlico, 2000 [1999]).
Berlin, Isaiah, *Three Critics of the Enlightenment: Vico, Hamann, Herder*, ed. Henry Hardy (Princeton: Princeton University Press, 2013).
Berman, David, *Atheism from Hobbes to Russell* (London: Routledge, 1988).
Bernstein, John Andrew, 'Shaftesbury's Optimism and Eighteenth-Century Social Thought', in Kors and Korshin (eds), *Anticipations of the Enlightenment in England, France, and Germany*, ch. 4.
Berriot, François, *Athéisme et athéistes au XVI siècle en France*, 2 vols (Lille: Atelier National de Reproduction des Thèses, 1977–1989 [photographic typescript]).
Berry, Christopher J., Maria Pia Paganelli and Craig Smith (eds), *The Oxford Handbook of Adam Smith* (Oxford: Oxford University Press, 2013).
Best, Ernest, *Ephesians, ICC* (London and New York: T&T Clark, 1998).
Besterman, Theodore, 'Reason and Progress', *SVEC* XXIV (1963), pp. 27–41.
Besterman, Theodore, *Voltaire* (Paris: Longmans, 1969).
Biener, Zvi, 'Newton's *Regulae Philosophandi*', in Eric Schliesser and Chris Smeenk (eds), *The Oxford Handbook of Newton* (Oxford: Oxford University Press, 2017, online): https://www.oxfordhandbooks.com/view/10.1093/oxfordhb/9780199930418.001.0001/oxfordhb-9780199930418-e-4
Biernacki, Loriliai and Philip Clayton (eds), *Panentheism across the World's Traditions* (Oxford: Oxford University Press, 2013).

Bietenholz, Peter G., *History and Biography in the Work of Erasmus of Rotterdam* (Geneva: Groz, 1966).
Bietenholz, Peter G., *Encounters with a Radical Erasmus: Erasmus' Work as a Source of Radical Thought in Early Modern Europe* (Toronto: University of Toronto Press, 2009).
Birch, Jonathan C. P., *Jesus in an Age of Enlightenment: Radical Gospels from Thomas Hobbes to Thomas Jefferson* (London: Palgrave Macmillan, 2019).
Black, J. B., *The Art of History: A Study of Four Great Historians of the Eighteenth Century* (London: Methuen, 1926).
Blake, William, *The Complete Poems*, ed. Alicia Ostriker (Harmondsworth: Penguin, 1977).
Blanchard, Shaun, *The Synod of Pistoia and Vatican II: Jansenism and the Struggle for Catholic Reform* (New York: Oxford University Press, 2020).
Blondel, Maurice, *The Letter on Apologetics* and *History and Dogma*, trans. and intro. Alexander Dru and Illtyd Trethowan (Grand Rapids, MI: Eerdmans, 1994).
Boas, George, 'In Search of the Age of Reason', in Earl Reeves Wasserman (ed.), *Aspects of the Eighteenth Century*, pp. 1–19.
Bodin, Jean, *Method for the Easy Comprehension of History*, trans. Beatrice Reynolds (New York: Columbia University Press, 1945).
Bolingbroke, Henry St John, Viscount, *Letters on the Study and the Use of History*, Letter VI: http://www.eliohs.unifi.it/testi/700/bolingbroke/letterVI.htm.
Bonhoeffer, Dietrich, *Letters and Papers from Prison*, ed. Eberhard Bethge (London: SCM Press, 1971).
Boswell, James, *Life of Johnson*, ed. R. W. Chapman (London: Oxford University Press, 1953).
Bourgault, Sophie and Robert Sparling (eds), *A Companion to Enlightenment Historiography* (Leiden: Brill, 2013).
Brack, O. M., 'Samuel Johnson and the Translations of Jean Pierre de Crousaz's "Examen and Commentaire"', *Studies in Bibliography* 48 (1995), pp. 60–84.
Brierley, Michael W., 'John Macquarrie's Panentheism', in Robert Morgan (ed.), *In Search of Humanity and Deity: A Celebration of John Macquarrie's Theology* (London: SCM Press, 2006), ch. 18.
Brinton, Crane, *Ideas and Men: The Story of Western Thought* (New York: Prentice Hall, 1950).
Brissenden, R. F. (ed.), *Studies in the Eighteenth Century II* (Toronto: University of Toronto Press, 1973).
Brockliss, Laurence and Ritchie Robertson (eds), *Isaiah Berlin and the Enlightenment* (Oxford: Oxford University Press, 2016).

Brown, John L., *The Methodus ad Facilem Historiarum Cognitionem of Jean Bodin: A Critical Study* (New York: AMS reprint, 1969 [1939]).
Brown, Stewart J. and Timothy Tackett (eds), *The Cambridge History of Christianity*, vol. 7: *Enlightenment, Reawakening and Revolution, 1660–1815* (Cambridge: Cambridge University Press, 2006).
Brown, Stewart J. (ed.), *William Robertson and the Expansion of Empire* (Cambridge: Cambridge University Press, 1997).
Brown, Stewart J., Peter B. Nockles and James Pereiro (eds), *The Oxford Handbook of the Oxford Movement* (Oxford: Oxford University Press, 2017).
Brumfitt, J. H., 'Introduction to Voltaire, *La Philosophie de l'histoire*', *SVEC* XXVIII (1963).
Brumfitt, J. H., *Voltaire: Historian* (Oxford: Oxford University Press, 1958).
Brumfitt, J. H., 'History and Propaganda in Voltaire', *SVEC* XXIV (1963), pp. 271–87.
Bryson, Gladys, *Man and God: The Scottish Enquiry of the Eighteenth Century* (Princeton, NY: Princeton University Press, 1945; repr. New York: Augustus M. Kelley, 1968).
Buckley, Michael J., *At the Origins of Modern Atheism* (New Haven, CT: Yale University Press, 1987).
Bullivant, Stephen and Michael Ruse (eds), *The Oxford Handbook of Atheism* (Oxford: Oxford University Press, 2013).
Bulman, William J. and Robert G. Ingram (eds), *God and the Enlightenment* (Oxford: Oxford University Press, 2016).
Bultmann, Christoph, 'Lessing and the Bible', in Ritchie Robertson (ed.), *Lessing and the German Enlightenment*, pp. 245–62.
Burckhardt, Jacob, *The Civilisation of the Renaissance in Italy* (London: Phaidon, 1965).
Burke, Edmund, *Reflections on the Revolution in France* (London: Dent; New York: Dutton, 1910).
Burke, Peter, 'A Survey of the Popularity of Ancient Historians, 1450–1700', *H&T* 5 (1966), pp. 135–52.
Burns, Arthur and Joanna Innes (eds), *Rethinking the Age of Reform: Britain 1780–1850* (Cambridge: Cambridge University Press, 2003).
Burns, R. M., *The Great Debate on Miracles from Joseph Glanville to David Hume* (Lewisburg, PA: Bucknell University Press, 1981).
Burson, Jeffrey D., *Rise and Fall of Theological Enlightenment: Jean Martin de Prades and Ideological Polarization in Eighteenth-Century France* (Notre Dame, IN: University of Notre Dame Press, 2010).
Burtt, E. A., *The Metaphysical Foundations of Modern Physical Science*, ed. Mineola, 2nd edn (London: Routledge and Kegan Paul; NY: Dover, 2003 [1932]).

Butler, Joseph, *Works*, ed. W. E. Gladstone, 2 vols (Oxford: Clarendon Press, 1896).
Butler, Joseph, *The Analogy of Religion, Natural and Revealed to the Constitution and Course of Nature, to Which Are Added, Two Brief Dissertations: On Personal Identity, and on the Nature of Virtue; and Fifteen Sermons* (London: Bell, 1889 [1736]).
Butterfield, Herbert, *The Origins of Modern Science* (New York: Free Press, 1965 [London: Bell, 1949]).
Byrne, Peter, *Natural Religion and the Nature of Religion: The Legacy of Deism* (London and New York: Routledge, 1989).
Cameron, Euan, *Enchanted Europe: Superstition, Reason and Religion, 1250–1750* (Oxford: Oxford University Press, 2010).
Cameron, Euan (ed.), *The New Cambridge History of the Bible. Volume 3, from 1450 to 1750* (Cambridge: Cambridge University Press, 2015).
Campbell, Tom, 'Adam Smith: Methods, Morals, and Markets', in Berry, Paganelli and Smith (eds), *The Oxford Handbook of Adam Smith*.
Caro, Hernán D., *The Best of All Possible Worlds? Leibniz's Philosophical Optimism and Its Critics 1710–1755* (Leiden: Brill, 2020).
Casaubon, Meric, *A Treatise Concerning Enthusiasme, as It Is an Effect of Nature, but Is Mistaken by Many for Either Divine Inspiration, or Diabolical Possession* (Gainesville, FL: Scholars' Facsimiles & Reprints, 1970 [1655; 2nd edn, 1656]).
Cassirer, Ernst, *The Philosophy of the Enlightenment*, trans. A. Koelln and J. P. Pettegrove (Princeton, NJ: Princeton University Press, 1951 [1932]).
Champion, Justin A. I., *Republican Learning: John Toland and the Crisis of Christian Culture, 1696–1722* (Manchester: Manchester University Press, 2003).
Chaplin, Chester F., *The Religious Thought of Samuel Johnson* (Ann Arbor, MI: University of Michigan Press, 1968).
Chappell, Vere (ed.), *The Cambridge Companion to Locke* (Cambridge: Cambridge University Press, 1994).
Chen, Jeng-Guo S., 'Providence and Progress: The Religious Dimension in Ferguson's Discussion of Civil Society', in Heath and Merolle (eds), *Adam Ferguson: Philosophy, Politics and Society*, ch. 11.
Church, Richard, *The Growth of the English Novel* (London: Methuen, 1951).
Clark, J. C. D., *Samuel Johnson: Literature, Religion and English Cultural Politics from the Restoration to Romanticism* (Cambridge: Cambridge University Press, 1994).

Clark, J. C. D., *English Society 1660–1832: Religion, Ideology and Politics during the Ancien Regime* [sic], 2nd edn (Cambridge: Cambridge University Press, 2000 [1985]).

Clark, J. C. D., *Thomas Paine* (Oxford: Oxford University Press, 2018).

Cobban, Alfred, 'The Enlightenment', in, J. O. Lindsay (ed.), *New Cambridge Modern History*, vol. 7, *The Old Regime, 1713–1763* (Cambridge: Cambridge University Press, 1957), pp. 85–112.

Cobban, Alfred, *Historians and the Causes of the French Revolution* (London: Routledge and Kegan Paul for the Historical Association, 1958).

Cobban, Alfred, *Rousseau and the Modern State*, 2nd edn (London: Allen & Unwin, 1964 [1934]).

Cobban, Alfred, 'The Enlightenment and the French Revolution', in E. R. Wasserman (ed.), *Aspects of the Eighteenth Century*, pp. 305–15.

Coffey, John, 'Scripture and Toleration between Reformation and Enlightenment', in Glaser (ed.), *Religious Tolerance in the Atlantic World: Early Modern and Contemporary Perspectives*, pp. 14–40.

Cohen, I. Bernard and George E. Smith (eds), *The Cambridge Companion to Newton* (Cambridge: Cambridge University Press 2002).

Cohn, Norman, *The Pursuit of the Millennium* (New York: Oxford University Press, 1970 [1957]).

Coleridge, Samuel Taylor, *Biographia Literaria or Biographical Sketches of My Literary Life and Opinions*, ed. George Watson (London: Dent; New York: Dutton, 1965).

Coleridge, Samuel Taylor, *Confessions of an Inquiring Spirit, Collected Works*, ed. Kathleen Coburn (Princeton, NJ: Princeton University Press; London: Routledge, 1976).

Collingwood, R. G., *Autobiography* (London: Oxford University Press, 1939).

Collingwood, R. G., *The Idea of History* (Oxford: Oxford University Press, 1946).

Collins, Gregory M., 'Edmund Burke on Slavery and the Slave Trade', *Slavery & Abolition: A Journal of Slave and Post-Slave Studies* 40.3 (2019), pp. 494–521.

Colman, John, *John Locke's Moral Philosophy* (Edinburgh: University of Edinburgh Press, 1983).

Connerton, Paul, *The Tragedy of Enlightenment: An Essay on the Frankfurt School* (Cambridge: Cambridge University Press, 1980).

Cornwall, Robert D. and William Gibson (eds), *Religion, Politics and Dissent 1660–1832: Essays in Honour of James E. Bradley* (Farnham: Ashgate, 2010).

Cottingham, John, *Cartesian Reflections: Essays on Descartes's Philosophy* (Oxford: Oxford University Press, 2008).

Crane, R. S., 'Anglican Apologetics and the Idea of Progress', *Modern Philology* 31 (1934), pp. 273–306, 349–82.
Cranston, Maurice and Richard S. Peters (eds), *Hobbes and Rousseau: A Collection of Critical Essays* (Garden City, NY: Doubleday, 1972).
Crocker, Lester, 'The Enlightenment: What and Who?', in Yolton and Brown (eds), *Studies in Eighteenth-Century Culture*, vol. 17.
Curran, Mark, *Atheism, Religion and Enlightenment in Pre-Revolutionary Europe* (Woodbridge: The Boydell Press, 2012).
Daniel, Stephen H., *John Toland: His Methods, Manners, and Mind* (Kingston, ON: McGill-Queen's University Press, 1984).
Daston, Lorraine, 'Probability and Evidence', in Garber and Ayers (eds), *The Cambridge History of Seventeenth-Century Philosophy*, vol. 2, ch. 31.
de Pauley, William Cecil, *The Candle of the Lord: Studies in the Cambridge Platonists* (London: SPCK, 1937; repr. Freeport, NY: Books for Libraries Press, 1970).
Del Prete, Antonella, Anna Lisa Schino and Pina Totaro (eds), *Philosophers and the Bible: The Debate on Sacred Scripture in Early Modern Thought* (Leiden: Brill, 2022).
Defoe, Daniel, *The Adventures of Robinson Crusoe*, with 30 Colour Plates by A. E. Jackson (London: Ward, Lock & Co., Limited, n.d. [1719]).
Defoe, Daniel, *The Fortunes and Misfortunes of the Famous Moll Flanders* (Oxford: Oxford University Press, 1971 [1722]).
Delvolvé, Jean, *Religion, Critique et Philosophie Positive chez Pierre Bayle* (Paris: Alcan, 1906; repr. New York: Burt Franklin, 1971).
Descartes, René, *Discourse on Method* and *Meditations*, trans. F. E. Sutcliffe (Harmondsworth: Penguin, 1968).
Devellennes, Charles, *Positive Atheism: Bayle, Meslier, d'Holbach, Diderot* (Edinburgh: Edinburgh University Press, 2021).
Di Rosa, Geneviève, *Rousseau et la Bible: Pensee du religieux d'un philosophe des lumieres* (Leiden: Brill Rodopi, 2016).
Diderot, Denis, *Selected Philosophical Writings*, ed. John Lough (Cambridge: Cambridge University Press, 1953).
Diderot, Denis, *Pensées philosophiques*, XII, in id., *Pensées Philosophiques/Lettre Sur Les Aveugles/Supplément Au Voyage de Bougainville* (Paris: Garnier-Flammarion, 1972 [1746]).
Diderot, Denis, *The Nun*, trans. Leonard Tancock (Harmondsworth: Penguin, 1974 [1792]).
Diderot, Denis, *Jacques the Fatalist*, trans. Michael Henry, intro. Martin Hall (Harmondsworth: Penguin, 1986).
Diderot, Denis, 'Prospectus': https://play.google.com/books/reader?id=f5hpqX0GdOUC&pg=GBS.PA2&hl=en_GB

Dilthey, Wilhelm, *Das Erlebnis und die Dichtung: Lessing-Goethe-Novalis-Hölderlin*, 16th edn (Göttingen: Vandenhoeck & Ruprecht, 1985).

Dixon, Thomas, Geoffrey Cantor and Stephen Pumfrey (eds), *Science and Religion: New Historical Perspectives* (Cambridge: Cambridge University Press, 2010).

Dodds, Gregory D., *Exploiting Erasmus: The Erasmian Legacy and Religious Change in Early Modern England* (Toronto: University of Toronto Press, 2009).

Donagan, Alan, 'Spinoza's Theology', in Garrett (ed.), *The Cambridge Companion to Spinoza*.

Donna, Diego, 'Hermeneutics and Conflict: Spinoza and the Downfall of Exegetical Interpretation', in Del Prete, Schino and Totaro (eds), *Philosophers and the Bible*, ch. 5.

Doyle, Phyllis, 'The Contemporary Background of Hobbes' "State of Nature"', *Economica* 21 (1927), pp. 336–55. https://doi.org/10.2307/2548403.

Doyle, William (ed.), *The Oxford Handbook of the Ancient Régime* (Oxford: Oxford University Press, 2012).

Dunn, John, *The Political Thought of John Locke: An Historical Account of the Argument of the 'Two Treatises of Government'* (Cambridge: Cambridge University Press, 1969).

Dupré, Louis, *The Enlightenment and the Intellectual Foundations of Modern Culture* (New Haven, CT: Yale University Press, 2004).

Eagleton, Terry, *Reason, Faith, and Revelation: Reflections on the God Debate* (New Haven, CT: Yale University Press, 2009).

Echeverria, Durand, 'The Pre-Revolutionary Influence of Rousseau's *Contrat Social*', *JHI* 33.4 (1972), pp. 543–60.

Edelstein, Dan, *The Enlightenment: A Genealogy* (Chicago: University of Chicago Press, 2010).

Edelstein, Dan, 'The Aristotelian Enlightenment', in Matytsin and Edelstein (eds), *Let There Be Enlightenment: The Religious and Mystical Sources of Rationality*, pp. 187–204.

Edsall, H. Sinn, 'The Idea of History and Progress in Fontenelle and Voltaire', *Yale Romanic Studies* 18 (1941), pp. 163–84.

Erasmus, Desiderius, *Enchiridion Militis Christiani* (London: Methuen, 1905; reprint of edn by Wynkyn de Worde, 1533 [1501]).

Erdozain, Dominic, 'A Heavenly Poise: Radical Religion and the Making of the Enlightenment', *Intellectual History Review* 27.1 (2017), pp. 71–96.

Farrington, Benjamin, *The Philosophy of Francis Bacon: An Essay on Its Development from 1603 to 1609 with New Translations of Fundamental Texts* (Liverpool: Liverpool University Press, 1964).

Febvre, Lucien, *The Problem of Unbelief in the Sixteenth Century: The Religion of Rabelais*, trans. B. Gottlieb (Cambridge, MA: Harvard University Press, 1982 [1942, 1947]).

Ferguson, Adam, *An Essay on the History of Civil Society*, ed. and intro. Duncan Forbes (Edinburgh: Edinburgh University Press, 1966).

Fergusson, David and Mark Elliott (eds), *The History of Scottish Theology, Volume II: From the Early Enlightenment to the Late Victorian Era* (Oxford: Oxford University Press, 2019).

Fergusson, David and Mark W. Elliott (eds), *The History of Scottish Theology, Volume III: The Long Twentieth Century* (Oxford: Oxford University Press, 2019).

Fergusson, David, 'Hume amongst the Theologians', in Fergusson and Elliott (eds), *The History of Scottish Theology, Volume II: From the Early Enlightenment to the Late Victorian Era*, ch. 21.

Ferrone, Vincenzo, *The Enlightenment: The History of an Idea*, trans. Elizabeth Tarantino (Princeton, NJ: Princeton University Press, 2015).

Fielding, Henry, *The History of the Life of the Late Mr Jonathan Wild the Great*, ed. and intro. George Saintsbury, *The Works of Henry Fielding*, ed. George Saintsbury, 12 vols, vol. 10 (London: Dent, 1893).

Fielding, Henry, *The History of the Adventures of Joseph Andrews and His Friend Mr. Abraham Adams*, intro. George Saintsbury (London: Dent; New York: Dutton, 1910 [1742]).

Fielding, Henry, *An Apology for the Life of Mrs. Shamela Andrews* (Oxford: Oxford University Press, 1981 [1741], with *Joseph Andrews*).

Fielding, Henry, *Amelia*, ed. David Blewett (Harmondsworth: Penguin, 1987 [1751]).

Fielding, Henry, *Tom Jones* (Ware: Wordsworth, 1992).

Fix, Andrew C., *Prophecy and Reason: The Dutch Collegiants in the Early Enlightenment* (Princeton, NJ: Princeton University Press, 1991).

Fleming, John V., *The Dark Side of the Enlightenment: Wizards, Alchemists, and Spiritual Seekers in the Age of Reason* (New York: W. W. Norton and Company, 2013).

Flint, Robert, *Historical Philosophy in France, French Belgium and Switzerland* (Edinburgh: Blackwood; New York: Charles Scribner's Sons, 1893).

Fontenelle, Bernard le Bovier de, *Les nouveaux Dialogues des Morts anciens* (Paris, 1724 [Amsterdam, 1683]).

Forbes, Duncan, *Hume's Philosophical Politics* (Cambridge: Cambridge University Press, 1975).

Forster, E. M., *Aspects of the Novel* (Harmondsworth: Penguin, 1962 [1927]).

Foster, Stephen Paul, *Melancholy Duty: The Hume-Gibbon Attack on Christianity* (Dordrecht: Kluwer, 2010).

Foucault, Michel, *The Foucault Reader*, trans. Catherine Porter, ed. Paul Rabinow (New York: Pantheon Books, 1984).
Fout, Jason A., *Fully Alive: The Glory of God and the Human Creature in Karl Barth, Hans Urs von Balthasar and Theological Exegesis of Scripture* (London and New York: Bloomsbury T&T Clark, 2015).
Frampton, Travis L., *Spinoza and the Rise of Historical Criticism of the Bible* (London and New York: T&T Clark, 2006).
France, Peter, *Diderot* (Oxford: Oxford University Press, 1983).
Francis, Keith A. and William Gibson (eds), *The Oxford Handbook of the British Sermon 1689–1901* (Oxford: Oxford University Press, 2012).
Frankel, Charles, *The Faith of Reason: The Idea of Progress in the French Enlightenment* (New York: Octagon Books, 1969 [1948]).
Franklin, Julian H., *Jean Bodin and the Sixteenth-Century Revolution in the Methodology of Law and History* (New York: Columbia University Press, 1963).
Fraser, Liam Jerrold, *Atheism, Fundamentalism and the Protestant Reformation: Uncovering the Secret Sympathy* (Cambridge: Cambridge University Press, 2018).
Fredman, Alice Green, *Diderot and Sterne* (New York: Columbia University Press, 1955).
Fussell, Paul, *The Rhetorical World of Augustan Humanism: Ethics and Imagery from Swift to Burke* (Oxford: Clarendon Press, 1965).
Gadamer, H.-G., *Truth and Method*, trans. and ed. Garrett Barden and John Cumming (London: Sheed and Ward, 1975).
Garber, David and Michael Ayers (eds), *The Cambridge History of Seventeenth-Century Philosophy*, 2 vols (Cambridge: Cambridge University Press, 2008).
Gardiner, Patrick, *The Nature of Historical Explanation* (Oxford: Oxford University Press, 1952).
Gardiner, Patrick, 'Historical Understanding and the Empiricist Tradition', in Bernard Williams and Alan Montefiore (eds), *British Analytical Philosophy* (London: Routledge and Kegan Paul, 1966), pp. 267–84.
Gardiner, Patrick, 'The Concept of Man as Presupposed by the Historical Studies', in Godfrey N. A. Vesey (ed.), *The Proper Study of Man*, Royal Institute of Philosophy Lectures, IV, 1969–1970 (London: Macmillan, 1971).
Gargett, Graham, *Voltaire and Protestantism* (Oxford: Voltaire Foundation, 1980).
Garrard, Graeme, *Rousseau's Counter-Enlightenment: A Republican Critique of the Philosophes* (New York: State University of New York Press, 2003).
Garrett, Don (ed.), *The Cambridge Companion to Spinoza* (Cambridge: Cambridge University Press, 1996).

Gascoigne, John, *Cambridge in the Age of the Enlightenment: Science, Religion and Politics from the Restoration to the French Revolution* (Cambridge: Cambridge University Press, 1989).
Gaskin, J. C. A., *Hume's Philosophy of Religion* (London: Macmillan, 1978).
Gaskin, J. C. A., 'Hume on Religion', in Norton (ed.), *The Cambridge Companion to Hume*.
Gay, Peter, *The Party of Humanity: Studies in the French Enlightenment* (London: Weidenfeld & Nicolson, 1964).
Gay, Peter, *The Enlightenment: An Interpretation, Vol. 1: The Rise of Modern Paganism* (London: Weidenfeld and Nicolson, 1966).
Gay, Peter, *The Enlightenment: An Interpretation, Vol. 2: The Science of Freedom* (London: Weidenfeld and Nicolson, 1970).
Gay, Peter, 'Why Was the Enlightenment?' in id. (ed.), *Eighteenth-Century Studies presented to Arthur M. Wilson* (Hanover, NH: University Press of New England, 1972).
Gay, Peter, *Style in History* (London: Jonathan Cape, 1975 [1974]).
Gibbon, Edward, *Autobiography* (London: Dent; New York: Dutton, 1911).
Gibbon, Edward, *The Decline and Fall of the Roman Empire*, abridged and intro. D. M. Low (Harmondsworth: Penguin, 1963).
Gibbon, Edward, *The Decline and Fall of the Roman Empire and Other Selections from the Writings of Edward Gibbon*, ed. H. R. Trevor-Roper (New York: Washington Square Press, 1963; London: New English Library, 1966).
Gibbon, Edward, *Essai sur l'étude de la littérature: A Critical Edition*, ed. Robert Mankin (Oxford: Voltaire Foundation, 2010).
Gibson, William, *Enlightenment Prelate: Benjamin Hoadly, 1676–1761* (Cambridge: James Clarke, 2004).
Gibson, William and Robert G. Ingram (eds), *Religious Identities in Britain, 1660–1832* (Farnham and Burlington, VT: Ashgate, 2005).
Gilley, Sheridan, 'Christianity and Enlightenment: An Historical Survey', *History of European Ideas* 1.2 (1981), pp. 103–21.
Ginsberg, Robert, 'David Hume versus the Enlightenment', *SVEC* LXXXVIII (1972), pp. 599–650.
Glaser, Elaine (ed.), *Religious Tolerance in the Atlantic World: Early Modern and Contemporary Perspectives* (Basingstoke: Palgrave Macmillan, 2014).
Gleick, James, *Isaac Newton* (New York: Vintage Books, 2003).
Glendinning, Victoria, *Jonathan Swift* (London: Hutchinson, 1998).
Goldie, Mark, 'Voluntary Anglicans', *The Historical Journal* 46 (2003), pp. 977–90.
Goldie, Mark and Robert Wokler (eds), *The Cambridge History of Eighteenth-Century Political Thought* (Cambridge: Cambridge University Press, 2006).

Goldsmith, Oliver, *The Vicar of Wakefield* (London and Edinburgh: Thomas Nelson, n.d.).
Gooch, G. P., *History and Historians in the Nineteenth Century* (London: Longmans, Green, 1928).
Gooch, G. P., 'Voltaire as Historian', in id., *Catherine the Great and Other Studies* (London: Longmans, Green, 1954), pp. 199–274.
Gore, Charles (ed.), *Lux Mundi: A Series of Studies in the Religion of the Incarnation*, 10th edn with additions by Gore (London: John Murray, 1890 [1889; 15th edition, 1904]).
Gossman, Lionel, 'Time and History in Rousseau', *SVEC* XXX (1964), pp. 311–49.
Goulbourne, Russell and David Higgins (eds), *Jean-Jacques Rousseau and British Romanticism: Gender and Selfhood, Politics and Nation* (London and New York: Bloomsbury, 2017).
Graham, Elaine, *Apologetics without Apology: Speaking of God in a World Troubled by Religion* (Eugene, OR: Cascade Books, 2017).
Gray, John, *Enlightenment's Wake: Politics and Culture at the Close of the Modern Age* (London and New York: Routledge, 1995).
Gray, John, *Isaiah Berlin: An Interpretation of His Thought; with a New Introduction by the Author* (Princeton, NJ: Princeton University Press, 2013 [1995]).
Green, F. C., *Rousseau and the Idea of Progress* (Oxford: Oxford University Press, 1950 [repr. Norwood Editions, 1978]).
Gregor Smith, Ronald, *J. G. Hamann 1730–1788: A Study in Christian Existence with Selections from His Writings* (London: Collins, 1960).
Gregor Smith, Ronald (ed. and intro.), *World Come of Age: A Symposium on Dietrich Bonhoeffer* (London: Collins, 1967).
Gregory, Jeremy, 'Transforming "the Age of Reason" into "an Age of Faiths"; or, Putting Religions and Beliefs (Back) into the Eighteenth Century', *Journal for Eighteenth-Century Studies* 32.3 (2009), pp. 287–306.
Gregory, Jeremy, 'Religion: Faith in the Age of Reason', *Journal for Eighteenth-Century Studies* 34.4 (2011), pp. 435–43 (Special issue: 'The State of the Discipline', ed. M. O. Grenby).
Gregory, Jeremy (ed.), *The Oxford History of Anglicanism, Volume II: Establishment and Empire, 1662–1829* (Oxford: Oxford University Press, 2017).
Gregory, Tullio, 'Pierre Charron's "Scandalous Book"', in Hunter and Wootton (eds), *Atheism from the Reformation to the Enlightenment*, ch. 3.
Grell, Ole Peter and Roy Porter (eds), *Toleration in Enlightenment Europe* (Cambridge: Cambridge University Press, 2000).
Grimsley, Ronald, *Rousseau and the Religious Quest* (Oxford: Clarendon Press, 1968).

Grimsley, Ronald, *Jean-Jacques Rousseau: A Study in Self-Awareness*, 2nd edn (Cardiff: University of Wales Press, 1969 [1961]).
Grimsley, Ronald, *The Philosophy of Rousseau* (Oxford: Oxford University Press, 1973).
Gunton, Colin E., *Enlightenment and Alienation: An Essay towards a Trinitarian Theology* (Basingstoke: Marshall, Morgan & Scott, 1985).
Gunton, Colin E., *The Three, the One and the Many: God, Creation and the Culture of Modernity* (Cambridge: Cambridge University Press, 2003).
Guy, Nathan, *Finding Locke's God: The Theological Basis of John Locke's Political Thought* (London and New York: Bloomsbury, 2019).
Guyer, Paul (ed.), *The Cambridge Companion to Kant and Modern Philosophy* (Cambridge: Cambridge University Press, 2006).
Haakonssen, Knud (ed.), *Enlightenment and Religion: Rational Dissent in Eighteenth-Century Britain* (Cambridge: Cambridge University Press, 1996).
Hacking, Ian, *The Emergence of Probability: A Philosophical Study of Early Ideas about Probability, Induction, and Statistical Inference* (Cambridge: Cambridge University Press, 1975).
Hales, E. E. Y., *Revolution and Papacy 1769–1846* (London: Eyre & Spottiswoode, 1960).
Hampshire, Stuart, *Spinoza* (Harmondsworth: Penguin, 1962 [1951]).
Hampson, Daphne, *Christianity and Feminism* (Oxford: Blackwell, 1990).
Hampson, Daphne, *After Christianity* (London: SCM Press, 1996).
Hampson, Daphne, *Christian Contradictions: The Structures of Lutheran and Catholic Thought* (Cambridge: Cambridge University Press, 2001).
Hampson, Norman, *The Enlightenment: An Evaluation of Its Assumptions, Attitudes and Values* (Harmondsworth: Penguin, 1968).
Hampson, Norman, *Will and Circumstance: Montesquieu, Rousseau and the French Revolution* (London: Duckworth, 1983).
Hardy, Nicholas, *Criticism and Confession: The Bible in the Seventeenth Century Republic of Letters* (Oxford: Oxford University Press, 2017).
Harris, Harriet, *Fundamentalism and Evangelicals* (Oxford: Clarendon Press, 1998).
Harris, James A., *Hume: An Intellectual Biography* (Cambridge: Cambridge University Press, 2015).
Harrison, Peter, *The Bible, Protestantism, and the Rise of Natural Science* (Cambridge: Cambridge University Press, 1998).
Harrison, Peter, *'Religion' and the Religions in the English Enlightenment* (Cambridge: Cambridge University Press, 1990).
Harrison, Peter, *The Fall of Man and the Foundations of Science* (Cambridge: Cambridge University Press, 2007).
Hartung, Fritz, *Enlightened Despotism* (London: Routledge and Kegan Paul, for The Historical Association, 1957).

Harvey, Van A., *The Historian and the Believer* (London: SCM Press, 1967 [1966]).
Haykin, Michael A. G., 'Evangelicalism and the Enlightenment: A Reassessment', in Haykin and Stewart (eds), *The Emergence of Evangelicalism*, ch. 2.
Haykin, Michael A. G. and Kenneth J. Stewart (eds), *The Emergence of Evangelicalism: Exploring Historical Continuities* (Nottingham: Apollos/Inter-Varsity Press, 2008).
Hazard, Paul, *The European Mind 1680–1715*, trans. J. Lewis May (Harmondsworth: Penguin, 1964 [1953]).
Heath, Eugene and Vincenzo Merolle (eds), *Adam Ferguson: History, Progress and Human Nature* (London: Pickering & Chatto, 2008).
Heath, Eugene and Vincenzo Merolle (eds), *Adam Ferguson: Philosophy, Politics and Society* (London: Pickering and Chatto, 2009).
Henry, John, *The Scientific Revolution and the Origins of Modern Science* (Basingstoke: Palgrave Macmillan, 2002 [2001; 3rd edn 2008]).
Hepburn, R. W., 'Hobbes on the Knowledge of God', in Cranston and Peters (eds), *Hobbes and Rousseau: A Collection of Critical Essays*.
Herbert of Cherbury, *The Life of Lord Herbert of Cherbury, Written by Himself and Continued until His Death* (London: Cassell, 1893).
Herbert of Cherbury, *De Veritate*, trans. Meyrick H. Carré (Bristol: University of Bristol Press, J. W. Arrowsmith, 1937; facsimile repr.: Thoemmes Continuum, 1999).
Herrick, James A., *The Radical Rhetoric of the English Deists: The Discourse of Skepticism, 1680–1750* (Columbia, SC: University of South Carolina Press, 1997).
Hill, David, 'Enlightenment as a Historical Process: Ernst und Falk and Die Erziehung des Menschengeschlechts', in Robertson (ed.), *Lessing and the German Enlightenment*, pp. 227–44.
Hill, W. Speed (ed.), *Studies in Richard Hooker: Essays Preliminary to an Edition of His Works* (Cleveland, OH: Case Western Reserve University Press, 1972).
Hindmarsh, D. Bruce, *The Evangelical Conversion Narrative: Spiritual Autobiography in Early Modern England* (Oxford: Oxford University Press, 2005).
Hindmarsh, D. Bruce, *The Spirit of Early Evangelicalism: True Religion in a Modern World* (Oxford: Oxford University Press, 2017).
Hinds, Hilary, *God's Englishwomen: Seventeenth-Century Radical Sectarian Writing and Feminist Criticism* (Manchester: Manchester University Press, 1996).
Hinkle, Nathan W., 'A Critique of the Enlightenment Doctrine on Progressivism through the Writings of Francis A. Schaeffer': https://core.ac.uk/reader/58824379.

Hobbes, Thomas, *Leviathan*, ed. and intro. C. B. Macpherson (Harmondsworth: Penguin, 1969).
Hoppit, Julian, 'Reformed and Unreformed Britain, 1689–1801', in Doyle (ed.), *The Oxford Handbook of the Ancient Régime*, ch. 29.
Horkheimer, Max and Theodor Adorno, *Dialectic of Enlightenment*, trans. John Cumming (New York: Herder and Herder, 1972; London: Allen Lane, The Penguin Press, 1973).
Horton, John and Susan Mendus (eds), *John Locke: 'A Letter Concerning Toleration' in Focus* (London: Routledge, 1991).
Hudson, Nicholas, *Samuel Johnson and Eighteenth-Century Thought* (Oxford: Oxford University Press, 1988/1990).
Hulliung, Mark, *The Autocritique of Enlightenment: Rousseau and the Philosophes* (Cambridge, MA: Harvard University Press, 1994).
Hulme, Peter and Ludmilla J. Jordanova (eds), *The Enlightenment and Its Shadows* (London: Routledge, 1990).
Hume, David, *Essays Moral, Political and Literary* (London: Grant Richards, 1903).
Hume, David, *Letters of David Hume*, ed. J. Y. T. Grieg, 2 vols (Oxford: Oxford University Press, 1932).
Hume, David, *The History of Great Britain: The Reigns of James I and Charles I*, ed. and intro. Duncan Forbes (Harmondsworth: Penguin, 1970 [1754]).
Hume, David, *Dialogues Concerning Natural Religion*, ed. Martin Bell (Harmondsworth: Penguin, 1990 [1779]).
Hume, David, *A Dissertation on the Passions; The Natural History of Religion*, ed. Tom L. Beauchamp (Oxford: Clarendon Press, 2007).
Hume, David, *An Enquiry Concerning Human Understanding*, VIII, part 1: https://davidhume.org/texts/e/8.
Hunt, Margaret R., Margaret Jacob, Phyllis Mack and Ruth Perry (eds), *Women in the Enlightenment* (New York: The Haworth Press Inc, 1984).
Hunter, Graeme, *Radical Protestantism in Spinoza's Thought* (Farnham and Burlington, VT: Ashgate, 2005).
Hunter, Michael and David Wootton (eds), *Atheism from the Reformation to the Enlightenment* (Oxford: Oxford University Press, 1992).
Hunter, Michael, *The Decline of Magic: Britain in the Enlightenment* (New Haven, CT: Yale University Press, 2020).
Huppert, George, 'The Renaissance Background of Historicism', *H&T* 5 (1966), pp. 48–60.
Huppert, George, *The Idea of Perfect History: Historical Erudition and Historical Philosophy in Renaissance France* (Urbana, IL: University of Illinois Press, 1970).
Hutcheson, H. R., 'Lord Herbert and the Deists', *The Journal of Philosophy* XLIII.8 (1946), pp. 219–21.

Iliffe, Rob, *Priest of Nature: The Religious Worlds of Isaac Newton* (New York: Oxford University Press, 2016).
Illingworth, J. R., *Divine Immanence: An Essay on the Spiritual Significance of Matter* (London: Macmillan, 1898).
Ingram, Robert G., 'The Weight of Historical Evidence: Conyers Middleton and the Eighteenth-Century Miracles Debate', in Cornwall and Gibson (eds), *Religion, Politics and Dissent 1660–1832*, pp. 85–109.
Insole, Christopher J., *The Intolerable God: Kant's Theological Journey* (Grand Rapids: Eerdmans, 2015).
Insole, Christopher J., *Kant and the Divine: From Contemplation to the Moral Law* (Oxford: Oxford University Press, 2020).
Israel, Jonathan, *Radical Enlightenment: Philosophy and the Making of Modernity 1650–1750* (Oxford: Oxford University Press, 2001).
Israel, Jonathan, *Enlightenment Contested: Philosophy, Modernity and the Emancipation of Man 1670–1752* (Oxford: Oxford University Press, 2006).
Israel, Jonathan, *Democratic Enlightenment: Philosophy, Revolution, and Human Rights 1750–1790* (Oxford: Oxford University Press, 2011).
Israel, Jonathan, *Revolutionary Ideas: An Intellectual History of the French Revolution from the Rights of Man to Robespierre* (Princeton, NJ: Princeton University Press, 2014).
Israel, Jonathan, 'Spinoza and Early Modern Theology', in Lehner, Muller and Roeber (eds), *The Oxford Handbook of Early Modern Theology, 1600–1800*, ch. 37.
Jacob, Margaret C., *The Radical Enlightenment: Pantheists, Freemasons and Republicans* (London: George Allen and Unwin, 1981).
Jacob, Margaret C., *The Scientific Revolution: A Brief History with Documents* (Basingstoke: Palgrave Macmillan, 2010).
Jacob, Margaret C., *The Secular Enlightenment* (Princeton, NJ: Princeton University Press, 2019).
Jacob, W. M., *Lay People and Religion in the Early Eighteenth Century* (Cambridge: Cambridge University Press, 1996).
James, Susan, *Spinoza on Philosophy, Religion, and Politics: The Theologico-Political Treatise* (Oxford: Oxford University Press, 2012).
Jantzen, Grace M., *God's World, God's Body* (London: Darton, Longman and Todd, 1984).
Johnson, Douglas (ed.), *French Society and the Revolution* (Cambridge: Cambridge University Press, 1976).
Johnson, J. W., *The Formation of English Neo-Classical Thought* (Princeton, NJ: Princeton University Press, 1967).

Johnson, Samuel, *Journey to the Western Islands of Scotland* and James Boswell, *Journal of a Tour to the Hebrides with Samuel Johnson LL.D.*, ed. R. W. Chapman (London: Oxford University Press, 1924).
Johnson, Samuel, *Lives of the Poets*, 2 vols (London: Dent, 1925).
Johnson, Samuel, *Selected Writings*, ed. Patrick Cruttwell (Harmondsworth: Penguin, 1968).
Johnson, Samuel, *The History of Rasselas, Prince of Abissinia*, ed. Paul Goring (Harmondsworth: Penguin, 2007).
Johnson, Samuel, *A Dictionary of the English Language* (1755): https://johnsonsdictionaryonline.com
Jordan, W. K., *The Development of Religious Toleration in England* (London: Allen & Unwin, 1938).
Joyce, James, *Ulysses*, ed. Jeri Johnson (Oxford: Oxford University Press, 1993).
Kant, Immanuel, *Critique of Pure Reason*, trans. J. M. D. Meiklejohn, ed. A. D. Lindsay (London: Dent; New York: Dutton, 1934).
Kant, Immanuel, *The Critique of Judgement*, trans. J. C. Meredith (Oxford: Clarendon Press, 1952).
Kant, Immanuel, *Religion within the Limits of Reason Alone*, trans. and intro. Theodore M. Greene and Hoyt H. Hudson, with a new essay 'The Ethical Significance of Kant's Religion' by John R. Silber (New York and London: Harper & Row, 1960 (1934]).
Kant, Immanuel, *Kant's Political Writings*, ed. H. B. Nisbet, trans. H. Reiss (Cambridge: Cambridge University Press, 1970).
Katz, David S., *God's Last Words: Reading the English Bible from the Reformation to Fundamentalism* (New Haven, CT: Yale University Press, 2004).
Kaufman, Walter, *Nietzsche: Philosopher, Psychologist, Antichrist* (Princeton, NJ: Princeton University Press, 1968 [1950]).
Keats, John, *Letters of John Keats*, ed. Frederick Page (London: Oxford University Press, 1954).
Kelley, Donald R., *Foundations of Modern Historical Scholarship: Language, Law and History in the French Renaissance* (New York: Columbia University Press, 1970).
Kelley, Donald R., 'The Development and Context of Bodin's Method', in Horst Denzer (ed.), *Jean Bodin: Verhandligen der internationalen Bodin Jagung in München* (München: Verlag C. H. Beck, 1973).
Kennedy, Gavin, 'Adam Smith on Religion', in Christopher J. Berry, Maria Pia Paganelli and Craig Smith (eds), *The Oxford Handbook of Adam Smith* (Oxford: Oxford University Press, 2013).
Kettler, David, *The Social and Political Thought of Adam Ferguson* (Columbus, OH: Columbus State University Press, 1965).

Killeen, Kevin, Helen Smith and Rachel Willie (eds), *The Oxford Handbook of the Bible in Early Modern England, c. 1530–1700* (Oxford: Oxford University Press, 2015).

Klein, Lawrence E. and Anthony J. La Vopa (eds), *Enthusiasm and Enlightenment in Europe, 1650–1850* (San Marino, CA: University of California Press, 1998).

Knott, Sarah and Barbara Taylor (eds), *Women, Gender and Enlightenment* (Basingstoke: Palgrave Macmillan, 2005).

Kołakowski, Leszek, trans. from Polish (1965) by Anna Posner, *Chrétiens sans Église: la conscience religeuse et le lien confessionnel au XVIIe siècle* (Paris: Gallimard, 1987 [1969]).

Kors, Alan Charles and Paul J. Korshin (eds), *Anticipations of the Enlightenment in England, France, and Germany* (Philadelphia, PA: University of Pennsylvania Press, 1987).

Kors, Alan Charles, *Atheism in France, 1650–1729. Vol. 1: The Orthodox Sources of Disbelief* (Princeton, NJ: Princeton University Press, 1990).

Kors, Alan Charles, *Encyclopedia of the Enlightenment*, 4 vols (Oxford: Oxford University Press, 2003).

Kors, Alan Charles, 'The Age of Enlightenment', in Bullivant and Ruse (eds), *The Oxford Handbook of Atheism*.

Koselleck, Reinhart, *Critique and Crisis: Enlightenment and the Pathogenesis of Modern Society*, trans. Keith Tribe (Oxford, New York and Hamburg: Berg, 1988 [1959]).

Kow, Simon, 'Politics and Culture in Hume's *History of England*', in Bourgault and Sparling (eds), *A Companion to Enlightenment Historiography*, ch. 2.

Koyré, Alexandre, 'The Significance of the Newtonian Synthesis', in id., *Newtonian Studies* (London: Chapman Hall, 1965).

Kramnick, Isaac, *Bolingbroke and His Circle: The Politics of Nostalgia in the Age of Walpole* (Ithaca, NY: Cornell University Press, 1992 [1968]).

Labrousse, Elisabeth, *Pierre Bayle*, 2 vols (The Hague: Nijhoff, 1963/1964).

Labrousse, Elisabeth, 'Reading Pierre Bayle in Paris', in Kors and Korshin (eds), *Anticipations of the Enlightenment in England, France, and Germany*, ch. 1.

Larmore, Charles, 'Scepticism', in Garber and Ayers (eds), *The Cambridge History of Seventeenth-Century Philosophy*, vol. 2, ch. 32.

Laursen, John Christian and Cary J. Nederman (eds), *Beyond the Persecuting Society: Religious Toleration before the Enlightenment* (Philadelphia, PA: University of Pennsylvanian, 1998).

Lecler, Joseph S. J., *Toleration and the Reformation*, 2 vols (New York: Association Press, 1960).

Legaspi, Michael C., *The Death of Scripture and the Rise of Biblical Studies* (Oxford: Oxford University Press, 2010).
Lehmann, William C., *John Millar of Glasgow 1735–1801: His Life and Thought and His Contributions to Sociological Analysis* (Cambridge: Cambridge University Press, 1960).
Lehner, Ulrich L., 'Catholic Theology and the Enlightenment', in Ayres, Volpe and Humphries, Jr, *The Oxford Handbook of Catholic Theology*, ch. 35.
Lehner, Ulrich L., *The Catholic Enlightenment: The Forgotten History of a Global Movement* (Oxford: Oxford University Press, 2016).
Lehner, Ulrich L. and Michael Printy (eds), *A Companion to the Catholic Enlightenment in Europe* (Leiden and Boston: Brill, 2010).
Lehner, Ulrich L., Richard A. Muller and A. G. Roeber (eds), *The Oxford Handbook of Early Modern Theology, 1600–1800* (Oxford: Oxford University Press, 2016).
Lessing, G. E., *Lessing's Theological Writings*, ed., trans. and intro. Henry Chadwick (London: Adam & Charles Black, 1956).
Lessing, Gotthold Ephraim, *Philosophical and Theological Writings*, trans. and ed. H. B. Nisbet (Cambridge: Cambridge University Press, 2005).
Levine, Joseph M., *Humanism and History: Origins of Modern English Historiography* (Ithaca, NY: Cornell University Press, 1987).
Levy, David M. and Sandra J. Peart, 'Adam Smith and the State: Language and Reform', in Berry, Paganelli and Smith (eds), *The Oxford Handbook of Adam Smith*.
Licata, Giovanni, '"The Law Inscribed in the Mind": On the Meaning of a Biblical Image in Spinoza's Theological-Political Treatise', in Del Prete, Schino and Totaro (eds), *Philosophers and the Bible*, ch. 11.
Lincoln, Andrew T., *Ephesians, Word Biblical Commentary* (Dallas, TX: Word Books, 1990).
Linton, Marisa, 'Dissent and Toleration', in Doyle (ed.), *The Oxford Handbook of the Ancient Régime*, ch. 20.
Livingston, Donald W. and James T. King (eds), *Hume: A Re-evaluation* (New York: Fordham University Press, 1976).
Livingston, James C., 'Henry Dodwell's *Christianity not Founded on Argument* Revisited', *JTS*, NS 22.2 (1971), pp. 466–78.
Lloyd, Genevieve, *Enlightenment Shadows* (Oxford: Oxford University Press, 2013).
Locke, John, *An Essay Concerning Human Understanding*, 2 vols (London: Dent; New York: Dutton, 1961).
Loewenstein, David and John Marshall (eds), *Heresy, Literature, and Politics in Early Modern English Culture* (Cambridge: Cambridge University Press, 2006).

Loewenstein, David, *Treacherous Faith: The Specter of Heresy in Early Modern English Literature and Culture* (Oxford: Oxford University Press, 2013).
Lough, John, *The Philosophes and Post-Revolutionary France* (Oxford: Clarendon Press, 1982).
Lovejoy, A. O., *Essays in the History of Ideas* (Baltimore, MD: Johns Hopkins University Press, 1948).
Löwith, Karl, *Meaning in History* (Chicago, IL: University of Chicago Press, 1949).
Lucci, Diego, *John Locke's Christianity* (Cambridge: Cambridge University Press, 2021).
Lund, Roger D. (ed.), *The Margins of Orthodoxy: Heterodox Writing and Cultural Response, 1660–1750* (Cambridge: Cambridge University Press, 1995).
McCloy, Shelby T., *Gibbon's Antagonism to Christianity* (London: Williams & Norgate, 1933).
McCloy, Shelby T., *The Humanitarian Movement in Eighteenth-Century France* (Louisville, KY: University of Kentucky Press, 1957).
McDaniel, Iain, *Adam Ferguson in the Scottish Enlightenment* (Cambridge, MA: Harvard University Press, 2013).
McDonald, Joan, *Rousseau and the French Revolution 1762–1791* (London: The Athlone Press, 1965).
McFague, Sallie, *The Body of God: An Ecological Theology* (London: SCM Press, 1993).
McGrath, Alister E., *The Making of Modern German Christology* (Oxford: Blackwell, 1986).
McGrath, Alister E., *Iustitia Dei: A History of the Christian Doctrine of Justification* [2 vols], *Vol. II: From 1500 to the Present Day* (Cambridge: Cambridge University Press, 1986).
McGrath, Alister E., *The Genesis of Doctrine: A Study in the Foundations of Doctrinal Criticism* (Oxford: Blackwell, 1990).
McGrath, Alister E. (ed.), *The Blackwell Encyclopedia of Modern Christian Thought* (Oxford: Blackwell, 1993).
McGrath, Alister E., *A Fine-Tuned Universe: Science, Theology, and the Quest for Meaning* (Louisville, KY: Westminster John Knox Press, 2011).
McGrath, Alister E., *Darwinism and the Divine: Evolutionary Thought and Natural Theology* (Oxford: Wiley Blackwell, 2011).
McGuinness, P., A. Harrison and R. Kearney (eds), *John Toland's Christianity Not Mysterious: Texts, Associated Works and Critical Essays* (Dublin: Lilliput Press, 1997).
MacIntyre, Alasdair, *After Virtue*, 2nd edn (London: Duckworth, 1988).
McMahon, Darrin M., *Enemies of the Enlightenment: The French Counter-Enlightenment and the Making of Modernity* (New York: Oxford University Press, 2001).

McManners, John, *The French Revolution and the Church* (London: SPCK, 1969).
McManners, John, *Death and the Enlightenment* (Oxford: Oxford University Press, 1981).
McManners, John, *Church and Society in Eighteenth-Century France*, 2 vols (Oxford: Oxford University Press, 1998).
Macquarrie, John, *In Search of Deity: An Essay in Dialectical Theism, Gifford Lectures, 1983–84* (London: SCM Press, 1984).
Mack, Phyllis, *Heart Religion in the British Enlightenment: Gender and Emotion in Early Methodism* (Cambridge: Cambridge University Press, 2008).
Mali, Joseph and Robert Wokler (eds), *Isaiah Berlin's Counter-Enlightenment* (Philadelphia, PA: American Philosophical Society, 2003).
Mandelbaum, Maurice, *History, Man and Reason: A Study in Nineteenth-Century Thought* (Baltimore, MD: Johns Hopkins University Press, 1971).
Mandelbrote, Scott, 'Newton and Eighteenth-Century Christianity', in Cohen and Smith (eds), *The Cambridge Companion to Newton*, ch. 14.
Mankin, Robert, 'Edward Gibbon: Historian in Space', in Bourgault and Sparling (eds), *A Companion to Enlightenment Historiography*, ch. 1.
Manuel, Frank E., 'From Equality to Organicism', *JHI* XVII.1 (1956), pp. 54–69.
Manuel, Frank E., *The Prophets of Paris* (Cambridge, MA: Harvard University Press, 1962).
Manuel, Frank E., *Isaac Newton, Historian* (Cambridge, MA: Belknap Press of Harvard University Press, 1963).
Manuel, Frank E., *Shapes of Philosophical History* (London: Allen & Unwin, 1965; repr. Aldershot: Gregg Revivals, 1993).
Manuel, Frank E., *The Religion of Isaac Newton* (Oxford: Clarendon Press, 1974).
Markus, R. A., *Saeculum: History and Society in the Theology of St Augustine*, 2nd edn (Cambridge: Cambridge University Press, 1988 [1970]).
Marsak, Leonard M., *Bernard de Fontenelle: The Idea of Science in the French Enlightenment* (Philadelphia: Transactions of the American Philosophical Society, 1959).
Marsden, George M., *Fundamentalism and American Culture: The Shaping of Twentieth Century American Evangelicalism 1870–1925* (Oxford: Oxford University Press, 1980).
Marshall, John, *John Locke: Resistance, Religion and Responsibility* (Cambridge: Cambridge University Press, 1994).

Marshall, John, *John Locke, Toleration and Early Enlightenment Culture* (Cambridge: Cambridge University Press, 2006).

Marshall, John and David Loewenstein (eds), *Heresy in Literature and Politics in Early Modern English Culture* (Cambridge: Cambridge University Press, 2006).

Marx, Karl and Friedrich Engels, *The Communist Manifesto*, ed. and intro. A. J. P. Taylor (Harmondsworth: Penguin. 1967 [1888]).

Mason, Haydn, *Pierre Bayle and Voltaire* (London: Oxford University Press, 1963).

Mason, John Hope, 'At the Limits of Toleration: Rousseau and Atheism', in Mostefai and Scott (eds), *Rousseau and L'Infâme: Religion, Toleration, and Fanaticism in the Age of Enlightenment*, pp. 239–56.

Masson, Pierre Maurice, *La religion de J.-J.Rousseau*, 3 vols (Paris: Hachette, 1916).

Matytsin, Anton M. and Dan Edelstein (eds), *Let There Be Enlightenment: The Religious and Mystical Sources of Rationality* (Baltimore, MD: Johns Hopkins University Press, 2014).

Mead, Margaret, *Coming of Age in Samoa: A Study of Adolescence and Sex in Primitive Society* (Harmondsworth: Penguin, 1943 [1928]).

Meinecke, Friedrich, *Historism* [sic]: *The Rise of a New Historical Outlook*, trans. J. E. Anderson (London: Routledge and Kegan Paul, 1972).

Merken-Spaas, G., 'The Social Anthropology of Rousseau's *Émile*', *SVEC* CXXXII (1975), pp. 137–81.

Mezei, Balázs M., Francesca Aran Murphy and Kenneth Oakes (eds), *The Oxford Handbook of Divine Revelation* (Oxford: Oxford University Press, 2021).

Michalson, Gordon E., Jr, *Lessing's 'Ugly Ditch': A Study of Theology and History* (University Park, PA: Pennsylvania State University Press, 1985).

Middleton, Conyers, *A Free Inquiry into the Miraculous Powers, Which Are Supposed to Have Subsisted in the Christian Church, from the Earliest Ages through Several Successive Centuries* (1749): https://play.google.com/books/reader?id=tXFPAAAAYAAJ&pg=GBS.PR34&hl=en_GB

Milton, John, *The English Poems of John Milton*, ed. H. C. Beeching (London: Oxford University Press, 1913).

Milton, John, *Areopagitica and Other Prose Works* (London: Dent; New York: Dutton, 1927).

Moberly, R. C., *Atonement and Personality* (London: John Murray, 1901).

Momigliano, Arnaldo A., 'Gibbon's Contribution to Historical Method', in id., *Studies in Historiography* (London: Weidenfeld & Nicolson, 1966), pp. 40–55.

Momigliano, Arnaldo A., *Classical Foundations of Modern Historiography* (Berkeley, CA: University of California Press, 1990).
Monod, Paul Kléber, *Solomon's Secret Arts: The Occult in the Age of Enlightenment* (New Haven, CT: Yale University Press, 2013).
Montaigne, Michel de, *The Complete Essays*, trans. and intro. M. A. Screech (Harmondsworth: Penguin, 1991).
Morgan, Teresa, *Roman Faith and Christian Faith: Pistis and Fides in the Early Roman Empire and Early Churches* (Oxford: Oxford University Press, 2015).
Morrison, James C., 'Vico and Spinoza', *JHI* XLI.1 (1980), pp. 49–68.
Mortimer, Sarah, *Reason and Religion in the English Revolution: The Challenge of Socinianism* (Cambridge: Cambridge University Press, 2010).
Mortimer, Sarah and John Robertson (eds), *The Intellectual Consequences of Religious Heterodoxy 1600–1750* (Leiden: Brill, 2012).
Mostefai, Ourida and John T. Scott (eds), *Rousseau and L'Infâme: Religion, Toleration, and Fanaticism in the Age of Enlightenment* (Leiden: Brill, 2009).
Muddiman, John, *The Epistle to the Ephesians*, Black's New Testament Commentaries, gen. ed., Morna D. Hooker (London and New York: Continuum, 2001).
Muhlack, Ulrich, 'German Enlightenment Historiography and the Rise of Historicism', in Bourgault and Sparling (eds), *A Companion to Enlightenment Historiography*, ch. 8.
Mulsow, Martin and Jan Rohls (eds), *Socinianism and Arminianism: Antitrinitarians, Calvinists, and Cultural Exchange in Seventeenth-Century Europe* (Leiden: Brill, 2005).
Munck, Thomas, *The Enlightenment: A Comparative Social History, 1721–1794* (London: Arnold; New York: Oxford University Press, 2000).
Munck, Thomas, 'Enlightenment', in Doyle (ed.), *The Oxford Handbook of the Ancient Régime*, ch. 25.
Nadel, George H., 'Philosophy of History Before Historicism', *H&T* III.3 (1964), pp. 291–315.
Nadler, Steven M., *Spinoza: A Life* (Cambridge: Cambridge University Press, 1999).
Newbigin, Lesslie, *The Other Side of 1984* (Geneva: World Council of Churches, 1983).
Newbigin, Lesslie, *Foolishness to the Greeks: Gospel and Western Culture* (Grand Rapids, MI: Eerdmans/London: SPCK, 1986).
Newbigin, Lesslie, *The Gospel in a Pluralist Society* (London: SPCK/ Grand Rapids, MI: Eerdmans/Geneva: World Council of Churches, 1989).

Newbigin, Lesslie, *Truth to Tell: The Gospel as Public Truth* (London: SPCK, 1991).
Newman, John Henry, *The Dream of Gerontius* (London: Bagster, 1908 [1865]).
Newman, John Henry, *An Essay on the Development of Christian Doctrine; The Edition of 1845*, ed. and intro. J. M. Cameron (Harmondsworth: Penguin, 1974).
Newton, Isaac, *The Principia: Mathematical Principles of Natural Philosophy*, trans. I. Bernard Cohen and Anne Whitman with Julia Budenz (Berkeley, CA: University of California Press, 1999).
Nichols, Bridget, ed., *The Collect in the Churches of the Reformation* (London: SCM Press, 2010).
Nicolson, Marjorie H., *Newton Demands the Muse* (Princeton, NJ: Princeton University Press, 1946).
Niebuhr, H. Richard, *Christ and Culture* (New York: HarperSanFrancisco, 2001[1951]).
Niebuhr, Reinhold, *Moral Man and Immoral Society: A Study in Ethics and Politics* (London: SCM Press, 1963).
Nietzsche, Friedrich, *Ecce Homo*, trans. Walter Kaufman (Harmondsworth: Penguin, 1979).
Nietzsche, Friedrich, *Human, All Too Human: A Book for Free Spirits*, trans. R. J. Hollingdale, intro. Erich Heller (Cambridge: Cambridge University Press, 1986).
Nisbet, Hugh Barr, *Gotthold Ephraim Lessing: His Life, Works, and Thought* (Oxford: Oxford University Press, 2013).
Noggle, James, *Unfelt: The Language of Affect in the British Enlightenment* (Ithaca, NY: Cornell University Press, 2020).
Noll, Mark (ed.), *The Princeton Theology 1812–1921: Scripture, Science, and Theological Method from Archibald Alexander to Benjamin Breckinridge Warfield* (Grand Rapids, MI: Baker, 1983).
Norton, David Fate (ed.), *The Cambridge Companion to Hume* (Cambridge: Cambridge University Press, 1993).
Nuovo, Victor (ed.), *John Locke: Writings on Religion* (Oxford: Oxford University Press, 2002).
Nuovo, Victor, *Christianity, Antiquity and Enlightenment: Interpretations of Locke* (Dordrecht: Springer, 2011).
Nuovo, Victor, *John Locke: The Philosopher as Christian Virtuoso* (Oxford: Clarendon Press, 2017).
O'Brien, Karen, *Narratives of Enlightenment: Cosmopolitan History from Voltaire to Gibbon* (Cambridge: Cambridge University Press, 1997).
O'Neil, Onora, 'Enlightenment as Autonomy: Kant's Vindication of Reason', in Hulme and Jordanova (eds), *The Enlightenment and Its Shadows*.

Oberman, Heiko A. and Thomas A Brady, Jr (eds), *Itinerarium Italicum: The Profile of the Italian Renaissance in the Mirror of Its European Transformations, Dedicated to Paul Oskar Kristeller on the Occasion of His 70th Birthday* (Leiden: Brill, 1975).

Osler, Margaret J., 'Religion and the Changing Historiography of the Scientific Revolution', in Thomas Dixon, Geoffrey Cantor and Stephen Pumfrey (eds), *Science and Religion: New Historical Perspectives*, ch. 4.

Oslington, Paul (ed.), *Adam Smith as Theologian* (London and New York: Routledge, 2011).

Packer, J. I., *Fundamentalism and the Word of God* (London: IVF, 1958).

Padgen, Anthony, *The Enlightenment and Why It Still Matters* (Oxford: Oxford University Press, 2013).

Pagliaro, H. E. (ed.), *Irrationalism in the Eighteenth Century* (Cleveland, OH: Case Western Reserve University Press, 1972).

Pailin, David A., 'Should Herbert of Cherbury be Regarded as a "Deist"?' *JTS*, NS, 51.1 (April 2000), pp. 113–49.

Paley, William, *A View of the Evidences of Christianity*, ed. Canon Birks (London: Religious Tract Society, n.d.).

Paley, William, *Natural Theology or Evidences of the Existence and Attributes of the Deity*; *The Works of William Paley, D.D* (London, 1825).

Palmer, R. R., *Catholics and Unbelievers in Eighteenth-Century France* (Princeton, NJ: Princeton University Press, 1939).

Pascal, Blaise, *Pensées*, ed. and intro. A. J. Krailsheimer (Harmondsworth: Penguin, 1995).

Passmore, John, *The Perfectibility of Man*, 2nd edn (London: Duckworth, 1970).

Passmore, John, 'The Malleability of Man in Eighteenth-Century Thought', in Wasserman (ed.), *Aspects of the Eighteenth Century*, pp. 21–46.

Pattison, Mark, 'Tendencies of Religious Thought in England, 1688–1750', in *Essays and Reviews*, 9th edn (London: Longman, Green, Longman, and Roberts, 1861), pp. 254–329.

Pennington, Madeleine, *Quakers, Christ, and the Enlightenment* (Oxford: Oxford University Press, 2021).

Perry, Ruth, *The Celebrated Mary Astell: An Early English Feminist* (Cambridge: Cambridge University Press, 1986).

Phillipson, Nicholas, *Adam Smith: An Enlightened Life* (London: Allen Lane, 2010).

Picard, Andrew, Myk Habets and Murray Rae (eds), *T&T Clark Handbook of Colin Gunton* (London and New York: T&T Clark, 2021).

Pocock, J. G. A., *The Machiavellian Moment: Florentine Political Thought and the Atlantic Republican Tradition* (Princeton, NJ: Princeton University Press, 1975).
Pocock, J. G. A., 'Clergy and Commerce: The Conservative Enlightenment in England', in R. J. Ajello et al. (eds), *L'Età dei Lumi: studi storici sul sul settecento europeo in onore di Franco Venturi* (Naples: Jovene Editore, 1985), vol. 1, pp. 523–68.
Pocock, J. G. A., 'Conservative Enlightenment and Democratic Revolutions: The American and French Cases in British Perspective', *Government and Opposition* 24.1 (Winter 1989), pp. 81–105.
Pocock, J. G. A., *Barbarism and Religion: The Enlightenments of Edward Gibbon, 1737–1764* (Cambridge: Cambridge University Press, 1999).
Pocock, J. G. A., *Barbarism and Religion, Volume Two: Narratives of Civil Government* (Cambridge: Cambridge University Press, 1999).
Pocock, J. G. A., 'Historiography and Enlightenment: A View of Their History', *Modern Intellectual History* 5 (2008), pp. 83–96.
Pocock, J. G. A., 'Within the Margins: The Definition of Orthodoxy', in Lund (ed.), *The Margins of Orthodoxy*, ch. 1.
Polanyi, Michael, *Personal Knowledge: Towards a Post-critical Philosophy* (London: Routledge, 1958).
Pollak, Ellen (ed.), *A Cultural History of Women in the Age of Enlightenment, Volume 4* (London and New York: Berg, 2013).
Pomeau, René, *La religion de Voltaire* (Paris: Nizet, 1956).
Pope, Alexander, *Poetical Works* (London: Frederick Warne, n.d.).
Popkin, Richard H., *The History of Scepticism: From Savonarola to Bayle*, 2nd edn (Oxford: Oxford University Press, 2003 [1960]).
Popkin, Richard H., 'Spinoza and Biblical Scholarship', in Garrett (ed.), *The Cambridge Companion to Spinoza*.
Porter, Roy, *Enlightenment: Britain and the Creation of the Modern World* (London: Penguin, 2000; USA *The Creation of the Modern Mind: The Untold Story of the British Enlightenment*, New York: W. W. Norton and Company, 2000).
Porter, Roy and Mikuláš Teich (eds), *The Enlightenment in National Context* (Cambridge: Cambridge University Press, 1981).
Preus, J. Samuel, *Spinoza and the Irrelevance of Biblical Authority* (New York: Cambridge University Press, 2001).
Principe, Lawrence M., *The Aspiring Adept: Robert Boyle and His Alchemical Quest; including Boyle's 'Lost' Dialogue on the Transmutation of Metals* (Princeton: Princeton University Press, 1998).
Principe, Lawrence M., *The Scientific Revolution: A Very Short Introduction* (Oxford: Oxford University Press, 2011).
Printy, Michael, *Enlightenment and the Creation of German Catholicism* (Cambridge: Cambridge University Press, 2009).

Rack, Henry, *Reasonable Enthusiast: John Wesley and the Rise of Methodism* (London: Epworth Press, 1989).
Radner, Ephraim, 'Early Modern Jansenism', in Lehner, Muller and Roeber (eds), *The Oxford Handbook of Early Modern Theology, 1600–1800*, ch. 28.
Rahner, Karl, S. J., *Theological Investigations*, vol. 21, trans. Hugh M. Riley (New York: Crossroad; London: Darton, Longman & Todd, 1988).
Rashdall, Hastings, *The Idea of Atonement in Christian Theology, Being the Bampton Lectures for 1915* (London: Macmillan, 1919).
Redwood, John, *Reason, Ridicule and Religion: The Age of Enlightenment in England 1660–1750* (London: Thames and Hudson, 1976).
Reed, T. J., *Light in Germany: Scenes from an Unknown Enlightenment* (Chicago: Chicago University Press, 2015).
Reedy, Gerard, S. J., *The Bible and Reason: Anglicans and Scripture in Late Seventeenth-Century England* (Philadelphia, PA: University of Pennsylvania Press, 2016 [1985]).
Reill, P. H., *The German Enlightenment and the Rise of Historicism* (Berkeley, CA: University of California Press, 1975).
Reventlow, Henning Graf, *The Authority of the Bible and the Rise of the Modern World* (London: SCM Press, 1984).
Richardson, Samuel, *Pamela; or, Virtue Rewarded* (Harmondsworth: Penguin, 1980 [1740]).
Ricoeur, Paul, *Lectures on Ideology and Utopia*, ed. G. H. Taylor (New York: Columbia University Press, 1986).
Rivers, Isobel, *Reason, Grace and Sentiment: A Study of the Language of Religion and Ethics in England, 1660–1780*: vol. 1, *Whichcote to Wesley*; vol. 2, *Shaftesbury to Hume* (Cambridge: Cambridge University Press, 1991/2000).
Roach, A. P. and J. Simpson, *Heresy and the Making of European Culture: Medieval and Modern Perspectives* (Farnham: Ashgate, 2013).
Robertson, John, 'The Scottish Contribution to the Enlightenment', in Wood (ed.), *The Scottish Enlightenment: Essays in Reinterpretation*, pp. 37–62.
Robertson, John, *The Case for the Enlightenment: Scotland and Naples 1680–1760* (Cambridge: Cambridge University Press, 2005).
Robertson, John, 'Women and Enlightenment: A Historiographical Conclusion', in Knott and Taylor (eds), *Women, Gender and Enlightenment*, pp. 692–704.
Robertson, John, *The Enlightenment: A Very Short Introduction* (Oxford: Oxford University Press, 2015).
Robertson, Ritchie (ed.), *Lessing and the German Enlightenment* (Oxford: Voltaire Foundation, 2013).

Robertson, Ritchie, *The Enlightenment: The Pursuit of Happiness, 1680–1790* (London: Allen Lane, 2020).

Rockwood, R. O. (ed.), *Karl Becker's Heavenly City Revisited* (Ithaca, NY: Cornell University Press, 1958).

Roddier, Henri, J.-J. *Rousseau en Angleterre au XVIIIe Siècle: L'oevre et l'homme* (Paris: Boivin, 1950).

Rosenthal, Jerome, 'Voltaire's Philosophy of History', *JHI* XVI.2 (1955), pp. 151–78.

Ross, Ian Simpson, *The Life of Adam Smith*, 2nd edn (Oxford: Oxford University Press, 2010 [1995]).

Rossi, Paolo, *Francis Bacon: From Magic to Science* (London: Routledge and Kegan Paul, 1968).

Roth, Dieter T., 'What ἐν τῷ κόσμῳ are the στοιχεία του κόσμου?' *Herv. teol. Stud* 70.1 (Pretoria, South Africa) January 2014: http://www.scielo.org.za/scielo.php?script=sci_arttext&pid =S0259-94222014000100036.

Rousseau, André Michel, *L'Angleterre et Voltaire*, SVEC, ed. Theodore Besterman, vols CXLV, CXLVI, CXLVII (Oxford: The Voltaire Foundation, 1976).

Rousseau, Jean-Jacques, *The Social Contract and Discourses*, trans. and intro. G. D. H. Cole (London: Dent; New York: Dutton, 1913).

Rousseau, Jean-Jacques, *Confessions*, trans. and intro. J. M. Cohen (Harmondsworth: Penguin, 1953 [1781]).

Rousseau, Jean-Jacques, *Lettres écrites de la montagne*; avec une préface de Henri Guillemin (Neuchâtel: Ides et Calendes, 1962).

Rousseau, Jean-Jacques, *Lettres écrites de la montagne*: https://books.google.co.uk/books?id=KX4HAAAAQAAJ&printsec=frontcover#v=o nepage&q&f=false.

Rousseau, Jean-Jacques, *The Social Contract*, trans. and intro. Maurice Cranston (Harmondsworth: Penguin, 1968).

Rousseau, Jean-Jacques, *Émile*, trans. Barbara Foxley, intro. P. D. Jimack (London: Dent; New York: Dutton, 1974).

Rousseau, Jean-Jacques, *Reveries of the Solitary Walker*, trans. Peter France (Harmondsworth: Penguin, 1979 [1782]).

Rousseau, Jean-Jacques, *Rousseau, Judge of Jean-Jacques, Dialogues*, ed. Roger D. Masters and Christopher Kelly; trans. Judith R. Bush, Christopher Kelly, and Roger D. Masters (Hanover, NH: Published for Dartmouth College by University Press of New England, 1990).

Rousseau, Jean-Jacques, *Letter to Beaumont, Letters Written from the Mountain, and Related Writings*, ed. Christopher Kelly and Eve Grace, trans. Christopher Kelly and Judith R. Bush (Chicago, IL: University of Chicago Press, 2012 [2001]).

Rubanowice, Robert J., 'Ernst Troeltsch's History of the Philosophy of History', *Journal of the History of Philosophy* XIV.1 (1976), pp. 79–95.
Ruether, Rosemary Radford, 'Prophets and Humanists: Types of Religious Feminism in Stuart England', *The Journal of Religion* 70.1 (1990), pp. 1–18.
Rummell, Erika (ed.), *Biblical Humanism and Scholasticism in the Age of Erasmus* (Leiden: Brill, 2008).
Russell, Paul (ed.), *The Oxford Handbook of Hume* (Oxford: Oxford University Press, 2016).
Sabine, George H., 'Hume's Contribution to the Historical Method', *The Philosophical Review* 15 (1906), pp. 17–38.
Sanna, Guglielmo, 'How Heterodox Was Benjamin Hoadly?' in Gibson and Ingram (eds), *Religious Identities in Britain, 1660–1832*, ch. 5.
Sewall, B. D., 'The Similarity between Rousseau's *Émile* and the Early Poetry of Wordsworth', *SVEC* CVI (1973), pp. 157–74.
Shackleton, Robert, 'Pope's Essay on Man and the French Enlightenment', in Brissenden (ed.), *Studies in the Eighteenth Century II*, pp. 1–16.
Sheehan, Jonathan, *The Enlightenment Bible: Translation, Scholarship, Culture* (Princeton, NJ: Princeton University Press, 2007).
Sheehan, Jonathan, 'Suffering Job: Christianity beyond Metaphysics', in Bulman and Ingram (eds), *God and the Enlightenment*, ch. 7.
Shils, Edward, *Center and Periphery: Essays in Macrosociology, Selected Papers of Edward Shils, II* (Chicago, IL: The University of Chicago Press, 1975).
Shils, Edward, *Tradition* (London: Faber, 1981).
Shils, Edward, *The Virtue of Civility: Selected Essays on Liberalism, Tradition, and Civil Society*, ed. Steven Grosby (Indianapolis, IN: Liberty Fund, 1997).
Schaeffer, Francis, *The Complete Works of Francis A. Schaeffer* (Illinois: Crossway Books, 1985).
Schargo, N. N., *History in the Encyclopédie* (New York: Columbia University Press, 1947).
Schleiermacher, F. D. E., *The Christian Faith*, trans. H. R. Macintosh and J. S. Stewart (Edinburgh: T&T Clark, 1928).
Schliesser, Eric, *Adam Smith: Systematic Philosopher and Public Thinker* (New York: Oxford University Press, 2017).
Schliesser, Eric, *Newton's Metaphysics: Essays* (Oxford: Oxford University Press, 2021).
Schmidt, James (ed.), *What Is Enlightenment? Eighteenth-Century Answers and Twentieth-Century Questions* (Berkeley, CA: University of California Press, 1996).

Scholder, Klaus, *The Birth of Modern Critical Theology: Origins and Problems of Biblical Criticism in the Seventeenth Century*, trans. John Bowden (London: SCM Press, 1990 [1966]).
Schouls, Peter A., *Descartes and the Enlightenment* (Edinburgh: Edinburgh University Press; Montreal: McGill-Queens University Press, 1989).
Scott, H. M. (ed.), *Enlightened Absolutism: Reform and Reformers in Later Eighteenth-Century Europe c. 1750–1790* (Basingstoke: Macmillan, 1989).
Scott, John T., 'Pride and Providence: Religion in Rousseau's *Lettre à Voltaire sur la providence*', in Mostefai and Scott (eds), *Rousseau and L'Infâme: Religion, Toleration, and Fanaticism in the Age of Enlightenment*, pp. 115–35.
Scott, Sir Walter, *The Lives of the Novelists* (London: Dent; New York: Dutton, 1910).
Seigel, Jerrold E., *Rhetoric and Philosophy in Renaissance Humanism: The Union of Eloquence and Wisdom, Petrarch to Valla* (Princeton, NJ: Princeton University Press, 1968).
Shaftesbury, Lord, *Characteristics of Men, Manners, Opinions, Times*, ed. Lawrence E. Klein (Cambridge: Cambridge University Press, 1999).
Shaftesbury, Lord, *Letter Concerning Enthusiasm*: https://oll.libertyfund.org/title/shaftesbury-characteristicks-of-men-manners-opinions-times-3-vols
Shaw, Jane, *Miracles in Enlightenment England* (New Haven, CT: Yale University Press, 2006).
Schwartz, Richard B., *Samuel Johnson and the New Science* (Madison, WI: University of Wisconsin Press, 1971).
Schwartz, Richard B., *Samuel Johnson and the Problem of Evil* (Madison, WI: University of Wisconsin Press, 1975).
Simon, Richard, *A Critical History of the Old Testament: Written Originally in French by Father Simon ... and since Translated into English by a Person of Quality. Histoire critique du Vieux Testament* (London: Walter Davis, 1682).
Simpson, James, *Permanent Revolution: The Reformation and the Illiberal Roots of Liberalism* (Cambridge, MA: Belknap Press of Harvard University Press, 2019).
Sirota, Brent, *The Christian Monitors: The Church of England and the Age of Benevolence, 1680–1730* (New Haven, CT: Yale University Press, 2014).
Smith, Adam, *An Inquiry into the Nature and Causes of the Wealth of Nations*, ed. Edwin Cannan, 2 vols (London: Methuen, 1904 [1776]).
Smith, David Dillon, 'Gibbon in Church', *JEH* 35.3 (1984), pp. 450–63.

Smitten, Jeffrey, 'William Robertson: The Minister as Historian', in Bourgault and Sparling (eds), *A Companion to Enlightenment Historiography*, ch. 3.

Smollett, Tobias, *Roderick Random* (London: Dent; New York: Dutton, n.d. [1748]).

Sorkin, David, *The Religious Enlightenment: Protestants, Jews, and Catholics from London to Vienna* (Princeton, NJ: Princeton University Press, 2008).

Southern, R. W., *Medieval Humanism* (Oxford: Oxford University Press, 1970).

Spellman, W. M., *John Locke and the Problem of Depravity* (Oxford: Clarendon Press, 1988).

Spinoza, Benedict de, *The Chief Works*, trans. and intro. R. H. M. Elwes (New York: Dover Publications, 1951).

Spinoza, Benedict de, *Ethics and On the Improvement of the Understanding*, ed. James Gutmann (New York: Hafner, 1949).

Spurlin, Paul Merrill, *Rousseau in America 1760–1809* (Alabama: University of Alabama Press, 1967).

Spurr, John, *The Restoration Church of England 1646–1689* (New Haven, CT: Yale University Press, 1991).

Stanlis, Peter J., *Edmund Burke: The Enlightenment and Revolution* (London and New York: Routledge, 2017 [1991]).

Stein, Howard, 'Newton's Metaphysics', in Cohen and Smith (eds), *The Cambridge Companion to Newton*, ch. 8.

Stephen, Leslie, *History of English Thought in the Eighteenth Century*, 2 vols (London: Harbinger, 1962 [1902]).

Stern, Fritz (ed.), *The Varieties of History: From Voltaire to the Present*, 2nd edn (London: Macmillan, 1970 [1956]).

Sterne, Laurence, *The Life and Opinions of Tristram Shandy, Gentleman* (London: Dent; New York: Dutton, n.d.).

Stewart, Philip, 'Are Atheists Fanatics? Variations on a Theme of Locke and Bayle', in Mostefai and Scott (eds), *Rousseau and L'Infâme*, pp. 227–38.

Stout, Jeffrey, *The Flight from Authority: Religion, Morality and the Quest for Autonomy* (Notre Dame, IN: Notre Dame University Press, 1981).

Stout, Jeffrey, *Democracy and Tradition* (Princeton, NJ: Princeton University Press, 2004).

Strauss, Leo, *Spinoza's Critique of Religion*, trans. E. M. Sinclair (Chicago: University of Chicago Press, 1997 [1965]).

Stromberg, Roland N., *Religious Liberalism in Eighteenth-Century England* (Oxford: Oxford University Press, 1954).

Suckling, N., 'The Enlightenment and the Idea of Progress', *SVEC* LVIII (1967), pp. 1461–80.

Sullivan, Robert E., *John Toland and the Deist Controversy: A Study in Adaptations* (Cambridge, MA: Harvard University Press, 1982).
Sutcliffe, Adam, 'Lessing and the German Enlightenment', in Robertson (ed.), *Lessing and the German Enlightenment* (Oxford: Voltaire Foundation, 2013), pp. 205–25.
Swift, Jonathan, *A Tale of a Tub and Other Satires* (London: Dent; New York: Dutton, 1909).
Swift, Jonathan, *Gulliver's Travels*, ed. Peter Dixon and John Chalker, intro. Michael Foot (Harmondsworth: Penguin, 1967 [1726]).
Sykes, Norman, *Church and State in the Eighteenth Century* (Cambridge: Cambridge University Press, 1934).
Taylor, Barbara, *Mary Wollstonecraft and the Feminist Imagination* (Cambridge: Cambridge University Press, 2003).
Taylor, Charles, *Sources of the Self: The Making of Modern Identity* (Cambridge: Cambridge University Press, 1989).
Taylor, Charles, *A Secular Age* (Cambridge, MA: Harvard University Press, 2007).
Teich, Mikuláš, *The Scientific Revolution Revisited* (Cambridge: Open Books, 2010).
Temmer, Mark J., *Samuel Johnson and Three Infidels: Rousseau, Voltaire and Diderot* (Athens, GA: University of Georgia Press, 1988).
Temple, William, *Nature, Man and God: Gifford Lectures 1932–33, 1933–34* (London: Macmillan, 1934).
Thomas Aquinas, *Summa Contra Gentiles (On the Truth of the Catholic Faith)*, 5 vols (Garden City, NY: Doubleday/Image Books, 1955).
Thomas Aquinas, *Summa Theologiae* (Blackfriars Latin/English edition; London: Eyre & Spottiswoode; New York: McGraw-Hill, 1964).
Thompson, W. D. J. Cargill, 'The Philosopher of the "Politic Society": Richard Hooker as a Political Thinker', in Hill (ed.), *Studies in Richard Hooker: Essays Preliminary to an Edition of His Works*, ch. 1.
Thomson, James, *The Seasons and the Castle of Indolence*, ed. James Sambrook (Oxford: Clarendon Press, 1972).
Thrale, Hester Lynch, *Thraliana: The Diary of Mrs. Hester Lynch Thrale*, vol. 1, ed. Katherine C. Balderson (Oxford: Clarendon Press, 1951).
Toland, John, *Christianity Not Mysterious: A Treatise Shewing That There Is Nothing in the Gospel Contrary to Reason, Nor above It: And That No Christian Doctrine Can Be Properly Call'd a Mystery*, facsimile edition with an introduction and textual notes by G. Gawlick (Stuttgart-Bad Cannstatt: Friedrich Fromann Verlag, 1964).
Tomaselli, Sylvana, *Wollstonecraft: Philosophy, Passion and Politics* (Princeton, NJ: Princeton University Press, 2020).
Torrey, Norman Lewis, *Voltaire and the English Deists* (Oxford: The Marston Press, 1963 [1930]).

Totaro, Pina, 'More on Spinoza and the Authorship of the Pentateuch', in Del Prete, Schino and Totaro (eds), *Philosophers and the Bible*, ch. 2.
Trevor-Roper, Hugh R., 'The Historical Philosophy of the Enlightenment', *SVEC* XXII (1963), pp. 1667–87.
Trevor-Roper, Hugh R., *Religion, the Reformation and Social Change* (London: Macmillan, 1967).
Trevor-Roper, Hugh, 'The Scottish Enlightenment', *SVEC* 68 (1967), pp. 1635–58.
Trevor-Roper, Hugh, *History and the Enlightenment*, ed. John Robertson (New Haven, CT: Yale University Press, 2010).
Trueblood, Elton (ed.), *Doctor Johnson's Prayers* (London: SCM Press, 1947).
Trueman, Carl S., 'Scripture and Exegesis in Early Modern Reformed Theology', in Lehner, Muller and Roeber (eds), *The Oxford Handbook of Early Modern Theology, 1600–1800*, ch. 12.
Tuck, Richard, 'The "Christian Atheism" of Thomas Hobbes', in Hunter and Wootton (eds), *Atheism from the Reformation to the Enlightenment*, ch. 4.
Turnbull, Paul, 'The Supposed Infidelity of Edward Gibbon', *The Historical Journal* 25.1 (1982), pp. 23–42.
Turner, Victor, *The Ritual Process* (London: Routledge and Kegan Paul; Chicago: Aldine Press, 1969).
Ullmann, Walter, *Medieval Foundations of Renaissance Humanism* (London: Elek, 1977).
Van Gennep, A., *The Rites of Passage* (London: Routledge and Kegan Paul, 1960).
Van Kley, Dale K., *The Religious Origins of the French Revolution: From Calvin to the Civil Constitution, 1560–1791* (New Haven, CT: Yale University Press, 1996).
Vance, Sylvia, 'History as Dramatic Reinforcement: Voltaire's Use of History in Four Tragedies Set in the Middle Ages', *SVEC* CL (1976), pp. 7–31.
Vanderburgh, William L., *David Hume on Miracles, Evidence, and Probability* (Lanham, MD: Lexington Books, 2019).
Vaughan, Charles Edwyn, *The Political Writings of Jean-Jacques Rousseau*, [French] 2 vols (Cambridge: Cambridge University Press, 1915; reduced photographic reprint, Oxford: Blackwell, 1962).
Vaughan, Frederick, *The Political Philosophy of Giambattista Vico* (The Hague: Martinus Nijhoff, 1972).
Venturi, Franco, *Utopia and Reform in the Enlightenment* (Cambridge: Cambridge University Press, 1971).
Vereker, Charles, *Eighteenth-Century Optimism: A Study of the Interrelations of Moral and Social Theory in English and French*

Thought between 1689 and 1789 (Liverpool: Liverpool University Press, 1967).

Verene, Donald Phillip, *Vico's Science of Imagination* (Ithaca, NY: Cornell University Press, 1981).

Verene, Donald Phillip, 'Giambattista Vico's New Science of the Common Nature of the Nations', in Bourgault and Sparling (eds), *A Companion to Enlightenment Historiography*, ch. 7.

Vico, G. B., *Autobiography*, trans. M. H. Fisch and T. G. Bergin (Ithaca, NY: Cornell University Press, 1944).

Vico, G. B., *The New Science of Giambattista Vico*, trans. T. G. Bergin and M. H. Fisch (Ithaca, NY: Cornell University Press, 1970 [1948]).

Voisine, Jacques, *J.-J. Rousseau en Angleterre à l' Époque Romantique: Les Écrits autobiographiques et la Légende* (Paris: Didier, 1956).

Voltaire, *Zadig* (London, ET: Chapman and Dodd, Abbey Classics, n.d.).

Voltaire, *Candide*, trans. John Butt (Harmondsworth: Penguin, 1947 [1759]).

Voltaire, *Lettres Philosophiques*, intro René Pomeau (Paris: Garnier-Flammarion, 1964).

Voltaire, *Philosophical Dictionary*, ed. and trans. Theodore Besterman (Harmondsworth: Penguin, 1971).

Voltaire, *Letters on England*, trans. Leonard Tancock (Harmondsworth: Penguin, 1980).

Voltaire, *L'Ingénu* (Cork: Ligaran, 2015 [1767]).

La Vopa, Anthony J., 'A New Intellectual History? Jonathan Israel's Enlightenment', *Historical Journal* 52 (2009), pp. 717–38.

Vyverberg, Henry, *Historical Pessimism in the French Enlightenment* (Cambridge, MA: Harvard University Press, 1958).

Wade, Ira O., *The Intellectual Development of Voltaire* (Princeton, NJ: Princeton University Press, 1969).

Wade, Ira O., *The Intellectual Origins of the French Enlightenment* (Princeton, NJ: Princeton University Press, 1971).

Wade, Ira O., *The Structure and Form of the French Enlightenment*, vol. 1 (Princeton, NJ: Princeton University Press, 1977).

Waldron, Jeremy, *God, Locke, and Equality: Christian Foundations in Locke's Political Thought* (Cambridge: Cambridge University Press, 2002).

Waligore, Joseph, 'The Piety of the English Deists: Their Personal Relationship with an Active God', *Intellectual History Review* 22 (2012), pp. 181–97.

Walsh, John, Colin Haydon and Stephen Taylor, *The Church of England c. 1689–c. 1833: From Toleration to Tractarianism* (Cambridge: Cambridge University Press, 1993).

Ward, Frances, *Why Rousseau Was Wrong: Christianity and the Secular Soul* (London and New York: Bloomsbury, 2013).

Ward, W. Reginald, *Christianity under the Ancien Régime, 1648–1789* (Cambridge: Cambridge University Press, 1999).

Warfield, Benjamin Breckinridge, *The Inspiration and Authority of the Bible*, ed. Samuel G. Craig (London: Marshall, Morgan & Scott, 1951).
Warman, Caroline, ed. and trans., *Tolerance: The Beacon of the Enlightenment* (Open Book Publishers, 2016).
Wasserman, Earl Reeves (ed.), *Aspects of the Eighteenth Century* (Baltimore, MD: Johns Hopkins University Press, 1965).
Waterman, Mina, *Voltaire, Pascal and Human Destiny* (New York: Octagon Books, 1971).
Watt, E. D., '"Locked In": De Maistre's Critique of French Lockeanism', *JHI* XXXII.1 (1971), pp. 129–32.
Watt, Ian, *The Rise of the Novel: Studies in Defoe, Richardson and Fielding* (London: Hogarth Press, 1987 [1957]).
Weil, Simone, *The Need for Roots: Prelude to a Declaration of Duties towards Mankind*, trans. Arthur Wills, preface T. S. Eliot (London: Routledge, 1952 [1949]).
Weinsheimer, Joel C., *Eighteenth-Century Hermeneutics: Philosophy of Interpretation in England from Locke to Burke* (New Haven, CT: Yale University Press, 1993).
Wertz, S. K., 'Hume, History and Human Nature', *JHI* XXXVI (1975), pp. 481–96.
Wesley, John, *Journals*, 4 vols (London: Dent; New York: Dutton, n.d.).
Westfall, Richard S., *Science and Religion in Seventeenth-Century England* (New Haven, CT: Yale University Press, 1958).
Westfall, Richard S., 'The Changing World of the Newtonian Industry', *JHI* 37.1 (1976), pp. 175–84.
Westfall, Richard S., *Never at Rest: A Biography of Isaac Newton* (Cambridge: Cambridge University Press, 1980).
Whelan, Ruth, 'Bayle, Pierre', in Kors (ed.), *Encyclopedia of the Enlightenment*, vol. 1, pp. 121–5.
White, Gilbert, *The Natural History of Selborne* (Oxford: Oxford University Press, 1937).
White, Hayden, 'The Irrational and the Problem of Historical Knowledge in the Enlightenment', in Pagliaro (ed.), *Irrationalism in the Eighteenth Century*.
White, Hayden, *Metahistory: The Historical Imagination in Nineteenth-Century Europe* (Baltimore, MD: Johns Hopkins University Press, 1973).
Wiles, Maurice, 'Newton and the Bible', in Ballentine and Barton (eds), *Language, Theology, and the Bible: Essays in Honour of James Barr*, pp. 334–50.
Willey, Basil, *The Seventeenth Century Background* (Harmondsworth: Peregrine, 1962 [1934]).

Willey, Basil, *The Eighteenth-Century Background: Studies in the Idea of Nature in the Thought of the Period* (Harmondsworth: Peregrine, 1962 [1940]).
Williams, Rowan, *Faith in the Public Square* (London and New York: Bloomsbury, 2011).
Williams, Rowan, *Lost Icons: Reflections on Cultural Bereavement* (London and New York: T&T Clark, 2003).
Wollstonecraft, Mary, *A Vindication of the Rights of Woman, A Vindication of the Rights of Men, an Historical and Moral View of the French Revolution*, ed. Janet Todd (Oxford: Oxford University Press, 1993).
Wolterstorff, Nicholas, 'Locke's Philosophy of Religion', in Chappell (ed.), *The Cambridge Companion to Locke*, ch. 7.
Womersley, David, *Gibbon and the 'Watchmen of the Holy City': The Historian and His Reputation, 1776–1815* (Oxford: Oxford University Press, 2002).
Wood, Paul (ed.), *The Scottish Enlightenment: Essays in Reinterpretation* (Woodbridge: Boydell Press, 2000).
Woolf, Leonard, *Growing: An Autobiography of the Years 1904–1911* (London: Hogarth Press, 1960).
Wordsworth, William, 'Lines Composed a Few Miles above Tintern Abbey, on Revisiting the Banks of the Wye during a Tour. July 13, 1798': https://www.poetryfoundation.org/poems/45527/lines-composed-a-few-miles-above-tintern-abbey-on-revisiting-the-banks-of-the-wye-during-a-tour-july–13–1798
Wykes, David L., 'The Contribution of the Dissenting Academy to the emergence of Rational Dissent', in Haakonssen (ed.), *Enlightenment and Religion: Rational Dissent in Eighteenth-Century Britain*, ch. 5.
Yandell, Keith E., 'Hume on Religious Belief', in Livingston and King (eds), *Hume: A Re-evaluation*.
Yarnell, Malcolm B., III, *Royal Priesthood in the English Reformation* (Oxford: Oxford University Press, 2013).
Yolton, J. and L. E. Brown (eds), *Studies in Eighteenth-Century Culture*, vol. 17, American Society for Eighteenth-Century Studies (East Lansin: MI: Colleagues Press; Suffolk: Boydell and Brewer, 1987).
Young, B. W., *Religion and Enlightenment in Eighteenth-Century England: Theological Debate from Locke to Burke* (Oxford: Oxford University Press, 1998).
Young, B. W., '"Scepticism in Excess": Gibbon and Eighteenth-century Christianity', *The Historical Journal* 41.1 (1998), pp. 179–99.
Young, B. W., 'Enlightenment Political Thought and the Cambridge School', *The Historical Journal* 52.1 (2009), pp. 235–51.

Young, B. W., 'Conyers Middleton: The Historical Consequences of Heterodoxy', in Mortimer and Robertson (eds), *The Intellectual Consequences of Religious Heterodoxy 1600–1750*, pp. 235–65.

Young, B. W., 'Theology in the Church of England', in Gregory (ed.), *The Oxford History of Anglicanism, Volume II*, ch. 21.

Young, E. J., *Thy Word Is Truth* (Edinburgh: Banner of Truth, n.d. [1957]).

Zagoria, Perez, *How the Idea of Toleration Came to the West* (Princeton, NJ: Princeton University Press, 2003).

Zalta, Edward N. (ed.), *The Stanford Encyclopedia of Philosophy* (Spring 2019 Edition): https://plato.stanford.edu/archives/spr2019/entries/.

Zaretsky, Robert, *Catherine and Diderot* (Cambridge, MA: Harvard University Press, 2019).

Yasukata, Toshimasa, *Lessing's Philosophy of Religion and the German Enlightenment* (Oxford: Oxford University Press, 2003).

Zilsel, Edgar, 'The Genesis of the Concept of Scientific Progress', *JHI* 6 (1945), pp. 325–49.

INDEX OF NAMES

Abelard, Peter 156
Acton, John Dalberg-Acton, 1st Baron 273
Adams, John 112
Addison, Joseph 8, 83, 87, 240, 283
Addison, Lancelot 209
Adorno, Theodor 10–12, 23–4, 53
Alexander, James 5 n. 9
Allison, Henry E. 331
Andrewes, Lancelot, Bishop 141
Anselm of Canterbury, St, Archbishop 40, 156, 236
Aquinas, Thomas, St 27, 46, 50, 80, 161–2, 177, 234, 306, 317
Aristotle 20–1, 81, 93
Arnold, Matthew 346
Astell, Mary 105–6
Aston, Nigel 8–9, 138, 146–7
Athanasius of Alexandria, St, Bishop 123
Atterbury, Francis, Bishop 218
Augustine of Hippo, St, Bishop 37, 40, 45, 50, 102, 128, 155, 236, 306, 334
Aulén, Gustaf, Bishop 156

Babbitt, Irving 56
Bach, J. S. 153
Bacon, Francis 10, 16–17, 20–1, 38, 67, 81, 85, 93, 116, 117–20, 125, 214, 224, 235, 238, 269, 280
Baillie, D. M. 156

Barnett, S. J. 130–1, 178, 239
Barr, James 224–5
Barrow, Isaac 268, 271
Barth, Karl 3, 35–6, 39, 175, 191–2, 198, 273, 301
Barth, Markus 352
Bayle, Pierre vii, ix–x, 21, 69, 88–90, 93, 101, 106, 126, 128–30, 134, 139–40, 149–50, 158, 176–7, 184–7, 205, 238, 250, 268, 279, 285, 294, 300, 307–8
Beaumont, Christophe de, Archbishop 196
Bebbington, David 221 n. 25, 222–3
Becker, Carl 94, 102
Beiser, Frederick C. 83–4
Bentham, Jeremy 98, 211
Berger, Carl 37
Bergson, Henri 28
Berkeley, George, Bishop 36, 82, 212–13
Berlin, Isaiah ix, 17, 58–65, 145, 258, 304
Berman, David 58, 202 n.156
Besterman, Theodore 101–3
Birch, Jonathan C. P. 107–8, 158–9
Black, J. B. 296
Blake, William 334
Blondel, Maurice 274, 325
Boas, George 84

Bodin, Jean 52
Bolingbroke, Henry St. John, Viscount 170, 187, 230, 241, 279, 287, 297
Bonaventure of Bagnoregio, St, Bishop 27, 162
Bonhoeffer, Dietrich 335–6, 342–5
Boswell, James viii, 81, 198–9, 201, 219
Boyle, Robert 18, 117, 125–6, 212, 238
Browne, Peter, Bishop 228
Brumfitt, J. H. 294–5
Buckley, Michael J. 174–5
Budé, Guillaume 52
Buffon, Georges Louis Leclerc, Comte de 96
Bulman, William J. 8–9, 209
Bulman, William J. and Ingram, Robert G. 149–52
Burckhardt, Jacob 50–1
Burke, Edmund 8, 57, 60, 68, 71–3, 87, 96, 106, 112, 199, 212–13, 240–1, 285, 289, 305
Burnet, Gilbert, Bishop 126, 268
Burns, R. M. 17
Burtt, E. A. 121
Butler, Joseph, Bishop 8, 50, 63, 83, 129, 157, 202, 207, 212, 234, 240, 254, 290
Butterfield, Herbert 115
Byrne, Peter 247

Calvin, John 39, 45, 156, 161, 176, 205, 236, 289, 319, 354
Campbell, John McLeod 156
Cappel, Louis 312
Caro, Hernán D. 168
Cary, Mary 104
Casaubon, Isaac 312
Casaubon, Meric 207, 269
Cassirer, Ernst 7 n.14, 145, 203, 276, 278

Castellio, Sebastian 21, 126
Catherine the Great, Empress of Russia 14–15, 74, 345
Cavendish, Margaret, Duchess of Newcastle 104–5
Cervantes, Miguel de 267–8, 269
Chadwick, Henry 327
Charles V, Emperor 294, 296
Charron, Pierre vii, ix, 21, 69, 88–90, 149, 176, 205, 254
Chillingworth, William 84, 234, 250
Church, Richard 261
Cicero, Marcus Tullius 21, 81, 93
Clark, J. C. D. 69, 138, 214–15, 236
Clarkson, Thomas 96
Clement XI, Pope 166
Clement of Alexandria 352
Coakley, Sarah 25
Cobban, Alfred 73–4, 162, 275–6, 292
Coleridge, Samuel Taylor 80, 324, 330–1
Collingwood, R. G. 144, 331
Collins, Anthony 230, 249
Colman, John 232
Condillac, Étienne Bonnot, Abbé de 19
Condorcet, Marie Jean Antoine Nicolas de Caritat, Marquis de 96, 103, 149, 230
Connerton, Paul 12
Cook, James 228
Cranmer, Thomas, Archbishop 353
Cranston, Maurice 187, 194
Crell, Jan 308
Crusius, Christian August 168
Cudworth, Damaris, Lady Masham 104
Cudworth, Ralph 104–5, 234

Daillé, Jean 250
D'Alembert, Jean-Baptiste le Rond 14, 38, 103
Dante Alighieri 195, 289
Dawkins, Richard 319
De Crousaz, Jean-Pierre 171
De Gouges, Olympe 107
De Maistre, Joseph 18–19
Defoe, Daniel 8, 257–9, 261
Deleyre, Alexandre 207–8
Descartes, René 7, 36, 39, 45–7, 48, 54, 62, 82–3, 118, 121–2, 125, 145, 176, 195, 269, 288
Devellennes, Charles 184–5
D'Holbach, Paul-Henri Thiry 61, 72, 96, 149, 179, 230, 345
Diderot, Denis 13–15, 60, 74, 103, 131–2, 149, 151, 179, 187–8, 208, 230, 245, 269 n.131, 297, 345, 348
Dilthey, Wilhelm 340
Doddridge, Philip 8
Dodwell, Henry (Younger) 230 n. 43
Donna, Diego 316
Douglas, Lady Eleanor 104
Doyle, William 19
Dryden, John 8, 87, 240
Dunn, John 232, 237
Dupré, Louis 50–5

Eagleton, Terry 12 n. 23
Echeverria, Durand 303
Edelstein, Dan 6
Edwards, Jonathan 224
Erasmus, Desiderius 21, 51–2, 68, 89, 176, 251, 269, 277
Erdozain, Dominic 139–40, 141, 174 n.74, 182
Evans, Gillian R. 48

Falkland, Lucius Cary, 2nd Viscount 84, 234, 268
Febvre, Lucien 176–7

Fell, Margaret 104
Ferguson, Adam x, 96, 109, 112–15, 285–6
Fergusson, David 109
Fichte, Johann Gottlieb 325
Fielding, Henry 8, 213, 259–60, 260–1, 263, 265–8, 270–1
Fisher, Samuel 183, 317
Fix, C. Andrew 184
Flint, Robert 295
Fontenelle, Bernard de 68, 98, 294
Forbes, Duncan 200
Forster, E. M. 259–60
Foster, Stephen Paul 201
Fox, George 104
Frampton, Travis L. 317
Franklin, Benjamin 199–200
Frederick the Great of Prussia 14, 74, 112, 345

Gadamer, Hans-Georg 20–1, 22, 23, 44
Galileo Galilei 54, 121, 125
Galloway, Allan D. 48
Gardiner, Patrick 333 n.114
Gatterer, Johann Christophe 282
Gay, Peter 4, 6, 14, 74, 75, 85–6, 102–3, 124, 162–4, 173, 280, 295, 305, 344
Giannone, Pietro 309
Gibbon, Edward 5, 69, 72, 74, 93, 97–8, 111, 112, 145, 187–8, 230, 240, 273, 280–2, 284–5, 290–1, 295, 296–300
Gibson, William 218
Gladstone, William Ewart, Prime Minister 251
Glanville, Joseph 117, 125
Godwin, William 106, 211
Goethe, Johann Wolfgang von 35, 136, 191
Goeze, Johann Melchior 321
Goldie, Mark 220

INDEX OF NAMES

Goldsmith, Oliver 263–4, 267–8, 270
Gooch, G. P. 293
Gore, Charles, Bishop 27, 314 n.120
Gossman, Lionel 301–2
Graham, Elaine 25, 55
Gray, John 63–5
Gray, Thomas 8, 87
Green, F. C. 100
Green, Thomas 72
Gregory, Jeremy 215–18
Gregory, Tullio 88–9 n. 55
Grell, Ole Peter and Porter, Roy 140 n. 8
Grimsley, Ronald 189 n.113
Grotius, Hugo 308, 312
Guicciardini, Francesco 280
Gunton, Colin E. 39–41, 44, 65
Guy, Nathan 232, 235–6

Haakonssen, Knud 69, 70
Hales, John 84, 234
Hamann, J. G. 18, 26, 60–3, 115, 161–2, 325–6, 334, 341–2, 343
Hampshire, Stuart 181
Hampson, Daphne 24–8
Hampson, Norman 140, 188, 199
Handel, Georg Frideric 8, 268
Hardy, Nicholas 312
Haydn, Joseph 153–4, 349
Hazard, Paul viii–ix, 75, 86, 126, 149–50, 275–6, 305
Hegel, Georg Wilhelm Friedrich 113
Helvétius, Claude Adrien 72, 96, 99, 149, 230
Herbert, Edward, 1st Baron of Cherbury 133, 210, 235, 251–5
Herbert, George 251
Herder, Johann Gottfried 18, 26, 60, 61, 80, 96, 113, 115, 273, 283, 305

Hindmarsh, Bruce 224
Hoadly, Benjamin, Bishop 218, 250, 266 n.121
Hobbes, Thomas ix, vii 36, 56–8, 74, 78–9, 91–2, 121, 125, 139, 158–9, 170, 176, 179, 239, 266 n.121, 268, 278, 307–9, 313
Hodge, A. A. 225
Hodge, Charles 225
Hogarth, William 267–8
Hooker, Richard 84, 141, 214, 234, 241, 268, 277, 309, 314
Horkheimer, Max 10–12, 23–4, 53
Hudson, Nicholas 212–13
Hulliung, Mark 13–14
Hume, David x, 5, 14, 16, 24, 62, 72, 84, 96, 100–1, 109, 111, 112, 189, 200–4, 206–7, 230, 242, 247, 273, 279–82, 284–8, 290–1, 296, 303, 305
Hutcheson, Francis 84, 99, 285–6
Hutcheson, H. R. 230

Illingworth, J. R. 27
Insole, Christopher J. 159–61
Israel, Jonathan I. ix, 4–6, 62, 69–70, 75, 86, 90, 126, 149–50, 158, 181, 187, 238–9, 308, 316

Jacob, Margaret C. 75, 76–80, 209 n. 3, 238–9
Jacob, William 218
Jefferson, Thomas, President 199–200
Jewel, John, Bishop 268
John of Leiden 205
Johnson, J. W. 298
Johnson, Samuel viii, 8, 68, 81, 83, 87, 96, 134, 157, 167, 170–2, 176, 187, 198–9, 201, 207, 212–13, 215, 217, 219, 234, 240–2, 260, 266, 319

Joseph II, Emperor of
   Austria-Hungary 14
Jurieu, Pierre 186–7
Justin Martyr, St 352

Kant, Immanuel x, 61, 83, 96,
   133, 159–62, 168, 230, 335–7,
   339–42, 345
Katz, David S. 313–14
Keats, John 197–8
Keble, John 123
à Kempis, Thomas 351
Kettler, David 114
King, William, Bishop 170
Kołakowski, Leszek 183
Kors, Alan Charles 177–8

La Mettrie, Julien Offray de 61,
   169, 179
La Peyrère, Isaac vii, 140, 141,
   183, 279, 307, 317
Labrousse, Elisabeth 186–7
Laud, William, Archbishop 141,
   202
Lavington, George 71–2
Law, Edmund, Bishop 170, 218,
   327
Law, William 8, 50, 81, 157, 212,
   230 n. 43, 234, 240
Le Clerc, Jean 134, 279, 307, 312
Legaspi, Michael C. 311–12
Leibniz, Gottfried Wilhelm von
   48, 82, 121, 149, 167–8,
   171–2, 180–1, 282, 324, 330
Lessing, Gotthold Ephraim x, 50,
   90, 115, 132, 273, 275, 279,
   282, 320–34, 348
Licati, Giovanni 317
Lloyd, Genevieve 1–2, 147
Locke, John vii, ix, 5, 19, 20–1, 38,
   48, 54, 56, 58, 70, 78, 81, 83,
   85, 98–9, 101, 105–6, 117–19,
   126, 130, 132, 134–5, 140,
143, 149, 158, 170, 206–7,
213, 214, 218, 221, 227–8,
231–8, 240–1, 258, 267, 269,
278, 283, 288, 294, 300
Louis XIV, King of France 34, 88,
   93, 143, 206, 258, 292–3
Louis XVI, King of France 71
Lucci, Diego 232–3
Lucretius, Titus Lucretius Carus
   93
Lund, Roger D. 178
Luther, Martin 25, 27, 45, 51, 61,
   129, 162, 176, 269, 289, 313,
   319, 320, 326, 343

Machen, J. Gresham 225
Machiavelli, Niccolò 280
MacIntyre, Alasdair 22, 23, 44
Mack, Phyllis 223–4
McManners, John 188
Macquarrie, John 28
Malebranche, Nicolas 36, 46,
   82–3, 269
Mandelbaum, Maurice 302
Mandeville, Bernard 213, 268
Manuel, Frank 123
Marie Antoinette, Queen of
   France 71, 106–7
Marlborough, John Churchill,
   Duke 258
Marshall, John 236–7
Marx, Karl and Engels, Friedrich
   73
Masson, Pierre 188–9
Meinecke, Friedrich 279, 287, 292
Mendelssohn, Moses 320
Michaelis, Johann David 279,
   311–12
Michalson, Gordon E. 326 n.142
Michelet, Jules 293
Middleton, Conyers vii, 248–51,
   300
Mill, John Stuart 113

Millar, John 109, 285–6
Milton, John 106 n.107, 126, 134, 153–4, 169, 348
Moberly, R. C. 156
Montaigne, Michel Eyquem, Sieur de vii, 21, 69, 74, 88–90, 149, 269, 294
Montesquieu, Charles Louis de Secondat 96, 112, 134, 194, 228, 230, 278, 284–6, 293–5, 303
More, Henry 125
More, Thomas 303
Mortimer, Sarah 308, 310
Munck, Thomas 210–11

Nadel, George H. 279
Napoleon Bonaparte, Emperor 62, 94, 112
Newbigin, Lesslie, Bishop 36–9, 40, 44, 65, 95
Newman, J. H. 49, 195, 251, 268, 298
Newton, Sir Isaac 17, 20–1, 38, 48, 82, 85, 106, 117, 121–4, 149, 161, 202, 212, 214, 218, 228, 231, 280, 286, 294, 347–8
Nicolson, Marjorie H. 124
Niebuhr, Reinhold 122
Nietzsche, Friedrich 89 n. 60
Norris, John 105, 227
Nuovo, Victor 232, 237

O'Neil, Onora 83
Oslington, Paul 111
Owen, John 233

Pagden, Anthony 149
Pailin, David A. 230, 254–5
Paine, Thomas 136, 230
Paley, William 239–40
Pannenberg, Wolfhart 161

Pascal, Blaise 89–90, 166, 175, 284, 289
Pattison, Mark 33
Paul, St 335–6, 337–9, 351–2
Pennington, Madeleine 15
Pocock, J. G. A. 5, 69–71, 145, 150, 250, 270, 280, 298–9, 309
Polanyi, Michael 37, 40–1, 44
Poole, Matthew 268
Pope, Alexander 8, 87, 169–72, 213, 267–8, 347–8
Porter, Roy 5, 140 n. 8, 142, 209–10, 270
Preus, J. Samuel 317–18
Price, Richard 211
Priestley, Joseph 99, 211, 298–9
Pseudo-Dionysius of Halicarnassus 279
Purcell, Henry 8
Pyrrho of Elis 88

Rabelais, François 269
Rahner, Karl, SJ 350–1
Ramsay, James 96
Ranke, Leopold von 276
Rashdall, Hastings 156
Ray, John 263
Redwood, John 86
Reedy, Gerard 312–13
Reid, Thomas 109, 225
Reill, P. H. 283
Reimarus, Hermann Samuel 323
Richardson, Samuel 8, 259–60, 263–4
Ricoeur, Paul 345–6
Robertson, John 5–6, 13, 60, 90, 104, 211–12, 307–8, 310
Robertson, Ritchie 132, 154–7
Robertson, William x, 113, 114, 201, 273, 281–2, 285–6, 288, 290, 295–7
Rochester, John Wilmot, Earl 135, 267

INDEX OF NAMES

Rousseau, Jean-Jacques viii, 13–14, 18–19, 26, 35–6, 56–8, 60, 63, 72–4, 82–4, 93–4, 96, 99–101, 106–7, 115, 131–3, 134, 143, 149, 162, 169, 173, 188–92, 193–4, 195–6, 197–200, 228, 230, 240, 269, 285–6, 300–4, 305, 346

Sacheverell, Henry 218
Sanchez, Francisco 347
Sancroft, William, Archbishop 105
Scaliger, Joseph Justus 269, 312
Schiller, Friedrich 113
Schleiermacher, F. D. E. 27, 342, 346
Scott, Sir Walter 259, 270–1
Selden, John 312
Seneca, Lucius Annaeus 81
Servetus, Michael 289
Sextus Empiricus 88
Shaftesbury, Anthony Ashley Cooper, 3rd Earl 102, 156, 170, 206–7, 230, 246, 267–8, 311
Sharp, Granville 96
Shaw, Jane 17
Sheehan, Jonathan 311–12
Sherlock, Thomas, Bishop 251
Shils, Edward 23–4
Simon, Richard A. vii, 278, 307, 311–12, 318
Simpson, James 140–2
Sirota, Brent 215
Smith, Adam x, 109–11, 206, 285–6
Smollett, Tobias 8, 261, 263–5, 267–8, 270
Socinus, Faustus 308
Sorkin, David 148–9
South, Robert 268
Spinoza, Benedict (Baruch) vii, ix, x, 36, 46, 48, 55, 61, 69, 80–3, 90–1, 106, 114, 122, 126, 130, 139–40, 149–50, 155–6, 158–9, 165, 176, 179–84, 185–6, 191, 273, 278, 279, 300, 306–9, 311, 313, 315–18, 324, 329–30
Stanlis, Peter J. 241 n.70
Stephen, Leslie 33, 166, 249–50
Sterne, Laurence 8, 87, 204, 263–4, 267, 268–70
Stewart, Dugald 109, 281
Stout, Jeffrey 44–7
Strauss, Leo 181–2, 315–17
Swift, Jonathan 83, 87, 176, 204–6, 213, 240–1, 262, 267–8
Sykes, Norman 220

Tacitus, Publius Cornelius 280
Taylor, Charles 234, 242–4, 336 n.1
Teich, Mikuláš 116
Temple, William, Archbishop 28
Thatcher, Margaret, Prime Minister 95
Thomasius, Christian 169
Thomson, James 124
Thucydides 279
Tillotson, John, Archbishop 69, 202, 234
Tindal, Matthew 230, 235, 240, 249, 268, 286–7
Toland, John 74, 235, 255–7, 300
Torrance, James B. 156
Torrance, Thomas F. 39, 156
Totaro, Pina 316
Traherne, Thomas 80–1
Trevor-Roper, Hugh (Lord Dacre) 5, 50–1, 69–70, 139–40, 291
Troeltsch, Ernst 300–1
Turgot, Anne Robert Jacques 103, 283, 289
Turner, Matthew 250

Valla, Lorenzo 52, 277
Van Kley, Dale K. 151

Vaughan, Frederick 306–7
Venturi, Franco 72, 102
Vico, Giambattista (G. B.) ix, 18,
    26, 60, 114–15, 143, 145–6,
    258, 273–4, 304–10, 332
Vives, Joannes 347
Voetius, Gisbertus 178–9
Voltaire (François-Marie Arouet)
    viii, 5, 14, 57, 60, 74, 82, 84,
    93–4, 96, 98, 101–3, 106,
    118–19, 121, 124, 131–3, 139,
    143, 149, 151, 162–3, 165–6,
    167, 169, 172–4, 175, 188,
    190–1, 200, 214, 228, 229–31,
    240, 269, 273, 284–6, 288,
    289–90, 291–7, 299, 301,
    318–19, 329, 345, 346

Wade, Ira O. 7 n.14, 124, 145,
    173–4
Waldron, Jeremy 232
Walsh, John, Haydon, Colin, and
    Taylor, Stephen 220
Warburton, William, Bishop
    170–1, 212, 240, 251, 267
Ward, Frances 56–7
Ward, W. Reginald 91, 145–6,
    178–9
Warfield, B. B. 225
Watson, Richard, Bishop 218
Watt, Ian 258–9, 263

Watts, Isaac 8
Wesley, Charles 157
Wesley, John 8, 16, 50, 71–2,
    83, 87, 155, 157, 167, 207,
    212–13, 223–4, 227–9, 240–1,
    251, 281–2
Westfall, Richard 123
Whiston, William 268
White, Gilbert 8, 261–3
Whitefield, George 153–4, 157,
    207, 265–6, 269
Whitehead, Alfred North 28
Wilberforce, William 96, 102
Willey, Basil viii
Williams, Rowan, Archbishop
    58–9, 65
Wolff, Christian 46, 48, 82, 149,
    168
Wollstonecraft, Mary 106–7, 211
Wolterstorff, Nicholas 232
Woolf, Leonard viii
Woolston, Thomas 230,
    266 n.121
Wordsworth, William 331
Wotton, William 204

Young, B. W. 87, 209, 219–20,
    249–50, 270
Young, Edward J. 226

Zwingli, Huldrych 176, 182–3